Dear Professor Learmonth,

Thanks for being my external examiner of my PhD thesis.

I would like to send this book to you, as a token of thanks to your advice and support!

Best Regards,

Joey Ng.

27/6/2023

Joey Kong Man Ng
The Successful Chinese Family Businesses

Management, Spirituality and Religion

Series Editor
Yochanan Altman

Volume 2

Joey Kong Man Ng

The Successful Chinese Family Businesses

—

An Archaeological and Anthropological Journey into Well-being

DE GRUYTER

ISBN 978-3-11-068457-5
e-ISBN (PDF) 978-3-11-068464-3
e-ISBN (EPUB) 978-3-11-068467-4
ISSN 2700-7790

Library of Congress Control Number: 2022941980

Bibliographic information published by the Deutsche Nationalbibliothek
The Deutsche Nationalbibliothek lists this publication in the Deutsche Nationalbibliografie; detailed bibliographic data are available on the internet at http://dnb.dnb.de.

© 2022 Walter de Gruyter GmbH, Berlin/Boston
Cover image: Ion Jonas, based on an idea by Yochanan Altman
Typesetting: Integra Software Services Pvt. Ltd.
Printing and binding: CPI books GmbH, Leck

www.degruyter.com

Preface and Acknowledgements

I am a Chinese living in my home city – Hong Kong – and working as an Assistant Professor at the Hong Kong Metropolitan University (HKMU). I obtained my PhD from the University of Nottingham in 2019. This book is based on my PhD thesis, which examines the topic of well-being. 'Well-being' is a contemporary term used by people around the globe to address how comfortable their lives are. Twenty years ago, I encountered this term for the first time when I was studying in Australia. I enrolled in a work-life balance course in the Master of Human Resource Management programme. As part of the course, I was asked to examine my own sense of well-being. This learning experience sparked my interest in this topic. I was quite determined to study well-being in my PhD thesis.

In the first year of my PhD, I felt a bit lost with how I was going to approach this topic. I had explored a number of methodologies, but I still could not identify a field that I felt passionate about and that challenged me. Until I read the works of Xu (2000), Banerjee (2003), Sparkes (2007), Ailon (2008) and Learmonth (2009), they inspired me to move towards the direction of Critical Management Studies (CMS). I realised the 'beauty' of CMS – constantly reflecting on the established mainstream management knowledge and practices and questioning what was taken for granted. Since then, I have strived to demystify the notion using a critical lens. I started by examining the assumptions behind the concept of well-being and questioning if such a Western concept could be applied in a Chinese context. My thesis consists of an archaeological and anthropological examination. The first part of the analysis draws from Foucault's (1972) *Archaeology of Knowledge* to examine the discursive (trans)formation of well-being. The second part is an ethnography which focuses on a Chinese perspective regarding the everydayness of life. I believe that as a researcher, I have an obligation to critique existing management assumptions and give a voice to the marginalised. That is how and why I finally chose CMS as the 'home' for my research. In light of the recent dynamic social movement in Hong Kong, this book not only offers an insight into the core values of Hong Kongers, but also dissects various layers of meaning in these values. I hope this book can lift up the voices of Hong Kongers, who were once marginalised in the discourse of well-being.

Although being a CMS researcher is exciting and meaningful, I also feel disconnected from other academics at work. It is quite difficult to find a CMS community in the business schools of Hong Kong. However, my enthusiasm sustains due to the presence of various angels in my life. First and foremost, I would like to express my sincere gratitude to my research supervisors, Dr Qi Xu, Dr Craig Shepherd and Dr Lorna Treanor for their continuous support along my PhD journey. I feel thankful for their patience, encouragement, immense knowledge and insightful comments. They consistently allowed my own interests and aspirations to flourish, but at the same time steered me in the right direction to make sure that the thesis was of appropriate standard and quality. My thesis would not have been possible without their passionate guidance, participation and enlightenment. I am gratefully indebted to them for their invaluable inputs and care.

I would also like to express my heartfelt gratitude to Professor Yochanan Altman for giving me the golden opportunity to turn my PhD thesis into a book. He offered me guidance and insights in polishing the proposal and content of this book. My warm thanks also go to Professor Mark Learmonth who was the external examiner of my thesis. With his inspiration, two conference papers based on my thesis were presented in the Annual Meetings of the Academy of Management (CMS Division) and one of the papers won The Best Student Paper award. Special thanks are due to Professor Stephen Cunnings, Dr Michelle Greenwood, Dr Ajnesh Prasad, Dr Eda Ulus and my reviewers for their constructive feedback. They offered me encouragement and insights in polishing my papers, as well as extending my future research. I am sincerely thankful to these senior academics for their mentorship and generous assistance.

Special thanks are due to Professor Alan Au, Dr Anthony Ko and Dr Lenis Cheung, my supervisors at work. Their kind understanding and support were important for me to finish my PhD studies while working full-time. I would also like to express my heartfelt appreciation to my fellow colleagues: Ms Sara Lau, Dr Maggie Chu and Mr Gaius Tam who have been always sympathetic, helpful and motivational. They provided me with a protected academic environment to pursue my research. They offered me unfailing comfort and reassurance whenever I lost my enthusiasm and confidence.

I must express my very profound appreciation to my family and close friends for their lively companionship and steadfast encouragement. Their presence definitely offers me an abundance of *xing fu* (living well). I am deeply grateful to them for tolerating my negative emotions whenever I experienced stress in the writing process. Last but not least, I thank God for being with me all the way, for never leaving me, for sending the above angels into my life and for loving me. I trust His grace is always sufficient for me; for His strength is made perfect in my weakness.

Contents

Preface and Acknowledgements — V

Chapter 1
Introduction — 1
1.1 A Western Perspective — 4
1.1.1 Hedonism — 4
1.1.2 Eudaimonia — 6
1.2 An Eastern Perspective — 13
1.2.1 Confucianism — 14
1.2.2 Daoism — 20
1.3 Lacunae in Well-being Research: Is Xing Fu Equivalent to Well-being? — 24
1.4 An Archaeological and Anthropological Journey into Well-being — 28

Chapter 2
Chinese Family Business — 32
2.1 Family Business in Hong Kong — 33
2.2 Chinese Family Business in Management Discourse — 34

Chapter 3
An Archaeological Examination of Well-being — 45
3.1 Discursive (Trans)Formation of Well-being — 45
3.1.1 Conditioning Texts of Well-being — 45
3.1.2 Well-being as an Object and a Concept — 49
3.1.3 Transformation — 53
3.1.4 Business Practice of Well-being — 55
3.2 Discursive (Trans)Formation of *Xing Fu* — 55
3.2.1 Conditioning Texts of Fu — 57
3.2.2 *Fu* as an Object and a Concept — 58
3.2.3 Transformation: From *Fu* to *Xing Fu* — 61
3.2.4 Business Practices of *Xing Fu* — 64
3.3 Between Well-being and *Xing Fu*: Any Discursive Space? — 64

Chapter 4
An Anthropological Journey in Chinese Family Business — 69
4.1 Managing Chinese Family Business — 71
4.2 Living Well in Chinese Family Business — 75
4.2.1 *Jia Ting* (Family) — 76
4.2.2 *Peng You* (Friends) — 92

4.2.3 *Kai xin gong zuo* (Happy work) —— 95
4.2.4 *Xin Zhong Fu You* (Being Rich at Heart-mind) —— 100
4.3 From Managing to Living —— 102

Chapter 5
A Cross-Cultural Analysis between the East and the West —— 109
5.1 Demystifying Chinese Notions —— 109
5.1.1 *Xing fu* (Living well) —— 109
5.1.2 *Xin* (Heart-mind) —— 120
5.2 Theoretical Dialogues —— 129
5.2.1 Sensation and Desires —— 130
5.2.2 Human Needs —— 132
5.2.3 Human Relations —— 137
5.2.4 Nature, *Yin/Yang*, Spontaneity —— 142

Chapter 6
Conclusion —— 146
6.1 Implications —— 146
6.1.1 Theoretical Implications —— 146
6.1.2 Methodological Considerations —— 153
6.1.3 Work Practices —— 157
6.1.4 Contribution —— 161
6.2 The Future of Well-being? —— 162

Appendices

Appendix A —— 167

Appendix B —— 187

Appendix C —— 217

Appendix D —— 221

References —— 225

List of Tables —— 247

List of Figures —— 249

Index —— 251

Chapter 1
Introduction

Well-being is made critical to business because the notion affects workers, management and organisations (Beer, Spector, Lawrence, Mills and Walton, 1984; Ho and Kuvaas, 2020; Noon, 1992; Salas-Vallina, Pasamar and Donate, 2021; Warr and Nielsen, 2018). In a mainstream well-being research, positivism and neo-positivism are the dominant epistemologies in which they treat well-being as if it is context-free and static. However, is well-being universally equivalent across cultures? What if the notion is culturally specific and transformative? This book argues that well-being is culturally specific and therefore the notion has to be contextualised. Well-being is suspected to be emerged specifically from a western culture and the notion might have changed over time. If this is the case, is well-being relevant to Chinese subject? Is well-being significant to Chinese family business? In response to these inquiries, a problem of essentialism is suspected in the literature. That means, well-being could be universally misappropriated in some Chinese contexts. For illustration, a Chinese term, *xing fu* 幸福 is often considered as an equivalent to well-being (Davis, 2005; Lu, 2001; 2010), even though the two concepts are culturally distinctive. Hence, this book argues that a Chinese subject could have been essentialised as an object of knowledge (Goody, 1996; Westwood, 2001; Xu, 2008) in the well-being discourse. If so, the Chinese is being deprived of its voice in the discourse. For that reason, this book seeks to diagnose and overcome essentialism in its research process. Two research questions (RQ) are formulated:

RQ 1: How does the discourse of well-being emerge and transform in a Chinese context?

RQ 2: Do members of family business in China (Hong Kong specifically) draw upon the discourse of well-being in their daily practices? If not, what relevant concepts do they refer to and make use of in a given time period?

The book positions itself within the critical management studies (CMS). Both archaeology and anthropology are deployed as the methodology. The first question is answered by way of an archaeological examination in which a close reference to Foucault's (1972) archaeology is drawn; while the second question is handled by way of an anthropological examination and upholding ethics in research. In particular, Geertz's (1973) 'thick description' is used to explore an indigenous voice.

The findings indicate that well-being is not a culturally universal concept. In the archaeological examination, essentialism is diagnosed when well-being is transformed into a Chinese context. Along the anthropological journey, the research subject – members of family business in Hong Kong, did not draw upon the discourse of well-being. Instead, they used multiple Chinese expressions, including *jia ting* (family), *peng you* (friends), *kai xin gong zuo* (happy work) and *xin zhong fu you* (being rich at heart-mind). These local expressions are further contextualised based on two Chinese concepts: *xing fu* (living well) and *xin* (heart-mind).

This book contributes to debates related to questioning well-being in cross-cultural management. Well-being is found to be insignificant in a Chinese context. The framework of well-being has limitations in explaining the research subject. Hence, the assumed universality of well-being is challenged. Misappropriating well-being in a Chinese context could imply a subtle colonisation of management ideologies and practices. In order to recover an indigenous voice, a discursive space is opened where a Chinese perspective is brought into the centre of discussion. In addition to the framework of well-being, the findings are re-interpreted from Chinese language and Chinese philosophies (including Confucianism and Daoism). In this way, this book sheds some light on the conditions of possibility for a Chinese theory. Hence, making a methodological contribution related to epistemology. At last, this book calls for diversity and reflexivity in management and research practices.

This book mainly consists of six chapters. Chapter 1 introduces the notion of well-being. To begin with, a western perspective of well-being is examined. The dominant philosophical conceptual frameworks of well-being mainly include Hedonism and Eudaimonia. Afterwards, the notion is explored from a Chinese perspective. *Xing fu* (which is a typical Chinese translation of well-being) is scrutinised from two Chinese philosophies, including Confucianism and Daoism. By contextualising *xing fu*, another layer of understanding about a Chinese perspective is revealed. This layer has often been neglected in the well-being literature. To recover such a layer of understanding about a Chinese subject, this book proposes a new conceptual framework that includes both western and Chinese perspectives of well-being and *xing fu* respectively. This hybrid framework aims to supplement the existing western view, fill in the lacuna in the literature and overcome the essentialist tendency in the well-being research. Its relevancy and applicability would be tested out through an archaeological and anthropological examination in a Chinese context – Family business in Hong Kong.

Chapter 2 examines the site of research. Chinese family business (CFB) in Hong Kong is chosen as the context in which well-being is examined. In order to provide an understanding of the research context, the management discourse related to CFB is being reviewed critically. The problems of objectification and essentialism are highlighted in the literature. Considering the problems, this chapter proposes to adopt Foucault's archaeology to account for change in discourse.

Chapter 3 is an archaeological examination of well-being in a Chinese context. This part demystifies the discursive (trans)formation of the two concepts: well-being and *xing fu*. The examination uncovers how well-being and *xing fu* are emerged and changed in the discourses. Significantly, the problems of objectification and essentialism are diagnosed. At the end of this chapter, a discursive space is opened. Within this space, an indigenous subject (such as a Chinese subject) is allowed to speak in its own expressions.

Chapter 4 is an anthropological examination – A 'thick description'. This chapter begins by highlighting views of the local Human Resource (HR) professionals regarding the notion of well-being. Their understanding of well-being is aligned with the archaeological examination in which it highlights well-being is a familiar language of HR professionals. Nevertheless, well-being is perceived not to be the same as *xing fu*. The archaeological and anthropological examination shows that treating *xing fu* as an equivalent of well-being would be problematic. Therefore, instead of applying well-being to the site, this ethnography explores expressions of the research subject based on its everyday lives. Four local expressions are revealed and contextualised, naming *jia ting* (family), *peng you* (friends), *kai xin gong zuo* (happy work) and *xin zhong fu you* (being rich at heart-mind). Towards the end of the chapter, four major practices of CFBs are presented, which include familial culture, absence of or resistance to strategy and management, striving to survive and moving on as life unfolds. These four practices represent an embodiment of the local expressions.

Chapter 5 is a possible extension of 'thick description' through a cross-cultural analysis between the East and the West. This chapter begins with a theoretical discussion of two Chinese notions: *xing fu* and *xin*. These two concepts are derived from the four local expressions found in the previous chapter. To move further, a dialogue is formulated. This is a dialogue between Hedonism, Eudaimonia, Confucianism and Daoism. Such a dialogue helps to identify similarities and differences among these perspectives.

Chapter 6 is a conclusion. Theoretical, methodological and practical implications of the study are drawn. For theoretical implications, the assumed universality of well-being is challenged given the study reveals essentialism in the well-being discourse. Hence, the insignificance of well-being in a Chinese context is implied. On the contrary, the benefits of exploring local expressions and concepts are spelled out. At the end, a cross-cultural analysis among different expressions and concepts is made possible. Regarding methodology, the study shows how both archaeology and anthropology can be deployed to diagnose and overcome essentialism respectively. The importance of ethics and reflexivity in research are also highlighted. 'Thick description' can be extended by a cross-cultural analysis through the use of a theoretical dialogue. As for work practices, some plausible suggestions concerning international human resource management (IHRM) and management research are offered. Business practitioners and researchers are encouraged to critically examine any global management concepts, theories, models, tools and even practices before applying them to any Chinese contexts. Diversity in management is advocated. After discussing implications, potential contributions are outlined. Lastly, limitations of the study are identified and directions for future well-being research are suggested.

1.1 A Western Perspective

Dictionaries, such as Cambridge dictionary, Oxford dictionary and Longman dictionary of contemporary English, define 'well-being' as the state of feeling comfortable, healthy, or happy. The World Health Organization (WHO) (1948) describes health as "a state of complete physical, mental and social well-being and not merely the absence of disease or infirmity" (p.100). The concept of well-being has been popularised since WHO has used it to define health. Implicitly, health does not simply mean an absence of illnesses, but also a positive attribute in life (Fleuret and Atkinson, 2007). Well-being is closely related to human flourishing and linked with daily life, opportunities for personal development and caring communities (WHO, 1986). Hence, well-being can be part of health (Wilcock, Arend, Darling, Scholz, Siddall, Snigg and Stephen, 1998). Nevertheless, from the perspectives of medical and physical sciences, the inclusion of well-being as part of health is challenging, because it is difficult to measure and explicate well-being (Wilcock et al., 1998). For instance, Pybus and Thomson (1979) conducted a research with a sample of 444 New Zealanders and found that their understandings of 'being well' include varieties of meanings, such as being full of life, feeling alive and vital, having energy and interest, as well as being able to do what one wants and enjoys. Blaxter (1990) carried out a survey with a sample of 9000 adults in the United Kingdom. Her findings highlight that the view of people in the context of health include the experiences of well-being, but their interpretations of well-being differ across one's life span and between genders. To further explore the notion of well-being, the next part examines its meanings from two philosophical views: Hedonism and Eudaimonia.

1.1.1 Hedonism

From Hedonic view, well-being refers to happiness or pleasure. In the fourth century B.C., a Greek philosopher, Aristippus, believes that the goal of life is to experience the maximum amount of pleasure. This approach towards well-being has been followed by many utilitarian philosophers. For instance, DeSade believes that the ultimate purpose of life is to pursue sensation and pleasure; Hobbes argues that happiness is derived from the pursuance of human appetites; and Bentham emphasises that good society can be built through maximising individual pleasures and self-interests. Hedonism assumes human organism is initially empty. Therefore, human beings need to gain meaning in life by seeking bodily pleasure, appetites and self-interests. Within this paradigm, well-being is essentially equivalent to Hedonism (Kahneman et al., 1999). Thus, maximising happiness is the same as maximising well-being (Deci and Ryan, 2008; Diener, Oishi and Tay, 2018; Lee, 2022).

Hedonism concerns with both physical and mental pleasures. The predominant view of Hedonism consists of (1) subjective happiness, (2) concern for pleasure versus pain and (3) good versus bad elements of life. One major theoretical construct of well-being is subjective well-being (SWB), which is developed by Diener (1984). Diener considers well-being as subjective since peoples are asked to evaluate their own sense of wellness. Although SWB is a broad category of phenomena regarding happiness (Diener, Suh, Lucas and Smith, 1999), it normally consists of three elements: life satisfaction, the presence of positive mood and the absence of negative emotion (Ryan and Deci, 2001). The operational assessment of SWB often includes measuring experiences that are related to positive affect, negative affect and degree of satisfaction regarding different aspects of life, such as marriage, health and work (Diener et al., 2018).

Generally, Hedonic psychology is built on the assumption that humans have a malleable nature. A typical model that builds on this assumption is the set-point theory. Set point theory is one of the dominant research paradigms in the field of SWB (Headey, 2008; 2010; Lee, 2022). The theory espouses that an adult level of SWB is held at a 'set point', where it does not change because individuals can adapt to most of the situations, except temporarily in the face of major life-events. The development of set-point theory usually provides account of linking three sets of variables: (1) stable person characteristics (including personality traits), (2) life events, and (3) measures of well-being (life satisfaction and positive affect) and ill-being (anxiety, depression and stress) (Headey, 2010). There are cumulative theoretical developments to supplement, extend or revise the set-point theory, such as the adaptation theory (e.g. Brickman and Campbell, 1971), the Easterlin Paradox (e.g. Easterlin, 1974), the personality theory (e.g. Costa and McCrae, 1980; Sirgy, 2021), the dynamic equilibrium theory (e.g. Headey and Wearing, 1989), the multiple discrepancies theory (e.g. Michalos, 1985) and the homeostatic theory (Cummins, 1995). Some studies (e.g. Diener et at, 2006; Headey; 2008; 2010) challenge the set-point theory. They show that certain personal aspects or life events, such as the unexpected death of a child (Wortman and Silver, 1987), repeated unemployment (Clark et al., 2004), marriage (Lucas et al., 2003), cosmetic surgery (Wengle, 1986; Frederick and Loewenstein, 1999), family life and health (Easterlin, 2005) and emotional reactivity (Huppert, 2005), can cause serious and apparently permanent changes in individual set-points. Therefore, Page and Vella-Brodrck (2009) and Headey (2008; 2010) argue that the set-point theory is seriously flawed. They demand a replacement of the set-point paradigm.

While the subjective measures of well-being focus on self-reported happiness and life satisfaction, the objective measure of well-being is related to economics (Wijaya, Kasuma, Tasenţe and Darma, 2021). In economics, the measures of well-being cover both macro and micro dimensions. At a macro level, economic researchers usually equate well-being with the material position of a country, which is usually measured by its Gross Domestic Product (GDP) (e.g. Kahnemann et al., 1999) or income per capita. Standard economic analysis generally assumes people's well-being increases with consumption of goods and services, which in turns, leads to a growth of utility. Conversely, other economic-related variables, such as unemployment, poverty and inflation would decrease well-being (Clark and Oswald, 1994; Oswald, 1997). For micro-level analysis, an economic determinant of well-being is the respective income of an individual. This measurement is also based on the supposition that income drives consumption and raises individual utility. According to the economic perspective, well-being is associated with materials (Conceição, and Bandura, 2008; Frey, 2021; Wijaya et al., 2021). However, it is arguable that well-being cannot solely be measured by GDP or income (Conceição, and Bandura, 2008). Giovannini, Hall and D'Ercole (2006) identify that the measurement of GDP has flaws. For instance, GDP does not account for market values of outputs, changes in asset values, externalities like pollution or depletion of natural resources, and non-market activities, such as housework or illegal activities. Most critiques argue that well-being is a multidimensional concept which encompasses all aspects of human life (Conceição, and Bandura, 2008). Hence, to understand well-being as multidimensional, non-economic indices (such as Quality of Life (QoL) and Human Development Index (HDI)) are created to complement GDP (Frey, 2021; Wijaya et al., 2021). These indices can include social and environmental indicators such as education, health and nutrition, environment (Giovannini, Hall and D'Ercole, 2006), value of leisure, damage of pollution (McGillvray, 2007), infant mortality, life expectancy, and adult literacy (Stanton, 2007). Regardless of these measures of well-being, Conceição, and Bandura (2008) contend that a single index tends to oversimplify a complex reality especially when the methodologies used to construct these assessments are not always transparent. Indices can possibly be manipulated by politicians (McGillivrary, 2007). This posts questions on the quality of data collected, which can make cross-country comparisons much more challenging (Conceição, and Bandura, 2008; Frey, 2021; McGillivrary, 2007).

Hedonism is one traditional approach to well-being. Nevertheless, there has been considerable amount of debates on equating Hedonic pleasure with well-being. The debates concern whether Hedonic happiness or utility can adequately define psychological wellness (Frey, 2021; Ryff and Singer, 1998). Eudaimonia is, therefore, endorsed as another view of well-being (Ryan and Deci, 2001).

1.1.2 Eudaimonia

Many philosophers, religious masters and visionaries consider that well-being is more than happiness. For instance, Aristotle uses the term '*Eudaimonia*' to indicate well-being (Aristotle, 1985). Eudaimonia is a Greek word, which signifies that human flourishing is the highest human good. Eudaimonia is a central concept in Aristotelian ethics. According to Aristotle, Eudaimonia refers to "well-being as distinct from happiness per se" (Ryan and Deci, 2001, p.145). In other words, being positively affective or satisfied does not necessarily mean being psychologically well. Aristotle perceives Hedonic happiness as a vulgar ideal that can imply humans to be slavish followers of their ever-increasing desires. His *'Nichomacean Ethics'* (1985), written in 350 B.C., posits that true happiness is found when one is expressing virtue – doing what is worth doing. He considers that virtue is the state of mind, which shows a disposition of choosing a mean. Any desire that is too extreme, excess or deficient would destroy virtues. Therefore, Aristotle clearly distinguishes the satisfaction of right and wrong desires. He recognises the importance of developing practical wisdom. He perceives rationality is imperative through virtuous training. Hence, he considers well-being as a process of preserving a mean, fulfilling one's virtuous potential and living according to one's inherent intention, rather than an outcome or end state.

According to Eudaimonia, being positively affective or satisfied does not guarantee well-being. Eudaimonia highlights that not all desires or outcomes, which are valued by an individual would lead to well-being. Based on Aristotelian view, Fromm (1979) argues that optimal well-being requires people to draw a distinction between purely subjectively felt needs and objectively valid needs. The subjectively felt needs are those desires that would only lead to momentary pleasure. They would not lead to psychological wellness if they are harmful to human growth. In contrast, objectively valid needs are always conductive to human growth. The realisation of any objectively valid needs could contribute to human development and wellness.

Maslow's (1943) hierarchy of needs can be used to illustrate Fromm's categorisation. Maslow identifies several levels of needs: physiological, safety, love, esteem, self-actualization needs. Later on, he further differentiates the self-actualization needs into four more levels: cognitive, aesthetic, self-actualization and self-transcendence needs (Maslow and Lowery, 1998) (see Appendix A: Fig. A1). Subjectively felt needs refer to the lower levels of needs, such as physiological and safety needs. They refer to those fundamental needs that are responsible for short-term pleasure but not for self-advancement. In contrast, objectively valid needs are associated with the higher levels of needs (such as esteem and self-actualisation). Self-actualisation refers to a tendency wherein an individual can comprehend his or her capabilities and attain self-fulfilment. While Hedonism seeks fulfilment on any levels of needs, Eudaimonia mainly targets on self-actualisation. "From the eudemonic perspective, subjective happiness cannot be equated with well-being" (Ryan and Deci, 2001, p.146), because subjective happiness can be attained by acquiring Maslow's (1943) lower level needs, which cannot actualise human potential. According to Eudaimonia, subjective happiness may not be able to promote wellness even though it produces pleasure.

Eudaimonia highlights the belief that humans naturally live for contentment. Eudaimonia aims to understand the conditions that enhance and diminish satisfaction (Deci and Ryan, 2008). Eudaimonia regards self-realization as the main route for contentment. Aristotle considers the highest human good is to realize one's virtues and potential. Unlike the assumption of human organism as empty which puts forth by Hedonism, Eudaimonia believes human beings initially have their own potential. Therefore, people live to uncover their human potential. If they realise those needs that contribute to their growths and developments, they would feel contented.

Many psychodynamically and humanistically oriented psychologists reflect Aristotle's view in their works (Jahoda, 1958; Ryff, 1989; Ryff and Singer, 2008). One of the first attempts to explore positive psychological functioning is by Jahoda (1958). Jahoda identifies six healthy psychological functioning: (1) acceptance of oneself, (2) accurate perception of reality, (3) autonomy, (4) environment mastery, (5) growth and development, and (6) integration of personality. Her contribution is significant in terms of the conceptualisation of mental health. Nevertheless, she did not develop a measurement of mental health (Peterson, 2006). Building on Jahoda's work, Ryff (1989) develops a lifespan theory of human flourishing, named psychological well-being (PWB). Ryff and Singer (2008) further present a multidimensional approach to measure PWB and separate PWB with SWB. PWB consists of six aspects of human actualisation: autonomy, environmental mastery, life purpose, personal growth, self-acceptance, and positive relatedness (Ryff and Singer, 2008). These six aspects define PWB theoretically and operationally and represent emotional and physical health.

Elements of PWB are personified in the concepts of individuation (Jung, 1933), self-actualisation (Maslow, 1943), adult development and realisation of virtues (Erikson, 1959) and maturity (Allport, 1961). For instance, Deci and Ryan (1985) develop the theory of self-determination (SDT) to embrace these concepts. They identify three basic psychological needs: autonomy, competence and relatedness. These needs are related to vitality (Ryan and Fredick, 1997) and self-congruence (Sheldon and Elliot, 1999). For Ryan and Deci (2000), fulfilling these needs is important to psychological growth, integrity and well-being. Waterman (1993) also relies on Eudaimonia and labels personal expressiveness (PE) as the circumstance in which peoples are able to feel alive. He found that PE was more strongly related to activities that could contribute to personal growth and development. While Hedonism pays little attention to autonomy, Eudaimonia accounts for the importance of authenticity, autonomy, competence, goals and efficacy (Brunstein, 1993; Carver and Scheier, 1999; McGregor and Little, 1998; Pancheva, Ryff and Lucchini, 2021). Hence, Eudemonic well-being refers to contentment of being fully functioning, rather than simply fulfilling desires.

(a) Comparison of Hedonism and Eudaimonia
Debate on Hedonic and Eudemonic approaches on well-being is intense. As illustrated in Tab 1.1, it shows differences between the two approaches. Discussions often relate to the nature of well-being: whether well-being is objective or subjective; stable or changeable; tangible or intangible and measurable or immeasurable.

Tab. 1.1: Hedonism Versus Eudaimonia.

Dimensions	Hedonism	Eudaimonia
Principle of well-being:	Being happy	Being fully functioning when one realizes his/her virtues and potential
Happiness and well-being:	Happiness is well-being Happiness is the goal of life – the end state.	Happiness is distinct from well-being Happiness is the by-product of well-being Well-being is a process of fulfilling one's virtuous potential, rather than the end-sate
Means to well-being:	Satisfy one's subjectively felt needs (i.e. desires that would lead to momentary pleasure) Obtain pleasure, avoid pain	Realize human objectively valid needs (i.e. wants that are conductive to growth and development) Demonstrate human potential
Assumptions:	Human organism is initially empty Humans live to obtain pleasure and sensation	Individuals initially have potential Humans live to uncover contentment through realizing their potential
Theoretical constructs in psychology:	Subjective well-being *Life satisfaction* *Presence of positive mood* *Absence of negative emotion*	Psychological well-being *Autonomy* *Environmental mastery* *Life purpose* *Personal growth* *Self-acceptance* *Positive relatedness*

In spite of the divergence between the two approaches, they can be complementary (Pancheva et al., 2021). For instance, Compton et al., (1996) examined the relationship among 18 indicators of well-being and concluded that Hedonic and Eudemonic foci could be both overlapping and distinct. Ryan and Deci, (2001) suggest that one defensible position of Hedonism is to use SWB as an operational definition of well-being but endorse the Eudemonic view of what fosters well-being. In that case, two approaches are used complementarily to generate a deeper understanding of well-being (Pancheva et al., 2021).

The two approaches can be complementary as they share similar ontological assumptions about human nature. Sullivan (1986) refers to 'human nature' as "the characteristics of mankind which generally enable us to distinguish humans from animals, from inanimate objects, and from social abstractions such as society or organizations" (p.535). The debates of human nature often lie in two issues: source and stability. The source relates to whether human is law-bound or self-bound. If human nature is the result of something external (such as biological, historical, cultural, or environmental forces etc.), it can be called law-bound. Conversely, if human nature is created through the course of sense-making and social interaction, it can be called self-bound. The stability dimension looks at whether human nature is malleable or not. Based on Sullivan's classification, both Hedonism and Eudaimonia assume that humans are to be bound by external forces and rules; however, their learning ability makes them malleable. First, humans are compelled by physical, chemical, psychological and social "law" (Sullivan, 1986). Based on this assumption, Hedonic and Eudaimonia approaches treat well-being as an 'external force' or 'law' that would influence human behaviours. In other words, humans are respondents to the 'external force of well-being'. That is why well-being is confined to have a definite and fixed prescription. To illustrate, well-being is defined as happiness or economic utility in Hedonism, while in Eudaimonia, well-being means an optimal psychological functioning. Second, humans are assumed to be malleable. Both Hedonic and Eudaimonia approaches presume humans have the ability and tendency to make themselves flexible and adaptable to external forces. For instance, the set-point theory in Hedonism suggests that individuals can maintain their set-points of SWB as they are able to familiarise themselves with external situations; whereas the needs theory in Eudaimonia suggests that human needs vary in accordance with different circumstances. Both approaches assume humans can freely adjust themselves in response to the external environment.

In examining the ontological assumptions of well-being, Christopher (1999) reveals that well-being (both SWB and PWB) is constructed based on the belief of individualism. Individualism considers each individual as a discrete entity. Accordingly, society is simply a collection of individuals, who are independent to each other. Each person has freedom to define and choose his or her own goals and interests. Needs fulfilment is seen as a natural function of human life. In other words, individual needs grant meanings and purposes that underline human behaviours. In that case, self is viewed as individualistic, independent, and autonomous. Hence, the notion of self with normative prescriptions for goodness is built upon "the ontological and liberal individualism" (p.141). For illustration, European Enlightenment gives rise to utilitarian individualism (Bellah et al., 1985), which emphasises on the pursuit of rational goals. Since Hedonism focuses on self-interest, utility and rationality, SWB is formulated on the basis of utilitarian individualism. Similarly, the Romantic Movement encourages expressive individualism through self-cultivation. Given that Eudaimonia values self-actualisation and seeks to uncover human potentials, PWB is based upon expressive individualism. After analysing the notion from Hedonic and Eudemonic perspectives, the next part examines well-being in organisational context.

(b) Organizational Studies of Well-being
Besides healthcare and psychology (Page and Vella-Brodick, 2009), attention to well-being is extended to work settings (Ho and Kuvaas, 2020; Salas-Vallina, Pasamar and Donate, 2021; Warr, 2011; Warr and Nielsen, 2018). Organisational studies of well-

being usually rely on Hedonic and Eudemonic approaches to develop concepts, models and theories (Shizgal, 1999). For instance, behavioural theories of rewards and punishments have been developed based on a Hedonic approach to well-being (Shizgal, 1999). One example is Vroom's (1964) expectancy theory. Vroom (1964) develops a model of work motivation that includes the components of valence, instrumentality and expectancy. Expectancy theory suggests that well-being is a desirable outcome which an individual expects to attain (Oishi et al., 1999).

Well-being is an important aspect of human resource management (HRM) (Beer et al., 1984; Ho and Kuvaas, 2020; Noon, 1992; Salas-Vallina et al., 2021). Beer et al. (1984) illustrate the relationship between well-being and HRM. Based on their model, employee and societal well-beings were treated as long-term consequences of HRM policies and outcomes. Well-being is perceived as a distinct consideration in HRM, because the concept represents both a factor and an outcome for HRM (Noon, 1992). Examinations of employee's well-being normally adopts measurements related to the subjective well-being (SWB) or/and psychological well-being (PWB) (Ho and Kuvaas, 2020; Salas-Vallina et al., 2021). A number of measurements are designed to measure employee well-being, such as job satisfaction (Ho and Kuvaas, 2020; Rode, 2004), affective well-being (Warr, 1987; 2011), work stress (Ho and Kuvaas, 2020; Liu, Siu and Shi, 2010), work-related affect (Daniel, 2019), burnout (Maslach, Leiter and Schaufeli, 2009), work attitudes, job security, physical and mental health and social integration (John, 2009; Salas-Vallina et al., 2021). Variables on different levels have been constructed to study their linkages with well-being.

Peter Warr provides extensive reviews on the concept of well-being in the workplace (Warr, 2019; Warr and Nielsen, 2018). Based on theoretical constructs of SWB and PWB, he constructs 'affective well-being' (AWB) as one of the components of mental health (Warr, 1987; 1990; 2007; 2009; 2011; 2019). AWB is considered as a domain, which is specifically measured in relation to work domain (job satisfaction and burnout), as well as life domain (life satisfaction and esteem). Warr (1990) presents AWB as a multi-dimensional construct, with two independent dimensions named "pleasure" and "arousal" (p.194). Along the two dimensions, he highlights six key indicators of affective well-being: displeased-pleased, anxious-contented, depressed-enthusiastic. These indicators are affected by job or organisational factors (working hours and organizational culture), dispositional factors (personality) and working attitude and behaviours (job security). Other aspects of mental health, which include competence, autonomy, aspiration and integrated functioning, can also determine an individual level of AWB.

Given the importance of well-being in management discourse, well-being is regarded as a significant aspect in family business (Ceja, 2009; Onnolee and Jennings, 2018). Ceja (2009) highlights that well-being is regarded as a driving force for family business. Well-being could impact the owner-entrepreneur's decisions to take part in the family business (Astrachan and Jaskiewicz, 2008), intention to exit from the venture, organizational commitment (Shepherd, Marchisio and Miles, 2009), ability to deal with challenging situations and intrinsic work motivation (Ceja, 2009; Onnolee and Jennings, 2018). Well-being could also influence whether the owner-entrepreneur can achieve family's goals, attain family's success and maintain family's commitment to the business (Astrachan and Jaskiewicz, 2008; Onnolee and Jennings, 2018). Hence, well-being could affect the quality of family's life (Danes, Zuiker, Kean, and Arbuthnot, 1999; Onnolee and Jennings, 2018). Furthermore, it could influence the family business in various ways, such as performance (Onnolee and Jennings, 2018; Shepherd et al., 2009), absenteeism (Stier, 1993), productivity (Danes, Leichtentritt, Metz, and Huddleston-Casas, 2000), achievement of business goals, supply of trustworthy human resources (Danes et al., 1999), and succession planning and training (Ceja, 2009). Generally, well-being could assert influences on human, social and financial aspects of family business and could generate impacts on individual, familial and business level.

Even though well-being is important to family business, there are remarkably few studies of well-being in family business literature. Individuals who engage in family businesses could have a work-family relationship pattern that is distinct from other kinds of businesses (Smyrnios, Romano, Tanewskil, Karofsky, Millen and Yilmaz, 2003). For instance, they usually have high control and flexibility over work (Chiu, 1998; Fan and Frisbie, 2009; Wu, Chang and Zhuang, 2010) and perform multiple roles in the same place (Ammons and Markham, 2004; Chiu, 1998). Given the unique characteristics of family business, well-being in family business is most likely different from the conventional view. For example, Hu and Schaufeli (2010) examine the impact of job insecurity and current remuneration on well-being of CFB workers. They found that downsizing and current remuneration were associated with organisational commitment and turnover intention through well-being (burnout and work engagement). Their findings were different from previous surveys conducted in OECD countries, wherein current remuneration was found to be less significant in compensating uncertainty (Clark, 2005). Hence, the notion of well-being needs to be contextualised in a family business environment.

Studies, such as Dodd (2011), Hu and Schaufeli (2010), Onnolee and Jennings (2018) and Rothausen (2009), have contextualised well-being in western family business. For instance, Rothausen (2009) develops a work-family fit model to examine the well-being in family business. Her model asserts that separating work and family was essential to address work-family balance in family business. Besides, Dodd (2011) further presents an occupational stress and health framework for western family firms. She illustrates that the special dangers faced by the western family business owner-managers include heightened risk of accident and poor physiological health. Nevertheless, the special benefits enjoyed by them are found to be higher task control, social support, evolutionary fitness and a rich accumulation of experiences. Onnolee and Jennings (2018) suggest that three enterprise-level strategies and three task-level practices of family business would strengthen familial well-being in terms of family member satisfaction and family system effectiveness. These studies illustrate that well-being could be important in family business.

However, can the notion be universally applied within the context of Chinese family business? Is there a Chinese well-being? In response to these inquiries, the next part attempts to scrutinise well-being from an Eastern perspective.

1.2 An Eastern Perspective

The notion of 'well-being' is itself a western concept with no exact Chinese equivalent. Lu (2010) notes that the word 'happiness' has not appeared in the Chinese colloquial language until recently. As suggested by Lu (2001; 2010) in most of his writings, the closest correspondent of the term, 'well-being' or 'happiness' in Chinese, is '*fu*'. More specifically, Davis (2005) in his '*Encyclopaedia of contemporary Chinese culture*', refers well-being or happiness as '*xing fu*'. To understand Chinese meaning of *xing fu*, it is helpful to consider this compound term in Chinese philology.

The compound *xing fu* is made up of two morphemes, *xing* 幸 and *fu* 福. *Xing* means lucky and fortunate (*xing yun* 幸運), while *fu* implies *you fu qi* 有福氣 (happiness). This may indicate that Chinese regard having luck and fortune as part of happiness. The word '*fu*' appeared as early as *jia gu wen* 甲骨文 (bone inscriptions) in Shang dynasty (from 1766 to 1122 BC) (Lu, 2001). At that time, *fu* implied to fill the container with wine and present it at the altar. As such, the original meaning of *fu* is to express human desires through worship of gods and prayers. It represents blessings from gods (Lu, 2001).

To further comprehend the meaning of a Chinese word, Wang Li (1982), a leading Chinese linguist of the 20th century, suggests analysing the meaning of each Chinese word through decomposition of its character. The character 幸 can be decomposed into two words: 土 and 干. 土 means earth, ground or soil. Here, 土 has been resembled. In fact, it should be originally referred to 夭. 夭 means early death, a person dies when he/she is young. For 干, if it is treated as a noun, it means a shield. The ancient Chinese view death as only a change in the rhythm of life. They believe that the deceased would continue life in *yin jian* 陰間 (the underworld), where their souls could be satisfied as if they were living in this world. Western connotation of underworld would possibly refer to the hell. However, from ancient Chinese perspectives, *yin jian* has a little negative undertone. Many luxurious burial gifts are found in the excavation of Shang's graves, because the ancient Chinese treat burial gifts as shields for the deceased. They are indicators of what constitute happiness. Therefore, unlike western emphasis on contentment in life, the Chinese concept of happiness includes pleasures both in this world and in *yin jian*. That means, Chinese also pay attention to happiness after life.

The character 福 can be decomposed into 示 (*shi*) and 畐 (*fu*). 示 means a sign, while 畐 indicates abundance. The two words put together to become 福 (*fu*), which means a sign of abundance. Further, 畐 is made up of the words 一 (*yi*), 口 (*kou*) and 田 (*tian*). 一 means the first. 口 refers to the mouth, which can have the connotation of eating. 田 stands for farmlands. Based on the composition of 畐, it implies that the first basic sign of abundance for the ancient Chinese was the farmlands. They relied on farmlands to provide adequate food for eating.

Moreover, there are *wu fu* 五福 (five signs of abundance) and *liu ji* 六極 (six sufferings) in Chinese. *Wu fu* refers to 一曰壽, 二曰福, 三曰康寧, 四曰有好德, 五曰好終命 (longevity, prosperity, peace and health, virtue and a comfortable death); while *liu ji* include 一曰凶短折, 二曰疾, 三曰憂, 四曰貧, 五曰惡, 六曰弱 (uncomfortable death, sickness, worries, poverty, wickedness and weakness) (*The Great Plan*, 11; in Zhao, 2003, p.38). 向用五福, 威用六極 (The hortatory use of the five [sources of] happiness, and the awing use of the six [occasions of] sufferings) are stated in the *Ancient Classics* (*The Great Plan*, 2; in Zhao, 2003, p.38). A popular greeting at Chinese New Year is 五福臨門, which means "May the five *fu* come beyond your door".

The meanings of *wu fu* are consistent with Lu's (2001) description concerning the Chinese concepts of happiness. His work discusses Chinese philosophical and folk views of happiness. He explains that *fu* consists of "material abundance, physical health, virtuous and peaceful life, and relief from death anxiety" (p. 409). In that sense, the signs of abundances include happiness across one's life span. Therefore, the nature of *xing fu* seems rather stable and long lasting.

According to the Cambridge Dictionaries Online, happiness can also be translated as '*kuai le*' 快樂 in Chinese. The compound of '*kuai le*' is made up of the morphemes, '*kuai*' and '*le*'. *Kuai* indicates fast, quick, soon and shortly, whereas *le* means joyful, jolly and happy. Therefore, based on motivation of transparent words, *kuai le* implies happiness for a short moment or happiness comes quickly. Despite the fact that both '*xing fu*' and '*kuai le*' can be translated as well-being or happiness, they are distinct from each other. From a linguistic perspective, *kuai le* is consistent with Hedonism. In contrast, *xing fu* represents happiness across the life span. To further comprehend Chinese perceptions of *xing fu*, the next part views *xing fu* from the two Chinese philosophical frameworks, including Confucian and Daoist perspectives.

1.2.1 Confucianism

Chinese philosophies have profoundly shaped its culture. Among many schools of thoughts, Confucianism and Daoism are the backbone of the orthodox Chinese culture. Confucius (551–472 B.C.) is the founder of Confucianism. Even though Confucius does not give prominence to *xing fu*, he spent a lot of time touring the states, educating his disciples on how to build good characters, and preaching to rulers on how to maintain social order. His teachings are mainly concerned with *ba mu* (the eight steps): (1) investigation of things, (2) extension of knowledge, (3) sincere in thoughts, (4) rectification of mind, (5) cultivation of moral characters, (6) establishment of a harmonious family, (7) governance of a state and (8) maintenance of harmony in the world (see Appendix A: Fig. A2). The Confucian ideal is to achieve societal harmony. In contrast, the mainstream approach to well-being focuses on individual happiness and self-actualisation. While examining Chinese sources of happiness based on folk psychology, Lu (2001) points out that Confucian tradition regards "contributing to society is the ultimate happiness, whereas hedonistic striving for happiness is regarded as unworthy and even shameful" (p. 411). Christopher (1999) also notes that western promotion of individualism, independency and autonomy can be regarded as a sign of selfishness and immaturity in many collectivist cultures. Thus, instead of focusing on personal happiness, the Chinese measure the quality of life by the contribution made to society and the community. Rather than promoting individual well-being, Confucian teaching is concerned more with relational or collective well-being. To further understand Confucian tradition, it is important to consider the following key concepts.

(a) De (Virtues)

Confucian teachings concern humanism and *de* (virtues 德). Confucius regarded the importance of spiritual happiness as more paramount than material satisfaction. Consistent with Aristotle's view, Confucius considers happiness could only be derived from having virtues. Confucius once said:

> The Master said, "With coarse rice to eat, with water to drink, and my bended arm for a pillow; I have still joy in the midst of these things. Richness and honours acquired by unrighteousness are to me as a floating cloud. (Analects: Shu R, 15; in Legge, 1949, p.200)

Confucius states that joy is independent of any external circumstances (Legge, 1949). He regards virtues as more valuable than wealth and social status (Yu, 1998). Hence, in the Confucian tradition, happiness is a by-product of being virtuous.

In addition, happiness is closely related to activities that build virtues. Confucius treats virtuous training as the focal point of achieving spiritual contentment. He regards learning as a source of pleasure (Analects: Xue Er: 1; in Legge, 1949, p.137). This perception is quite similar to Eudemonic recognition of growth and development. Both Confucius and advocates of Eudaimonia believe that individuals could develop virtues through self-cultivation, which means that learning can augment one's well-being. Although both Eudemonic and Confucian frameworks see virtuous cultivation as important, their focal points of teaching are different. Based on Eudemonic perspective, self-determination theory concentrates on aspects like rationality, free agency and individual rights (Ryan and Deci, 2000). On the contrary, Confucian appeal of virtues emphasizes *ren* 仁 (benevolence), *yi* 義 (appropriateness), *li* 禮 (ritual propriety), *zhi* 智 (acting wisely) and *xin* 信 (fidelity). These five virtues are closely linked.

i. Ren (Benevolence)

Ren is considered as the principal virtue in Confucian tradition (Cheung, 2011). Other virtues are built upon the foundation of *ren*. *Ren* is normally translated as 'benevolence' or 'humanity'. This means *ren* is related to human kindness wherein one showcases that act of kindness to others. *Ren* concerns with cultivating love and building relations with people. It implies that one cares for the well-being of others (Cua, 1998). It is an other-regarding virtue that lays the ground and justification for altruism (Lu, 2001), to such an extent others become an end, rather than a mean. As such, interpersonal relationships are the central places where one can acquire *ren* (Tu, 1985a). Therefore, "self may not be defined by itself alone, but rather is situated between people" (Chang and Holt, 1996, p.1493). Significantly, self is being constructed interdependently with others (Lu, 2008). This is different from individualism discussed earlier, where self is seen as independent. The Confucian notion of self is based upon social relations (Cheung, 2011; Liu and Yu, 2021).

According to the Confucian teaching, there are five cardinal relations, named *wu lun* (五倫). Mencius suggested that w*u lun* includes: (1) a ruler and a subject (superior and subordinate), (2) father and son (parent and child), (3) husband and wife, (4) elder brother and younger brother (siblings) and (5) friends (Bockover, 2010). The five relations are interdependent. Among *wu lun*, three of the relations belong to the family. Indeed, Confucian tradition places great emphasis on family (Ames, 2009). It sees family as a place for cultivating and extending *ren* (Herr, 2003).

> Benevolence is the characteristic element of humanity, and the great existence of it is in loving relatives
> (Doctrine of the Mean, 20:5, in Legge, 1949, p.405)

Here, the degree to which *ren* is developed requires people to love their families. Even if the relationship between a ruler, subject and friends are not within family ties, they are based on a family model (King and Bond, 1985). For instance, the word 'country' in Chinese is *guo jia* 國家 (country family), which means that the Chinese perceive their country as a family; and the Chinese could sometimes call friends as *xiong di* 兄弟 (brother), which implies that friends must be treated as close as brothers (Cheung, 2011). The concept of *jia* 家 (family) can be extended, including non-kin ties that are established through appropriate mutual exchange (Chang and Holt, 1996). The concept of family is not bound by biological fact.

Cultivating *ren* is one of the most significant aspects of Confucian teaching. Ames (2009) translated *ren* as "authoritative conduct", "to act authoritatively" or "authoritative person" (p.370). In *Mengzi*, it states:

> Benevolence (ren) is the tranquil habitation of man, and righteousness (yi) is his straight path
> (Mengzi: Li Lou I: 10; in Legge, 1985)

The quote suggests that righteousness is a way to encourage *ren*. Thus, an individual requires to perform *yi* (appropriateness) and *li* ((ritual propriety) for attainment of *ren*. The virtue: *yi* is therefore closely related to *ren*.

ii. Yi (Appropriateness)

Yi means 'appropriateness', as the perspective of something being right is dependent on one's role and context (Hall and Ames, 1987). *Yi* relates to one's social status or roles (Cheung, 2011). The Confucian concept of self is placed within the social nexus (Chang and Holt, 1996), thus, the concept of self-worth and self-acceptance rely upon the appropriateness of one's social behaviours. Based on Confucian teaching, the status or role of an individual is defined by *wu lun* (the five cardinal relations). Each role has its own rights, duties, obligations and responsibilities. For instance, Mencius points out that a ruler needs to act appropriately to maintain social order (*Mencius: Liang Hui Wang I, 7,* in Legge, 1985). According to Confucians, the fulfilment of the physical needs of the citizens is an appropriate duty of the ruler.

Moreover, *yi* directs people away from egoism. Confucius perceives one of the qualities of *jun zi* 君子 (a virtuous person) is to pursue *yi* and does not seek ego advantages (Cheung, 2011). For Confucius, *jun zi* refers to a person who possesses *yi* and acts in accordance with *li* (ritual propriety). *Jun zi* would attain *yi* through *keji* (self-discipline) (Hall and Ames, 1987). If one can maintain self-discipline, they would not focus on their personal gains. *Mengzi* states that *jun zi* (a virtuous person) would be delighted when (1) his parents are both alive and brothers are not anxious; (2) he has no shame and (3) he is able to acquire, teach and nourish talents (*Mengzi: Jin Xin I, 20;* in Legge, 1985).

iii. Li (Ritual Propriety)

Originally, *li* refers to sacrifice to the ancestors or spirit. The worship of ancestors is known to be a ritual of some kind (*li*). However, later on, *li* represents the rules that govern one's attitudes and conducts. It does not only indicate "what is appropriate?", but also "doing what is appropriate" (Ames, 2009, p.380). Confucian teaching emphasises "observing ritualised roles and relationship" (*shou li* 守禮) (Ames, 2009, p.122). *Mencius* asserts:

> between father and son, there should be affection; between sovereign and minister, righteousness; between husband and wife, attention to their separate functions; between old and young, a proper order; and between friends, fidelity.
> (Mencius: Teng Wen Gong I, 4; in Legge, 1985)

The above rules (*li*) guide individuals to act in an appropriate manner within a social relationship. They define appropriate behaviours and set boundaries for individuals to perform various roles in *wu lun* (the five cardinal relations). One could accomplish *ren* (benevolence) through *li*, because *li* represents being respectful to others (Cheung, 2011). For instance, in order to instil affection within the relationship between a father and son, both must act in accordance with *li*. The son would, therefore, demonstrate filial piety (love and respect for the parents and ancestors), while the father would show concern and care towards his son.

Within the Confucian tradition, family is a crucial platform for the observation of ritualised roles and relationship. *Li* should begin in the family (Ames, 2009). The virtue of *xiao* 孝 is generally translated as *'filial piety'*. Ames (2009) deciphers *xiao* as *"familial deference"* (p.122). He clarifies that *xiao* represents the kind of respect that is different from *'piety'* and *'paterfamilias'*. *'Piety'* can have a religious connotation, while *'paterfamilias'* may imply hierarchical differences. In Confucian teaching, individuals have *xiao* neither because of God's command nor hierarchical obedience. Indeed, *xiao* is a kind of *li* in the family. In Confucian tradition, family is the central point of focus within the life of an individual, thus, one would act in accordance to *xiao* by preserving and expanding the prosperity and vitality of his or her family (Lu, 2001). This further asserts that the well-being of the family would be an essential concern for an individual.

Similarly, if friends behave based on *li*, they would ensure fidelity. Fidelity implies honesty and sincerity (*xin* 信). In fact, *xin* does not only refer to being honest and sincere, it also indicates the trustworthiness and reliability of an individual (Cheung, 2011). So Zi Xia (Tzu-hsia) regards " . . . in his intercourse with his friends, his words are sincere" *(Analect: Xue Er, 7;* in Legge, 1949, p.141). While blood relations demand obligations, *xin* would be the basis of friendship. Even though friendship is the only form of relation in *wu lun* (five cardinal relations) that involves equality, *xin* is an important criterion that governs friendship.

iv. Zhi (Wisdom)

Zhi is often translated as wisdom. The Confucian concept of *zhi* does not only represents one's ability to distinguish between right and wrong (Mote, 1971), but also refers to the ability to understand the situation, their roles and proper interaction with others (Cheung, 2011). It implies knowledge to act in accordance with *ren, yi* and *li*. If one can cultivate *ren* (benevolence), possess *yi* (appropriateness) and perform *li* (ritual propriety) appropriately, one can attain *zhi* (wisdom). Therefore, the four virtues are inter-related. Confucian teachings advocate that achieving the four virtues would help a person to realise *dao* (the human way).

(b) Dao (The Human Way)

Dao means 'the way' (Cua, 1975). The Chinese compound term *'dao de'* 道德 can be translated as 'ethics', which indicates that *dao* (the way) and *de* (virtues) are closely interlinked. Hansen (1993) explains the relationship between *dao* and *de*. *De* are the virtues that would consist of human character traits, skills and disposition; while *dao* is the social way that guides a person to realise their virtues within the human system (i.e. individual, family or state). Hence, a person can obtain virtues from comprehending *dao* (the way). Furthermore, Confucius perceives *dao* as the goal and the ideal of human being (Wong, 2011). *Dao* in Confucian teaching refers to 'the human way' (*ren dao* 人道) (Zhang, 2002). *Ren dao* refers to the way human beings should live (Wong, 2011).

To envision *dao* is to appreciate the value of *harmony* (Wong, 2011). Li (2008) explains that the principle of harmony (*he* 和) comes from the Chinese cookery which emphasises that a dish should be made with an appropriate mixture of ingredients to produce a harmonious deliciousness (Ames, 2009). The *Doctrine of the Mean*, treats harmony as a central concept. It specifies that being *zhong yong* 中庸 (equilibrium: being balanced and upright) is the way to achieve harmony (Li, 2008, p. 425). Confucius once said "Perfect is the virtue which is according to the Constant Mean" (*Analects: Yung Ye*, 27; in Legge, 1949, p.194). This implies that people need to act in accordance to the mean and maintain equilibrium in their daily activities (Ames, 2009). Most of the virtues in the Confucian framework focus on the attainment of harmony within an individual, among others and also in the world (Wong, 2011). For instance, *li* (ritual propriety) specifies the appropriate behaviours of various roles in order to maintain harmonious social relationships. Hence, following *li* could enable harmony (Ames, 2009).

(c) Summary: How Would Confucians Express Xing Fu?

To conclude, in Confucian teaching, *xing fu* does not relate to transient and sensual pleasures. Confucius stresses on collective welfare (including family, society and the entire human race) rather than individual interests. *Xing fu*, in the similar manner, represents a collective well-being, instead of individual well-being alone.

In addition, *xing fu* refers to being virtuous. The four *de* (virtues) are *ren* (benevolence), *yi* (appropriateness), *li* (ritual propriety) and *zhi* (wisdom). These virtues can be obtained through virtuous training. One can achieve happiness through self-cultivation and learning with friends. *Ren* (benevolence) acknowledges the intrinsic goodness of love and care to others. *Li* (ritual propriety) and *yi* (appropriateness) provide guidance in order to behave appropriately in the realm of a social relationship. *Zhi* (wisdom) involves one's knowledge in putting *ren*, *yi* and *li* into practice. Thus, in such a manner, the idea of self is identified in relations to others (Chang and Holt, 1996; Hwang and Chang, 2009). Therefore, *xing fu* lies in the social nexus.

In Confucian teachings, *dao* (the human way) is about one's life goal. To realise *dao*, one must cultivate *de* (virtues) and maintain harmony in different aspects. Hence, according to *dao* (the ideal of human life), the attainment of *xing fu* can be considered as a by-product of being virtuous, maintaining harmony and living in accordance to *dao* (the ideal of a good human life).

1.2.2 Daoism

Daoism (also as Taoism) is another philosophical tradition in ancient China, founded in the sixth century B.C. Lao Zi is the founder of the Daoist tradition. To explore Lao Zi's philosophy, it is essential to understand the following concepts.

(a) Dao: The Way of Nature

Similar with Confucian tradition, *dao* is a key concept within the Daoist framework as well. Nevertheless, Morris (1994) specifies that the interpretations of *dao* between Confucius and Lao Zi are distinct. He highlights that Confucius focuses on *ren dao* (the human way), while Lao Zi stresses *dao* as "the way of nature" (p.110). He interprets Lao Zi's concept of *dao* in naturalistic terms, meaning that *dao* represents the pattern of nature. Lao Zi considers *dao* as the origin of the world. *Dao* is nameless and without any forms (*Dao De Jing*, 25; in Legge, 1891a).

How does *dao* come into existence? For Lao Zi, *dao* first manifests itself as *wu* 無 (non-being) making it formless in nature. Then, it gives birth to all possibilities and realises them as *you* 有 (beings). 'Being' (*you*) refers to the Heaven and Earth; and 'non-being' (*wu*) refers to *dao*. The Heaven and Earth are initially created by *dao*. How does *dao* create all things?

> The Dao produced One; One produced Two; Two produced Three; Three produced All things. All things leave behind them the Obscurity (out of which they have come), and go forward to embrace the Brightness (into which they have emerged).   (Dao De Jing, 42; in Legge, 1891a)

In the quote above, "One" refers to *qi* (energy). Originally, *dao* creates *qi* (energy). Morris (1994) describes *qi* as "vital pneuma", "life-force" or "energy" (p.104). Then, *qi* becomes the source of two opposite forces: *yin* 陰 and *yang* 陽. *Yin* and *yang* complement each other in producing things (Cheung, 2011). *Yin* represents darkness, whereas *yang* represents brightness. The whole system of the world is built around the dynamics of these two forces. Hence, *yin* can be associated with 'the earth', 'cold' and 'femininity'; while *yang* can be associated with 'the heaven', 'heat' and 'masculinity'. Ames (2009) explains the linkage of *yin* and *yang* with *wu* (non-being) and *you* (being) respectively. *Wu* and *you* are relative and interdependent concepts. That means *wu* is relative to *you*, and vice versa. Although *yin* and *yang* are seen as opposite, they represent two complementary facets of existence (Morris, 1994). They are not isolated. Indeed, they are mutually interdependent. For instance, happiness has emerged due to existence of unhappiness, and vice versa (Lu, 2010). Everything or phenomena have two sides: *yin* and *yang*. Therefore, well-being and ill-being are embedded within a never-ending relationship of interdependence. Each depends on the other for existence, contrast and meaning (Lu, 2010).

Yin and *yang* also symbolise the importance of harmony. Neither *yin* nor *yang* exists in pure form. A balanced proportion between *yin* and *yang* has to be presented in every aspect of beings. Therefore, it indicates that a balance between happiness and unhappiness should be maintained in life (Lu, 2010). How can harmony be maintained? Daoist tradition perceives that all things should be processed in accordance with their own natural order. If everything is allowed to go its own way, the harmony of the world will be maintained (Morris, 1994).

Daoist tradition treats *dao* as the way of life, wherein the individuals need to forsake their egos and pursue the order of nature. Thus, rather than controlling or regulating other things or people, Daoist tradition recognises self by harmonising everything in accordance to the natural rhythms and pattern of the world (Cheung, 2011). Daoist tradition advises people to embody themselves in nature. While Confucian framework constructs self within the social nexus, Daoist framework relates self as an integral part of the nature (Cheung, 2011).

In order to follow the pattern of nature (*dao*), one needs to manifest *de* (potency). *De* in Daoist framework is different from Confucian regards in the context of moral virtues. Kaltenmark (1969) notes that Daoists refer to *de* as the potency of an individual to realise itself within nature (in Lai, 2007). Such potency is obtained from *dao* since human beings come from *dao* (Cheung, 2011). The close connection between *de* and *dao* explicitly implies the importance of maintaining the natural order of things.

In Daoist tradition, any individuals who possess *de* (potency) are called *zhen ren* 真人, which means a real or true person (Morris, 1994). *Zhen ren* (a real or true person) would manifest *de* (potency) by dropping their egos and cultivating a way of living that is harmonious with the nature. They would not interfere with the natural order of things (Cheung, 2011). They would preserve *zi ran* (nature, spontaneity).

(b) Zi ran (Nature, Spontaneity)

For Daoist tradition, the way to attain *dao* is to preserve *zi ran* 自然 (nature, spontaneity). Lai (2007) explores the two dominant interpretations of *zi ran*. One is to understand *zi ran* as 'nature'. This interpretation suggests that everything should be attained in their 'natural state'. Another interpretation is to refer *zi ran* as 'spontaneity'. In Chinese, *zi* (自) means 'self' and *ran* (然) indicates 'so', thus *zi ran* literally refers to "so-of-itself" (Liu, 2009, p.226). This suggests that individuals need to have mental space for spontaneity, they should refrain from interference and do not impose unnecessary constraints on any individual or situations. Lai (2007) further highlights the differences in these two interpretations with an example:

> People model themselves on the earth, the earth models itself on Heaven, Heaven models itself on Dao, and Dao models itself on zi ran. (Dao De Jing, 25; in Liu, 2009, p. 227)

It suggests that a series of links culminate to *zi ran*. If *zi ran* is interpreted as 'nature', this would mean that every individual, the Earth, the Heaven and *dao* itself are ideally modelled on the basis of the nature. Everything should follow the pattern of nature. From this perspective, the natural world is an absolute value or ultimate principle. In contrast, if *zi ran* means 'spontaneity', it draws attention to the uncontrived movement and changes that occurred within the natural environment. In response to these changes, the condition of beings is to be spontaneous, meaning humans should not disturb the pattern of nature and jeopardise harmony in the nature (Cheung, 2011). Even though, there are fundamental differences between the two interpretations of *zi ran*, both of them emphasise on the importance of following the pattern of nature. Therefore, both explanations are supported in the *Dao De Jing*.

(c) Wu wei (Non-assertive Action)

To maintain *zi ran*, one needs to practice *wu wei* 無為 (non-assertive action). The most relevant translation of *wu wei* is 'non-action' or 'doing nothing'. However, Morris (1994) argues that such translation can be misleading. He considers that *wu wei* is more related to a non-assertive action, instead of an excuse for not doing anything nor not daring to act. *Wu wei* is an attitude of mind that one seeks harmony with the nature, rather than in rebellion against *dao* (the way of nature). It represents non-interference and tolerance towards what exists and whatever comes (Villaver, 2007). It suggests that people to defer responses, fit into the environment and follow things as they are, so that confrontations to any obstacles are not necessary (Cheung, 2011). It is an effortless action that enables individuals to respond spontaneously to any situations or circumstances. Therefore, it is a response that preserves *zi ran* (spontaneity).

How can one practice *wu wei*? *Wu wei* requires individuals to have an open mind (Cheung, 2011). It requires people to "forgetting of one's own life/self" (Villaver, 2007, p.2). The individuals need to let go of their personal desires and pre-conceived preferences. They should not urge for fulfilling their wants and needs. They can follow the pattern of nature, and accept what life gives them. Only by living harmoniously with *dao* (the way of nature), they can feel happy, safe and secure.

(d) Summary: How Would Daoists Express Xing Fu?

Daoist framework promotes an attitude towards the natural world. It advocates people to follow the pattern of nature. Self can only be recognised through the harmonisation within the natural rhythms (Cheung, 2011). Therefore, Daoist tradition considers living harmoniously with *dao* (the way of nature) which would lead to true happiness. With *yin* and *yang* philosophy, it indicates that the relationship between well-being and ill-being are interdependent. Therefore, one needs to maintain a balance between happiness and unhappiness in life (Lu, 2010).

To live in accordance to *dao*, one needs to manifest in *de*, which refers to the potency of the individual to realise itself within the nature. Individuals also need to allow for spontaneity or naturalness (*zi ran*) by practicing *wu wei* (non-assertive action) in life.

(e) Is there any Chinese well-being?

Lu (2010) studies Chinese well-being. His endeavour is among the first to bridge the gap between conventional theories of SWB and Chinese perception on happiness. First, he concludes that for Chinese, happiness is prominently conceptualised as a harmonious state of existence, wherein one maintains a harmonious relationship with oneself and the environment. Such harmony requires an individual to (1) feel satisfied, (2) be the agent of his or her own happiness, (3) regard spiritual enrichment as more important than material satisfaction, and (4) maintain a positive outlook towards the future. Second, he highlights the dialectical relationship between happiness and unhappiness. Thus, happiness and unhappiness are perceived as the two sides of the same coin, wherein one side depends on the other for significance and existence. He explains that Chinese prefer to maintain a balance between happiness and unhappiness in life. Third, he describes that Chinese believe that the pursuit of happiness derived from discovery, contentment, maintaining gratitude, giving, sharing, serving others and self-cultivations.

Based on the above findings, Lu and Gilmour (2006) develop the individual-oriented and social-oriented cultural conceptions of SWB scales (ISSWB). ISSWB does not only consist of conventional aspects of SWB, which is based on the individualistic notion of self, but it also incorporated the East Asian view of self as a relational being. The social-oriented cultural conception SWB is composed of two distinct characteristics: role obligations and dialectical balance. For role obligations, it is based on the Confucian teaching that happiness can be obtained through fulfilling social role obligations and disciplined self-cultivation. For dialectical balance, it is built upon Daoist concept of *yin* and *yang*, which suggests that people should not pursue happiness in excess of unhappiness, and vice versa. Lu and Gilmour (2006) show that Chinese possess stronger social-oriented SWB than Americans, while Americans have stronger individual-oriented SWB. Their study clearly indicates that there are cultural differences in well-being.

Most importantly, ISSWB explores the possibility of a bicultural self. Lu and Gilmour (2006) found that both individual-oriented and social-oriented SWB coexisted among Chinese and American students. This may suggest that different cultural systems could actually coexist at the individual level. Therefore, Lu and Yang (2006) propose the Chinese bicultural self-model. They highlight that Chinese would be influenced by the western culture. Thus, the modern Chinese self-system can be inculcated with both individualistic and social orientations. While examining the bicultural self-model, Lu (2009) found that the aspects of independence and relatedness were both strongly valued among the Taiwan youngsters. Lu, Kao, Chang, Wu and Jin (2008) also highlight that the bicultural self is prevalent among both the mainland Chinese and Taiwanese, with the former endorsed aspects of the individual-oriented self in a more determined manner than the latter. Their study indicates Chinese may face dilemma between individual-oriented self and social-oriented self. Therefore, Lu (2010) encourages more systematic and fine-grained investigations on examining the dynamic process of such cultural integration, social changes and psychological transformation in Chinese society. Given research on Chinese well-being is still in its infancy stage, he suggests researchers to have a moral obligation and maintain cautiousness to any social transformations. In response to his call, this book pays attention to the hybridity of the subject and the dynamics of change in the discourses of well-being and *xing fu*. Both western and Chinese perspectives are taken into account in order to better understand the Chinese subject.

This section offers further layer of meaning about *xing fu*. Such a layer is often being ignored in the mainstream framework of well-being. Hence, it highlights there are weaknesses in a mainstream approach to well-being. Next section further examines these lacunae in well-being research.

1.3 Lacunae in Well-being Research: Is Xing Fu Equivalent to Well-being?

Positivism and neo-positivism are the main epistemologies in well-being research. This argument is aligned with the analyses of Leppäaho, Plakoyiannaki and Dimitratos (2016) and Steffy and Grimes (1992), who found that positivism and neo-positivism are the prevailing research methodologies in Organisational Psychology and Family Business. The key assumption of the positivist view is that the "social world exists externally and its properties should be measured through objective methods, rather than being inferred subjectively through sensation, reflection or intuition" (Easterby-Smith, Thorpe and Lowe, 1991, p.22). Therefore, to positivists, "science is value-free" and the "observer is independent" (Easterby-Smith et al., 1991, p.27). Researchers that follow the positivist paradigm would gather facts, collect statistical data, look for causality and laws, and measure the frequency in which certain patterns occur (Harvey and MacDonald, 1993). They aim to develop and confirm general laws and theories that govern the relationship between various observable variables.

Neo-positivism is a modification of positivism. Neo-positivists rely upon qualitative methods to inductively develop description of pattern, relationships and causal propositions to explain and predict behaviours. Even though neo-positivism rejects falsifications and is in favour of induction, neo-positivism is deeply rooted in positivism. Both positivists and neo-positivists treat "knowledge as a correspondence of representations and the reality" and "knowledge production rests on a privileging of the consciousness of the researcher who is deemed capable of discovering the 'truth' about the world of management and organizations through a series of representations" (Knights, 1992, p.515). They seek to develop theories that aim to represent the empirical reality; construct conceptual frameworks based on various isolatable constituent variables to provide abstract representation of 'thing' or event assumed to be out there; and hypothesise relationships between variables. They assume that theory can be generated from the standpoint of the researchers (i.e. observers) who stand 'outside' the situations.

Positivism and neo-positivism have contributed to knowledge as these two methodologies are able to highlight the significance of well-being in organisational contexts. However, the possible weaknesses of positivism and neo-positivism are: (1) their restriction on "ontological potential" (Steffy and Grimes, 1992), and (2) limited degree of reflexivity (Jack, Calas, Nkomo and Peltonen, 2008). First, ontological and epistemological questions are largely assumed to be irrelevant in the positivist or neo-positivist research, since inquiries tend to be confined within those propositions that are empirically testable or observable (Steffy and Grimes, 1992). Criticism is generally confined to questions on the internal rules of method. For instance, positivists and neo-positivists seek understanding of well-being as if it was a 'law-like' process which influences human behaviour. They primarily focus on variables that affect well-being, whereas the ontological nature of well-being itself becomes a secondary issue which is rarely examined (Sarvimaki, 2006; Simsek, 2009). The practice of systematising and universalising scientific theories in positivism and neo-positivism, can "turn people *(subject)* into things *(objects)*" (Madigan, 1992, p. 266).

From the positivist perspective, the ontological assumption of well-being is confined to be predetermined, law-bound and static. For instance, cross-cultural examinations on well-being is always cross-sectional which assumes well-being is fixed in nature (Chandler and Lyon, 2001; Diener, Suh, Smith, and Shao, 1995; Kontinen and Ojala, 2010; Veenhoven, 2000b). Both Hedonism and Eudaimonia have a similar ontological assumption on human nature, a Modern Man, which assumes that human beings would be bound by external forces. In that case, well-being is seen an 'external force' or 'law' that has the capability to influence human behaviours. However, a definite and lawful prescription of well-being as an external force can neglect the lived experience of human beings, since well-being could be socially constructed through interaction between peoples in a particular situation and within a particular historical and cultural context (Calestani, 2009). Could well-being be dynamic, flexible, interactive and political? Could well-being be (re)created through human interactions in different time and space and with different people? Giving well-being a fixed description or meaning may restrict its ontological potential. There is limited attention to generate detailed description about the dynamic social process in formulating and transforming well-being.

In the examination of international management (IM) discourse, Jack et al. (2008) consider that IM has remained firmly rooted in traditional-functionalist-positivism. Such a research approach has little reflexivity on its epistemological position. Their critique applies to a cultural understanding of well-being. Positivists seldom acknowledge their own participation in the constitution of social reality (Knights, 1992). They have a tendency to be un-reflexive about their ontology, epistemological strategy and the representation they produce. For instance, Christopher (1999) observes that the

Hedonism and Eudaimonia may actually *"illuminate the Euro-American cultural roots"* (p.141) and could have little relevance to the *Other's* (non-western) cultures. The theoretical constructs of subjective well-being (SWB) and psychological well-being (PWB) may constitute a social reality that is based on individualism. Misrepresentation and misunderstanding could result, if the prevailing components of SWB and PWB are transplanted to *the Other's* culture. Hence, Christopher questions such cultural-free theories or assessments of well-being. He argues that the concept of well-being is inherently culturally rooted. Therefore, he claims that an "understanding of psychological well-being necessarily relies upon moral visions that are culturally embedded and frequently culture specific" (p.149).

Building upon Christopher's argument, Lu (2010) explains that the notion of self is intricately linked with one's perception of well-being. Lu argues that well-being is derived from the notion of self, which carries "cultural mandates in a culturally mandated manner" (p.334). By this, Lu emphasises that the perception of well-being is built upon the construction of self, which varies across cultures. For instance, Lu highlights that the Chinese locate self within social relationships and therefore their "social expectations" are "finely integrated into their sense of well-being" (p. 293). The Chinese view self as part of social nexus and nature (Lu, 2008). In contrast, Americans consider self as being independent; they "uphold personal happiness as the supreme value of life, and blatantly assert individual agency against social restrictions" (p. 294). Thus, Lu contends, "culture serves as a major force shaping the way people conceptualize the self, think about happiness, and cope with difficulties and upheavals in life" (p.290). Hence, if a mainstream framework of well-being is brought to a Chinese context, its assumed universality is questioned. In that case, the voices of a Chinese subject could be marginalised. For illustration, cross-cultural examinations of well-being often exhibit that the Chinese have lower degree of happiness than westerners (Diener, Diener and Diener, 1995; Helliwell, Huang, Wang and Norton, 2021; Veenhoven, 2000a). Diener et al.'s (1995) cross-cultural research with students in South Korea, Japan, China and United States explored differences in reported subjective well-being (SWB). They found that students in East Asia appeared to have lower SWB than their American counterparts. Chinese students were found to be less familiar with the notion of SWB, and therefore, appeared to have less concern for SWB. China is ranked below 50 in The World Happiness Report in 2017–2020 (Helliwell, Huang, Wang and Norton, 2021).

Why does research often show that the Chinese have lower degree of happiness? One reason is the word 'happiness' does not appear in Chinese colloquial language until recently (Lu, 2010). Although the research of well-being in Chinese societies has progressed, most of the studies are typically conducted based on western ideas, cultural tradition and instrumentation (Liu and Yu, 2021; Luo and Chou, 2020). Hedonism or Eudaimonia are always exclusively adopted to interpret the Chinese perspectives of well-being (Luo and Chou, 2020). In examining the conventional approach to well-being, Lu (2010) considers that the mainstream research may have twisted the Chinese culture in order to show psychological equivalence to western theoretical framework. This could be one major shortfall of the mainstream framework. With regards to this, it is important to scrutinise Chinese culture through its local language and intellectual traditions (Liu and Yu, 2021). In Section 1.2, an additional layer of meaning of *xing fu* is revealed, in which it implies that *xing fu* may not be exactly the same as well-being. Nevertheless, this layer of knowledge is often being neglected because *xing fu* is often treated as a direct equivalent of well-being in the literature. In order to recuperate such a Chinese perspective of *xing fu*, a proposed conceptual framework (see Tab. 1.2) that includes both well-being and *xing fu* is formulated. Both concepts will be demystified and contextualised through an archaeological and anthropological examination.

Tab. 1.2: Proposed Conceptual Framework.

Dimensions	A Western Perspective		An Eastern perspective	
Philology:	**Well-being** The state of feeling comfortable, healthy, or happy. The World Health Organization (WHO) (1948) describes health as "a state of complete physical, mental and social well-being and not merely the absence of disease or infirmity" (p.100)		***Xing fu*** (幸福) Lucky and fortunate Durative, stable, long-lasting Blessings from the supernatural Harmonious Pleasures in and after life ***Kuai le*** (快樂) Fast, quick, momentary, short-lived happiness	
Philosophy:	Hedonism	Eudaimonia	**Confucian framework**	**Daoist framework**
Focus	Individualism		Be virtuous Social relations Collective welfare	Pattern of Nature
Concept of self	Individualistic, autonomous and independent		Relational and interdependent	Self as part of the Nature
Life goals	Be happy	Actualize human potential	Observing or acting according to the way of Heaven (*tian dao*)	Live in accordance to the way of Nature (*dao*)
Ways to well-being	Obtain pleasure Avoid pain	Realize human potential, growth and development	Cultivate virtues (*de*) Maintain harmony in social relations	Manifest the potency (*de*) to realize oneself within the nature Allow for spontaneity (*zi ran*) Practise non-assertive action (*wu wei*)

Tab. 1.2 (continued)

Dimensions	A Western Perspective		An Eastern perspective	
Psychology:	Subjective well-being (SWB)	Psychological well-being (PWB)	Socially-oriented SWB: Role obligations	Socially-oriented SWB: Dialectical balance

1.4 An Archaeological and Anthropological Journey into Well-being

The review of well-being literature raises issues related to the knowledge production of well-being. The book suspects that *xing fu* could probably be misappropriated in the well-being discourse. To address this issue, the book explores conditions of two possibilities: (1) the conditions that made the discourse of well-being possible in a Chinese context and (2) the conditions that could make a Chinese voice possible in management discourse. Both archaeology and anthropology are used as the methodology. An archaeological examination is taken to handle RQ 1 (i.e. 1st possibility); while an anthropological examination is conducted to answer RQ 2 (i.e. 2nd possibility). In other words, the first part of analysis (see Chapter 3) will explore the discursive (trans) formations of well-being in a Chinese context; while the second part of the analysis (see Chapters 4 and 5) will explore a Chinese perspective on everydayness of life.

(a) An Archaeological Examination

In the first part of the investigation, an archaeological examination is conducted to analyse the discursive (trans) formation of well-being. In this examination, well-being is treated as a discursive concept. Drawing from Foucault's (1972) *Archaeology of Knowledge*, the conditions, rules and changes that shape the discourse of well-being are revealed. Foucault's archaeology provides a tool to examine the discursive practices that produce the knowledge of well-being in a Chinese context. For illustration, Xu's (2000) archaeology of quality is one example. She demonstrated that "how 'quality' and 'standard' may have become discursive objects" (p.427) in the discourse of *Total Quality Management*. Following Xu's (2000) approach, this book establishes well-being and *xing fu* as discursive objects and examines their (trans)formation in the discourse. Foucault (1972) pointed out that:

> to describe the formation of the object of a discourse, one tries to locate the relations that characterize a discursive practice (pp.44–48)

1.4 An Archaeological and Anthropological Journey into Well-being — 29

Here, Foucault refers 'the relations' as "a group of relations establish between authorities of emergence, delimitation and specification" (p.46). To be more specific, it is a group of "discursive relations" (p.47) that "offer its objects of which it can speak . . . in order to deal with them, name them, analyse them, classify them, explain them, etc" (p.46). "These relations characterise not the language used by discourse, nor the circumstances in which it is deployed, but discourse itself as a practice" (p.46). Foucault perceives "discourses as practices obeying certain rules" (p.138). Hence, archaeology examines "the groups of rules that are immanent in a practice, and define it in its specificity" (p.46). For Foucault, discursive practice is particularly formulated by and for a particular group. In this case, archaeology provides a ground for the argument that there is no universal or objective knowledge of well-being. The formation of well-being can be culturally and historically distinctive.

Foucault (1972) identifies "five distinct tasks" (p.160) of archaeology. These tasks imply "what archaeology wishes to uncover is primarily – in the specificity and distance maintained in various discursive formation" (p.160). In short, archaeology is an examination of (1) discursive formation and (2) transformation through (3) different thresholds (Appendix A: Notes A1). Based on the key elements in Foucault's archaeology, how can research put his archaeology into operation? Some researchers have followed Foucault's archaeology to examine management knowledge. For example, Jacques (1996) exhibited a history of American management discourse and contextualised the conditions that gave rise to 'the employee'. Xu (1997) provided a supplementary account on *total quality management* (TQM) discourse. She examines the discursive emergence, formation and transformation of TQM and its knowledge production. She maps out the 'generation of texts' (p.167) as shown in Tab. 1.3.

Tab. 1.3: An Archaeology of TQM (Xu, 1997).

Generation of texts	Description on each level of texts
Conditioning text	Texts formulate earlier than the 1st order text (p.179)
1st order texts	"the original texts on total quality control (TQC)" (p.167) written by guru
2nd order texts	"introductory texts on TQM written by QM experts and/or academics" (p.169)
3rd order texts	"research projects" (p.170) on TQM
4th order texts	"for the consumption of the general public" (p.179)

Building on Xu's (1997) 'orders of TQM texts' (p.166–200), this examination traces the discursive (trans)formation of well-being. It aims to uncover the rules that govern every layer of the discourse as highlighted in Tab. 1.4. The procedures are developed on the basis of Xu's (1997) 'orders of TQM texts', but its focus of archaeological analyses is varied from that of Xu (1997). This book places its centre of interest on the (trans)formation of a concept, whereas Xu (1997) examines the making up of a discourse. Xu (1997) treats TQC texts (i.e. the precondition of TQM discourse) as the 1st order of text and placed the 2nd order of text (i.e. trace of TQM) as the centre of TQM discourse "where 'TQM knowledge' appears as operational guideline" (p.172); while the archaeological operation in this study (1) puts any precondition(s) of an object in the layers underneath its formation (i.e. conditions of texts and conditioning texts); and (2) traces how an object is emerged, formed (i.e. in 1st layer of texts) and transformed into a concept (i.e. in 2nd layer of texts). Following Foucault's sequence of discursive formation, an object is formulated before the formation of a concept. Hence, the movement from 1st layer to 2nd layer uncovers the conditions that an object is 'recorded, described, explained and elaborated' (p.167) into a concept. The 3rd layer of texts signifies any transformations of a concept. One needs to pay attention to the thresholds whenever examining the movements along different layers of the texts. Similar to Xu's analysis, the 4th layer of texts is for knowledge consumption. For this book, the context lies in the realm of business management. Therefore, knowledge consumption could refer to any business practices related to the concept of well-being.

Tab. 1.4: An Archaeology of Well-being.

Generation of texts	The archaeology of well-being
Layers underneath the origins	Conditioning texts of well-being; Conditions that gave rise to the texts
1st layer texts: Formation of a discursive object	Formation of *well-being* as an object
2nd layer texts: Formation of a discursive concept	Formation of *well-being* as a concept
3rd layer texts: Transformation of a concept	The discursive transformation of *well-being*
4th layer texts: Business practice of a concept	Business practices of *well-being*

The archaeology examines the discourse of well-being. Such an analysis relies on previous texts, which are past records that have been lying there, kept or assembled by others. In other words, archaeology is a historical analysis in which it is unable to reveal any empirical findings on the local expressions. Therefore, to answer the second research question, one needs to get close with the research subject and be sensitive to its expressions, including its own language and lived experience. This task would be achieved through an anthropological study.

(b) An Anthropological Examination

In the second part of the investigation, an anthropological study is carried out to explore the significance of well-being in a Chinese context and uncover some indigenous expressions. These social expressions are scrutinised through 'thick description' (Geertz, 1973), including their richness of intentions, thoughts and meanings. Christopher (1999) suggests that any understandings of well-being need to be based on the *'moral vision'*, rather than solely relying on theories and measures of well-being that are developed in the west. He suggests alternative methodologies to contextualise individual perceptions of being well. In response to his call, a critical ethnography would be appropriate for this research as it does not only allow me as the researcher to get close to a Chinese subject, but also emphasise reflexivity in order to uphold ethics in research.

The fieldwork began in March 2012 and finished in December 2015. Four field sites are chosen and all of them are small family businesses. The data are obtained mainly through a combination of methods, including participant observation, informal conversation, documentary and photographs, interpretive field notes and diary and semi-structured interviews. The interviewees are ranged from the owners, family workers, family members and employees in family businesses, as well as local Human Resource professionals in multinational corporations. The details of the research design and fieldwork are described in Appendix B: Notes B1. After the fieldwork, I transcribed the interview records, consolidated all the data and then analysed the data (Appendix B: Notes B2). I use thematic analysis to sort out the ethnographic data. Thematic analysis is a process for locating codes and themes in qualitative information (Boyatzis, 1998; Braun and Clarke, 2006) (see Appendix B: Tab. B7). The empirical data of the ethnography is classified into themes. These themes are initially presented through a 'thick description' (Geertz, 1973) in Chapter 4. 'Thick description' may potentially help to generate an in-depth understanding of the research subject. Afterwards, a cross-cultural analysis among different perspectives (i.e. Hedonism, Eudaimonia, Confucian and Daoist teachings) are made in Chapter 5. First, a Chinese subject's voice is put at the centre of the discursive space. Their expressions are first interpreted through a mainstream framework of well-being (mainly Hedonism and Eudaimonia) and then through a Chinese perspective, namely Confucian and Daoist frameworks. Here, the Chinese language and its intellectual traditions can be the key resources to understand a Chinese subject (Westwood, 2004). Second, each perspective (i.e. Hedonism, Eudaimonia, Confucian and Daoist teachings) would initiate a dialogue (see Section 5.2). The dialogue begins by highlighting the crucial ideas and concerns from a particular framework. Then, space will be provided for other perspectives to speak as an equal partner, and respond to any focal points of interest being raised. Hence, a theoretical dialogue among various perspectives is initiated. Hopefully, the dialogue enables each side to better understand one another and shed some light on understanding the research subject – members of Chinese family businesses (CFB) in Hong Kong.

Chapter 2
Chinese Family Business

Chinese family business (CFB) in Hong Kong is the context in which well-being and *xing fu* are scrutinised. In order to provide an understanding of the research context, this chapter examines the management discourse of CFB. The problems of objectification and essentialism are highlighted in the literature review. Foucault (1972) describes objectification as a discursive practice that "transforms human beings into (objectified) subjects" (p.777). While reviewing Redding's (1990) account of CFB, Xu (2008) considers that a non-western subject is often unwittingly made as an object of knowledge for analysing the western theories. Similarly, Westwood (2001) diagnoses the occurrence of essentialism in his examination of management discourse. According to him, essentialism is "a reductive strategy" (p.258), in which the Other (a non-western subject) is being appropriated and positioned as a "counterpoint" (p.250) to the Self (the west). In that case, any cultural differences between the Other and the Self are essentially exaggerated, amplified, aggravated or distorted without rendering much significance to the Other. For instance, in the literature (such as in the works of Chen, 1995; Chen, Zhou, He and Fu, 2020; Luechapattanaporn and Wongsurawat, 2021; Mosbah and Wahab, 2018; Poutziouris, Wang and Chan, 2002; Redding, 1990; Redding, 2000; Whiteley, 1992; Wong and Chau, 2020; Yu, 2001), CFB is often constructed with distinctive management features, including small in scale, defensive and unprofessional. These representations can portray a negative image of CFB and are considered to be incomplete or even incorrect (Xu, 2008).

Are the practices of CFB really falling behind the western professional management? Or are these negative connotations of CFB an evident of an essentialist tendency in the management discourse? Could these misrepresentations impede the development of Chinese management? Under what conditions could a Chinese management theory become possible? This book offers an answer to these questions via archaeology. Michel Foucault's (1972) *Archaeology of Knowledge* is drawn to reveal and dissect essentialism in the discourse, because his archaeology can account for discursive changes and trace a sequence of "conditions of possibility" (Foucault, 1979, Preface: p.xxiv) that gives rise to a discourse. In other words, his archaeology could be a way to examine how and when essentialism could have taken place within the discourse.

This chapter first discusses the roles of CFB in Hong Kong, which is helpful in understanding the broader context of the research. Then it critically reviews CFB in management discourse and highlights the problems in the literature. In dealing with the problems, a new research direction that accounts for change is proposed.

2.1 Family Business in Hong Kong

By 2021, Hong Kong had a population of 7.48 million people wherein 3.87 million of them were included in the labour force (Census and Statistics Department, 2021). Among the working population, 5.2% were self-employed (Census and Statistics Department, 2021). The percentage of self-employed has been growing. Small and medium-sized enterprises (SMEs) constitute over 90% of business enterprises in Hong Kong (ECIC, 2005; The Hong Kong Institute of Directors, 2014; Wong and Chau, 2020). Most of them are family businesses, in which they are controlled, managed and operated by entrepreneurs and their family members (ECIC, 2005; King and Peng, 2007; The Hong Kong Institute of Directors, 2014; Wong and Chau, 2020; Zheng, 2002). Chiu (1998) defines a family business as any business that involves family members in shared ownership, management, or labour on a continuing basis. Approximately 70% of the listed companies on the Hong Kong Stock Exchange are family-controlled and they constitute for over 80% of GDP in Hong Kong (Wong and Chau, 2020). Some well-established local family businesses have been in operation for over three generations, such as *Lee Kam Kee, Yu Yan Sang* and *Kwong Sang Hong*. Hence, CFB plays a dominant role in the economic development of Hong Kong.

Most employees in Hong Kong have worked in CFBs before they are employed by the multinational corporations (MNCs) (The Hong Kong Institute of Directors, 2014). Their work expectation in MNCs could be most likely derived from their previous work experience in CFBs. Hence, the indigenous practices of CFB could be regarded as a reference for MNCs, especially when international human resource management (IHRM) is regarded as a biggest challenges for foreign companies doing business in China (The EU SME Centre, 2015; Liu and Yu, 2021). Very often, MNCs face difficulties in attracting and retaining talent in China (Cooke, Saini and Wang, 2014; The EU SME Centre, 2015). Some of the so called 'best practices' in Human Resource Management (HRM) are ineffective in managing Chinese employees (Ariss and Sidani, 2016; Liu and Yu, 2021). For instance, employee assistance programs are often universally used for improving employee well-being. However, these HR initiatives have been found as less attractive to Chinese employees, because the concept of work-life balance is less relevant to them (Xiao and Cooke, 2012). Their work motivation is influenced by different incentives and disincentives (Xiao and Cooke, 2012). If MNCs want to attract and retain Chinese talents effectively, it would be useful to understand the work practices of CFB for the development of a contextualised HRM approach in China (Ariss and Sidani, 2016; Cooke et al., 2014; Liu and Yu, 2021; Xiao and Cooke, 2012).

2.2 Chinese Family Business in Management Discourse

The paradigm of family business research has been developing since the last 20 years wherein the mainstream enquiries concentrate in western contexts (Dess, Pinkham and Yang, 2011; Sharma, 2004; Zahra, Klein and Astrachan, 2006). Nevertheless, the rapid economic development in Asia (particularly in China and the Southeast Asia) leads to the development of research in the context of Chinese family business (CFB). Loy (2012) and Wong and Chau (2020) present a comparative review on CFB. According to their reviews, most of the studies examine the business, management and financial aspects of CFBs, which mainly includes business growth, competitiveness, management culture, professionalism, performance and internationalism. In addition, the importance of 'family' in constructing the daily lives and practices of CFB is emphasised. *Strategy* and *management* are major areas of investigations in CFB discourse (Loy, 2012; Wong and Chau, 2020).

CFB is often constructed with distinctive features within the realm of structure, strategy and management. For instance, CFB is usually characterised as small and medium in scale, in which its management prefers centralised decision making (Mosbah and Wahab, 2018; Redding, 1990; Redding, 2000; Whitley, 1992), flexible work system (Yu, 2001), paternalistic leadership (Luechapattanaporn and Wongsurawat, 2021; Mosbah and Wahab, 2018; Redding, 1990; Sheer, 2013 Whitley, 1992; Yu, Wang, Bai and Li, 2018), patriarch family culture (Luechapattanaporn and Wongsurawat, 2021; Mosbah and Wahab, 2018; Minkes and Foster, 2011; Yu and Kwan, 2015) and strong stability with limited long-term planning, growth and innovation (Chen, 1995; Chen et al., 2020; Luechapattanaporn and Wongsurawat, 2021; Poutziouris et al., 2002; Redding, 1990; Redding, 2000; Whitley, 1992; Yu et al., 2018); while individuals working in CFB are usually devoted to the business wholeheartedly, due to their intrinsic characteristics of being cost-conscious (Chen et al., 2020; Redding, 1990; Redding, 2000; Yu, 2001), diligent (Luechapattanaporn and Wongsurawat, 2021; Minkes and Foster, 2011), nepotic, loyal and obligated to family business and committed to prosperity (ECIC, 2005; Luechapattanaporn and Wongsurawat, 2021; Redding, 1990; Redding, 2000; Sheer, 2013; Whitley, 1992; Zheng, 2002). While these features are often generalised among CFB around the world (Luechapattanaporn and Wongsurawat, 2021; Mosbah and Wahab, 2018), it is also important to highlight any significant differentiations of the oversea CFB (OCFB) around the diaspora (Loy, 2012; Redding, 2000).

In the literature of family business, Gordon Redding is a prominent researcher who has made a significant contribution to the knowledge of CFB management (Carney and Jaskiewicz, 2015). Therefore, it is necessary to critically analyse his work, *'The Spirit of Chinese Capitalism'* (1990). The aim of Redding's (1990) study is to examine the notion of economic culture that is prevalent in CFB, particularly to the OCFB in Southeast Asian diaspora. He conversed with 72 executives, mainly in Hong Kong, Taiwan, Singapore and Indonesia. His study pays tribute to Max Weber

(1958) by underlining his work, *"The Protestant Ethics and the Spirit of Capitalism"* (Redding, 1990: Preface vii). Redding perceives the nature and management of OCFB as a cultural artefact, and based on this assumption, he describes the management ideologies of OCFB as: *"paternalism", "familism", "hierarchy", "personalistic relations", "reciprocity", "nepotism", "limited trust to employees"* and *"strategic and financial caution"* (Redding, 1990: p.145). He considers that the mentioned characteristics are shaped by three key surroundings which are inherited from the Chinese culture: *"paternalism", "personalism" and "insecurity"* (p.144). As a result, he characterises the typical organisational structure of OCFB as *"small scale"* with *"product or market specialisation", "low standardisation", "low role specialisation", "strong workflow formalisation", "centralization"* and *"emphasis on line rather than staff"* (p.154). For Redding, the OCFB relies greatly on *"extensive networking", "relational contracts", "interlocking directorship" and "strategic alliances"* (p.144) and concentrates on *"centralised planning and control", "tight financial and production management", "informal and pragmatic personnel management"* and *"vestigial marketing"* (p.145). Redding describes the above features as 'the Chinese family business management'. He concludes that OCFB has its own distinct managerial mechanism that is substantially different from western professional management, bureaucracy and neutralisation.

Are there any weaknesses and gaps in the above CFB discourse? To answer this question, below shows a critical review of the management discourse:

(a) Interrogating Management Discourse

A tendency of objectification and essentialism is identified in the management discourse of CFB. Objectification and essentialism are issues raised by the critical perspective. In order to understand the two issues, it is necessary to examine the critical management studies.

i. Objectification

Poststructuralism can be regarded as an intellectual movement that was initiated by Michael Foucault and Jacques Derrida in the 1960s. It represents a radical disintegration from structuralism that was once a dominant mode of ideology in Europe since the early 1900s. Structuralism has been formulated on the works of a linguist, Ferdinand de Saussure, who is regarded as 'the father of structuralism'. In his lecture notes, *Course in General Linguistics*, he states that:

> A language is a system in which all the elements fit together, and in which the value of anyone element depends on the simultaneous coexistence of all the others. (de Saussure, 1983, p. 113)

According to the above proposition, he believes that a scientific model of language is connected with a system, which has an underlying structure of rules and codes. Blackburn (2008) describes structuralism as:

> the belief that phenomena of human life are not intelligible except through their interrelations. These relations constitute a structure, and behind local variations in the surface phenomena there are constant laws of abstract culture.

To a limited extent, structuralism views "language as a close and complete system" and studies phenomenon "with the law-like precision of a science" (Radford and Radford, 2005, p. 67). In such a case, structuralism tends to study the state of language or phenomenon at a particular moment and overlooks the changes that occurred with time. Such shortcoming gave rise to the post-structuralist movement.

Post-structuralism does not only provide critiques on structuralism but also reveal the diversity of discourse (Xu, 1997). This mode of thinking asserts that to understand any given object, it is imperative to scrutinise both an object/a phenomenon itself and its knowledge system. That is to say, the post-structuralist approach examines the production of knowledge. Poststructuralist writers seek to have a critical self-reflection on how the western knowledge is produced and have altered over time. Michael Foucault (1972) is a typical poststructuralist who studies the production of knowledge. His works refer to the critical studies of social institutions. One of the most influential themes in his works is power, knowledge and subjectivity (Townley, 1993). In *"The subject and power"* (1982), he notably observed the formulation of discursive objects. He asserts that *'objectification'* is a discursive practice that "transforms human beings into (objectified) subjects" (p.777). He highlights three modes of objectification: (1) scientific classification; (2) dividing practice (p.777) and (3) subjectification (p.778). Scientific classification refers to "the modes of inquiry which try to give themselves the status of sciences" (p.777). For example, Foucault explains that while analysing wealth and economics, labours were chosen as the subjects; they were objectified as a productive subject. The second mode of objectification is "dividing practice" (Foucault, 1982, p. 777), wherein the subject that exhibits differences would be divided socially or physically through objectification. This practice is tolerated, justified and even legitimised as the social group that gives power to scientific claims (Madigan, 1992). Foucault uses the mad versus the sane and the sick versus the healthy, to illustrate that an individual is given a social and personal identity in the process of objectification and categorisation. He suggests that the mode of inquiry can support and legitimise dividing practice. Scientific evidence is generated to exaggerate or mythologise the differences between groups, which allows and supports the supremacy of dominant group over the others (Curtis and Harrison, 2001). The third mode of objectification is subjectification, "the way a human being turns himself into a subject" (Foucault, 1982, p.778). For this mode, Foucault takes the domain of sexuality to examine "how men have learnt to recognise themselves as subjects of "sexuality"" (p.778). This objectification is different from the previous two modes. Under this scenario, the person is taking an active role in the process of self-formation. It is a self-understanding process that individuals would conduct and monitor themselves in accordance with the interpretations of their cultural norms (Madigan, 1992). Foucault relates objectification to the issue of power, because the human subject is located within power relations when knowledge is produced.

Johannes Fabian follows up with similar concern in his epistemological critique of anthropology: *"Time and the Other: How Anthropology Makes its Object"* (1983). He associates the issue with *'allochronism'* (p.32) – the traditional forms of ethnographic representation would lead to the suppression of the subject's voice via *"denial of coevalness"* (p.31). He explains that such a denial is due to the epistemological position of the researchers. He criticises that the positivist approach would require the researchers to employ a given theory for organising the observed phenomenon. In such a way, the theory or the category of the theory is adopted to study *the Other's* culture. Any aspects of *their culture*, which are not covered in the theory, might be treated as unimportant or irrelevant. In other words, the positivist approach focuses on what *our theory* allows us to say about *their culture*. It requires anthropologists to locate their subject in the discursive space of *the theory*. As a consequence, the subject is made to be *an object of knowledge* for examining *the theory* and the representations would be lack of critical self-reflection. Fabian regarded such a constitutive phenomenon as distancing and reifying the subject as an inherent object of the anthropologist's observation. For Fabian, such allochronic discourse is a product of ethnocentrism, which is considered as a vehicle of western self-domination and a political act, because the non-western *Other* is ethnographically depicted as "primitive" or "savage" (p.77).

With reference to Fabian's *allochronism*, Levinas' ethics, China's economic culture and language, Xu (2008) generates a critical review of Redding's (1990) *'The Spirit of Chinese Capitalism'*. She suspects Redding's examination on Chinese family businesses has underpinned *'the theory'* of Weber's cultural thesis and therefore the interpretation of overseas Chinese was not devoid from Eurocentric tendency. Redding has created a "collectivist form of capitalism" (Goody, 1996, p.7) and "has appropriated the subject into an object of knowledge" to testify Weber's *"The Protestant Ethics and the Spirit of Capitalism"* (1958) (Xu, 2008, p.261). Xu highlights that Redding treated his subject as *"data"* for theorising, instead of being his interlocutors (p.252), because he was conversing with "those economists who discount culture in explaining economic activities" (p.252), rather than the overseas Chinese entrepreneurs. Therefore, she considers such an approach as a process of *objectification* (i.e. making the subject as the object of knowledge), which can "interrupt the subject's continuity, deprive its voice and deny its capacity for dialogue" (p.242). Her critique of *objectification* can be parallel to the problem of *essentialism*, raised by the postcolonial perspective.

ii. Essentialism

Said (1978) draws from Foucault's idea on dynamics of power and knowledge to develop the concept of *'Orientalism'*. He describes *'Orientalism'* as

> a style of thought based upon an ontological and epistemological distinction made between "the Orient" and (most of the time) "the Occident". (p.2)

Here, 'the Orient' is referred to *the Other's* culture, particularly in the Near East (the Middle East), whereas 'the Occident' is regarded as Europe (or the west). Said perceives *Orientalism* as a discourse. He argues that knowledge is formulated through discursive social practices which create a representation of the object of knowledge. Individuals would follow these practices for communication, understanding and acceptance. He demonstrates how knowledge of the Orient's culture is constructed by the Occident. *Orientalism* enables one to "understand the enormously systematic discipline by which European culture was able to manage – and even produce the Orient politically, sociologically, militarily, ideologically, scientifically, and imaginatively during the post-Enlightenment period" (p.3). Said articulates *Orientalism* as follows:

> Orientalism, a way of coming to terms with the Orient that is based on the Orient's special place in European Western experience. (p. 1)

Orientalism implies "European culture gained in strength and identity by setting itself off against the Orient as a sort of surrogate and even underground self" (Said, 1978, p.3). Said argues that "because of Orientalism the Orient was not (and is not) a free subject of thought or action" (p.3). Though he emphasises the west's encounter with the Middle East only, his logic of argument could be extended to other European colonial expansions.

In addition to Said (1978), Gayatri Chakravorty Spivak is another significant contributor to postcolonial perspective. Spivak addresses a range of issues, particularly history and historiography, feminism, philosophy and literature. She assays the colonial discourse of history (Spivak, 1981). She posits that literal history is being devised and educated without the awareness about the danger of imperialism and its cultural representations. She considers historical narratives that are formulated based on the coloniser's perspectives and assumptions, as a form of "planned epistemic violence" (Spivak, 1985, p. 264). In other words, history can be formulated as an imperialist representation of a given object (Young, 2004). Spivak (1988) essentially focusses on the subordination in the South Asian society and the 'Third World'. She highlights how the history of South Asia is being misconstrued and represented; her works question the western fantasy on homogenising the historical narratives of the subaltern. She is one of the earliest scholars who acknowledges the danger of *strategic essentialism* in the subaltern studies.

Similarly, Jack Goody (1996) argues that there is an Eurocentric bias in the western historical writings about the East. He takes Redding's (1990) account of

Chinese family business as an example to illustrate his argument. Redding focusses on Needham's work to examine the Chinese culture and society. However, Goody is aware of the weaknesses in Needham's perception of the Chinese society. Goody (1996) challenges the assumptions in European histories and social theories, particularly on the notion of rationality. While rationality has enabled "the uniqueness" (p.4) of the west to modernise, such a concept has differentiated the East as "static" and "backwards" (Goody, 2012, p.118). He argues that there are minimal differences between the East and the West in terms of mercantile activity during the medieval and early colonial periods. Yet, Redding asserts his analysis based on European rationality. Therefore, Goody (1996) argues that:

> If you start with contemporary Europe or European science as the point of reference, everything else is bound to be deviant, as lacking something. That is the general problem for contemporary European historians looking backwards or elsewhere. Difference takes on a somewhat negative evaluation, since recent European science becomes the norm and everything else is found wanting, a failure that needs accounting for. (p. 153)

Goody criticises Redding's work because "it fails to allow for the lexical generativeness of language" and "gives insufficient recognition to the historical development" (p.46). He perceives Redding's description on CFB as an overly "holistic view of man and his society", wherein the *Greek rationality* and *European science* are used "to qualify men and culture" (p.46). Yet, the indigenous (Chinese) language, logic and social changes are ignored. In that case, even though Redding's tone is sober, his representation of the Confucian management in CFB is constructed with European bias.

Nandy is another significant contributor of postcolonial thought. His works primarily concentrate on "the psychology of colonialism" (Prasad, 2003, p.14). Nandy (1983) scrutinises that "the colonisation of the mind and imagination effected under the colonial situation" (Prasad, 2003, p. 15). That is to say, the colonisers altered the minds, values and cultural priorities within the colonised society. Rather than regarding the coloniser as the winner while the colonised as the loser, Nandy considers that both parties are victims of colonialism. On one hand, the colonised is perceived as a victim as the coloniser marginalised it. On other hand, this victim could construct the west based on its own imageries, myths and fantasies. For instance, Nandy observed how Indians (the colonised) could develop a strategy of survival, evaluate, judge and make choices for the sake of their own purpose. As a result, a plurality of ideologies is often accommodated within their lifestyles.

In the light of Nandy's ideological plurality and Said's Orientalism, Homi Bhabha reveals ambivalence in the colonial discourse. He highlights that the relationship between the coloniser and colonised is even more politically complicated than Said's interpretation of Orientalism (Young, 2004). He identifies the notions of 'ambivalence', 'mimicry' and 'hybridization'. Bhabha (1984) follows on the same idea of mimicry as perceived by Jacques Lacan to reveal the ambivalence of the coloniser; the colonial subject is often constructed in a way that is "almost the same", but still different (i.e. "not quite" or not completely white) (p. 126). That means, mimicry implies the coloniser has a greater loss of control since the construction of the colonial because *the Other* constitutes only a partial representation of the coloniser, which is actually "incomplete" and "virtual" (p. 127). Bhabha (1996) regards such "partial culture" as something like "'culture's in-between', bafflingly both alike and different" (p. 54). Partial culture implies the colonial power has its limitations. Cultural clash and borderline negotiations over cultural differences are possible. Therefore, Bhabha perceives the colonised is an agent of menace to the coloniser in an unconscious manner. Building on the above argument, Bhabha (1985) develops a concept of hybrid and describes the colonised as the hybrid. He considers that the partial representation of the coloniser indicates the hybridity of its object and the impact of colonial power can be perceived as the production of hybridisation which undermines the colonial influence. He highlights that hybridisation represents a strategy that reverses colonial domination and enables native resistance and subversion. Hybridisation implies how colonialism formulates another culture, which is blended in-between the coloniser and colonised. This new culture locates in the "Third Space of enunciations" – an in-between space where essentialist opposition, contradiction, ambiguity, negotiations and hybridity are taken place (Bhabha, 1994, p.56). In reviewing Bhabha's works, Young (2004) highlights that Bhabha has provided a solution for Said (1978) who was unable to show how Orientalism could be articulated within the phenomenon of cultural differences.

The postcolonial thought are not only confined within the fields of history and psychology. Spivak's idea of *strategic essentialism* is applied in business management. Robert Westwood is a key management researcher who focuses on critical international management and organisational studies. While examining the comparative management, Westwood (2001) regards *essentialism* as:

> a reductive strategy wherein the 'Other's' (non-western) subjectivity is constructed by a Western discourse which claims to speak authoritatively and definitively about what constitutes that subjectivity. (p.258)

Anshuman Prasad is another management researcher who focuses his research on postcolonial ideas, organisational culture and ideology, workplace diversity and multiculturalism, resistance and empowerment in organisations. Prasad (2003) refers *'essentialism'* to:

> the idea that any specific group of objects or people (e.g., a race, gender, or class) is marked, identified and defined by pure, immutable, and transhistorical characteristics and essences that inhere in the specific group in question, and that determines the fundamental and unique nature of that group. (p.25)

To further examine the problem of *essentialism*, Westwood (2001) discovers three strategies that are devised by the west to appropriate *the Other* in the dominant discourse, which include: (1) dragging *the Other* into the dominant discourse and generating a misrepresentation of their worldview; (2) representing *the Other* in a way that enabled the west "to capture, lay out and make sense of *the Other*" (p.249); and (3) silencing and marginalising *the Other* through "repression, oppression or denial of the existence of any counterpoint to the dominant group" (p.250). These strategies place and interpret *the Other* within the conditions of economic, political and cultural context that are determined and controlled by the west. Specifically, they amplify, exaggerate and distort the perceived cultural differences through essentialising the crucial nature of a particular group of people. As a consequence, *the Other* is made "accessible", "comprehensible" (p.248) and manageable by the western audience. For example, the representations of Japan have been problematic in the west, because Japanese culture of "'pragmatic' has turned into 'unprincipled, 'group norms' has become 'conformity', 'discipline' has twisted to 'regimented', and 'paradox' has framed as 'contradiction'" (Westwood, 2001, p.261). By essentialism, the West could also "reaffirm its own value and power" (p.248). In other words, *the Other* is positioned as a "counter-point" (Westwood, 2001, p.250) to the west, without any meaningful specificity attached to *the Other*.

While contemplating the discourse of comparative management, Westwood (2001) diagnosed an *essentialist* tendency in Redding's work. He observed that Redding displayed a certain continuity of the colonial project. He highlighted that Redding's study was based upon the premise that the Chinese have different cognitive thinking on aspects such as "causality, time, self, probability and morality" (p.263). For instance, Redding claimed that Chinese thinking was formulated on the basis of practical, pragmatic and concrete perception, rather than abstract logic. This implied that Chinese was incapable of western professional management. As a result, CFBs were usually being associated with a negative connotations, such as CFBs are usually small in scale and non-complex in organisational structure in which they have not been able to keep pace with modernisation (Xu, 2008). That is why Westwood (2001) considers Redding has essentialised the Chinese culture. To sum up, Redding perhaps unwittingly made a partial representation of CFB by:
(1) ignoring the Chinese language, logic and social changes (Goody, 1996),
(2) essentialising the Chinese culture (Westwood, 2001) and
(3) objectifying his subject (the overseas Chinese) (Xu, 2008).

Despite the relevancy of Redding's (1990) research on CFB, its degree of reflexivity is often questioned. To a certain extent, his work is formulated within the concept of structuralism while he examined the underlying structure of rules and codes that governed the Confucian management of CFB. His work portrays a sense of timeless quality (Xu, 2008), assuming that Chinese culture and society does not change over time. The above diagnosis highlights problems in Redding's approach to his Chinese subject. These problems could possibly appear in the Orthodox studies of international business management (Westwood, 2001), as well as in the well-being literature. As mentioned in the previous chapter, majority of well-being studies assume the concept is static and context-free. The Chinese term, *xing fu*, is used as an equivalent to well-being. However, is *xing fu* the same as well-being? This book argues that they are culturally distinctive concepts. It suspects that a Chinese subject could have been essentialised as an object of knowledge (Goody, 1996; Westwood, 2001; Xu, 2008) for testifying a western notion of well-being. The Chinese subject could have been marginalised with a comparatively lower level of well-being (Diener et al., 1995; Helliwell, Huang et al., 2021; Veenhoven, 2000a). If this is the case, the original meaning of *xing fu* could have been discounted in the well-being discourse. In other words, the Chinese perspective of *xing fu* could have been made silence in the well-being literature. Under such a condition, is it possible for researchers to found a concept or/and theory on a Chinese subject? If not, what are the conditions for making a Chinese theory possible? To answer these questions, the book aims to explore the conditions in which management researchers could move away from an essentialist tendency. How? Instead of assuming discourse is context-free and static, change should be taken into account.

(b) Accounting for Change

How can research account for change? As suggested by the post-structuralists, one way account for change is to examine the history of discourse (Cummings, Bridgman, Hassard and Rowlinson, 2017; Foucault, 1972). Michel Foucault, particularly in his writing, '*Archaeology of Knowledge*' (1972), adopts archaeology to scrutinise change in discourse. His archaeology "tries to define those discourses themselves" (p.138) and seeks "a differential analysis of the modalities of discourse" (p.139), "defines types of rules for discursive practices" (p.139) and provides "systematic description of a discourse-object" (p. 140). In other words, archaeology investigates the conditions that give rise to discourse and examines discursive transformations. It uncovers the rules of discursive (trans)formations and highlights "the analysis of the rules proper to the different discursive practices" (p.207). In short, archaeology is "a discourse about discourse" (p.205).

What is the objective of archaeology? The purpose of archaeology is "to uncover the regularity of a discursive practice" (p.145) through revealing "relations between discursive formations and non-discursive domains (institutions, political events, economic practices and processes)" (p.162). It "seeks to discover that the whole domain of institutions, economic processes, and social relations on which a discursive formation can be articulated" (p.164). Foucault (1972) specifically explains that:

> Its purpose is to map, in a particular discursive practice, the point at which they are constituted, to define the form that they assume, the relations that they have with each other, and

the domain that they govern. In short, its purpose is to maintain discourse in all its many irregularities; and consequently to suppress the theme of a contradiction uniformly lost and rediscovered, resolved and forever rising again, in the undifferentiated element of the Logos.

(pp.155–156)

What are the potential benefits of archaeology? How could archaeology contribute to the management discourse? Archaeology helps management research to move away from the structuralist tendency and avoid the problems of *objectification* and *essentialism*. Foucault (1972) asserts that "history is now trying to define within the documentary material itself unities, totalities, series, relations" (p.7) based on the tradition of 'structural analysis' (structuralism). However, he is uncertain over "the possibilities of creating totalities" (p.8) and questions these representations of historical continuity. He considers that "once these immediate forms of continuity are suspended, an entire field is set free" (p.26). How can one break away from such chronology? Rather than describing a linear sequence of events, Foucault scrutinises history based on the conditions or rules that govern the discursive (trans)formations. He assumes that the epistemological strategies and tactics can regulate knowledge production and can aid to define the parameters and shape the function of the knowledge products. Therefore, he uses archaeology to search "for the origin, for formal a *prioris*, for founding acts" that regulate discourse and describe the ruptures of a discourse. In such a way, archaeology is able to break down historical unity and hence "free history from the grip of phenomenology" (p. 203). As a consequence, archaeology provides an additional research approach to management history (Cummings et al., 2017). Another advantage of archaeology is that it offers a possible way to dissect the problems of *objectification* and *essentialism* in management discourse. Archaeology takes discourse as not only texts but practices (Foucault, 1972; Jacques, 1996). It examines discursive practices and treats them as conditions or rules governing a discourse. Hence, archaeology helps to investigate what conditions constitute to *objectification* and *essentialism*.

How about the critiques of archaeology? The critiques of Foucault and justifications of using his archaeology are explained in Appendix A: Notes A2. Various researchers have followed Foucault's archaeology to examine management knowledge. For instance, Jacques (1996) exhibits a history of American management discourse and contextualised the conditions that gave rise to 'the employee'. He argues that management knowledge has been developed by "indigenizing 'organisational science' itself as a discourse shaped by its culture of origin" (p. xiii). There is no universal or objective knowledge and therefore management is arguably 'historically and culturally specific' (Jacques, 1996). His archaeological analysis offers a critical self-reflection of western management. Xu (1997) also uses Foucault's archaeology to offer a supplementary account of total quality management (TQM) discourse. She examines the discursive emergence, formation and transformation of TQM and its knowledge production. She highlights the importance of archaeology as:

> it enables us to appreciate a radically dislocating effect to 'positive knowledge' or to a familiar mode of thought. (p.428)

Her archaeological examination offers a contribution to knowledge by "allowing historical detail to be played out on the central stage" (p. 429). Her analysis is able to "give voice to what established procedures for 'positive knowledge' have been unable to deliver" (p.427). Therefore, archaeology is able to uncover the rules governing the management discourse and show how they could or/and continually affect the present world. Paradoxically, examining the past may guide one to find a plausible resolution. Therefore, the first part of analysis in this book is an archaeological examination of well-being, in which it seeks to: (1) diagnose the problems of *objectification* and *essentialism* in the well-being discourse, (2) search for a possible solution to the problems and (3) open a new avenue for management research, where the previously deprived voice can be account for.

To conclude, this chapter has given a brief account of CFB. The dominant representation of CFB focuses on western logic of *'management'* and *'strategy'* because CFB is often construed with distinctive features that are dissimilar or even inferior to western professional management. In regard to *objectification* and *essentialism*, some poststructuralist and postcolonial researchers (such as Goody, 1996; Westwood, 2001; Xu, 2008) have already considered the above as a partial representation of *the Others* which implies a sense of structuralism, a timeless quality in the literatures of CFB and well-being. Considering the problems, this book proposes to adopt Foucault's archaeology to account for change in discourse. Through archaeology, a solution and a new direction to management research can be offered.

Chapter 3
An Archaeological Examination of Well-being

This chapter addresses the first research question – *How does the discourse of well-being emerge and transform in a Chinese context?* Here, well-being and *xing fu* are considered as discursive concepts. The archaeological examination scrutinises well-being per se and examines its knowledge production. The examination makes a contribution to knowledge by showing well-being is culturally distinctive and dynamic; and locating objectification and essentialism in the well-being discourse. More importantly, a suggestion to deal with objectification and essentialism will be offered.

The analysis will first demystify a mainstream framework of well-being in a Chinese context. Next, the formation of fu and how it is transformed to xing fu are examined. As discussed in Section 1.4, Foucault's (1979) archaeology of knowledge is operationalised through five layers of texts (see Tab. 1.4). Lastly, implications from the archaeological examination are drawn.

3.1 Discursive (Trans)Formation of Well-being

The notion of well-being is based upon Hedonism and Eudaimonia. These two philosophical approaches are related to the ideas on happiness. Therefore, texts on happiness could be regarded as conditioning texts for well-being.

3.1.1 Conditioning Texts of Well-being

This section illustrates the formation of happiness as a discursive object and the subsequent emergence of well-being (see Fig. 3.1: Layers underneath the origin). Based on Foucault's (1972) archaeology, one could examine a discursive formation by defining the formation of an object. Therefore, the analysis begins by looking at how happiness is formed as a discursive object. First, the conditions that allowed happiness to emerge on the surface are examined. Due to the experience of wars, some sophists started questioning the existence and power of gods and goddesses in the mid-5th century. This was the time when consciousness of happiness was emerged. After the Greco-Persian Wars, philosophers began to pay attention to human lives. For instance, Socrates (469BC – 399BC) often argued eloquently with his students regarding the topics of human lives, including souls, virtues and knowledge. His thoughts on these areas had influenced many of his students, such as Plato, Aristippus and Antisthenes. These intellectuals came from aristocratic backgrounds and therefore provided them with the status and authority to discuss, argue and teach within the community. This situation constituted a precondition for happiness to emerge as a discursive object particularly within the discourse of philosophy, in which Aristotle (Plato's student) attempted to explore the meaning of happiness in ancient Greece. He had thoroughly examined happiness in his writing: *Nichomachean Ethics* (1985). This was the moment when happiness, was firstly emerged as an object in philosophy. At the same time, his texts on eudaimonia became conditioning texts for well-being.

Second, the appearance of happiness is made possible through a "grid of specification" (Foucault, 1972, p.42). In ancient Greece, different types of happiness are "being divided, contrasted, related, regrouped, classified, derived from one another" (Foucault, 1972, p.42) as objects in the discourse of political science. Aristotle (1985) defined various objects related to happiness and formed grids of specification for differentiations (see Tab. 3.1). These grids of specification became a condition that allowed happiness to develop as a discursive object.

Third, the formation of happiness is made by "the authorities of delimitation" (Foucault, 1972, p. 41). As specified by Aristotle (1985),

> the best and most pleasant life is the life of the intellect, since the intellect is in the fullest sense the man. So this life will be the happiest. (p.331)

In ancient Greece, only the intellectuals were qualified to speak about happiness. They were the ones who had the authority to talk about happiness since their lives were perceived to be the happiest. In that case, education could be considered as 'the institutional site' (Foucault, 1972) wherein the intellectuals created the discourse on happiness. Aristotle (1985) even highlighted that:

> Education in goodness is the best undertaken by the state . . . this (being a good man) can be achieved by living under the guidance of some intelligence or right system that has effective force. (p.337–338)

At that time, politicians were the key audience, receiving the knowledge of happiness because they were qualified to practice happiness via the means of law. That is why Aristotle (1985) differentiated the roles between sophists and politicians as follows:

> But as for political science, although the sophists profess to teach it, not one of them practices it; that is done by politicians, and they would seems to do it from a sort of ability aided by experience rather than by the exercise of reason. (p.340)

That means, the intellects were qualified to make and teach the discourse of happiness for the politicians through education; while the politicians were qualified to experience and practice happiness through law. Discourse on happiness at that time was made for the politicians to regulate and control the public. As Aristotle (1985) said:

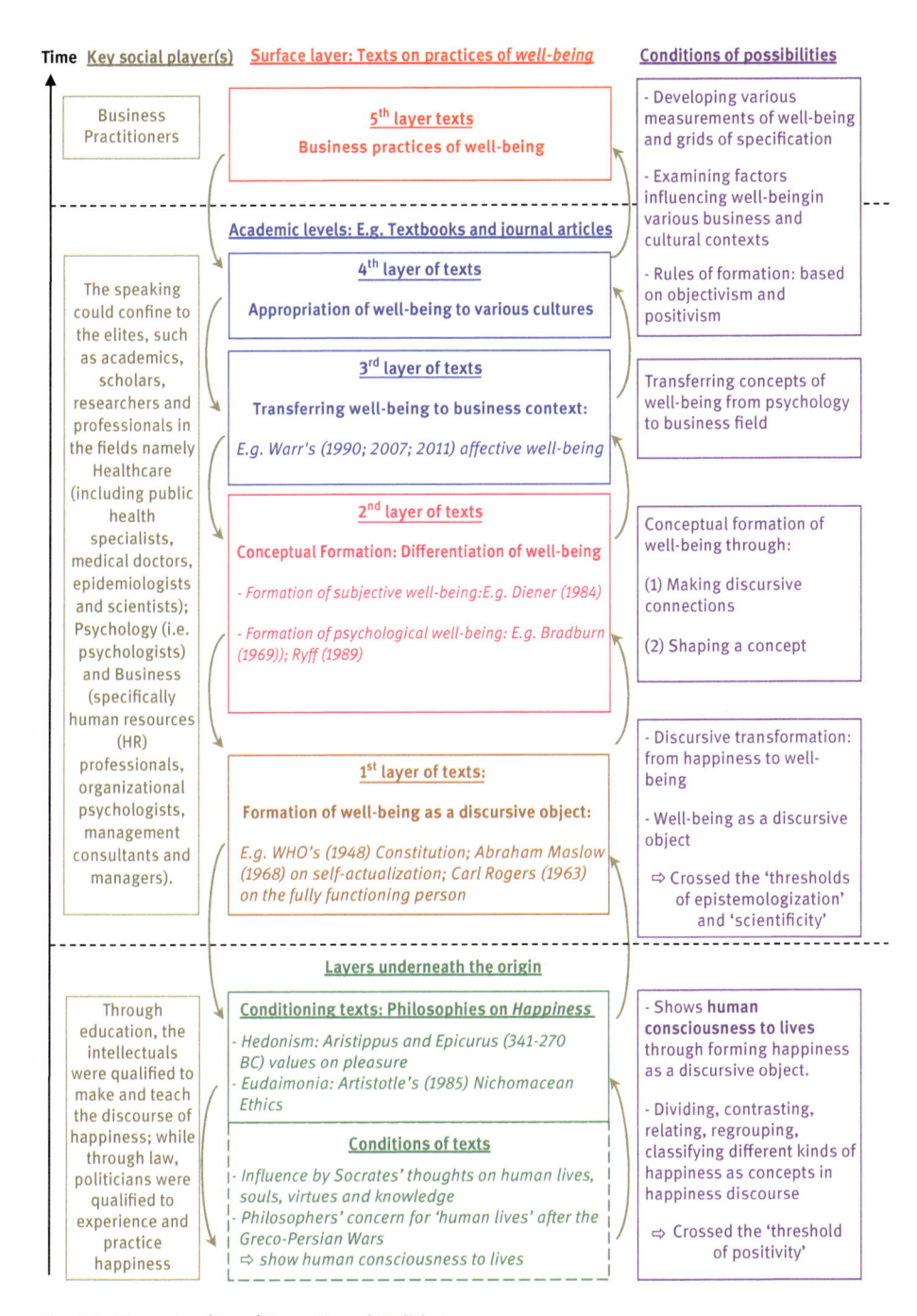

3.1 Discursive (Trans)Formation of Well-being — 47

Time	Key social player(s)	Surface layer: Texts on practices of *well-being*	Conditions of possibilities
↑	Business Practitioners	**5th layer texts** Business practices of well-being	- Developing various measurements of well-being and grids of specification - Examining factors influencing well-being in various business and cultural contexts
	The speaking could confine to the elites, such as academics, scholars, researchers and professionals in the fields namely Healthcare (including public health specialists, medical doctors, epidemiologists and scientists); Psychology (i.e. psychologists) and Business (specifically human resources (HR) professionals, organizational psychologists, management consultants and managers).	Academic levels: E.g. Textbooks and journal articles **4th layer of texts** Appropriation of well-being to various cultures	- Rules of formation: based on objectivism and positivism
		3rd layer of texts Transferring well-being to business context: E.g. Warr's (1990; 2007; 2011) affective well-being	Transferring concepts of well-being from psychology to business field
		2nd layer of texts Conceptual Formation: Differentiation of well-being - Formation of subjective well-being: E.g. Diener (1984) - Formation of psychological well-being: E.g. Bradburn (1969)); Ryff (1989)	Conceptual formation of well-being through: (1) Making discursive connections (2) Shaping a concept
		1st layer of texts: Formation of well-being as a discursive object: E.g. WHO's (1948) Constitution; Abraham Maslow (1968) on self-actualization; Carl Rogers (1963) on the fully functioning person	- Discursive transformation: from happiness to well-being - Well-being as a discursive object ⇨ Crossed the 'thresholds of epistemologization' and 'scientificity'
	Through education, the intellectuals were qualified to make and teach the discourse of happiness; while through law, politicians were qualified to experience and practice happiness	Layers underneath the origin Conditioning texts: Philosophies on *Happiness* - Hedonism: Aristippus and Epicurus (341-270 BC) values on pleasure - Eudaimonia: Aristotle's (1985) Nichomacean Ethics Conditions of texts - Influence by Socrates' thoughts on human lives, souls, virtues and knowledge - Philosophers' concern for 'human lives' after the Greco-Persian Wars ⇨ show human consciousness to lives	- Shows **human consciousness to lives** through forming happiness as a discursive object. - Dividing, contrasting, relating, regrouping, classifying different kinds of happiness as concepts in happiness discourse ⇨ Crossed the 'threshold of positivity'

Fig. 3.1: Discursive (Trans)Formation of Well-being.

> The science that studies the supreme Good for man is politics . . . Clearly this description fits the science of politics; for it is political science that prescribes what subjects are to be taught in states, and which of these different sections of the community are to learn, and up to what point . . . Such, then, is the aim of our investigation; and it is a kind of political science. (p.64)

At that time, studies on happiness were regarded as a crucial aspect within the realm of political science. Since happiness has been formed as an object in political science, its discourse began to form.

According to Foucault's (1979) sequence of thought, a concept is formed when its discourse has crossed the "threshold of positivity" (p.186). Happiness has become a concept when various distinct systems for formation of statement are put into operation via "forms of co-existence" (p.57). That is to say, Hedonism and Eudaimonia were two schools of thoughts that had been co-existed in the ancient Greece. Hedonism was founded by Aristippus (the student of Socrates) and championed by Epicurus (341–270 BC); while Eudaimonia was founded by Aristotle. They were individual schools of thought and each represented a distinct system where statements about happiness were formed and operated. This was the moment when happiness was first perceived as a sort of positive knowledge, because both Hedonism and Eudaimonia were co-existed to serve as 'general principles' or 'models' of happiness. By this, happiness is transformed into a concept.

According to Foucault (1972),

> knowledge is that of which one can speak in a discursive practice, and which is specified by that fact: the domain constituted by the different objects that will or will not acquire a scientific status. (p.182)

Hence, the knowledge of happiness in ancient Greece, was not the sum of things thought to be true, but the whole set of practices, singularities and deviation which could be presented within the discourse of political science. At that period, the role of happiness discourse could reflect and strengthen the status, authority and functions of the intellects since they were qualified to speak, guide and teach others (in particular, the politicians) to live well. Therefore, the conversations of happiness among the intellects in various schools of thought (mainly Hedonism and Eudaimonia) in ancient Greece, was a reflection of their social status, authority and functions in the society. As a consequence, the discursive formation of happiness (both as an object and a concept) was made possible by a group of relations established between: (1) the life and status of the aristocracy and intellects; (2) the authority of the intellects and politicians; (3) the roles of the intellects and politicians; (3) the authority of the academic institutions and government; (4) the roles and functions of the academic institution and government; (5) the systems of classification for sciences or faculties and philosophy; and (6) the systems of specification in philosophy and psychology.

Tab. 3.1: Grids of Specification of Happiness (Aristotle, 1985).

Objects of happiness	Grids of specification on objects of happiness					
The life (p.68)	Pleasure		Political		Contemplative	
The goods (pp.70–78)	Substance (God or mind)	Quality (The virtues)	Quantity (What is moderate)	Relation (What is useful)	Time (Opportunity)	Place (Habitual)
		Means			Ends	
	External		Of the soul		Of the body	
The virtues (p.90)	Intellectual				Moral	
The soul (pp.88–89)	Rational				Irrational	
	Good				Bad	
	Continent				Incontinent	

3.1.2 Well-being as an Object and a Concept

(a) Formation of Well-being

Foucault (1972) defined that an object "may give birth simultaneously or successively to . . . objects without having to modify itself" (p.44). In this way, happiness gave birth to an object, named 'well-being'. The following layer of texts represented the transformation of happiness to well-being (see Fig. 3.1: 1st layer of texts). In 19th century, happiness was a philosophical concept that appeared not just within the discourse of political science; but also in varied fields, such as healthcare, psychology and business management. For instance, the following excerpt highlights the importance of happiness in healthcare:

In 1948, World Health Organization (WHO) describes in its Constitution:

> THE STATES Parties to this Constitution declare, in conformity with the Charter of the United Nations, that the following principles are basic to the happiness, harmonious relations and security of all peoples: Health is a state of complete physical, mental and social well-being and not merely the absence of disease or infirmity. (WHO, 1948, p.1)

Here, well-being was regarded as a state of health which serves as basic to happiness. Hence, the relationship between happiness, health and well-being was emphasised in healthcare.

Psychology is another major field where the concept of happiness flourishes. From 1950s to 1960s, the American public and community of scientific psychologists exhibited strong interest over the issues of psychological growth and health (Ryan and Deci, 2001). Happiness had become a hot topic within the field of psychology, in particular humanistic psychology, such as the works of Abraham Maslow (1943) on self-actualisation and Carl Rogers (1963) on the fully functioning person (Harrington, 2013; Huppert and Linley, 2011). Since the late 19th century, the discourses of happiness and well-being have been put into the subfield of Positive Psychology (Harrington, 2013). Seligman and Csikszentmihalyi (2000) highlighted that "the aim of positive psychology is to . . . focus [on] building positive qualities" (p.5) and well-being is classified as one key positive qualities in lives. Their paper became one of the seminal papers in Positive Psychology. Similarly, Haworth and Hart (2007) emphasised that "well-being offers a paradigm that allow those in academic, policy and user field to focus on positive outcomes, and how best to realize them" (p.1). Even Seligman (2011) highlighted that: "I now think that the topic of positive psychology is well-being" (p.13). Since then, well-being has become a major discursive object in Positive Psychology.

Based on Foucault's (1972) archaeology, well-being has become a discursive object when the discourse of happiness crossed the "threshold of epistemologization" (p.187) and "threshold of scientificity" (p.187) in the science of psychology. After the World War II, psychology has become a science which focused heavily on healing (Seligman and Csikszentmihalyi, 2000). Kashdan, Baswas-Diener and King (2011) highlighted that although Hedonic and Eudemonic approaches to examine happiness might make sense for the philosophers, they are less appropriate to the science of psychology. They argued that:

> Eudaimonia and Hedonic happiness are intriguing philosophical concept . . . While they are entirely appropriate to the philosophical traditions in which they were produced, these concepts do not translate well to modern scientific and empirical inquiry . . . While philosophers have often emphasised the different types of happiness, social scientists must consider the best available empirical evidence when making arguments. (p.330–331)

They stressed that "as scientists we draw on research to . . . examine the validity of the notion that feeling good about one's life is unlikely to provide a reliable assessment that one is happy for the right reasons" (p.319). They believed that the science of psychology needs to provide "a unique approach to issues about the nature of happiness in the good life", and that "scientific methods and empirical attention to mental status add a new perspective on the historical dialogue on happiness" (p.332). Hence, in order to make research on happiness sound more scientific in the discourse of psychology, another object, 'well-being' was introduced in 1984 by Ed Diener. Diener (1984) published on the construct of 'subjective well-being' (SWB). Later in 1989, Carol Ryff, introduced another construct called 'psychological well-being' (PWB). Thus, these were key moments in the field of psychology when happiness was transformed to well-being.

In Diener's (1984) and Ryff's (1989) productions of SWB and PWB, well-being has been made as 'a construct' to differentiate itself from its predecessor, happiness (Seligman, 2011). As a construct, well-being could have "several measurable elements" and "each of the elements is a measurable thing" (Seligman, 2011, p. 15). In such a manner, psychologists made the object of well-being as 'a construct' for the science of psychology, "and thus one of the great dividing lines of happiness and well-being research was born" (Huppert and Linley, 2011, p.7). Since then, research on well-being has been regarded as a scientific discourse which emphasises on its measurement, validity, coherence and functionality. It stresses on the significance of scientific models, critiques, or verification. Hence, well-being as an object was born because it has crossed the "threshold of epistemologization" and "threshold of scientificity" (Foucault, 1972, p.187).

Why was it necessary to create a new name called well-being? In her archaeological analysis on the transformation of TQC to TQM, Xu (2000) provides an answer. She explains that "to distinguish a discourse from its earlier version, a change of name is necessary" (p. 431). Thus, to differentiate the discourse of political sciences from the healthcare and psychological discourse, a creation of an object named, well-being is necessary. This is the moment when well-being as a discursive object firstly emerged. Xu (2000) argues further:

> A conventional view holds that, if the world is constituted of 'thing', the enterprise of enquiry must be on or of 'things'; they constitute a first order, whereas links or relationships constitute the second. (p.432)

In the light of this, the coming-into-being of well-being could be made possible through the creation of its name, which had diverted the psychology discourse to examine the 'essence' of such a 'thing', given its formation emerges only in discourse. Hence, well-being provides scholars with 'a scientific language' for talking about such an object (Kashdan, el al., 2011, p.317).

Who are qualified to speak about well-being and where is the speaking taken place? Haworth and Hart (2007) specified that researchers, educators, policy makers and politicians are all interested in well-being "consciously or subconsciously, as together we create well-being" (p.1). Kashdan et al. (2011) further specified that "the search for something 'better' than SWB or better form of happiness connotes a potential elitism, that the Good Life is an experience for individual who have attained some transcendence from everyday life" (p.331). In that case, the speaking could be possibly confined to the elites, such as academics, scholars, researchers, professionals, politicians and government officials who work in the fields of Healthcare (including public health specialists, medical doctors, epidemiologists and scientists), Psychology (i.e. psychologists) and Business Management (specifically human resources (HR) professionals, organizational psychologists, management consultants and managers). Academic institutions, governments, inter-governmental organizations (such as World Health Organization organized by United Nations) and professional bodies (such Psychology Associations and HR Association) are the 'institutional site' wherein such speaking takes place. Since the formation of Positive Psychology, various associations, networks, and databases have been established to encourage the discourse of well-being. For instance, an International Positive Psychology Association (IPPA) and an European Positive Psychology Network have been formed to promote regular conferences and publications; a World Database of Happiness Research in Europe is freely offered on the internet at http://www.eur.nl/

fsw/research/happiness; the Centre for applied Positive Psychology (CAPP) has been established to offer assessment and development tools to examine the potentials and strengths of individuals, teams and organizations (Haworth and Hart, 2007). Even searching on the term 'well-being' in Psychinfo can result in over 28,000 citations (Ryan and Deci, 2001). Hence, the formation of the new field, Positive Psychology, has not only granted a discursive space for the object of well-being to emerge, but has also positioned well-being in a manner that leads to its flourishment.

(b) Well-being as a Concept

Foucault (1972) defines 'the procedures of intervention' as a way to uncover the formation of concepts (p.58). He explains that "these procedures are not in fact the same for all discursive formations; those are used (to the exclusion of all others), the relations that link them and the unity thus created make it possible to specify each one" (pp.58–59). Well-being could be made a concept (particularly in the discourse of Psychology) through the two procedures of intervention: (1) making discursive connection and (2) shaping the concept of well-being through interpretations (see Fig. 3.1: 2nd layer of texts). First, the concept of well-being is formed through successive connection of Hedonic happiness with subjective well-being; and Eudemonic happiness with psychological well-being. Foucault (1972) traces the formation of concepts through "forms of succession", in which "a set of rules for arranging statement in series, an obligatory set of schema of dependence, of order, and of succession, in which the recurrent elements that may have value as concepts were distributed" (p.57). Based upon his idea on succession, the sets of rules governing the discourse of Hedonic happiness and Eudaimoina have amalgamated to the discourses of SWB and PWB respectively. How did such succession take place? Xu (2000) highlighted that by creating "links" between "quality control" and "quality management", "one shapes a discursive space" (p.429). With her argument, one could trace a discursive transformation from happiness to well-being by delineating the discursive connections between them. Kashdan el al. (2011) highlighted that Hedonic and Eudemonic happiness "are the most useful way to frame contemporary research in well-being" (p.330), because "it is the very link between Eudaimonia and Hedonics that justifies the psychologists' place at the table in the discussion of the Good Life" (p.332). Therefore, making a discursive connection of Hedonic happiness with SWB; while Eudaimonia with PWB is another mode of discursive formation. This mode of discursive formation allows SWB and PWB to be formulated in sets of successions that are instilled with similar predecessors, such as, Hedonic and Eudemonic happiness respectively. Hence, concepts of well-being are formed based on this form of succession.

Second, given well-being is made as 'a construct' in research, Seligman (2011) highlighted that "enumerating the elements of well-being is our (academics and psychologists) next task". Since well-being is formed as an object, academics and psychologists have been keen on operationalising well-being through their interpretations.

Various elements of well-being have been measured and examined which led various exclusive objects to devise the concept of well-being. Such operation is similar to Xu's (2000) metaphor of making a snowball through adding a 'patch' to a concept. She highlighted that:

> Another mode of discursive formation is through shaping concepts. Like making snowballs . . . One adds a 'patch' to a concept so that a desirable shape emerges . . . One common procedure is interpretation. (p.433)

How have they made a snowball? A snowball is created through the development of different measurements and "grids of specification" (Foucault, 1972, p.42). For example, 'living standard' is considered as another discursive object that allows the assessment of well-being through measurements such as Quality of Life (QoL), Human Development Index (HDI) and living standard index etc.. Various grids of specification have been used which have led to the development of various object of well-being. For example, there are differentiations on health, as health includes physical, mental and social well-being; subjective well-being versus psychological well-being in the discourse of psychology; and well-being in various contexts such as in business/work (e.g. affective well-being, job satisfaction, work-life balance and stress etc.); in family (e.g. familial relation, familial climate and familial health etc.); and in society (e.g. economic wealth, technological advancement and human development etc.). While devising this snowball, well-being is measured, divided, contrasted, related, regrouped, and classified into different degrees, levels and kinds. In such a manner, well-being is incorporated into various fields of scientific and empirical discourses, including Healthcare, Psychology, and Business Management.

The above analysis shows that the discursive formation of well-being is made possible by a group of relations established between: (1) the status and authority of the academics, governments and professionals in Healthcare, Psychology and Business; (2) the roles of the academics, governments and professionals in these fields (3) the authority of the academic institutions, governments, inter-governmental organizations and professional bodies; (4) the roles and functions of the academic institutions, governments, inter-governmental organizations and professional bodies; and (5) the systems of verification, classification and specification in these fields.

3.1.3 Transformation

The discursive transformation of well-being can take place by transferring the concept to different commercial and cultural contexts. Along this direction, well-being is made as a global concept, which seems to be universally applicable across any businesses and cultures.

How did well-being transfer to Business field? Well-being has devised into a number of discursive objects in Business field (see Fig. 3.1: 3rd layer of text). For instance, initially, job satisfaction emerged in Sales and Marketing during 1920s (Wright, Emich and Klotz, 2017); Quality of Work Life (QWL) was introduced during 1960s (Jacques, 1996); and affective well-being was developed by Warr in 1990s (1990; 2007; 2009; 2011) to assess the importance of well-being in the workplace. These objects were successively formed to indicate a shift of attention to employee well-being, which is an advance concept in the Management discourse.

How did such a transformation of management knowledge occur? During the examination of the management knowledge from 19th century to 21st century, Jacques (1996) provided a probable answer for the question. He classified management history into five themes, including Taylor's scientific management; Hawthorne studies on organisational behaviours; Weber's structural consideration; integrated perspectives and a paradigmatic science of behaviours in organisations. The movement from Taylorism to the Hawthorn studies represented a transformation in management knowledge – from mechanic engineering to informal organisations. This transformation in management discourse has been made possible with the rise of industrial-organisational psychology (I/OP). The first textbook of I/OP was published by Munsterberg in 1910. At that time, most of the psychologists working in this area were based in universities and were responsible for defining the tone and structure of I/OP (Landy, 1997; Link, 1924). Jacques (1996) reflected that:

> the entry of industrial psychology into the discourse of employee was a point from which the extensive interpenetration of the university and the organisation began to produce a distinct product. Industrial psychology was the first institution of management to be enunciated primarily by academics. (p.140)

In this case, psychologists rather than management engineers were the key individuals who generated and monitored the discourse of management knowledge. The academic bodies and laboratories, instead of the industrial units, turned out to be the institutional site of management discourse. The above change represents a discursive transformation in management.

I/OP followed the Positive Movement of Psychology. As a consequence, Positive Psychology has extended to business arena, such as positive organisational behaviours (POB), positive organisational scholarship (POS) and positive human resource management (PHRM) (Wright, 2007). Along the same lines as Positive Psychology, I/OP is placed upon sound and scientific techniques. Its ontologies and epistemologies have again transferred to the management discourse. Jacques (1996) called this transformation as "phenomenological shift" (p.141):

> The convergence of Scientific Management with the vocational, employment managers' and industrial psychology movements indicated and accelerated a profound shift in reality of work. Because of the strong influence of German idealism in this transformation. I will refer to it as the 'phenomenological shift'. It was manifested in a decentering of the material and economic aspects of work in favour of an emphasis on work as what would today be called a social construction. (p.140)

Steffy and Grimes (1992) further specified that positivism and neo-positivism were the dominant modes of engagement in I/OP. Under such practices, employee well-being was assumed to be a 'real' object that could be tested through scientific methods. In this case, the subject (the employee) was treated as an object of knowledge to testify the notion of employee well-being in management discourse.

More significantly, well-being is applied to various cultural contexts through appropriation (see Fig. 3.1: 4th layer of text). Using Chinese context as an example, well-being was being directly translated as *'xing fu'* in Chinese. However, is *xing fu* emerged from well-being? Are the two concepts identical? Do they have the same origin? If not, would there be a tendency of objectification and essentialism along the discursive transformation? If so, how and when did these problems occur? In order to provide answers to these questions, Section 3.2 examines the discourse of *xing fu* and demystifies its formation and transformation.

3.1.4 Business Practice of Well-being

How did well-being shape business practices? The fifth level of texts indicates the discourse of well-being practices in work (see Fig. 3.1: 5th layer of texts). After the First World War, the employees (i.e. the army in that period) were encouraged to apply I/OP in the workplace (Jacques, 1996). With the influence of Positive Psychology and Hawthorn studies, employers and managers changed their focus to *employee well-being* and positive human resource management (HRM). They paid attention to variety of positive HRM practices, including employee involvement, work-life balance initiatives, wellness programs, employee assistance programs, family-friendly policies, employee satisfaction surveys etc. (Ballard and Grawitch, 2017; Burke, 2017; Jacques, 1996; Warr and Nielsen, 2018; Wright et al., 1997). These interventions were designed to improve employee well-being, generate a healthy work environment and build up performance (Warr and Nielsen, 2018) and public reputations, such as being Employer-of-Choice and award-winning organisations given by the American Psychological Association (APA) (Ballard and Grawitch, 2017). At the same time, these recognitions could be served as standards or expectations for employees in relation to their desired work lifestyle or well-being (Warr, 2017). That is why these interventions are often regarded as part of the 'best practices' in HRM.

3.2 Discursive (Trans)Formation of *Xing Fu*

Xing fu is made up of two Chinese words: 'xing' 幸 and 'fu' 福. Therefore, one needs to trace the (trans)formation of *fu* in order to examine the discourse of *xing fu* (see Fig. 3.2).

56 — Chapter 3 An Archaeological Examination of Well-being

Time	Key social player(s)	Surface layer: Texts on practices of *xing fu*	Conditions of possibilities
↑	Business Practitioners	**5th layer of texts** — *Business practices of xing fu*	- The entire rules of formation used in the mainstream concept of well-being are being copied and applied to the Chinese contexts ⇨ Crossed a 'threshold of epistemologization'
	The academics, governments and professionals in fields such as healthcare, psychology and business	Academic levels: E.g. Textbooks and journal articles **4th layer of texts:** *Appropriation of well-being to various Chinese contexts*	
	Enlightenment thinkers in early period of Qing Dynasty	**3rd layer of texts:** *Discursive transformation: From fu to xing fu* - Advance knowledge of *fu* through rationality and scientific methods	- 'Rationality' and 'scientificity' have become the new rules of formation governing the discourse of *fu* ⇨ Crossed the 'threshold of scientificity'
	Intelligentsia class: Itinerant intellectuals who were qualified to speak, guide and teach others (in particular, the monarchs) to live well	**2nd layer of texts** — *Conceptual Formation: Differentiation of fu* - Hundred schools of thoughts were formed in the Spring and Autumn and Warring States Period (770 BC to 221 BC) ➔ Major ones included Confucian, Mohism, Taoism, Legalism, Sophists, Military Treatises, Yin and Yang, Divine Farmer, Coalition Persuaders and Selecticism. - Each school of thought formed its own concept of *fu*	- Each school of thought had developed its own 'guidelines' and 'model' of living. - The concept of *fu* was formed and perceived as a kind of positive knowledge ⇨ Crossed the 'threshold of positivity'
	Oracle priests lost their discursive power over politics. The kings of Zhou were qualified to speak and create the discourse of *fu* as perspectives for governance.	**1st layer of texts:** *Formation of fu as a discursive object:* - The discursive object of *fu* 福 was first appeared in The *Book of Documents (The Great Plan)*. In Chinese, the book is known as *Shang Shu (Hong Fan)* 《尚書.洪範.》	- Mapping the birth of *fu* as a discursive object - The sources of *fu* is being divided into five sources and being contrasted with the six evils
	Oracle priests, who were qualified to speak and provide guidance to the rulers on any matters related to lives	Layers underneath the origins **Conditioning texts:** - "Bone inscriptions" found on the burial gifts of the graves of kings in Shang Dynasty : words and symbols related to the weal and woe of mankind at that time	- Shows **human consciousness to lives** through the dimension of spirits

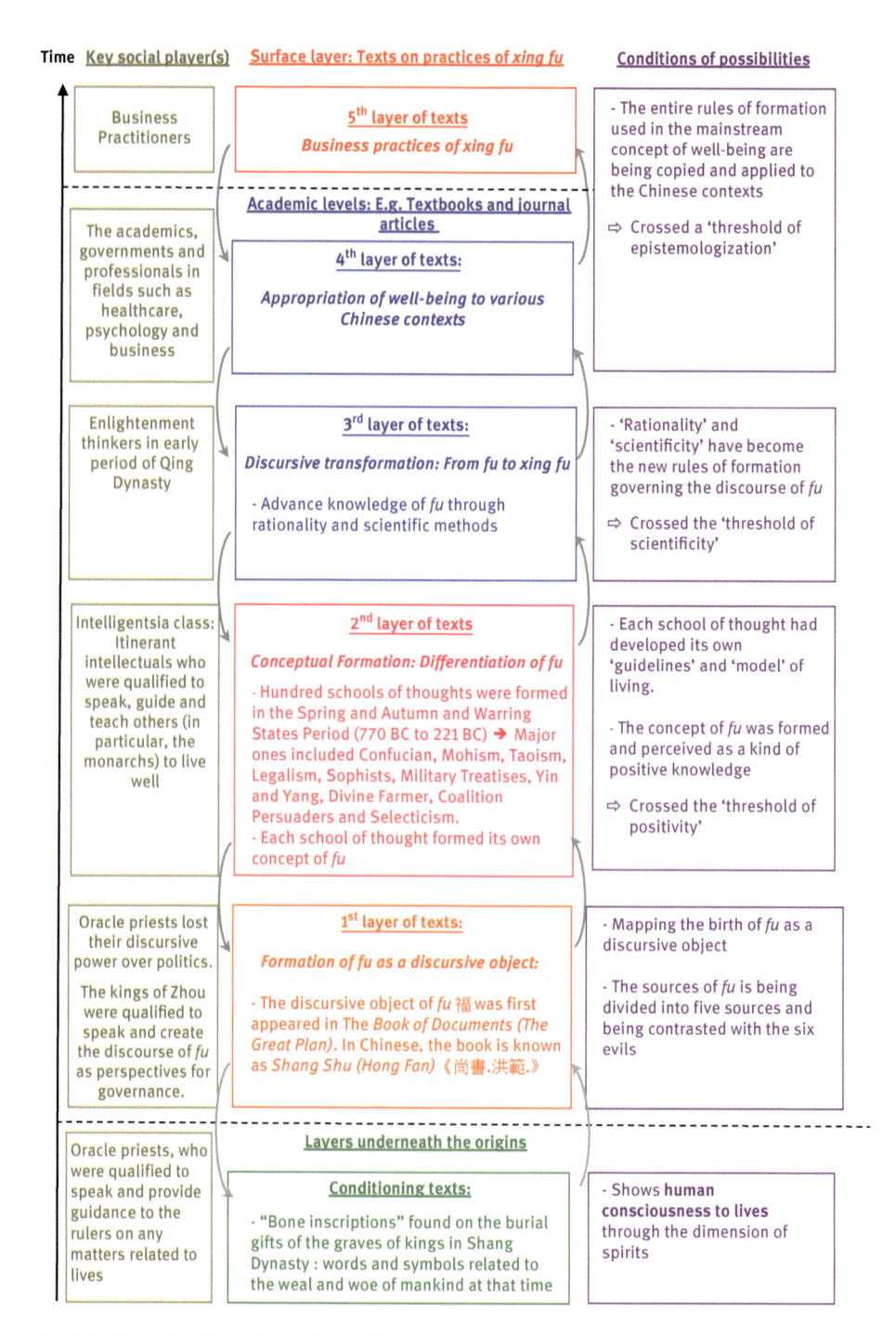

Fig. 3.2: Discursive (Trans)Formation of *Xing Fu*.

3.2.1 Conditioning Texts of Fu

The word, *fu* 福 was first appeared as bone inscription in ancient China before it was being transformed to a modern term, *xing fu*. These bone inscriptions were found on the burial gifts in the graves of Shang's kings. They had become conditioning texts of *fu* and *fu* (as a discursive object itself) was originally emerged in the Spring and Autumn and Warring States Period (770 BC to 221 BC). Wolfgang Bauer (1976), a German sinologist, identified that:

> The "bone inscriptions" from the Shang dynasty . . . show quite clearly on what depended the weal and woe of mankind or, perhaps more accurately, of the aristocracy of the time. (p.4)

Those bone inscriptions were related to human concerns on "nature events of all kinds such as rain and sunshine, floods, the failure of harvests, and the right time for hunting and fishing". During that period, Chinese believed in spirit and seek for spiritual "advice sought in all human affairs such as the sending of envoys, the founding of cities, sacrifice to the spirits of nature and the dead, military expedition, illnesses and dreams" (Bauer, 1976, p.4). Consequently, in Shang dynasty, the Chinese consciousness of lives was emerged through the dimension of spirits (see Fig. 3.2: Layers underneath the origins).

What were the conditions that gave rise to those bone inscriptions? During Shang dynasty, Shang's rulers relied on the oracle priests to understand life on earth and the underworld. Bauer (1976) specified the social roles of the oracle priests in Shang:

> The oracle priests thus became indispensable guides in a world divided into wilderness and civilization, this world and the beyond . . . They intend to provide guides for action in the Here and Now. (p.5–6)

At that time, the oracle priests were qualified to speak and guide the rulers for a living. They "had formed a kind of second government up to that time because their predictions had also influence politics" (p.12). To maintain their status and power that could influence politics, the priests built up the consciousness of life on earth and the underworld through the dimension of spirits. They used the "bone inscriptions" as a means to understand the will of the spirits and guide the Shang's rulers to live well. As a result, the consciousness to live well was once built and governed by the oracle priests given "their position as councillors of the king and as men whose word was all powerful" (p.12). They were the ones who were considered qualified enough to speak and provide guidance and counsel to the rulers on matters related to living.

3.2.2 *Fu* as an Object and a Concept

(a) Formation of Fu

This part traces the formation of *fu* as an object (see Fig. 3.2: 1st layer of texts). According to Foucault (1972), the formation of an object could be demystified based on three steps: (1) mapping the first of its emergence; (2) analysing the grid of specification; and (3) describing the authorities of delimitation (p.41). First, the discursive object of fu was primarily appeared in The Book of Documents (The Great Plan) during the Zhou dynasty. In Chinese, the book is known as *Shang Shu* (*Hong Fan*). The invasion of Zhou led to the downfall of the Shang dynasty and eventually the rule of Zhou took the title of King and attained a position to perform rites of his own. As a result, the oracle priests began to lose their power and significance in politics. Bauer (1976) described that the decline of oracle priests as follows:

> They literally lost their entire existence – at least the existence which they had always considered ideal, i.e. their position as councillors of the king and as men whose word was all-powerful. The new rulers had sufficient confidence in themselves to eliminate them (i.e. the oracle priests) rigorously from this position. At the same time, they were intelligent enough to continue occupying them in the administration as slave officials of a sort. (p.12)

Instead of relying on the oracle priests, the king of Zhou focused on 'morality', because he would like to make the citizens, particularly those who formed the nobility to believe that such a change in the leadership was justifiable (Bauer, 1976). Hence, The Book of Documents (The Great Plan) described the conversation between the first king of Zhou (i.e. Zhou Wu Wang) and the former Shang's prince named Jizi. Zhou Wu Wang once visited Jizi to gain his advice on leadership and government. Jizi told the king of Zhou the nine principles of governance, known as nine divisions in the Great Plan. Among the nine divisions, the five *fu* (i.e. five sources of happiness) were listed as the ninth division. Here Jizi emphasised the importance of:

> the hortatory use of the five (sources of) happiness, and the awing use of the six (occasions of) Suffering. (Shang Shu: Great Plan, 2, in Legg 1985)

Hence, this was the moment when *fu* firstly emerged in *Shang Shu* (*Hong Fan*) as a discursive object in Zhou dynasty.

Second, the appearance of fu has been made possible due to 'the grid of specification' (Foucault, 1972, p.42). The grid of differentiation consists of three aspects:
1. the sources of *fu* are classified into five ways:

> of the five (sources of) happiness. The first is long life; the second, riches; the third, soundness of body and serenity of mind; the fourth, the love of virtue; and the fifth, fulfilling to the end the will (of Heaven). (Shang Shu: Great Plan, 11, in Legg 1985)

2. the occasions of suffering are classified into six evils:

    Of the six extreme evils, the first is misfortune shortening the life; the second, sickness; the third, distress of mind; the fourth, poverty; the fifth, wickedness; the sixth, weakness.
    (Shang Shu: Great Plan, 11, in Legg 1985)

3. the five sources of *fu* are made in contrast to the six evils.

Hence, the above systems of classifications could be a condition that allowed fu to emerge as an object.

Third, the formation of fu as an object was devised by "the authorities of delimitation" (Foucault, 1972, p,41). In Zhou dynasty, the empire was regulated and governed by kings who paid attention to moral governance. They engaged actively in political propaganda. The conversation between Zhou Wu Wang and Jizi, was where *fu* firstly emerged as a discursive object to indicate the principles of moral governance. In this case, the kings of Zhou were the ones who were deemed qualified enough to speak, generate and discuss the discourse of *fu*. They formulated fu as an important perspective for governance within the political circle. Hence, government and political circle were considered as "the institutional site" (Foucault, 1972) in which the rulers made the discourse of *fu*.

(b) Fu as a Concept

The concept of *fu* was formed (see Fig. 3.2: 2nd layer of texts) when it crossed the "threshold of positivity" (Foucault, 1972, p.186). Such formation can be defined through "forms of co-existence" (Foucault, 1972, p.57). In ancient China, the rulers and officials were appointed according to the hierarchical system in place, while the land was allocated to the regional lords through the Fengjian system. In Zhou dynasty, the nobles were chosen on the basis of their birth and thus enjoyed the privilege of being officials for generations, disregarding of their abilities and capabilities. As a consequence, the commoners had limited chance to pursue a career within the political circle. In other words, the social status of an individual was determined by birth, rather than his/her ability. Nevertheless, the situation began to change since the Spring and Autumn and Warring States Period (770 BC to 221 BC). At the beginning of the Spring and Autumn period, Zhou king had lost his power. Therefore, warring regional lords (such as Qi Huan Gong, Jin Wen Gong, Chu Zhuang Wang and Qin Mu Gong) began to compete amongst themselves for survival. To further strengthen their power, they aggressively looked for skilful and literate officials and teachers who could offer them advice on economic, military and cultural developments. Since then, the officials were recruited on the basis of their merits rather than their birth.

Those commoners and literates who came from minor nobles would win the favour of the monarchs by engaging in the imperial examination and using their talents and abilities to participate actively in the political circle. Hence, they were regarded as the intelligentsia class (*shi* 士) and gradually became the pillar of society. Such change in the system created a condition for private schools to prosper. Lecture tours started to become popular. One typical example is Confucius, who was a literate at that time. He travelled throughout China, hoping to share his political and ethical ideas with the warring regional lords, who might hire him and implement his ideas. By the time of the Warring States period (476BC and 221 BC), the monarchs continued to seek intellectuals and patronise them. Such social reform stimulated various thinkers and led to a "Hundred School of Thoughts" (*zhu zhi ba jia*) emerged, which provided a condition for various schools of thought to formulate their own concepts of *fu*.

The "Contention of a Hundred Schools of Thoughts" (*bai jia zheng ming*) was marked as the "Golden Age" in the Chinese history of thoughts. Those major schools include Confucianism, Mohism, Daoism, Legalism, Sophists, Military Treatises, Yin and Yang, Divine Farmer, Coalition Persuaders and Selecticism. Each school of thought was inculcated with its own distinct perspectives on political and social issues such as governance, war, diplomacy, society, human life and the world. In fact, each school of thought embodied its own connotation of *fu*. To analyse each school's perspective of *fu*, Wang (2008) wrote a thesis to describe the evolution of the concept of *xing fu* held by different schools of thought over different historical stages. He highlighted that the concept of happiness in Confucianism emphasises on moral satisfaction; Mohism focuses on utilitarian happiness with pleasure-sharing and altruism; Legalism regards benefits as the essence of happiness; and Daoism concentrates on naturalistic happiness. The Hundred Schools of Thoughts co-existed during that period. Each school of thought represented a single system where statements related to *fu* are formed and operated during the Spring and Autumn and Warring States period. This was the moment when the concept of *fu* was formed and perceived as positive knowledge, where each school of thought had developed its own 'guidelines' and 'model' of living. Here, the object of *fu* has transformed into a concept.

During that period, the formation of *fu* as a concept, is made possible by a group of relations established between: (1) the life and status of various social classes and the intelligentsia class; (2) the authority of the intelligentsia class, the schools of thought and rulers; (3) the roles of the intelligentsia class, the schools of thought and rulers; (4) the authority of the schools and government; and (5) the roles and functions of the schools, government and imperial examination system.

For Foucault (1972), "knowledge is that of which one can speak in a discursive practice, and which is specified by that fact: the domain constituted by the different objects that will or will not acquire a scientific status" (p.182). Based on his argument, the knowledge of *fu* in the Spring and Autumn and Warring States period, is not the sum of what was thought to be true, but the whole set of practices, singularities and deviation of which one could speak in the discourse. During that period, the consciousness of *fu* was initially made within the intelligentsia class who learnt and taught about the social and political matters such as governance, wars, diplomacy, social relations and roles. The role of discourse on those issues was made to reflect and strengthen the status, authority and functions of the intelligentsia class, as they were the ones who were qualified enough to speak, guide, counsel and teach others (in particular, the monarchs) to live well.

Thinkers of each school of thought came from various social groups. For instance, Confucius and Lao Zi came from minor nobles; Divine Farmer were driven by agriculturists; Legalism represented the rising landlords; Military Treatises were made of the military experts; and Coalition Persuaders were mainly consisted of diplomats. Henceforth, each school of thought was formed and developed according to the values and interests of a particular social group in which its thinkers belonged to. In that case, the discourse on *fu* was made in order to protect and strengthen the position, roles, interests and benefits of various social groups. The debates on *fu* among the intelligentsia class in the Hundred Schools of Thoughts, could be a reflection of their social class, status, authority and functions in the society at that period of time.

3.2.3 Transformation: From *Fu* to *Xing Fu*

Following Foucault's analysis of transformation, the discursive transformations of *fu* take places in two stages: (1) advancing knowledge of fu through rationality and scientificity (see Fig. 3.2: 3rd layer of texts) and (2) transforming from fu to xing fu (see Fig. 3.2: 4th layer of texts). In stage 1, that is during the Spring and Autumn and Warring States period, the concept of fu was developed. At that time, the discourse of fu was formed without the development of a scientific status. However, the rules of formation had begun to change since the late Ming dynasty. Such a change in the rules represents what Foucault (1972) calls: a discursive transformation. How did the rules change? What were the new rules of formation? In the late Ming and early period of Qing dynasty, Chinese intellectuals (Huang Zongxi, Gu Yanwu and Wang Fuzhi) were inspired by the movement of Enlightenment that took place in Europe in the late 17th century. They were influenced by western thinking (such as individualism, rationality and capitalism) and began to challenge the ideas and systems of Chinese traditions, ethics and beliefs. For instance, they criticised the *fengjian* system and despotism. Some intellectuals also questioned the Confucian deontological concept of *fu* which was rooted mainly on social relations and virtues (Wang, 2008). These intellectuals preferred to analyse the knowledge of *fu* through rationality and scientific methods. As a result, they reconstructed the concept of *fu* from "balanced multidimensional" perspectives to "the relation of rationality, justice and commonweal" (Wang, 2008, p.III). In that case, 'rationality' and 'scientificity' became the new rules of formation that governed the discourse of *fu*. According to Foucault's (1972) archaeology, the discourse of *fu* at that moment "complied not only with archaeological rules of formation, but also certain laws for construction of propositions" (p.187). In other words, this discursive transformation has crossed the "threshold of scientificity" (p.187) and it was made due to the power and status of the Chinese Enlightenment thinkers, because they were qualified to speak and argue for such a change of rules at that time.

In stage 2, *fu* is transformed to *xing fu*. The rise of the Chinese Enlightenment thinkers (such as Kang You Wei, Liang Qi Chao, Tan Szu Tung and Yan Fu) provided for an environment wherein various western ideas of capitalism, individualism, rationality, equality, freedom and democracy generated a deep impact upon the modern Chinese discourse of *fu*. This is the time when western theories of happiness and well-being were made appropriate to the Chinese contexts. Consequently, the discourse of fu has transformed to a stage where it has crossed the "threshold of epistemologization" (Foucault, 1972, pp.186–187). In Wang's (2008) thesis on the evolution of *xing fu*, he highlighted:

> In modern times of China, facing the historical task of saving the nation from subjugation and ensuring its survival, new thinkers advocated moral revolution, formed concept of happiness featured by seeking pleasure and escaping from bitterness on the basis of Western theory of happiness and pleasure, which became the most influential mainstream concept of happiness. And it was generally and reasonably expounded in the period of May 4th Movement of 1919.
> (p.III)

Wang's (2008) analysis pointed out that the western discourse of well-being was transferred to the modern Chinese context. Since then, well-being was regarded as the mainstream concept of *xing fu*, especially in the Chinese academic institutions, governments, inter-governmental organizations and professional bodies. When academics, scholars and researchers transferred the concept of well-being to the Chinese context, the most common procedures of intervention used is transplantation. That means, the entire rules of transformation which were used in the framework of well-being are being copied and applied to the Chinese context. One illustration could be: well-being is being translated as *xing fu* (Lu, 2001; 2010; Davis, 2005), making *xing fu* as the direct equivalent of well-being. Since then, both well-being and *xing fu* have adopted the same grids of specification. For instance, the discourse of *xing fu* is made possible by the classification between subjective well-being (in Chinese, it is directly translated as *zhu guan xing fu gan* 主觀幸福感) and psychological well-being (in Chinese, it is directly translated as *xin li xing fu gan* 心理幸福感). By using this transplantation, the rules governing the formation of any empirical and scientific discourses of well-being (mainly positivism and objectivism) are also applicable to the discourse of *xing fu*. Within this layer of texts, *xing fu* could be measured, divided, contrasted, related, regrouped and classified into different degrees, levels and kinds across various Chinese contexts. At the same time, *fu* was changed to a term called '*xing fu*'. Since then, the statements of *xing fu* are articulated and validated according to the norms of verification and coherence operated in the discourse of well-being. The discourse

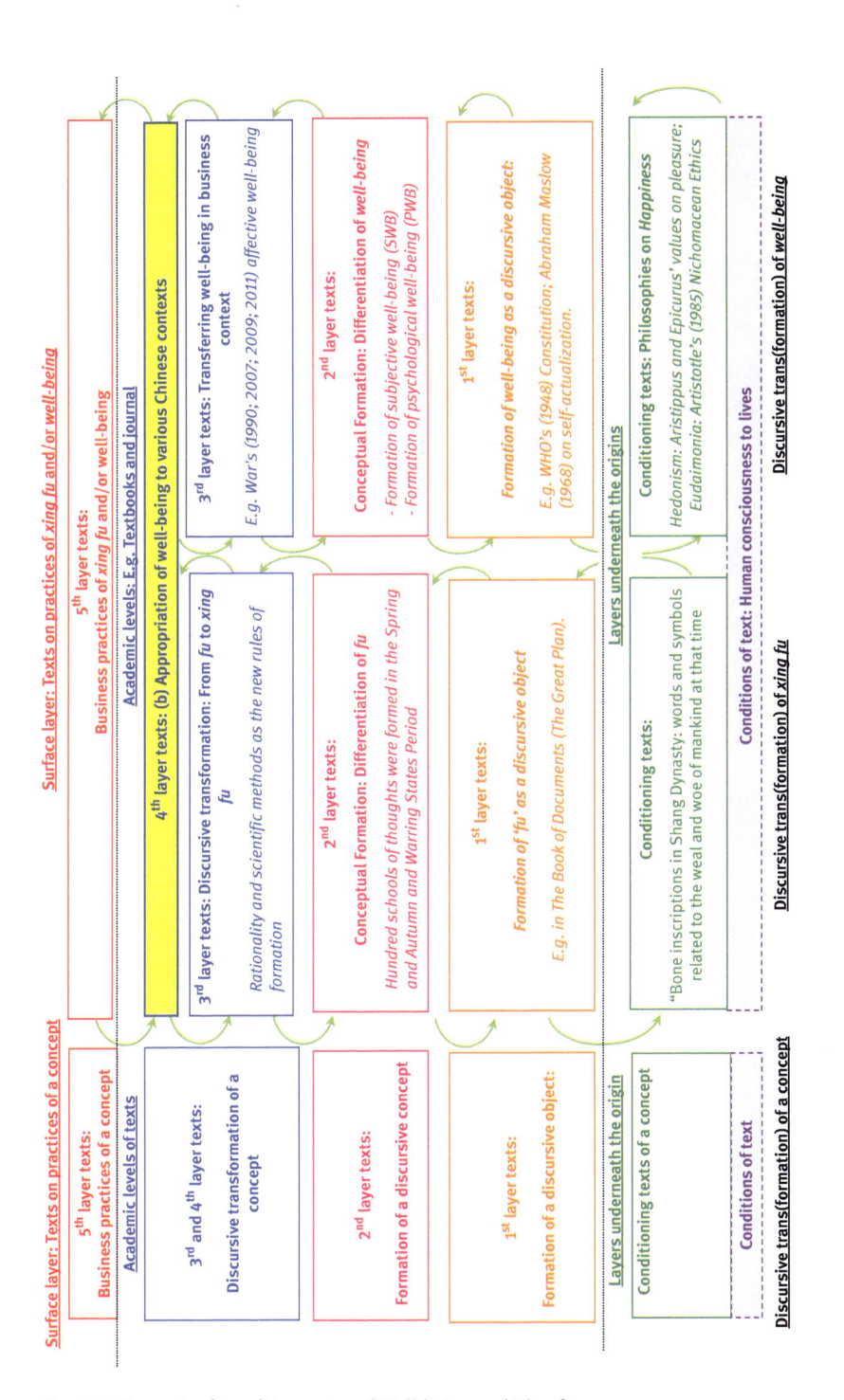

Fig. 3.3: Discursive (Trans)Formation of Well-being and *Xing fu*.

of well-being has eventually served as a dominant function (as a model, a critique, or a verification) over the knowledge of *xing fu* (Foucault, 1972). *Xing fu* is subsequently governed by the same set of rules of formation in the well-being discourse. This is the moment when the discourses of well-being and *xing fu* have been merged together (see Fig. 3.3: 4th layer of texts). According to Foucault's (1972) archaeology, this level of text represents a discursive transformation, because the discourse of fu has crossed a "threshold of epistemologization" (pp.186–187). Under this level of discourse, transformation from well-being to *xing fu* was occurred.

3.2.4 Business Practices of *Xing Fu*

Since *xing fu* is made as an equivalent to well-being in 1900s, the two concepts have been applied interchangeably in many Chinese workplaces. In the management discourse, business practices of *xing fu* often correspond to the positive human resource management practices designed for employee well-being. However, would the practices of *xing fu* be different in the Chinese family business (CFB)? How far would the members of CFB draw upon the discourse of well-being in their daily lives? To answer these questions, Chapter 4 is an anthropological study that explores the lived experience of a Chinese subject in CFB.

3.3 Between Well-being and *Xing Fu*: Any Discursive Space?

This part derives implications from the above archaeological examination. The archaeology uncovers 'a' sequence of rules that govern the discourse and examined the possibility of it impacting the present world. The examination considers well-being as a discursive object. With such an assumption, a discursive space is created to examine the discourse of well-being.

From the archaeological examination, two additional ontological possibilities of well-being are revealed. First, well-being is dynamic (rather than fixed) in nature, given it has gone through a series of transformation in the discourse. Well-being has emerged from a discursive object to a concept and has been applied to various fields and cultural contexts. Second, well-being is culturally distinctive, rather than context-free. Well-being is originated from the Eurocentric philosophies on happiness. Hence, the knowledge generated is "culturally and historically specific" (Jacques, 1996, p.vii). With the above two additional characteristics of well-being, this book makes a contribution to knowledge by revealing more ontological possibilities of well-being.

Furthermore, this archaeological study diagnosed two problems in the well-being discourse: (1) objectification and (2) essentialism. Foucault (1982) classified objectification into three modes: (1) scientific classification; (2) "dividing practice" (p.777) and (3) "subjectification" (p.778) (see Section 2.2). These three modes of objectification can be found in the well-being discourse. First, the science of psychology relies on tactics, such as 'objective', 'reliable' and 'accurate' measurement and statistical analysis (Steffy and Grimes, 1992) to examine the validity of well-being. These tactics treat well-being as an authentic and 'real' scientific object. As a consequence, inquiries of well-being tend to emphasise on social norms and individual differences based on variables of interests (Madigan, 1992). With the scientific practice of measuring individual well-being, human is turned to be an object. For instance, when examining employee well-being (see Fig. 3.1: 3rd layer of texts), employees (who were supposed to be the subject) have become an object of knowledge to testify well-being at work. Foucault perceived this practice of classification as "an individualizing and a totalizing form of power", because it turns human into an object of knowledge and "ignores individuals, looking only at the interests of the totality" (p.782). He criticized that:

> There is nothing " scientific" in this (that is, a dogmatic belief in the value of scientific knowledge), but neither is it a skeptical or relativistic refusal of all verified truth. What is questioned is the way in which knowledge circulates and functions, its relations to power. (p.781)

Hence, the notion of well-being is not externally 'given', but produced historically through the elements of power and knowledge (McGillivray, 2005) produced by the key social players.

Second, the dividing practice can be found in the positivist and neopositivist approaches to well-being. The rationale of these epistemologies tends to create individual as an analysable and describable object that can be objectively assessed, judged, measured, categorised and compared (Townley, 1993). For instance, the major psychological or economic measurements of well-being tend to classify individuals hierarchically along the predetermined scales, such as index of happiness, index of well-being, Quality of Life (QoL) and Human Development Index (HDI) (UNDP, 2007). These scales divide peoples or countries with labels based on the grids of specification such as well-being versus ill-being, wealth versus poverty, health versus illness, and developed country versus the Third World. The dividing practice can be seen as a tool adopted by the disciplinary power to "gaze at, scrutinize, classify and count individual characteristics and behaviours" (Steffy and Grimes, 1992, p.192).

Third, the dominant discourse of well-being emphasises on the economic benefits that can be gained from the discussed subject. For instance, the benefits for business can include variables like reduction in absenteeism, improved performance, employee engagement and retention (see Fig. 3.1: 3rd layer of text). Drawing from Foucault's idea of subjectification, McGillivray (2005) highlighted that positivist and functionalist discourses of organisational wellness are increasingly legitimated. In such discourse, the rationalisation and function of wellness are encouraged to an extent that the concept of well-being plays a significant role in shaping the employee's lifestyle and behaviour. In other words, well-being can become a "commodity", "fashion" or "culture" that can induce employees to commit themselves to an organisation (Burrell, 1992, p.73). Under such perspective, the concept of well-being has been internalised by human beings. Individuals would take initiatives to make themselves as a subject and practice well-being since well-being is deemed to be a norm that is desirable in lives. For instance, employees view work-life or work-family balance as a desirable lifestyle and demand family-friendly initiatives in the workplace (see Fig. 3.1: 5th layer of texts).

With regards to Foucault's three modes of objectification, the discourse of well-being can be seen as a way to legitimise dominant knowledge group, divide individuals and shape individual's behaviours and identity. For instance, based on Foucault's ideas of governmentality and the subject, McGillivray (2005) provided an analysis on the discursive social practices of organisational wellness (OW). He challenged that while the managerial discursive practices of OW were regarded as 'productive', 'transformative' and 'performative' (p.125) to any individuals, businesses and societies, they have neglected the heterogeneity of employee responses. Therefore, he suggested to identify various subject's positions, "ranging from employees who utilise wellness facilities to realise their own projects of the self, to those who fail to recognise the value of discourses of wellness in their entirety" (p.135), and give each of them a voice.

The problem of essentialism is dissected through the archaeology of well-being. Jacques (1996) argues that management knowledge has been developed by "indigenizing 'organizational science' itself as a discourse shaped by its culture of origin" (p. xiiii). Well-being is rooted with Eurocentric beliefs on happiness. Therefore, well-being is a culturally bounded concept. Originally, well-being was not significant to the Chinese culture, because as shown in the archaeology of *xing fu* (see Fig. 3.2), Chinese has its indigenous prescription of *fu*. Well-being and *xing fu* were originally emerged as two individual discursive objects with separate conditioning texts (cultural origins). They were perceived as two distinctive concepts in their formations (see Fig. 3.3). Nevertheless, essentialism (Westwood, 2006) has occurred along their transformations. When, how and why did it happen? The archaeological examination provides an answer. During the period of May 4th Movement in 1919, the Chinese Enlightenment thinkers promoted western ideas (such as individualism, rationality and democracy etc.) which provided a condition for academics, scholars and researchers to directly transfer the concept of well-being to the Chinese context. In the 4th layer of text (see Fig. 3.3), the appropriation of well-being to various Chinese contexts has begun. Under this level of discourse, *xing fu* is made as a direct equivalent of well-being even though the two concepts were inherently and culturally distinctive. This was the moment when essentialism appeared in well-being discourse because the Chinese (the Other) was being dragged into the dominant discourse of well-being, while the existence of the Chinese concept – *fu*, was denied. Subsequently, the indigenous views on *fu* were silenced in the well-being discourse. While the concept of well-being has been widespread globally, the Others' voices on what they think to be good are rarely heard. In other words, the discourse of well-being could represent an insidious form of colonisation and marginalisation. As an implication, the archaeological examination in this chapter makes a methodological contribution by offering a way to dissect the objectification and essentialism in the well-being discourse.

Are there any ways to avoid objectification and essentialism in the discourse? Is decolonisation possible? Xu (2000) explains in her archaeological examination:

> Paradoxically, asking questions backward does allow me to think forward. Not only does a way of thinking produce knowledge, its production cannot be separated from its discursive condition. (p.447)

She highlights that even though archaeology deals with history of discourse, it allows the people to learn from the past and think in an advanced manner. To learn from the past, the archaeological examination reveals that any formation of a concept and its knowledge production would be "culturally and historically specific" (Jacques, 1996, p. vii). Each discursive concept is entailed with its own cultural orientation and is formed historically within a particular set of conditions. Hence, this book claims that transferring a western concept to any Other's cultural context could run the risk of dragging the Other (the subject) as an object for illustrating or testing western ideologies and eventually lead to objectification and essentialism. This assertion is aligned with Xu's (2008) position in her critical appraisal of Redding's The Spirit of Capitalism. She has exhibited how Redding's subject is made an object of knowledge to testify Weber's thesis. As a consequence, "the subject's continuity is interrupted, its voice deprived and its capacity for dialogue denied" (p.242). In order to avoid objectification in the research process, shall we not place the Other within the well-being discourse? If so, where could we possibly locate the Other? The book suggests opening a discursive space, where the voices of the Other could be heard and conversations with the west could be made possible.

Is there any discursive space outside the interface of well-being? This book opens 'a' discursive space outside the well-being discourse. In Xu's (1999) examination of quality management discourse, the name, TQM is demystified as "an arbitrary linguistic sign" (p.659) which enables the possibility of substitutions. In her analysis, three possibilities of substitution could be considered: (1) Same name can be used for separating events and engendering different identities; (2) Different names can be used for similar events or practices; and (3) 'Something' (i.e. other names) can be appeared in between these names. Building on her statement, the name, 'well-being' can be regarded as an arbitrary linguistic sign as well. Although 'happiness' is changed to 'well-being' due to the purpose of differentiating well-being from the earlier discourse of happiness, well-being is indeed discursively connected with Hedonic happiness and Eudaimonia. Hence, well-being can arguably be regarded as another name, representing similar images of happiness (i.e. the 2nd probability made in Xu's (1999) analysis). Similarly, 'xing fu' is made as another name for the concept of well-being in the discourse. In this light, 'well-being' "is merely one of a number of possible names" (Xu, 1999, p.665). Numerous names could appear in the discourse; some names are recently formulated while some are old names that have disappeared due to the discursive transformation (Xu, 1999). Some names are for different images or practices; whereas some names are different but for similar images or practices. There are also certain names that go in between 'names'. In that case, there is a discursive space outside the discourse of well-being, wherein different arbitrary linguistic signs are made possible.

Then, where can researchers find a discursive space outside the boundary of well-being? Where is the interstitial space in a discourse? According to the archaeological examinations, one common condition that can give rise to happiness, well-being and *fu* is human consciousness to lives (see Fig. 3.3: Conditions of texts). In other words, it is the human consciousness to lives that leads to the formations of happiness, well-being and *xing fu*. Under this condition, human consciousness to lives could lead to various distinctive cultural expressions. There is 'an' interstitial space in between happiness, well-being and *xing fu*, where numerous discursive objects and concepts, illustrating human consciousness to lives, could have possibly been formed with various specific historical and cultural contexts. For example, 'Suma Jakana' in Bolivia (Calestani, 2013) and 'ikigai' in Japan (Mathrews, 2010). This interstitial space allows other cultural objects and concepts to emerge and transformed. Within such a discursive space, cross-cultural examinations among various discursive objects and concepts are made possible (see Fig. 3.4). As a result, instead of dragging the Other to the discourse of well-being, researchers could locate the Other in such an interstitial space.

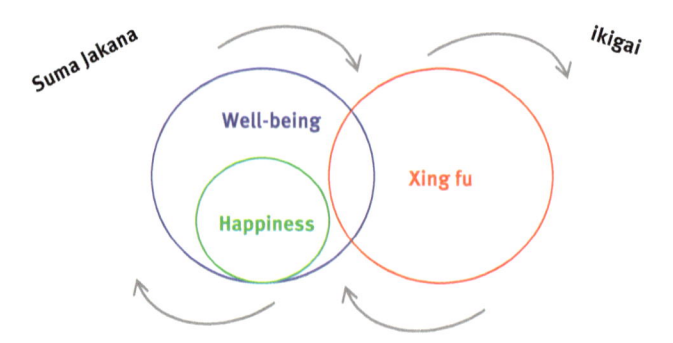

Fig. 3.4: A Discursive Space 'Outside' Well-being Discourse.

How could researchers locate the Other in the discourse without objectifying or essentialising the subject? This book suggests taking a critical ethnography to study the Other. The 'thick description' in the next chapter explores an indigenous (a Chinese) perspective on living well in Chinese family business.

Chapter 4
An Anthropological Journey in Chinese Family Business

The archaeological examination (see Chapter 3) shows that well-being is brought to business management and become a well-known concept particularly in Human Resources Management (HRM), Industrial/Organisational Psychology (I/OP) and Professional Business Management fields. This indicates that in the management discourse, the speaking is possibly confined to the business elites, naming Human Resource Professionals (HRP), I/OP practitioners and managers. Similarly, this anthropological journey also illustrates that the notion is well-known to the local HRP, I/OP practitioners and managers who work in Multinational National Corporations (MNCs). All of them are familiar with the term *well-being*. They can explain well-being as follows:

> From the staff perspective, well-being refers to the totality of physical state, mental state and psychological state . . . (Well-being) is referring to the positive state . . . so it's a positive physical state, mental state, as well as psychological state . . . and also positive relationship (with others)! Positive state means 'healthy', that means physically healthy, mentally healthy and psychologically healthy. That what well-being means."   (Mr. Peter)

> 'Well-being' is referring to something that would make one feels satisfied or happy. 'Well-being' is more related to the employee benefits . . . and even employee relations. . . . I would think (well-being) is equivalent to 'job satisfaction'!   (Ms. Paris)

> In general, 'well-being' is: do you feel happy in work? . . . We (My company) offered work-balance week last year. During that week, (it) offered many healthy snacks, activities . . . (Employees feel free to) turn off (the office's) light and leave (work) earlier etc.   (Mrs. Pansy)

> 'Well-being' is 'work-life balance' . . . Yes, you need to maintain work-life balance in both physically or mentally . . . That's why my company offers work-life balance leave . . . By nature, it's a kind of benefits to the employees.   (Mrs. Hestia)

> 'Well-being' . . . um . . . is . . . that's to say, you are . . . are feeling comfortable. I mean, by all (aspects), including eating, healthy (in) psychological state, (and) physical body, all aspects.
>   (Patricia)

> 'Well-being' is very (related to) material aspect. It is because Western often views well-being as (equivalent to) something material, such as job satisfaction, how much salary do you have . . . If you look at (well-being in) a country, (it is referred as) social welfare, benefits, GDP . . . That is whether you are rich or not, how many poverty index is it? . . .   (Pauline)

The above responses show that the concept of 'well-being' is quite well-known to the HR professionals and management in the MNCs in Hong Kong. Nevertheless, some of them expressed that well-being is not exactly the same as *xing fu*, or vice versa. Here are their comments:

> Using xing fu to describe work? Em . . . or should it used to describe (one's) whole (life) . . . Em . . . Very strange! Xing fu . . . should include many aspects. (If)Everything is very good, I think (you) can call (you are) xing fu. So, **xing fu does not seem to be the same as well-being.**
> (Paris)

> **Xing fu and well-being, to my feeling, (they are) very different things!** You would feel: Wa, (I'm) very xing fu!; But you wouldn't feel: (I'm) very well-being! Xing fu includes more elements . . . (such as) have energy to breath, or have energy to work . . . this is already very satisfied, very xing fu! At the very beginning, I won't take 'well-being' to be translated as 'xing fu'.
> (Patricia)

> 'Well-being' is not a word that enters deeply into my heart! This is a word that comes from foreign (countries)! I know this English word only when I had entered university. (This is a word that) I did not use it as an expression when I was small. So, I especially feel strange when I use this word! May be because I encounter this word only when I studied Psycho(logy) . . . In contrast, I know the term, 'xing fu', when I was small. I would use it (xing fu) to express myself, such as when I feel satisfied, I have a family who loves me, I feel healthy in all aspects . . .
> (Pauline)

> I was a bit surprised of this translation (i.e. 'well-being' is being translated as 'xing fu')! That is (if talking about) work aspects, I don't use xing fu (to describe work). (Rather, I) may use 'job satisfaction', or 'positive mind-set'. Xing fu is usually used to describe a little woman . . . associated with you have cars, have flats, have doggies, (you) don't have any worries nor pressure! Once you need to work, you are not xing fu. Because you have work pressure! Besides, xing fu is not said by yourself, it needs to be said by others: (That is) How do others perceive you?
> (Pansy)

The above feedback shows even some of the local HR professionals and management do not agree on taking *xing fu* as if it is equal to well-being. They think that well-being and *xing fu* are two distinct concepts in which each has its own cultural usage and meaning. Their view is aligned with the archaeological examination. Well-being is not exactly the same as *xing fu*. The findings from both archaeological and anthropological examinations reinforce the need to justify *xing fu* as an equivalent of well-being.

This anthropological examination carries further to ask: *Do members of family business in China (Hong Kong specifically) draw upon the discourse of well-being in their daily practices? If not, what relevant concepts do they refer to and make use of in a given time period?* To answer this research questions, I observed and participated in the informants' daily lives. The findings reveal that the informants used alternate local expressions, instead of well-being. These expression(s) are written according to various aspects of life. Nevertheless, the narration may appear to be scattered and fragmented. Every night, I recalled the experiences of a particular day and wrote the diary. Various pieces of memories would be scattered in the mind and while recollecting those thoughts, I ended up writing down every tiny piece of details. This writing experience was similar to the daily lived experience of me and the informants. On one hand, the narration in this chapter revealed our expressions in life. On the other hand, in making sense to our lives, doubts, puzzles, ambivalence and pressures would sometimes appear. Hence, the complexity of life is highlighted.

My ethnography began at the end of December 2011 when I returned to Hong Kong to start data collection. This chapter richly describes and analyses my anthropological journey – the findings of the ethnography. Through a 'thick description' (Geertz, 1973), the context of each family business, the practices and lived experience of the research subject are scrutinised in detail. Chinese family businesses in Hong Kong are chosen as my field site to investigate whether their members would draw upon the discourses of well-being in their everyday practices. I first give a brief general background of each company which describes the context of Chinese family business in Hong Kong. Then I go into participants' lives and look at how they would live well in their family businesses. Other expressions are explored to describe their works and daily lives. Lastly, I further interpret their lives into four kinds of practices. These practices represent an embodiment of their expressions, which can offer an additional layer of understanding to Chinese family business without essentialising them based on western professional management.

4.1 Managing Chinese Family Business

This section introduces each family business and its main characters. Totally, four field sites (FB 1, 2, 3 and 4) are chosen. These four companies are small-sized businesses, with less than 30 employees. In fact, most of them are micro-enterprises which have less than 10 employees. The following description briefly explains how the owners started the businesses and their daily operations.

(a) FB 1 (An Education Centre)

FB 1 is the first chosen site. Since this was the first attempt to conduct a site visit, I was nervous and cautious. FB 1 is an education centre which provides tutorial services mainly for the primary school pupils. Ada was the successor of FB 1. She was in her early 40s and was a friend of one of my close contacts, Gigi. Ada and Gigi were classmates and they studied in the same secondary school. Ada graduated with a degree in business in London. In the first dinner with Ada, she shared the story about how FB 1 has been started and evolved. Here is her story: The business started in 1996. Before opening FB 1, her father (Mr. Alex) owned a store, which was a family business from his parents. With the instruction of his parents, Mr. Alex decided to pass the business to the fourth wife of his father and became a taxi driver. Few months later, his wife (Mrs. Alice) initiated to start a new business because she would like to *'find another way to generate income for the family, instead of solely relying on her investment in the stock market'*. More importantly, *'she (Mrs. Alice) realized there was a demand for private tutoring, because at that time, there were two kids from our jiu jie fang* 舊街坊 *(previous neighbourhood) who had come to our home and asked us (Ada and her elder sister) for tutorship . . . '.* That was how Mrs. Alice started the business.

On 1 March 2012, I started the company visit at FB 1. FB 1 is situated at the Eastern district where I had lived for almost 20 years. On the first day of visit, Ada explained the daily business operation while showing me around the centre. The company mainly involved the following staff:

- 6–8 full-time employees: An owner (Mrs. Alice), a family worker (Ada), 5 full-time teachers (Audrey, Amy and Ann; while Ally and Abegail were resigned in October and November 2012 respectively) and Mrs. Ashley who is responsible for clerical assistance and pantry work.
- 10–15 part-time teachers on seasonal demand, such as Ms. Averi, Ms. Alysia and Ms. Abbey.

(b) FB 2 (A Dance Studio)

This business is a dance studio which offers various dance courses, including ballet, Chinese dance, jazz, hip pop, K pop, rhythmic gymnastics and yoga. It has been functioning since September 2013. It was first owned by two partners, Betty and Bonnie. Both of them were in their late 30s. Betty was single while Bonnie was married with a three-year old daughter. Betty had a larger percentage of ownership. Three months after the start of the business, Betty found it difficult to maintain the operation due to the limited amount of financial capital. Hence, she invited her past superior, Bob, to invest in the business as a limited partner. He would mainly provide FB 2 with sufficient source of capital and seldom participates in its daily operation.

The journey of FB 2 begins when Betty and Bonnie intended to start a business together. Here is our conversation:

> I asked them: *I thought you two would start the business through franchise!*
>
> Betty replied with an anger tone: *Sigh! Don't mention about the franchise! We have turned down the franchise partnership . . . But we have found a place for our studio and signed the lease contract for two years already. In that case, we still need to open the studio by ourselves. We have already made our hair wet.* (已經洗濕個頭) *(meaning: We have already started the business, we can't stop it immediately)*

The above conversation captured how Betty and Bonnie began the business. Since Betty and Bonnie had signed the lease contract, they decided to run the business by themselves. The studio has started its operation since September 2013. Once the studio had opened, Betty and Bonnie were busy in arranging office facilities, designing course schedules, hiring full-time staff and planning for promotion etc. As their close friends, I would regularly visit their studio and offer assistance in reception.

During the fieldwork, FB 2 mainly involves the following staff:
- Betty, Bonnie and Bob are the owners
- 2 full-time employees: Brenda and Blossom (but they were terminated after the first three months of employment)
- 1–2 Part-time teachers, such as Ms. Bessy

(c) FB 3 (A Jade Accessory Maker)

This business was focussed on jade accessory making. It was a kind of craftsmanship that was once very popular in Hong Kong in 1960s to 1980s. It was owned by a sole proprietor, Uncle Carl. He was in his 60s and has a wife (Auntie Connie), two sons and a daughter.

I started visiting FB 3 since 1st January 2013. FB 3 was situated in the same district as FB 1. Uncle Carl and Auntie Connie were living in a residential building under the home ownership scheme. Uncle Carl's flat is situated right next to the lift on the 8th floor. There was a *tu di gong shen wei* (a spiritual tablet representing the God of Earth) placed outside his flat. It was a flat with around 550 square meters. When entering the flat, I saw the kitchen and his work station. His work station was located right next to the entrance door with a bench, a high chair and a light. The bench was made of a hard rock with dark grey colour. Rulers, pencils, erasers and various tools for carving were placed on the right-hand side of the bench. A machine for polishing jades was placed in the middle of the bench, with many small semi-polished jades scattered around. A bowl of water was always placed on the lower left-hand corner. Uncle Carl would usually dip the jade in the water for a few seconds before showing it. On the left-hand side, there was a cupboard with many small drawers. Different kinds of semi-finished and finished jade accessories were classified and put into these drawers. Underneath the bench, there were stocks of large jade stones. They were all wrapped with newspapers and were scattered on the floor. Auntie Connie once commented: *"This is his (Uncle Carl's) work station where no one in the family is allowed to reach. Ha . . . You see, things are arranged in a messy manner. I guess only he (Uncle Carl) could be able to identify the things he needs to use."*

On each visit, I would go to Uncle Carl's home first, engage in a social conversation and observe him while he was working in his station. I would also have lunch or tea with them. Afterwards, I would visit Uncle Carl's retail store, which was a leased market stall issued by the government. The stall was in the marketplace, where it was located right next to where Uncle Carl lives. It was a marketplace with several storeys. Uncle Carl retail store was located on the third floor. The stalls in this floor sold mainly clothes and accessories. They were arranged according to rows. His store was located in the last stall of the first row. The store was around 100 square meters, which was much larger than his work station at home. Inside the stall, there were two cupboards with window. They were placed as an 'L' shape.

His finished jade-made accessories are placed inside the cupboard. The customers were able to browse the goods through the windows. At the back of the stall was another work station. The setting of this work station was almost the same as that at his home. Next to his work station was another table. A water bottle and a cup are always placed on the table. Above the table, a paper fish, which was made from red pockets, was hanging from the ceiling. Uncle Carl was quite satisfied with such the environment of this stall. He commented with comfort: *"This stall is much better than my previous one! It offers bright lightings, a sink with a water tap and an air-conditioned environment. Its area is much larger than the old stall."*

(d) FB 4 (A Fashion Boutique)

FB 4 is the last chosen site for this research. FB 4 is a business that focuses on fashion design, production and retails. It is a fashion label which offers clothes that are gender-neutral. FB 4 was owned by two partners: Doris and Dave. Doris is in her mid-40s; while Dave is in his late 50s. Doris is a fashion designer who has created her own design label since 2006; while Dave is a businessman. Doris was an employee of Dave's company. Dave's business was originally focused on garment manufacturing. In 2009, he planned to expand its business to both food and fashion industries. Therefore, he hired Doris and gave her a primary responsibility of developing a sport fashion label for his company. Nevertheless, with her efficiency, passion and diligence, Doris has become a right-arm to Dave after a few months of her employment. She helped Dave to manage the company, including both food and fashion businesses. Until 2014, she has partnered with Dave, to start FB 4 – a fashion business. They have opened a fashion boutique at PMQ.

The boutique finished its renovation and began its operation in the late April 2014. On 3rd May 2014, I was asked by Doris to look after the store. The store is situated in one residential unit of PMQ. PMQ was once the Police Married Quarters in 1951, but it has been revitalised in 2010. Since then, it has become a site for creative industries (PMQ, 2015). The lightings inside the shop are made of a number of white water pipes. A pair of iron stands and shelves is placed at the two sides the wall, for displaying products. A few wooden boxes are put on the shelves for storing stock. A sound bar is hanged on the left-hand side of the wall, with a purpose of playing sound and music. At the middle-bottom of the room, a glassed table with iron stands is hanging from the ceiling. This is where the cashier is placed. A changing room is situated on the left of the cashier, while a sewing machine is placed on the right-hand side. The area behind the cashier is a workstation. There is a big wooden table in the workstation. Doris normally uses the station for designing, ironing, sewing and doing administrative works. The design of the shop is likeable and reflects a feeling of simplicity, but yet stylish and durable. The interior design of the shop matches with the company's fashion style.

4.2 Living Well in Chinese Family Business

How did the members of Chinese family businesses live in Hong Kong? Do they draw upon the discourses of well-being? I did not find the term *well-being*, to be spontaneously expressed during the field visits. It is doubtable whether well-being is a familiar language or a significant issue to the locals who work in small family businesses. Even though some of my informants (usually those with tertiary education qualification, such as Ada, Betty, Doris and Hestia) may understand the idea of well-being, they do not agree that such an idea can be entirely applicable to their lives. For instance, in one of my social chat with Ada, she asked about my research progress and the details of my topic. In our discussion, she made the following comments:

> Yes, 'the balance' talked by the foreigners are different from the local view of balance. Foreigners work for four days only. But, here, maybe (we) see work as lives. Indeed, people who talk about balance are most probably those already have had a certain degree of wealth. That's why they can seek for (a quality of) lives. Those grassroots do not talk about 'balance'. The demand (for balance) depends on different people. (Ada)

From Ada's comments, she thinks that the idea of *'work-life balance'* cannot be entirely applicable to the local lives of the grassroots. Her view is similar to the following comments made by Hestia:

> (For) Small-sized firms, especially family businesses, everyone is 'one foot kick' (one is responsible for all duties and tasks). Hence, 'well-being' is not a matter (to them). I think foreign-invested firms must have this so called 'well-being', because they are relatively more easy-going, are more open-minded. (They) do not (only focus on) working (even though) they sit down (in the office) . . . (However), Chinese would work very hard once they have sat down. They strive to work (for their own businesses) because family businesses are their own businesses. They need to monitor the financial performance. They are more anxious on the financial performance, rather than their own well-being. I mean, they won't even think of well-being (as an issue) to their lives. (Hestia)

Hence, well-being is not entirely applicable to the lives of the informants who work in the local family businesses, because they could not afford the luxury of work-life balance given they need to work hard for survival.

I found that management language is scarcely spontaneously used in Chinese family businesses. After months of field visits, an absence of well-being discourse became apparent. Such a finding is similar to Learmonth's (2009) examination of argument regarding avoiding the colonization management language among the clerks in a UK hospital's medical records library. Given it is obvious that management language and concepts are seldom practiced in Chinese family businesses (particularly for small and medium-sized enterprises (SMEs) in Hong Kong), the focus of this ethnography is on working with indigenous expressions (in terms of both language and practices) used by a Chinese subject in everyday lives.

If members of Chinese family businesses in Hong Kong do not draw upon the discourse of well-being, what relevant concepts do they refer to and make use of in their daily practices? The archaeological examination (see Chapter 3) opens up a discursive space, where it allows various cultural expressions to be articulated. The following description reveal some key terms/concepts expressed by the research subject. Each expression has its own contextual meaning and highlights the aspect of life that the informants regarded as important. As a local, these expressions are of no stranger to me. They were arranged according to their frequency of occurrence and importance. Besides using language, the subject lived well through their daily practices. These practices represent the embodiment of their expressions (see Appendix C: Tab. C1).

4.2.1 Jia Ting (Family)

During the fieldwork, I lived with a local family who is one of my close contacts. The head of this family was Mr. Isaac, who passed away in his early 70s in 2013. He worked in a *wu jin pu* (a metal work store) during his lifetime, which was a family business succeeded from his father. He and his wife (Mrs. Cindy) have seven daughters. I stayed with the couples and two of their daughters. They often shared their lifetime stories with me. Living with them allowed me to grasp, experience, participate and comprehend the local daily lives. They are my central family and were regarded as the most important aspect of my life. Similarly, most of the informants expressed '*jia ting*' (family) as their most important aspect of lives.

Mr. Peter, who was working as a Human Resources Director in a medium-sized trading firm, thought there is a difference between foreign and Chinese families:

> (In) Foreign countries, most of the children would leave their families when they have grown up. However, for Chinese, they emphasize on xiao (filial piety). Therefore, (for Chinese) **familial relationship is very important!**

Bonnie in FB 2 even highlighted that:

> (If I need) To prioritize the order of importance, for sure, it would be my family, indeed . . . I think ever since I was little, I know my family is the most important . . . I can only think of family (as the most important aspect of my lives)!

From the observation on how FB 1, 2, 3 and 4 operated, it could be posited that all of them demonstrated a degree of **'familial' culture that blurred the boundary between family and company**. Below are evidences that illustrate family is embedded in their daily work:

FB 1: Work like a family
My general impression about the people in FB 1 was they were working like a family, with Mrs. Alice as their family head. **'Go and ask Mrs. Alice'** is the phrase I would usually hear, which highlighted Mrs. Alice was the authority of FB 1. Mrs. Alice was the owner of FB 1 and was in her late fifties. She always wore a smile on her face whenever she walked around the centre. Everyone in the centre was polite to her. Instead of calling her name, everyone would show respect to her by calling her "Mrs. Alice". People in FB 1 never criticised Mrs. Alice directly. Once the tutorial started, Mrs. Alice would walk around to oversee the operation. As the owner of the business, she took up the leadership roles: for being the decision makers, problem solver or conflicts handler, performance monitor as well as spokesperson. By taking these roles, she gained authority and respect from everyone, including the staff, pupils and guardians. For that reason, she represented a head of the family.

With a family head, the next question is: Who are or could be regarded as family members? The answer could depend not only on biological criteria, but also on one's position and seniority in FB 1. While FB 1 is led by Mrs. Alice, it is managed by a family member (Ada) and three full-time teaching staff (namely Audrey, Amy and Ann). Since Ada is Mrs. Alice's daughter, she is biologically regarded a key family member (and most likely the successor) of FB 1. She is mainly responsible for administration, marketing and management in the main centre, such as arranging teaching schedule, designing teaching curriculum and materials, making marketing leaflets, recruiting and selecting new staff, collecting tuition fees, giving out receipts and picking up phone calls etc. Although she is responsible for administrative and managerial tasks, she also engages in teaching and sometimes cleaning and maintenance. For teaching, she is mainly responsible for classes, such as Chinese and English composition, artwork and cookery classes. These classes are usually held on Saturday or during the summer holidays. Since she is the youngest daughter of Mrs. Alice, the staff and pupils in the centre would normally call her "*xi jie jie*" (Little sister)". This appellation does not only indicates her distinct identity, it also create a strong familial atmosphere in the daily operation of FB 1.

Mrs. Alice, Ada, the full-time teaching staff (such as Amy, Audrey and Ashley) and the female part-time teachers who have been working here for more than two years (such as Averi and Abbey) were working like a family. They are able to chat freely and happily among themselves. They can enjoy the freedom to handle their own personal and familial matters at work. These practices forms a casual working environment and builds a strong 'familial' culture.

Teachers does not only discuss familial issues in the workplace, they would also treat their pupils as their own children. The teachers would usually call their pupils: '*a zi*' (sons) or '*a nu*' (daughters) or '*xiao bao bao*' (little precious dear). Calling their pupils as their own kids conveys a strong familial atmosphere. I felt at home and became part of the family when Amy made the following comments after I have been visiting the site for almost 6 months:

> You have joined as being part of us! (You) are our zi ji ren 自己人 (one of us)!

The recognition as *'zi ji ren'* (being one of us) provided me with much freedom. Due to their acceptance, my nervousness and uneasiness disappeared as time passed. Nevertheless, my ambivalence was augmented because *zi ji ren* implies a reciprocal obligation. Since then, I offered assistance and was given some teaching and clerical duties occasionally.

FB 2: My own baby

> Because (we) really start from . . . we start from zero . . . from thinking about the name of the studio, then design the logo, then design the leaflets, manage renovation . . . yes . . . yes . . . because from the beginning to the end, (everything) is done by two of us (Betty and Bonnie), so **it (FB 2) is just like my own baby** . . . I would not give it up!

The above was a comment given by Betty. This showed how she felt about the business. Her expression reflected her mental and personal attachment to this business. She treated this business as if it were her own baby. Knowing her great passion, she and Bonnie were determined to continue this business even when they encountered much financial burden at the beginning. They insisted to hold on the business by cutting as much cost as possible. In order to save cost, they had stopped hiring any full-time staff and tried to handle almost every task by themselves. Both Betty and Bonnie would be willing to try their very best to look after 'this baby' regardless the potential challenges.

FB 3: Home office
Uncle Carl has his workstation both at home and in the stall. While I was observing his workplace, I noted that he had the following daily routine:

> Uncle Carl works from Monday to Friday. Every morning (at around 9:30 a.m.), he goes to the marketplace and opens the stall. Sometimes, he would stay in the window counter to serve customers. In the time when there are no customers, he would stay back in his workstation and continue producing jade accessories. Auntie Connie, who has quitted her job to become a full-time housewife, would go to the marketplace to buy food in each morning. Then she would go home to prepare lunch. At around 12:00 noon, Uncle Carl would close the stall and go back home to have lunch with Auntie Connie. After lunch, he would take a rest for around 30 minutes. Then he would sit at his work station at home and make jade accessories again. He stays at home to work until 4:00 p.m. Then he would go back to the marketplace again and open his retail stall. He chooses to open the stall in every morning and evening because these are the periods when the marketplace would be most crowded with customers. When there are not many customers, he sometimes would chat with the neighbours in the next stalls. They are selling baby clothes. At around 9:00 p.m., he closes the stall and go back home for dinner. After dinner, he would sit on the sofa and watch television with Auntie Connie. At around 11p.m., he would go to sleep.

Based on the above description, Uncle Carl keeps working irrespective of whether he is at home or in the stall. The setting of his work station at home is similar to that in his stall (office). Hence, in terms of production, there is not much difference between home and office in FB 3.

FB 4: Family helper
Doris hires a part-time staff, Ms. Daisy, to look after the shop occasionally. Daisy is in her 20s and is currently studying fashion design in the Hong Kong Polytechnics University. She would offer assistance to Doris in terms of store operation and some designing works. I met Daisy for few times only, because Daisy would not work if I was available to look after the boutique in the weekend. Doris treated me as a family helper to look after the boutique, when she needed to attend classes during the weekend. Only when I was not available to offer help, Doris would ask Daisy to work. Every time when I would be the family helper for Doris, she would leave me a WhatsApp message, listing the things that needed to be taken care of.

Hence, the culture and operations in FB 1, 2, 3 and 4 highlight that *jia ting* (family) played an important role in the businesses. *Jia ting* is the key part of the informants' lives, no matter they were at work or at home.

(a) Xing Fu Jia Ting (Good Family)
Jai ting is the most important aspect of life for most of the informants. In that case, my next question would be: *What is/are the Chinese concept(s) related to a good family?* The Chinese concept – '*xing fu*' is usually used to describe a good family. This expression had been appeared in several occasions of my fieldwork:

Occasion 1 (in FB 1)
'Amy was teaching one primary three pupils in doing the Chinese composition on the topic of "My family". She taught the pupil to use the term "xing fu" to describe the fact that the pupil has a good family'.

Occasion 2 (in FB 1)
'Ada gave me the latest marketing brochure. It lists and describes all courses that the centre will offer in the coming summer holidays. During summer holidays, the centre would offer some interests classes, such as drawing, painting, artwork and cookery courses. One description of an artwork in the brochure caught my attention. It states "幸福小兔音樂盒" *(a music box with a xing fu rabbit)*. Here, the term 'xing fu', is used to describe a female rabbit that wears a wedding dress with a bright smile.*

Occasion 3 (in FB 2)
'I have a Whatsapp chat group with my close secondary schoolmates. Betty and Bonnie were part of this group. We always have social chats via this platform. Today, while all of us were still working, one of our secondary schoolmates chatted with us through Whatsapp. She told us that she was now having a spa in the Peninsula Hotel. This was one of her wedding gift. She has just married to a Singaporean guy. She has resigned and was preparing to leave Hong and relocate to Singapore. Bonnie commented "Wow! You are xing fu shao nai nai (a wife who can enjoy life and does not need to bear any financial burden). Then Betty also replied "Yes, You are very xing fu! What a good life!"'

Occasion 4 (in FB 4)
Doris told me: "Xing fu is . . . may be I have the best wife or husband, then I have some very guai zi nu (good son(s) and daughter(s)) . . . This is a typical xing fu . . . "

Based on the above occasions, the local concept of 'xing fu' was often related to a good marriage (occasion 2, 3 and 4) or/and a good family (occasion 1 and 4). It is a concept that is particularly used within the context of *jia ting* (family).

Since *xing fu* is a key Chinese concept of family, I further examine how the informants look at *xing fu*. I asked: *What does xing fu mean to the locals? When would they express xing fu? How would they feel xing fu?* To answer the above questions, the following expression(s) were revealed to illustrate the cultural meaning of *xing fu*:

i. Qi Zheng (Complete Orderly)
This was the phrase expressed by Mrs. Cindy, to describe her desired life in a family. This expression seems to capture her feeling of loss when her husband had passed away. She emphasised that:

> I think a desired life is . . . the whole family needs to be qi qi zheng zheng(complete orderly) . . .

Qi qi zheng zheng is also known as *qi zheng*. *Qi zheng* can be referred as *wan zheng*, which means perfectly complete. Here, for Chinese, it means having a complete family that consist of a father, a mother and children.

Brenda was once a full-time Chinese dance teacher in FB 2. She expressed a similar thought when she was asked about what made up a happy family. She indicated that:

> "My second (important aspect of lives) is jia ting. Need to have a happy family. . . that is (it consists of) having a good partner, daddy, mother, da jia yi qi (A big family stays together)."

Her expression highlighted the importance of having a good partner to make up a family which involves a father and a mother. Indeed, the Chinese term 'xing fu' (which appeared in occasion 2, 3 and 4) is mostly used within the context of marriage. Hence, finding a partner to marry is a fundamental step for making up a *xing fu jia ting* (good family).

1. Build a Family with Children

Marriage can be regarded as an important life goal for some of my female informants. For instance, Alysia was a part-time teacher at FB 1. She was in her early twenties and was hired as she was referred by her friends who had been working in FB 1 for a long time. I was assigned by Mrs. Alice to work with Alysia since she was not familiar with the working procedure in FB 1. After working with her for a few times, we became familiar with one another (in local term: *shu*). When I asked her about her future aspirations, she answered: *"I would like to become a flight attendant. In particular, I want to work in Emirate. This airline provides opportunity for me to stay in Dubai, the place where there are a lot of rich men. My target is to diao jin gui"*. Literally, *diao jin gui* in Chinese means fishing for a golden turtle. Golden turtles in Chinese represent rich men. Therefore, the whole phrase implies 'marrying a rich man'. Alysia's answer showed that marriage was one of her life goals. In particular, *diao jin gui* (marrying a rich man) seems a way that can make her feel *xing fu*. Without commenting on the feasibility of her goal, I was amazed at her courage and openness to reveal such thoughts to me.

While *diao jin gui* provided Alysia with hope and motivation in life, the urgency for finding a right partner for marriage could sometimes create pressure, particularly to some single females who are already over 30 years old. I did experience such anxiety, particularly when there are negative buzzwords on women who are unmarried. For example, *'zhong nu'*, which is a term to describe women who are middle-aged and single; while *'sheng nu'* refers to women that are leftover (remain single). These buzzwords bear a negative connotation over single females who are over 30 years old. Mrs. Cindy often urged me to get marry. She often said to me, *"You need a husband who can walk with you for the rest of your life. I really want you to be xing fu. You know, I can't walk with you for the rest of your life. One day, I would die"*. Even Betty, who was still single, often said to Bonnie, *"You don't need to worry about future life because you have already shang an (landed) (meaning: got married already and can rely on her husband)"*. Betty noticed a sense of urgency in getting married, particularly when her mother urged her to get married. For instance, her mother had brought her to walk around the *tao hua yuan* in the *tian hou miao* (Tin Hau Temple) during the Chinese New Year. *Tao hua yuan* literally means the garden of the peaches of immortality. Chinese believes that *tao hua* (The queen of Sky) can bring luck in love. Some of our friends would eager to refer single males to us. Although Betty and I wished to get married and make up a *xing fu jia ting* in the near future, it is mentally exhausting to attend those planned dating arrangements.

'*Qi zheng*' could also refer to having children in a *jia ting*. Hestia was working as a manager in local bank which can be considered as a multinational corporation.

After she got married, she was eager to have a baby. Therefore, she visited a Chinese doctor and took Chinese medicine regularly. She hoped that taking Chinese medicine could improve her physical health condition, which in turns may increase the chance of getting pregnant. However, she also shared with me her difficulties in striving for pregnancy: *"It's really not easy! The process is really stressful. It's just like a cycle which you work hard for it, but you fail and then you work hard again! Every day, I also need to keep monitoring my health and temperature. There are a lot of works to be done . . ."*. On one hand, she strived for building a *wan zheng jia ting* (a complete family) with parents and children. On the other hand, she encountered many failures and frustration in the process. While the concept of *'qi zheng'* or *'wan zheng'* represent a *jia ting* with children, there are people who do not aim to have children. For instance, although Ada had often persuaded Gigi to have a baby, Gigi and her husband, Daniel, have never planned to have one. Gigi stayed firm with her view, *"Having children require much responsibility! We (she and her husband) don't see there is any need for us to have any kids"*.

Not only having a child could constitute a *wan zheng jia ting*. Ada further emphasised the importance of having both a son and a daughter in a *jia ting*. She made the following comments when Audrey got pregnant with her second child: *"She (Audrey) wants a son this time . . . because you nu you zi jiu xi ge hao zi* (have a daughter and a son is a word of *hao*). Literally, the Chinese word, *hao*好 (good) is made up of two words: *nu*女'a woman' and *zi*仔 'a son'. It originally means it would be a good thing if a woman gives birth to her son. Nevertheless, Ada's expression even implies that it is good to have a daughter and a son in a family. She recognised the value of having both a daughter and a son in a *jia ting*. Therefore, she was excited to get pregnant with a boy (her second child) in 2014 given her first child was a girl.

Mrs. Eden, whose husband (Mr. Edmond) had succeeded the family business from his father, showed similar preference over the gender of her second child. When she got pregnant, she chatted with me in a dinner: *"Of course, we (she and her husband) want it to be a girl. We have Eric (her son's name) already . . . so this time, we want it to be a girl!"* Therefore, her expression shows that having children (including at least *yi zi yi nu* (one son and one daughter)) would constitute to be a typical *xing fu jia ting* (good family).

ii. Yang Jia (Feed a Family)

Yang jia 養家 (Feed a family) is a concept related to the responsibility and obligations in Chinese families. Literally, it refers to feeding a family. Gender could have specific roles in supporting a family. While female informants expressed concern for marriage and having children; the male informant, Uncle Carl highlighted his responsibility as a financial supporter in his family. Here is Uncle Carl's story of how he entered the field of craftsmanship in order to feed his family:

FB 3: Craftsmanship for a living
Before Uncle Carl entered into this field, he had worked in various occupations, such as selling lively poultry, fish balls and fruits in the market, food-processing and wholesales and oil spouting for cars and more. Until 1968, one of his relatives referred him to the field of craftsmanship. At that time, there were two kinds of craftsmanship available for him to learn: denture or jade accessories. Among the two options, he has chosen jade accessories. He started as an apprentice and learnt from his *shi fu* (a master) for four years. He recalled his experience of apprenticeship: *"Normally we entered the field with a very low salary. At the beginning, (my salary) was $15 each month, including meals and accommodation. At that time, I slept on a piece of wood only . . . Working hours started from 10 a.m. to 10 p.m. Being an apprentice in the past had long working hours. Normally, at the first few months, there would be no holidays. The first and fifteen days of lunar month did not require to work at night. (After I) Had worked (there) for around half a year, then it started to offer (me) holidays. (I could take two-day leaves. That means taking leave on the first and fifteen days of lunar month . . . At the beginning, (I) only responsible for doing some simple tasks. Wait until you (I) gained more knowledge on jade, then shi fu (my master) would teach you (me) more . . .* **It (This craftsmanship) is the techniques for maintaining my future lives. Learn yin men shou yi (one kind of craftsmanship), so (I) don't have to worry the basic living in the future**". His experience of apprenticeship demonstrated his hard-work and great assiduity.

After the apprenticeship, Uncle Carl began his business as a jade accessory maker. At the beginning, his sources of customers were mainly referred by his *shi fu* and he paid the commission fees to his *shi fu*. By that time, his *shi fu* helped him to build network and contact with the suppliers and customers, so that he would later on contact them by himself. Since then, he had focused on the wholesales business of jade accessories. After 1994, the wholesale industry of jade products had started declining. At that time, he had a large surplus of the finished products. Therefore, he decided not to solely focus on wholesale business and started the retail business. He opened a retail stall in the same district where he was living and rented a market stall issued by the government. The stall was located in a temporary marketplace and was made of iron panels. It was 30 square meters in area without water supplies and air-conditioning. He ran that retail stall in the temporary marketplace for six years. It was in 2000 that the government built a new marketplace with storeys. Afterwards, he was able to move to his current market stall where it had a larger space and better facilities. His stall is opened from morning to afternoon. He ended his story with a pleasant tone: *"Now, the business is mainly relied on shu ke (the acquainted customers . . . (My current lives is) so-so . . .* **At least (I was) able to guo dao sheng huo, yang dao jia** *(maintain lives and feed the family) . . . As for your Auntie (Auntie Connie), she needs to look after a lot of household matters"*. His comments suggested that he expected his wife to be responsible for handling household issues, while he would take up the role of maintaining a living for his *jia ting*. In that case, being able to maintain a living for a *jai ting* was regarded as another important aspect of good family.

Mrs. Cindy had a similar thought as that of Uncle Carl. She insisted the importance of *'you fan shi, you qian xi '* (Have food to eat, have money to spend). It is understandable that both Uncle Carl and Mrs. Cindy regarded the ability to maintain a living as an important aspect of life. Uncle Carl and Mrs. Cindy share the same family; Mrs. Cindy is Uncle Carl's elder sister. Their father left the family in their teenage. Without the support of their father, it was their mother who took the sole responsibility to provide livelihood to their family. At that time, Uncle Carl and Mrs. Cindy needed to quit the school and go out for work in order to earn money and support their family. They had experienced hunger and homelessness in their childhood. That was why they regarded *yang jia* (feed family) as a major familial obligation.

The value of *yang jia* is not only restricted to those who are married and have children. Even Brenda recognised the importance of having a stable income for her family. She expressed: *"It's important to have economic foundation, (so that) lives would not be too (financially) difficult in the family"*. Hence, she regarded that *'having a stable job'* was what she and her boyfriend were looking for.

1. Mai lou (Buy a Place)

Once Brenda was able to earn a living, she set her next life goal, which is to buy a residential place. *'Living in a residential place where I (she) like(s)'* was regarded as her most important aspect of life. Doris also recognised that it was necessary to have a residential place for living. She commented: *"Xing fu also means you lou shu (having a residential place for living)"*.

Similarly, Betty and Bonnie had concern over their respective residential living. They paid attention to where their customers lived. They intentionally chose to locate their dance studio in a district where there are various high-class residential buildings. They hoped that families with relatively high income would be their target customers. Bonnie would sometimes sit near the windows and stare blankly at those high-class residential buildings. She would dream that one day, she could live in one luxury flat nearby. To be more practical, I and Betty created an 'Investment chat group' through Whatsapp. This was a communication platform among our close friends. We could exchange and update news related to property market and discuss our investment plans. All the participants in this Whatsapp group shared their interest in owning a place for living (in Chinese, it is called as *mai lou*) and paid attention to the local property market. This showed that being able to **buy one's own place** was a typical way to feed a family.

Although having a residential place to live is important, having enough financial capability of *mai lou* is another concern. Such concern could become a burden for some locals, especially when the current property market has been overheating. Even though, the Hong Kong government has imposed new housing policies (which are locally referred as *la zhao (spicy policy)*) that target on stabilising the property market rate, they are being criticised as not being effective in cooling down the market. Betty and Doris further complained that *"these so called la zhao are not helping us to shang che"* (Literally, *shang che* means getting on the car). Locals refer the term as getting on the property ladder. Both Betty and Doris feel worried as they found it difficult to get on the property ladder. While buying one's own place is important to them, the purchase process could also make them feel frustrated.

2. Shape Quai (Good) Children

In addition to providing physical and financial supports to their families, another key responsibility of local parents would be on facilitating the whole person development of their children. That means, shaping their children to be good is particularly important for local parents, teachers in schools and educational institutions and governments. Since FB 1 and FB 2 are classified as educational centres, they take responsibility in shaping their students to be good. What do local parents and teachers mean by 'good children'? I noticed that the local word – *quai* 乖, is often used to describe a good child. Literally, *quai* means obedient and well-behaved. *Quai* is a term used for complimenting a child who has appropriate discipline, behaviours and performance. Indeed, the teaching approach of FB 1 reflects one key obligation of teachers is to train their students to become *quai*. According to the observations in the field visits, I characterised the teaching styles adopted by the teachers in FB 1 as rigorous, disciplinary, with appropriate amount of autonomous, all-rounded, focusing on mutual respect, politeness and humbleness, preventing selfishness and arrogance, training on responsibility and independence and motivating based on both positive and negative reinforcements. Hence, the teaching of FB 1 reflects a local perception of a *quai* (good) child. This means a *quai* child should be all-rounded, good at both academic and non-academic aspects, obedient, self-disciplined, independent, polite, respectful, humble and generous.

How can local parents and teachers shape their children to be *quai*? *'Ying zai qi pao xian'* (Literally means: Win at the starting line), is one buzzword that was being quoted in the website and Facebook page of FB 2. FB 2 use this phrase in its promotion. *Ying zai qi pao xian* is an expression that describes the process by which local parents try to shape their children to be all-rounded (good) by offering them with abundant resources for development. FB 2's mission statement is *'Our academy focuses on children's healthy growth, our formal dance training aims to ensure that students have a healthy physical development'*. Its mission highlights the importance of enabling children to have healthy growth and physical development.

The advertising brochures of FB 1 also stresses on shaping children to be good in every aspect of lives. The brochure highlights that its educational centre offers: 全方位補習班 (Holistic and comprehensive regular class), 一站式服務 (One stop service) and 尖子班 (Top students class). FB 1 puts emphasis on providing a one-stop tutorial service to students, so that they would become all-rounder and top students in their schools. They do not only offer tutorials to improve student academic performance. They also offer classes on developing student interest on non-academic areas (such as arts, cooking and playing chess etc.). These classes aim to develop the interests and potentials of students in different areas. Hence, in order to meet the demand of local parents and teachers, both FB 1 and FB 2 target on shaping children to be all-rounder by offering a comprehensive development for the children.

iii. Jian Kang (Being Healthy)

Jian kang 健康 refers to being physically and mentally healthy. The health condition of family members could be another important aspect that constitutes a good family. Mrs. Cindy always emphasised: *"The most important is everyone (in the family) is jian jian kang kang (being healthy) . . . I wish that each of my children has good health"*. Likewise, Doris (being Mrs. Cindy's fourth daughter) regarded *xing fu* is related to *'fu mu jian kang'* (father and mother are healthy).

The concern for *jian kang* (healthiness) is reflected in the social interaction among the participants. Here are some examples:

Example 1 (in FB 1)

People in FB 1 showed care to each other's health. For instance, Ada showed care to Amy whenever Amy was feeling unwell or caught cold. Ada would help Amy to buy cream and lotion online, knowing that Amy would get skin allergy in winter. Members in FB 1 would often refer doctors among themselves. For instance, Mrs. Alice and Ada referred a *tie da yi shi* (Chinese medical bonesetter) to me when they were aware about my foot injury. Hence, in FB 1, health became one common topic for social chats.

Example 2 (in FB 3)

In FB 3, Uncle Carl would protect his family's health by not allowing his wife to work in the field because the nature of his work could cause severe injuries easily. He explained *"I don't allow my wife (Auntie Connie) to help me because I don't want her to get hurt"*. He showed me the scars on his hands to illustrate that it was dangerous to use those tools and machines. Although those scars represented the hardship he had encountered in his career, they also symbolised his care for his family.

1. Physical Exercises and Good Sleep

How can the locals maintain *jian kang* (healthy)? One common way to maintain *jian kang* is by doing physical exercises. Mrs Cindy has a habit of doing morning exercise in the park. Every day, she wakes up at around 6 o'clock in the morning, brushes her teeth and gets dressed with sportswear. Then, she walks to the park next to her home. In the park, she does some morning exercises (mainly stretching and jogging) for around an hour. Afterwards, she goes to the Chinese restaurant to meet her neighbours and have morning tea with them. Mrs. Alice has similar habit too. In one of our causal conversation, she mentioned:

> (I) always feel sick . . . like feeling dizzy, like that. With this symptom . . . (I) need to do exercises in the morning. (There should be) no problem (if it only takes) half an hour . . . I would walk by the seaside . . . (My) mood would be quite good. (There are) some people doing exercise too. (I) can say hello to them (and chat with them for a while).

Mrs. Alice asserts that doing exercises helped her to maintain good blood circulation, mental health and social life. Hence, she thinks that physical exercise is essential to maintain *jian kang*.

Another symptom of being healthy is to have good sleep. Both Mrs. Cindy and Pansy associate *xing fu* with sleeping well:

> Able to sleeping well is the most xing fu　　　　　　　　　　　　　　(Mrs. Cindy)

> Sleeping is the time when I think that I'm the most xing fu. (It is)Because you don't need to think, so comfortable　　　　　　　　　　　　　　(Pansy)

Uncle Carl has suffered from insomnia in the past due to stress. He took medicine in order to sleep well at night. However, he found that relying on medicine is not an impactful way to release stress or to maintain *jian kang*. Below is how he shared his experience of reducing stress:

> The most jian kang (healthy) (activity) is to do exercises . . . (I) must maintain healthy through doing exercises. (Doing exercises) can reduce stress. I would go hiking and running . . . Now, (I) can sleep well . . . Currently is the time when I can sleep more stable

Uncle Carl considers that being able to sleep calmly and orderly is important to *jian kang*. He thinks that physical exercises can help him to release stress and enable him to have a good sleep. Hence, based on his experience, doing exercises (such as running and hiking) can enable him to have a better sleep. This is how he has stayed healthy both physically and spiritually.

iv. Ping Jing (Peace and At Ease)

Ping jing is an expression used by Blossom when she described *xing fu*. Her expression indicates that *xing fu* can be related to *ping jing (feeling peaceful and at ease)*. She further explained: *"(Ping jing is) Do not have many worries . . . do not need any excitement . . . I want ping jing . . . jian dan kai xing fu (simple xing fu) . . . jian dan kai kuai lei (simple happiness) is xing fu . . . wu bao fu (no burden) . . . "*. She felt peace spiritually when she did not have any worries, excitements and burdens. She preferred to have simple happiness: *"To be herself; work as she likes; and dance from her heart"*.

Similarly, Pansy who is also aged between mid-twenties, described that *"xing fu (means), you don't need to worry. You don't have any burdens. I already think (that) is hao hao (very good)"*. Hence, both Blossom and Pansy thought *xing fu* refers to when there was worries nor burdens in lives.

When would the informants feel *ping jing* – without worries and burdens? Below are some expressions on when the informants could feel *ping jing*:

FB 1: Tai ping (Peace and stability)
Both Mrs. Alice and Ada valued *"tai ping"* (peace and stability). For them, *tai ping* refers to they can maintain a stable operation without losing the education license. One major challenge for FB 1 is to maintain its education license through complying with statutory requirements on private schools. Ada thought it was difficult to comply with the statutory requirement. She described: *"The most terrible is (we) always worry and afraid of government official check"*. This frightening experience reflects that they seek for *tai ping* (stability) in running the business.

FB 2: No monetary pressure
Financial burden was a key aspect of lives that would make Betty and Bonnie felt pressured. In the first half year of business, Betty was often worried: *"Indeed, if there is no financial pressure, actually it's really quite kai xin (happy) (to run FB 2)"*. In other words, Betty felt worried due to the financial pressure in running FB 2. She would feel *kai xin* (happy) if she could get rid of the financial burden.

FB 3: Ping wen (Peace and stability)
Uncle Carl described his current life with comfort: *"(My life is) Ping ping wen wen (peace and stable) . . . I'm at a semi-retired stage, so semi-retiree won't work for long. (Otherwise) it would be very exhausting. (I have) Changed to make myself be less stressful. (I) Won't be too attached to whether it has business or not"*. This indicated that Uncle Carl is comfortable with his stable life wherein he does not need to work for long hours and worry about the business.

FB 4: Be relaxed
Doris shared the kind of lives she is looking for: *"Be relaxed . . . I wish to be not so busy . . . then I can try other things . . . things that are not related to work. I will try to study cookery"*. She would feel relaxed if her work is not too busy. Then, she can have some time to learn other things, such as cookery.

Based on the above expressions, one could feel *ping jing*:
(1) when the business is *tai ping and ping wen* (stable) (FB 1 and FB 3);
(2) when he/she does not bear any financial burden and stress (Betty and Uncle Carl);
(3) when he/she is less busy in work and feels relaxed (Uncle Carl and Doris).

1. Rituals and Gestures

How can locals feel *ping jing* (or *ping an*) (spiritually peaceful and secure)? One common way to enable the informants feel *ping an* is by performing rituals. Some typical local rituals are: worshiping ancestors and *feng shui*. Mrs. Cindy has been following these rituals since she was young. She insisted to install a worship table in her new home, even though all of her daughters are Christians and they do not believe in these rituals. She puts incense into a censer every morning and evening. She would also burn joss paper and incense as a way to offer sacrifice to the ancestors. When asked about the reasons for following these rituals, she asserted that:

> You know what? You can hardly understand! That's my responsibility! That's what I need to do! If I don't do that, I would feel insecure! Just let me do that if you want me to feel an xin!

Hence, her answer indicated that performing rituals is her responsibility. She intends to fulfil such responsibility because these rituals would make her feel secure and *an xin* (spiritually peaceful and comfortable).

The worship of the ancestors is not religiously followed by the seniors only. In fact, many local young adults would follow such custom as well. One typical example is cutting the roasted pork to worship gods when one starts a business and opens a new branch. In the opening of FB 2, Bonnie had arranged a series of worship ceremony. First, before the opening, she asked a *feng shui* specialist to inspect the new branch. She followed the specialist instructions by placing some *feng shui* ornaments in the branch, hoping that would facilitate the financial performance of the business. Then, in the opening, she worshiped the four corners of the branch by placing four censers in each corners of the wall and putting incenses into those censers. Lastly, she bought a whole set of roasted pork, cut it for ancestor worship and shared it with all the guests. She made sure that all these rituals were done at the beginning of the opening ceremony. Although Betty is a Catholic, she followed these rituals. Below is her explanation on why she followed these ritual:

> Bonnie, her family and my family said it was necessary to perform all these worships. Yes, I don't believe it. However, they (Bonnie and their family members) would be more an xin if they had performed these rituals and followed what the feng shui specialist has asked us to do. Otherwise, they may complain when the studio had poor performance.

Betty showed concern for her friend (Bonnie) and their family members (mainly the parents of both Betty and Bonnie). She explained that she performed these worships not for her own sake, but rather for the sake of her friends and family. She performed all the above rituals given she would like Bonnie and their family members to feel *an xin* (spiritually peaceful and comfortable) and worry less about the performance of the studio.

Another common way to make locals feel *ping an* is through gestures, such as wearing some symbolic accessories. That is one of the reasons why FB 3 can be sustainable in the market. Uncle Carl shares his knowledge and experience about his business:

> You know, people wear jade accessories because these products bear some symbolic meaning to one's life. They can bring hao yi tou (good fortune) to the person wearing it.

FB 3 can be sustainable since many locals hold a belief that wearing jade accessories can bring good fortune to them. With these accessories, they would feel more secure towards their future.

2. No Strategy: Jian Bu Xing Bu (See One Step, Take One Step)

Since the informants value *ping wen* (peace and stability), such value is embedded in their business practices. One significant practice that represents the embodiment of *ping wen* is that they do not adopt a particular business strategy. They simply *jian bu xing bu*. *Jian bu xing bu* is a Chinese expression, which literally means 'see one step, take one step'. It implies a specific practice in which the informants would act as their businesses go along. Instead of having specific planning, strategies nor management, they claimed that they would see how things go and plan the next step. Such a practice enables the informants to maintain peace spiritually since they **moves along as life unfolds**. Below are how they describe their ways of running the businesses:

FB 1: Act in the right timing

When I inquired about the business strategies for running FB 1, Ada's response is as followed:

> (We use) **no special strategies, (nor) plans.** (We) **do** (the business) **as it goes along**. (We) see how things go and then plan (our) next step. That is: **shun zhu qu zuo** (do as it goes along), **jian bu xing bu** (see one step, take one step)

The above expression indicates that there were no special strategies or plans involved in managing FB 1. I would consider Ada's expression: **shun zhu qu zuo** (do as it goes along) and *jian bu xing bu* (see one step, take one step) as her specific business practices. That is to say, she would see how things go and plan the next step accordingly. This implies that Mrs. Alice and Ada prefer to act in the right time. But, when is the right time to act? In general, there are three occasions in which they considered them as the right time to act: Occasion 1 – when it is necessary for them to act; Occasion 2 – when there is an opportunity; or Occasion 3 – when there are no obstacles. Their response to these three occasions shows that they prefer to manage the business through right timing. For instance, regarding to the business development, they would prefer slowing down the expansion process, wait and see how the business goes. They prefer using the least amount of effort to let the the business grows and develops in its right time.

FB 2: Jian bu xing bu (See one step, take one step)

As the business was becoming more financially stable, Betty and Bonnie were asked to recall their experience in the previous year to analyse if they could be able to elaborate on the business strategy opted. Betty answered the question immediately:

> **No strategy** . . . (we) **are jian bu xing bu (See one step, take one step)'** . . . Every day, a lot of things (are happening) . . . with variety! (There are) Many problems emerged, (and there are problems) you have never thought of . . . That's why we have to always change and adapt.

Rather than strictly following certain rules and procedures, both Betty and Bonnie are willing to change and adjust their ways of running the business. In other words, without a definite strategy, they prefer running the business flexibly.

FB 3: No perfect plan

> (I) followed the market to see what the customers like . . . so, (I) **don't have any perfect plan to do this** (business).

This was Uncle Carl's response when I asked him for the strategy in running the business. Uncle Carl's answer portrays his flexibility in carrying out the business.

FB 4: Keep going until opportunities arise

> (There is) **No specific point** (of time to start the business). It (has started) only because (this business) is (what I) ongoing (continuously) want to do . . . to have my own brand label and fashion business . . . To achieve this, I didn't set a particular time frame for myself . . . what I did is **simply do, do and do** . . . .

The above statement was Doris's comment on recalling the time period and reason of opening FB 4. Her expression clearly indicates her persistence in living up her dream. Even though Doris did not have a precise plan for the commencement of her business, she kept working for it. She **simply worked and waited until an opportunity came** and she grabbed it. Below is her description on how she started FB 4:

> Indeed, I'm not a person with good planning. . . . **In fact**, (I can) **not say** (I'm) **strategically doing** (such) **business**. . . . Yes, (what I can do) is **simply walking slowly: walk and walk** . . .

The above reflects that Doris did not claim to have any good planning nor strategy in the management. She prefers to keep moving until opportunities come.

4.2.2 *Peng You* (Friends)

Beside *jia ting* (family), *peng you* (friends) is another aspect of life that the informants had regarded as important. Bonnie has once commented: *"Peng you (Friends) is also very important, because I myself do not know many friends. (But) We have known each other since we were small. (Betty) is very important to me"*. In fact, both Betty and Bonnie regarded *peng you* as the second important aspects of their lives (which is right after *jia ting* and marriage). Betty even made a post on her Facebook, saying: *'(Friendship is indifferent. But compare with love, (friendship is) more long-lasting. We do not need to bother whose love is more. (We) Do not need to always accompany each other. However, every time when (we are) in need, friends always stand by (our) side)'*. Betty's post shows she values friendship.

(a) Xin (trust)
What counts as *hao peng you* (good friends)? Below are my roles of being a good friend to Better and Bonnie: (1) Being a listener to whom they can share their worries and thoughts, especially when they are encountering difficulties in lives; (2) Being an opinion sharer, who can discuss all sorts of matters and exchange the views with them truthfully; (3) Being a helper, who always provide them support whenever in need (e.g. being their receptionist, first customer and referee etc.); and (4) Being a cheerer, who try to cheer them up whenever they are perturbed and disappointed about the business. These roles symbolize that we are friends. We can *xin* (trust) and rely on each other. Therefore, *xin* is regarded as an important element in friendship.

(b) *Work with Peng You*
The significance of *peng you* is reflected in the four family businesses (FB 1, 2, 3 and 4), given they have chosen to start the businesses with their friends. The importance and obligation of *peng you* do not only show in a business partnership (FB 2 and FB 4), but also in business operation and practices (shown in FB 1, 2 and 4) and apprenticeship (FB 3). Here are the examples:

FB 1: Hire shu ren (acquaintance)
Ada (being the only family worker at FB 1) has the management authority in the recruitment and selection of teachers. The key selection criterion in FB 1 is *xin* (trust). Hence, referral is the most preferred recruitment and selection channel in FB 1. Majority of the full-time staffs in FB 1were referred by *'shu ren* 熟人*'* (acquaintance). Mrs. Alice had often asked me: *"Do you have any shu ren (acquaintance) to recommend?"* For Mrs. Alice and Ada, *shu ren* means their relatives, close friends or *jiu jie fang* (previous neighbourhood). They thought:

With three to four full-time staff who are trustworthy enough, the business has become more stable.

Amy, Ann and Audrey are the full-time staffs who Ada regards as trustworthy. Amy was in her mid-twenties while Ann was in her early-thirties. Both Amy and Ann have worked at FB 1 for almost 8 years and both of them were referred by *shu ren* (acquaintance). With the long years of service, they have built trust with Mrs. Alice and Ada.

How about the management in the branch? The branch is mainly managed by Audrey who is the secondary schoolmate of Ada's elder sister. Audrey is in her late 40s, married and has two kids. Ada explained why the branch centre was managed by Audrey:

> This centre (the branch centre) is managed by Audrey, because my family trusts her very much. It is due to her long years of friendship with my elder sister. We trust her very much!

Hence, the daily operation of the two centres was managed by Audrey, Amy and Ann. Even though they do not have any biological relation with Mrs. Alice, they can be regarded as family members of the business due to their loyalty and trustworthiness. They also asked *shu ren* for assistance, maintenance and renovation during the peak seasons or summer. Therefore, the significance of the friendship is reflected in the operation and practice of FB 1.

Indeed, the value of *xin* is embedded in the daily operation of FB 1. In FB 1, "**No need management! Everyone would zi dong bo** *(work automatically) Teachers and pupils . . . everyone would zi dong bo (work automatically)because all of them have worked (here) for a long time, (they) are familiar with the operation here.*" This comment was induced by Ada, which captures the work practice in FB 1. According to Ada's comments, staffs were expected to take the initiative to work. That means, once you are regarded as part of the family, you would have an obligation to facilitate the daily operations.

FB 2: Rely on zi ji ren (ingroup members)

Among the four field sites, FB 2 starts based on the friendship between Betty and Bonnie. Betty chose to start FB 2 with Bonnie because *"(Bonnie) is my (her) secondary schoolmates. We (They) are already very shu to each other. I (She) think(s) the most important is to find a partner whom you (she)* **xin de guo** *(trustworthy).* Given that FB 2 did not start through franchise, Betty and Bonnie have to handle everything by themselves. They had to search for a right way to run the business, sometimes through trial and errors, sometimes by learning from mistakes and most of the time by seeking advice and assistance from *shu ren*. The operation of FB 2 relies heavily on the network and support their *peng you*:

(The workforce is) **mainly come from our common friends . . . so** (we) **want to find some xin de guo kai zi ji ren** (people who we regarded as part of us and trustworthy) **. . . The most important are to find someone xin de guo** (trustworthy). (Betty)

Therefore, as their close friends, I was regarded as *'zi ji ren'*. They have told me the door password and have given me the office key in case I need to give office support at any time. They perceived that it was important to *'find some xin de guo kai zi ji ren'* (ingroup members who are trustworthy), who were *'mainly come from (their) common friends'*, given they had an unpleasant experience in hiring and managing the full-time staff. At first, FB 2 had hired two full-time staffs: Brenda and Blossom. Both Brenda and Blossom were hired as a full-time teacher with a fixed monthly salary. They designed the teaching curriculum and conducted the classes. Besides teaching, they were also responsible for any office support, such as handling clerical works, reception and answering phone calls etc. A month later, Betty and Bonnie found it difficult to manage the performance of the two full time staffs. For example, in our informal chats, they often complained: *"She (Brenda) sometimes would be late at work"*; *"She (Brenda) often forgot to specify our company's name when receiving phone calls"*; *"I don't know why her (Brenda's) class is too unstructured. She seems didn't follow the teaching plan"*; *"She (Blossom) did not tidy up the studio after the Yoga class"*; *"She (Blossom) showed her unwillingness to teach this class. Seems I need to beg her to teach. But she is employed with salary!"*. Given the business was under financial burden, Betty and Bonnie decided to terminate the two full-time employees after 3 months. After the termination, Betty told me with a sense of release: *"I think recruiting, managing full-time (employees) is very troublesome!"*

FB 3: Take care shi fu (master)
Peng you (Friends) are not bound within peers. Friendship is also important in the apprenticeship. In FB 3, Uncle Carl pays high respect and gratitude to his *shi fu* (master). For instance, his last year of apprenticeship was called *bu shi* (a supplementary), when the apprentice would work for the *shi fu* (the master) and help the *shi fu* to earn money. Uncle Carl said with respect: *"Because shi fu (the master) have taught you (me) a lot of things, bu shi is (I) help shi fu to do more works, earn more money . . . The best reward is shi fu is willing to teach you (me) things, then I could be able to finish learning."* That was why he tried to do more works and earn more money for his *shi fu* in the year of *bu shi*. He also took responsibility to look after his *shi mu* (the master's wife) after the death of his *shi fu*.

FB 4: Work wholeheartedly
In FB 4, Doris showed thankfulness to Dave (her boss). Doris felt grateful for the trust and recognition of Dave, because he appreciated her works. Doris is responsible for all the tasks in FB 4 (no matter is an operation, administration, production, marketing

and promotion, human resources management, accounting or logistics etc.) even though she did encounter the following challenges in management:

> I guess the challenge is coming from yourself . . . I guess it lies in the management . . .

Her comments reflect that she regards "management" as a challenging and difficult task. Doris found it challenging to manage the following three aspects: (1) fashion design, (2) production and (3) retail. Although these tasks are closely related, they can create conflicts in terms of management as well.

The lives of Uncle Carl and Doris demonstrate that *peng you* can be extended to relations between master and disciple (in FB 3) and between the boss and employee (in FB 4). These social relations can play an important role in one's lives.

4.2.3 *Kai xin gong zuo* (Happy work)

Kai xin gong zuo 開心工作 (happy work) is the wish made by Mrs. Cindy. She wished her children can '*kai kai xin xin chu qu zuo ye*' (go out to work happily). Brenda prioritised that having a '*hao gong zuo*' (good work) as the third important aspect of her life. Hence, *gong zuo* (work) is another important aspect of the lives for my informants. Doris even made '*work as part of herself*':

FB 4: Work as part of self

Doris is always the key person who manages FB 4 and works in the shop. Most of the time, Doris is the only person who looks after the shop. When the shop has a manageble amount of customers, Doris would usually work in the work station behind the cashier. Her works include: Developing new designs, setting the price lists, creating the price tags and labels, ironing the clothes, sewing, managing the stocks via the computer system, communicating with the manufacturers through emails etc. In Cantonese, her role could be described as *yi jiao ti*. This term is literally referred as '*one foot kick*', which means a person who is responsible for all the duties and tasks at work. In FB 4, Doris is the one who is responsible for everything.

My impression of Doris is that she is quite a workaholic. She usually goes out to work at 9 o'clock in the morning, and came back home late, around 10 o'clock at night. When she comes back home, she would then take the dinner which her mother prepares for her. Once she has finished her 'late' dinner, she would keep working in front of her computer till midnight and goes to sleep at around 3 a.m. I appreciate her diligence and passion towards her work. Even Dave showed gratitude to her in the opening of FB 4. He made a comment to Doris in front of her family: "*Doris is very hard-working and capable! She always keeps working. I wonder if she eats nor sleeps! Thanks for her diligence!*" From his compliment, I could understand why Dave treats her as his right-arm, leaving much important management duties to her. It is because she is hard-working, loyal, trustable and capable.

One day, I asked Doris casually: "Why do you work like a workaholic?" She gave me the following response:

> Indeed, I think . . . I think this work has already become part of me. It has been a very large . . . very large part of me. Because (this business) already is my own business. It's not saying I'm now working for somebody or a company. It is my own business. Given it's my own business, I want to do it well and make it successful. I guess . . . **if (your work) does not become part of you, you can hardly work.**

Her answer demonstrates her strong devotion towards work. It is such devotion that keeps her and her business (FB 4) alive. Given *gong zuo* (work) becomes part of my informants' lives, my next questions would be: What shapes a *hao gong zuo* (good work)? How would one feel *kai xin* (happy) towards his/her work? To answer these questions, here are several expressions used by the informants to express what made them feel *kai xin* (happy) at work:

(a) *You Xing Qu (Have Interest) and Zhong Yi (Like)*

You xing qu (have interest) and *zhong yi* (like) are two important expressions used by my informants to describe *hao gong zuo* (good work). Below shows their expressions related to *hao gong zuo* (good work):

> Brenda described that "One hao gong zuo is: I myself would **you xing qu** *(have interest)* over such work."

> Betty explained how she started FB 2: "because I myself **zhong yi** *(like)* dancing very much . . . He (Her father) thinks that it is good that I can work according to my **xing qu** *(interest)*. He is very supportive."

> Uncle Carl chose to be a jade accessory maker because: "I (He), from the beginning to the end, **xi huan** *(like)* jade accessory making . . . zui kai xin (The happiest) is I **zhong yi** *(like)* this occupation."

> Doris recalled: "since I was in the school (that is in secondary school and university), I recognised that I **zhong yi** *(am fond of)* fashion design . . . then I feel that I would like to know more about (this field) . . . I think (I have) the passion and talent in here (this field). I always have a feeling that if I don't work (in this field), I would somehow feel sorry for my dad and mum. So . . . I want to work (in this field)"

The above expressions indicate that **you xing qu** (have interest) and **zhong yi** (like) are important elements that shape a *hao gong zuo* (good work). In particular, Doris emphasised that she *zhong yi* (is fond of) her work as a fashion designer because of her passion and talent in that field. In her view, passion and talent are natural gifts from her parents. Hence, she would disappoint her parents if she would not fully utilize her talent at work.

(b) You Man Zu Gan (Have Satisfaction)

You man zu gan (have satisfaction) is another expression that indicates why one could feel *kai xin* (happy) at work. Betty expressed she gained *kai xin* (happiness) over her work when she saw the pupils were dancing happily:

> You man zu gan (have satisfaction) is the little kids won an award . . . Indeed, not only because of getting the award. It is (because of) seeing those kids. (I) Hao kai xin (Very happy) that (we) have tried very hard to choreograph a dance . . . then you (I) saw those five pupils. (Seeing they are) Very united . . . very happy . . . enjoy very much the process (of dancing). Then (I) would be hao kai xin. (very happy)

(c) Chuang Zuo (Creative Work)

Chuang zuo (creative work) is another key element that enables my informants to feel *man zu* (satisfied). *Chuang zuo* (creative work) is critical and relevant to some of my informants. The significance of *chuang zuo* (creative work) is especially emphasised in FB 2, 3 and 4, because their nature of business is related to art and design:

FB 2:
Brenda expressed that: "A hao gong zuo (good work) is to do some **chuang zuo** (creative work). Can give more to others; can inspire more people . . . (Such as) art . . . That is to say, demonstrate **chuang zuo** (creative work), **chuang yi** (creativity)!"

FB 3:
Uncle Carl explained the main reason why he *zhong yi* (likes) his work: "A finished product is (originally) started from (a stone that was) not beautiful. Then through (my) **xin ji** (hard work) and **chuang yi** (creativity), the stone is sculpted into a perfect product . . . Sometimes, the clients keep praising (me), (saying my) products are good. This would (give me) hao you man zu gan (much satisfaction)."

FB 4:
Doris expressed that: "zui kai xin (the happiest experience) always comes from that man zu gan (satisfaction) . . . That is I want to have the **chuang zuo kong jian** (room for creativity) . . . Then when you (I) look at those products that you yourself (I myself) feel satisfied, and receive some compliments from others, your man zu gan (satisfaction) would be very great."

The above expressions indicate *chuang zuo* (creative work) is an important aspect of work (as reflected in FB 2, 3 and 4). *Chuang zuo* (Creativity) shapes the informants' sense of *man zu gan* (satisfaction). They would be *kai xin* (happy) particularly when their *chuang zuo* (creative works) are being recognised and praised.

(d) Work hard and bear xin ku (hardship): Strive to Survive

In contrast to *kai xin* (happiness), how would one express hardship towards his/her work? '*Xin ku*' (hardship) is an expression used by the informants when they felt difficult in work. *Xin ku* (Hardship) is supposed to be in contrast to *kai xin* (happiness). How do the informants handle *xing ku* (hardship) at work? Even if the work is not always easy, my informants would still work hard. This positive attitude shows that they are able to live well because they are working hard to overcome difficulties in lives. Below shows how the informants strive to survive by overcoming challenges and hardship at work:

FB 1: Liu de qing shan zai, na pa mei chai shao (Stay on the green mountain, do not afraid of no wood to burn)

In 2013, I witnessed how the centre had gone through another official supervision conducted by the Department of Health, Fire Service Department and Building Department. In order to fulfil the supervision requirements, two centres were required to be renovated. While the centres were under renovations, I chatted with Mrs. Alice, regarding how she responded to such official supervision. She replied: *"now, engaging in tutoring business would encounter many problems: one (problem) is the expensive rental fee, another (problem) would be getting a license . . . And so, we currently reduced the number of pupils . . . Anyway, never mind, (we can) plan further later!* **Liu de qing shan zai, na pa mei chai shao** (stay on the green mountain, do not afraid of no wood to burn)".

"*Liu de qing shan zai, na pa mei chai shao*" was the comment made by the owner (Mrs. Alice) in a time of challenge, which seems to capture her core value for survival. This is a Chinese proverb. Literally, it means 'stay on the green mountain, do not afraid of (there is) no wood to burn'. That implies, as long as (we) are able to survive and maintain existence in the market, (we) will not be afraid of having no revenue to stay alive. Even though FB 1 has gone through several challenges since 1996, Mrs. Alice's comments gave me a deep impression that she had a strong sense of striving in the time of difficulties. Hence, such persistence to survive and thrive suggests why she would be able to operate FB 1 in this fast-moving world for 18 years.

FB 2: Shou zhu xian (Hold on to survive first)

Betty and Bonnie have been looking for clients. In the beginning, Betty and Bonnie seemed quite optimistic about their business future. Nevertheless, the business was still having a deficit after it had been operating for three months. There were only a few clients who come from the artist's studio next door. I could feel the worries of Betty and Bonnie, every time when I visited the company. Bonnie sighed for a number of times in our social chats: "*Sigh! (The business is) Really very quiet! Indeed, (we) really need to find (more) new clients. (If we) Rely on friends (only), we can hardly survive for long!"* She even said: *"Sigh! Now the only way is to **shou zhu xian** (hold on to survive first) . . . (We) Have started (the business), (we can) only continue doing it . . . maybe I need to ask my mum to lend me more money"*. Her expression – *shou zhu xian* (hold on to survive first) reflects her persistence to survive.

A few weeks later, Bonnie told me her new idea: *"Need to have a tight control on budgeting . . . (Since we) kai wu dao yuan, jiu yao jie liu xian (have not been able to find more sources of revenue, (we) need to reduce expenses first)"*. With this new strategy, they had reduced expenses in several ways: (1) terminated all full-time staff and hired part-time staff, (2) tightened the marketing budget and focused on a few key promotional channels and (3) designed and printed the marketing posters and leaflets by themselves rather than hiring an advertising agency. With these practices to reduce expenditure, FB 2 had become more financially stable. This story illustrates how FB 2 strived to maintain its existence in the market.

FB 3: One man band (Zi ji zuo)

This is my impression of how Uncle Carl worked at FB 3. He did not recruit any employees. Everything is done by him. In order to reduce cost in recruiting and retaining staff, Uncle Carl would rather be **'one man band'.** He told me: *"So now, I would try to **zi ji zuo** (do it by myself)"*. Auntie Connie seldom participates in the business because Uncle Carl does not allow her to do so. He would rather handle the business all by himself, so that Auntie Connie could concentrate on household matters. Uncle Carl once commented: *"Now, I would rather do it all by myself. (I) hope that (doing it by myself) would reduce (staff) cost. Hence, (my) working hours would be quite long."* Even though being an one man band is never easy, he feels proud of himself given he is able to finish all the tasks on his own.

FB 4: Gong fu (effort) and xin ji (heart-mind)

Instead of focusing on strategic management, Doris would rather rely on her own hard work. Whenever I met her in the retail store, she would be busy in working, such as ironing clothes, buttoning, designing new clothes via her computer notebook, making procurement, serving customers, doing accounting works etc. In one weekend, I went to her store as usual. When I walked into the shop, I saw her trimming the thread ends. When she saw me, she said:

> Therefore, indeed, doing fashion this industry is . . . really require (me to) spend a lot of **xin ji** (heart-mind; effort) . . . You see, even for trimming the thread ends, also need to spend a lot of **xin ji** (heart-mind; effort). . . . Also for choosing cloth, even for choosing which threads . . . also require (me to) spend so much **gong fu** (effort) (and) **xin ji** (heart-mind; effort). Therefore, doing fashion this industry, really is not an easy task. (Producing) A garment is (required) (me) a lot of **gong fu** (effort) (and) **xin ji** (heart-mind; effort). That is why it is sold at such a price. (This work) Is not easy!

Doris needs to closely monitor every detail in work. She has emphasised that her work requires her to spend a lot of *gong fu* (effort) and *xin ji* (heart-mind). She has repeated the following phrases: '*xin ji*' for three times and '*gong fu*' for twice. This shows she would put much *xin ji* (heart-mind) and *gong fu* (effort) in work.

The above stories demonstrate the subject's strong willingness to bear any hardship at work. They would strive to survive in the market by: (1) persistently being able to maintain existence in the market, (2) trying to handle most of the tasks by themselves, and (3) working hard with their *xin ji* (heart-mind) and *gong fu* (effort).

4.2.4 *Xin Zhong Fu You* (Being Rich at Heart-mind)

Some locals (particularly the youth) regard *xin zhong fu you* (being rich at heart-mind) as another important aspect of life. I found this expression from the following casual conversation with Doris when I asked her when she could feel *xing fu*:

> That's NOT about: (If) you have much money, you would feel xing fu. Indeed, (if) you don't (have money,) you would then become xing fu. You know that is (if) you don't have (it), you are (rather) xing fu. (It is) Because that satisfaction does not come from external. But money or materials are always come from external sources, right? . . . This is similar to taking drugs! (If you have) relied on it (the drugs), indeed you have already lost your own self. It's about (a matter of) control! Indeed, once you can't control yourself (and rely on something externally given), you can't take control of your own happiness. (That's why) **xin zhong fu you** . . . yes! **xin zhong fu you** is alright!

Doris's expression: "*xin zhong fu you*" is another local buzzword. This term originates from the lyrics of a local song with the verse: "Hunger for being rich at heart-mind; do not intentionally chase for reputation and benefits". This term is normally used to describe the current local youth (new generation) who do not demand things that are of material existence. They could rather look for being rich at heart-mind, such as freedom, democracy and social justice etc. For instance, the previous Financial Secretary of Hong Kong, Mr John Tsang Chun Wah, has used this phrase to praise the new local generation. In his speech, he mentioned:

> After hundreds of years of development, Hong Kong's economic capability has already been positioned at the top tier of the world. Hong Konger, especially the new generation, looks for something outside the material life; (they are) rather "hunger for richness in heart". This is a mature social behaviour!

After the speech, he uses this phrase for a second time in order to make further complements to the local youth. He appreciated the local youth who have tried to make use of various forms of social enterprises to make their dreams come true and change the world. Hence, this phrase has become a local buzzword, which also symbolises the life goal that the local youth would like to pursue in order to get a good and successful living.

When would the local youth have *xin zhong fu you* (being rich at heat-mind)? During the fieldwork, I found that the local expression: '*Wo yao zhen pu xuan*' (I want real universal suffrage) is often expressed by the local youth to indicate their demand for *xin zhong fu you* (being rich at heart). *Wo yao zhen pu xuan* is the slogan that expresses the local appeal for a real universal suffrage in the election of Chief Executive in 2017 and forming the Legislative Council in 2016. A majority of the locals rejected the 831 decision, made by The Standing Committee of the National People's Congress (SCMNP), not only expressing their views verbally but also through the provision of art and design. The yellow ribbon is used to symbolize the demand for real universal suffrage in Hong Kong. In particular, the graphic of yellow ribbon with a black colour as a background (see Appendix C: Fig. C1) is used to show the disagreement over the use of any violence suppressed by the Hong Kong Police in the Umbrella Movement in 2014. How did *zhen pu xuan* (real universal suffrage) mean to the informants? Around 75 percent of my informants have Facebook and nearly 53 percent of them had changed their profile picture as shown in Fig. C1 to express the support towards the real universal suffrage. Five of the informants have even posted the slogan of '*Wo yao zhen pu xuan*' (I want real universal suffrage) as their status on Facebook. The above verbal or graphic expressions reflect the fact that *zhen pu xuan* (real universal suffrage) is rather relevant in the lives of the informants living in Hong Kong. Social protest is one of the significant ways in which the locals could voice out their concern for better life to the central government.

Nevertheless, some locals expressed the acceptance of the 831 decision. Mrs. Cindy expressed her view over the *zhong yang zheng fu* (Literally means the central government. It refers to the government in Beijing):

> Given zhong yang zheng fu (the central government) would never change, dai zhu xian (take it first) would be necessary.

Indeed, '*dai zhu xian*' is a local expression that is first suggested by Chief Secretary, Carrie Lam, to promote an acceptance of the 831 decision. This term literally refers as "pocket it first". It means 'let us take the 831 decision first', so that local voters can have a chance to vote for their own Chief Executive in 2017.

Both Uncle Carl and Auntie Connie had similar thoughts. Uncle Carl even lamented:

> Sigh . . . Let's dai zhu xian (pocket it first) given it has already led to she hui si lie (social cleavage).

Social cleavage refers to the division of people into various social groups based on their views and voting preferences. When the social cleavage is applied to the local political situation, it is translated in Chinese as *she hui si lie* (breaking down the social harmony due to the differences between the people's views and voting preferences). It is an expression that bears negative connotation against the people supporting *zhen pu xuan* (real universal suffrage).

4.3 From Managing to Living

This section aims to interpret the above business practices adopted by the four family businesses. The literature review (see Chapters 1 and 2) highlights the problem of *essentialism* in the mainstream research on the Chinese family business (CFB) and well-being. With the critiques given by the post-colonial thoughts, this book avoids *essentialism* by offering interpretations based on both mainstream and Chinese perspectives. The following interpretation starts with a familiar approach (a mainstream perspective) to understand the business practices adopted by the four family businesses. While it seeks understanding based on the mainstream perspective, it also reveals possible weaknesses and restrictions when the data are interpreted based on the mainstream. In responses to those flaws and limitations, the analysis then moves to interpret the same data through Chinese language and two major Chinese philosophies (the Confucian and the Daoist traditions) so as to (1) reveal an alternative perspective or/and (2) to provide an additional layer of understanding.

From the data in the last section, the local expressions have shaped the practices within the four firms (see Appendix C: Tab. C1). Those major practices include:
(a) Familial culture: Blurring boundary between business and family
(b) Absence of/Resistance to strategy and management
(c) Strive to survive
(d) Move on as life unfolds

(a) Familial Culture: Blurring Boundary between Business and Family

As revealed in Section 4.2.1, the informants are working like *'a family'* (FB1) and treating the business as their *'own baby'* (FB 2) or even *'part of self'* (FB 4). They treat home as office or vice versa (*'Home office'* in FB 3) and often rely on *'family helpers'* (FB 1 and 4). If these values and practices are to be interpreted based on the mainstream discourse on CFB, such way of work would be interpreted as 'a business management' with features of "paternalism" (Chen et al., 2020; Luechapattanaporn and Wongsurawat, 2021; Mosbah and Wahab, 2018; Redding, 1990; Redding, 2000; Whiteley, 1992; Sheer, 2013), "familism", "nepotism" and "personalism" (Redding, 1990, p. 145). Similar to a typical CFB in the management discourse, the family businesses in this study have a patriarch family leadership and culture (Luechapattanaporn and Wongsurawat, 2021; Minkes and Foster, 2011; Yu and Kwan, 2015), adopt centralization (Redding, 1990, p. 154) with ownership and control being held among the family members, and rely on "relational contracts" and "reciprocity" (Redding, 1990, p. 144). "Informal", "sparse" and "pragmatic", could be used to commonly describe the personnel management of the family businesses (Chen et al., 2020; ECIC, 2005; Mosbah and Wahab, 2018; Redding, 1990; Redding, 2000; Sheer, 2012; Whiteley, 1992; Yu et al.,2018; Zheng, 2002). Hence, their management would most possibly be concluded as 'unprofessional' with "low standardization" and "low role specialization" (Redding, 1990, 154).

Although the above analysis seems to be quite aligned with the typical description of CFB in the management discourse, it is questionable that the subject views business as a separate sphere that requires 'professional management'. Given they work like *'a family'* (FB1), treat the business as their *'own baby'* (FB 2) or *'part of self'* (FB 4), work in *'home office'* and rely heavily on *'family workers'*, these practices over their work (or business) indicate that the informants regard their work (or business) as part of their families or selves. Why do they treat work (or business) as part of their families or selves? The answer could be explained by the Confucian perspective. In the Confucian teaching, self is constructed within the social nexus in which it is relational and interdependent (Chang and Holt, 1996; Hwang and Chang, 2009). Among different relation, the Confucian tradition strongly focuses on family (Ames, 2009). Three of the five cardinal relations (*wu lun*) are belonged to the family. Besides, the Chinese concept of *'jia'* (family) does not only bind by biological relation. Even though the relations between a ruler and the subject and friends do not lie within the family ties, they are developed according to the family model. *Jia* can be extended to non-kin ties through appropriate mutual trust (*xin*) and exchange (Chang and Holt, 1996). The Chinese treats *guo jia* (state or country) as family. *Zhi guo* 治國 (the governance of *a country*), is therefore regarded as part of the familial duties of a ruler. In the findings, the subject regards work (or business) as a way to maintain a living for their families. For example, Mrs. Alice starts FB 1 because she needs to *"find another way to generate income for the family"*. Uncle Carl engages in FB 3 as he needs to maintain *"a basic living"* for his family. Hence, it is understandable that the subject regards work (or business) as part of family and self. 'Business strategy' and 'professional management' produced in the business management discourse are usually used in the work (or business) context rather than in the familial nor personal lives. If the subject regards work (or business) as part of family or self, are 'business strategy' and 'professional management' still meaningful to them? Would they adopt any 'strategies' and 'professional management' in their familial or personal lives? The answers to these questions are provided in the next part.

(b) Absence of/Resistance to Strategy and Management

As shown in last section, the informants aim at *"liu de ging shai zai"* (FB 1), *"shou zhu xian"* (FB 2), *"zi ji zuo"* (FB 3) and work based on *"gong fu (effort) and xin ji (heart-mind)"* (FB 4). All of them indicated that they had *"no plans"* at all. If these expressions have to be interpreted based on the mainstream management discourse on the Chinese family business (CFB), such way of running a business could be typically scrutinized as *defensive*. CFB, in the management discourse adopts a classic business strategy termed as defensive (Mosbah and Wahab, 2018; Redding, 1990; Redding, 2000; Whiteley, 1992). Under such a defensive business strategy, CFB would usually have a *"tight financial and production management"* (Redding, 1990, p. 145) and little ambition to seek for further growth and expansion (Chen, 1995; Chen et al., 2020; Luechapattanaporn and Wongsurawat, 2021; Mosbah and Wahab, 2018; Poutziouris et al., 2002; Redding, 1990; Redding, 2000; Whiteley, 1992). Therefore, according to the mainstream discourse, FB 1, 2, 3 and 4 are regarded as "small-scaled" (Redding, 1990, p. 154) which only focus on maintaining daily operation for business survival. Besides, findings show that the informants would *"jian bu xing bu"* (FB 1 and 2) and "follow the customers' preferences and reactions" (FB 3 and 4). Based on the mainstream discourse, these strategies could be seen as overly stable with limited long-term planning (Chen, 1995; Chen et al., 2020; Mosbah and Wahab, 2018; Poutziouris et al., 2002; Redding, 1990; Redding, 2000; Whiteley, 1992). Hence, in the mainstream discourse, the business strategies adopted by FB 1, 2, 3 and 4 could be characterized as *defensive*, *stable* and *short-term*.

Although the above interpretation is common within the management discourse on CFB, the question lies on whether the subject regards such a living approach as 'a business strategy'. Does the use of 'business strategy' apply to them? Do they familiarize with what is so called 'business strategy'? As mentioned in 4.2, the informants revealed specifically that they ran the business with *"no strategies"* (FB 1, 2 and 4) nor *"any perfect plan"* (FB 3). That means, they regard 'business strategies and plans' are unnecessary and non-applicable to them. If the term, 'business strategy' is alien to them, the interpretation that they are using a defensive, stable and short-term strategy would possibly become a misrepresentation of their lives. Such a misrepresentation has neglected the abstracts in Chinese language and logic (Goody, 1996); has made the characteristics of CFB essential with negative connotation as being small, defensive and short-term focused (Westwood, 2001). In other words, it has objectified the Chinese subject to test the western concepts and theories of 'strategic management' (Xu; 2008). In order to avoid the above misrepresentation that would lead to the problem of *essentialism*, this research pays attention to the local language, its logic, values and the traditions.

Intrinsically, the findings show that the subject regards 'management' as *"no need"* (Ada, FB 1), *"troublesome"* (Betty, FB 2) and even *"a challenge"* (Doris, FB 4). Uncle Carl (FB 3) even did not mention the word, 'management' at all. That means, the informants think using 'management' in work is unnecessary, difficult and challenging. Their expressions reveal that they do not think 'management' is meaningful to their lives. They did not talk about 'management' spontaneously. They did not adopt 'management' in their lives. Some of them even resist to 'management'. Why do they seldom or even never mention 'management' spontaneously? Why do they think it is unnecessary to adopt 'management' in their lives? Why do some of them even resist to management? Their responses to 'management' could be explained by the Chinese language and traditions. Firstly, the word, 'management' is definitely not a Chinese word. Geert Hofstede (1993) examines the history and evolution of 'management' when he tries to differentiate management practices across countries. In his examination, the linguistic origin of the word is from Latin, *manus*, hand, via the Italian *maneggiare*, which is the training of horses in the *manege*. Subsequently, its meaning was extended to skill of handling in general. The word also became associated with the French *menage*, household, as an equivalent of "husbandry" in its sense of the art of running a household. The theatre of present-day management contains elements of both *manege* and *menage* and different *menages* and cultures may use different accents" (p.82). From Hofstede's examination of the history of 'management', the word is originated from not only a single foreign language, but a plethora of languages (starting from Latin and Italian, and then associated to French and English). Later on, 'management' is further developed as 'a process' by Adam Smith in 1776 and Scientific Management by Frederick Taylor in 1911 (Hofstede, 1993). Until now, 'management' is being developed as 'a concept', 'a science' and 'a field of study'. Various ways to 'management' are being created in the discourse, such as quantitative approach, behavioural approach, system approach and contingency approach (Robbins and Coulter, 2010). Although 'management' is well-developed and spread to other Asian countries, it is not originated from the Chinese language and traditions. 'Management' is seen as a foreign language to the Chinese. That is why the word, 'management' is not spontaneously being mentioned and adopted by some of the informants.

Secondly, 'management' is seen to be unnecessary to the subject because 'management' has never become an approach to living in Chinese philosophies, such as Confucian and Daoist tradition. In Confucian teaching, human approach to social lives should be governed by *yi* (appropriateness). In Confucian teaching, each role has its own rights, duties, obligations and responsibilities within a particular context. If the locals follow *yi* in their works, they would fulfil their roles as well as the duties by themselves. In that case, it is not essential to use 'management' to exercise any monitoring and control (e.g. scientific management), nor encourage motivation (e.g. human resource management). This explains why Ada (FB 1) thinks it is not necessary to adopt 'management' given "everyone would *zi dong bo* (work automatically)". She believes the staff in FB 1 would follow *yi* as their approach to work. Besides, the Daoists practice *wu wei* (non-assertive action) works on a daily basis. Based on *wu wei*, the Daoist leadership would avoid any coercive policies and practices that would discourage or restrict people from being spontaneous. Given 'management' requires implementation of any coercive policies and practices in work, Daoists would probably avoid using 'management' in lives. Hence, the concept of '*wu wei*' in Daoism can also explain why the subject does not exercise 'management' in work (or business).

Thirdly, 'management' is being seen as *"difficult"* and *"a challenge"* by some of the subjects. Why did they have such feeling towards 'management'? One possible account for this local response could refer to Bhabha's (1985; 1990; 1994) concepts of 'ambivalence', 'mimicry' and 'hybridization' within the post-colonial thoughts. Bhabha highlights the ambivalence of the colonizer because the colonial Other was constructed in a manner that was only a partial representation of the colonizer, instead of portraying the real image. Hong Kong was colonized by Britain, therefore the locals' knowledge, values and thinking will be influenced by the colonizer. In the critiques towards Redding's (1990) The Spirit of Chinese Capitalism, Xu (2008) draws research to pay attention to the subject's "hybrid" legacy:

> It is the colonial nineteenth century as part of the subject's "hybrid" legacy, and the interviewees' sense of being both "Chinese" and the product of a society once run by outsiders. Hence, one discerns both favourable feeling towards Chinese tradition and for western institutions as well as criticism, predicament, and tension in terms of power, control and identity. (p.266)

Some of the informants view management as *"difficult"* and *"a challenge"* because of their "hybrid" legacy – they experience tension when they live with both local traditions and knowledge on 'management'. It is no doubts that some locals, especially the younger generation, often acquire western values and knowledge on 'management', while they treasure and live according to many Confucian and Daoist values. For instance, Betty, Bonnie (FB2) and Doris (FB 4) understand 'management' very well because they have been studied business subjects since they were in secondary schools. With adequate business knowledge, they understand the value and importance of management. Both of them understand about personnel management, cost control and time management, etc. At the same time, they also treasure and live according to many Confucian and Daoist values, such as Betty and Bonnie treasuring *zi ji ren*, rely *xin* (trust) and valuing harmony; while Doris strives to survive (*zi qiang bu xi*) by spending a lot of *gong fu* (effort) and *xin ji* (heart-mind; effort) in her work. With favourable feeling towards Chinese traditions, as well as adequate knowledge on 'management', they feel that exercising 'management' in their family businesses would create tensions in work. For instance, Betty and Bonnie found it difficult to impose any control and monitoring to their staff, because they would like to maintain harmony. Besides, in dealing with the challenges of managing different aspects of the business, Doris did not implement any strategies. On a contrary, she chose to work based on her *gong fu* (effort) and *xin ji* (heart-mind). Based on these two examples, the subject's responses reveal that implementing 'management' could violate harmony, *tian dao* (the way of Heaven) and *wu wei* (non-assertive action) in Confucian and Daoist teachings respectively. Hence, they express management as *"difficult"* and *"a challenge"*.

If the subject does not focus on 'management', what could be their real concern in lives? In the findings, the subject have mentioned terms such as *"basic living"*, *"liu de ging shai zai"* and *"jian bu xing bu"* etc.. These local expressions are all related to the "livings" or "approaches to living" of the respondents. In other words, they are simply concerned about 'life'. As mentioned in the last part, the subjects treat work (or business) as part of their families and their own selves. The concept of self is socially constructed (Chang and Holt, 1996; Hwang and Chang, 2009), and they work (or do business) in order to maintain a living for their families. That means they are more interested on maintaining 'a living' for their families, rather than 'management'. They care about 'life' (or 'a living') due to the local traditions. Both the Confucian and the Daoist traditions are regarded as 'philosophies of living' (Xu, 2008, p.258). That is to say, they target on providing meaning to human lives and teaching people the appropriate ways of living, rather than 'management'. For example, in the Confucian teaching, the cultivation of human virtues in daily lives are, including *ren* (benevolence), *yi* (appropriateness), *li* (ritual propriety) and *zhi* (acting wisely), while the Daoists encourage humans to live according to the nature. Since 'life' (or 'a living') is the main concern of the subject, the next section seeks an understanding their ways of living, which are embedded in their business practices. It explores the local lives with alternative themes: (1) Strive to survive and (2) Move on as life unfolds.

(c) Strive to Survive

The local expressions: *"liu de ging shai zai"* (FB 1), *"shou zhu xian"* (FB 2), *"zi ji zuo"* (FB 3), *"gong fu (effort) and xin ji (heart-mind)"* (FB 4) reveal that my research subject has been **striving to survive**. They work hard in order to maintain a living for survival. For instance, Mrs. Alice has been maintaining the survival of FB 1 for 20 years; Betty and Bonnie are willing to take compromises to retain their clients, so that FB 2 could *"shou zhu xian"* (hold on to survive); Uncle Carl starts FB 3 so that he does not need *"to worry the basic living in the future"*; and Doris can start FB 4 because *"(this business) is (what she) ongoing (continuously) want to do"*. Their behaviours can be interpreted by one Chinese idiom: '*zi qiang bu xi*'. The Chinese idiom translates that one strives with unremitting efforts. Therefore, striving continuously in order to survive could be seen as an ultimate life goal of the subject.

This life goal can be interpreted by the Confucians as "positive self-striving", one key characteristic of *jun zi* (a virtuous person) (Xu, 2008, p. 270). In the Confucian teaching, *ren dao* (the human way) is treated as one's life goal (see Section 3.2.2). *Ren dao* symbolizes how human should live on *di* (the Earth, the material world). Hence, *ren dao* represents a moral ideal of an entire human life. What does a moral ideal mean in the Confucian teaching? A moral ideal in Confucian teaching refers to a sage who understands *dao* and lives according with it. Then, how can one become a sage? To become a sage, one must cultivate *de* (virtues). That means lifelong self-cultivation of *de* is necessary. When one attained *de* with a high degree of standard, he/she is regarded as *jun zi* (a virtuous person). According to *Yi Jing*, *zi qiang bu xi* is one characteristic of *jun zi*:

> Xiang Zhuan: Heaven, in its motion, (gives the idea of) strength. The superior man, in accordance with this, nerves himself to ceaseless activity. (Yi Jing: Qian, 1; in Legge, 1985)

The above indicates that *jun zi* must strive positively and ceaselessly. Hence, the subjects struggle towards survival can be understood as *zi qiang bu xi* (positive self-striving), one of the key virtues that a *jun zi* would be accustomed to.

(d) Move on as Life Unfolds

The Chinese language of *"jian bu xing bu"* (FB 1 and 2) and *"follow the customers' preferences and reactions"* (FB 3 and 4) portrays that the subjects believe that **moving on as life unfolds** is indeed important. That means, they live by following the way of the Nature. This approach to living can be understood by the Daoist teaching, as it inspires humans to live according to *dao* (the way of Nature) (see Section 1.2.2). Daoists encourage humans to allow for spontaneity (*zi zhenran*), i.e. humans should live in accordance with the pattern of the Nature. In fact, both the Confucian and the Daoist thoughts are known to be inspired by *Yi Jing*. Xu (2008) translated the above opening line of *Yi Jing* as "Heaven moves eternally. *Jun zi* who follows its way strives unceasingly" (p.270). With regards to the Chinese language, logics and traditions, she thoroughly interprets the line as follows:

> In Chinese, "Heaven" refers to nature. Humans are part of nature. Therefore, they follow nature's way. Here, the order Tian di jun zi/ren suggests, firstly, to position "human (jun zi/ren) in nature's movement; and secondly, to learn from nature's way in one's positive striving.
> (Xu, 2008, p.270)

Based on Xu's explanation, *jun zi* (a virtuous person) has to follow the pattern of Nature while they strive positively and unceasingly. That is why the subject responds to live by acting spontaneously to any happenings being occurred (i.e. *jian bu xing bu*). For instance, Ada runs FB 1 by *"shun zhu qu zuo* (do as it goes along)". Mrs. Alice and Ada prefer to act at the right timing. That is to say; they would suspend an act until there is an opportunity or wait until there is no obstacles. Doris also starts FB 4 with no particular point of time. She simply keeps working until a chance is at her disposal, and she grabs for it. Hence, the informants walk according to the natural pattern of life. They strive to survive by following the pattern of Nature – act through the right moment when there is an opportunity or no obstacles. This approach to living is regarded as positive, because this is how a *jun zi* would live on the Earth, the material world (*di*) – lives according to the Nature's way along one's positive striving.

Chapter 5
A Cross-Cultural Analysis between the East and the West

The data in Chapter 4 highlights two alternate local expressions of: (1) *xing fu* and (2) *xin*. These two Chinese concepts have their inherent meanings and they are embodied in the subject's daily lives. As illustrated in Tab. 5.1, it summarises the themes derived from the data which reflects the contextual meanings of these two Chinese concepts. As mentioned in Section 4.2.1, *xing fu* is expressed within a particular context – in a marriage and family. Hence, such a contextual term highlights that the informants value social relations. In particular, they regard *jia ting* (family) and *peng you* (friends) as the most important aspects of their lives. Therefore, this chapter begins by scrutinising *xing fu* within the familial context. Next, *kai xin gong zuo* (see Section 4.2.3), and *xin zhong fu you* (see Section 4.2.4) are expressed to indicate how the informants work and live well in society. Both expressions contain an expression – *xin*. *Xin* has its specific connotations (Li, Ericsson and Quennerstedt, 2013; Zhang, 1993). Hence, the meanings of *xin* from various philosophical perspectives are uncovered. This chapter aims to contribute to knowledge by shedding light on an indigenous perspective.

The first section of this chapter presents a theoretical discussion of the local expressions. The two Chinese expressions: *xing fu* and *xin* are explored from both western and Chinese perspectives. Each expression is scrutinised initially via the notion of well-being from a mainstream framework. The discussion reveals possible boundaries when the data is analysed from a mainstream (western) approach. Afterwards, the same expressions are interpreted through Confucian and Daoist frameworks – so as to offer further layers of understanding. The second part of the chapter draws the four perspectives into dialogues. By engaging them in conversations, the section aims to highlight the similarities and the differences between different perspectives and further demystify the notion of *xin*. Such knowledge may help westerners and Chinese to better understand each other.

5.1 Demystifying Chinese Notions

5.1.1 *Xing fu* (Living well)

Xing fu is the first expression to be analysed. This term is used to describe *jia ting*. To my subject, *jia ting* (family) is the most important aspect of life. This compound is made of two morphemes: '*jia*' and '*ting*'. *Jia* is written as 家. The character 家 can be seen as 宀 and 豕. 宀 represents a roof; 豕 symbolizes pigs (豬). In Ancient China, people feed pigs for a living, and they would live with pigs. Feeding pigs is part of daily lives. That means, 家 may be under a roof – a home. As for ting, it is written as 庭. 庭 signifies a courtyard, spacious hall or yard. This implies the place for living. Both *jia* and *ting* are therefore literally referred to the home of a family. In other words, jia ting 家庭is simply 'family'.

Why does the research subject regard family as the most important aspect of life? How can one explain such a view based on the notion of well-being? Hedonism values family if individuals are able to derive happiness from their families. From an utilitarian perspective, family can be a means for obtaining pleasures and self-interests. That is why people would desire to have a good family. Likewise, Eudaimonia also believes that family can be significant to one's life. According to Maslow's (1943) hierarchy of needs, familial relation is classified as a social need. Humans seek to have a favourable relationship in order to fulfil their social needs. Hence, good familial relation could contribute to positive relatedness, which is part of psychological well-being. Although from such a perspective, one can see the significance of family, they never perceive family is the most necessary element of human life. Based on Maslow's (1943) theory, social need is characterised as a lower order of need (a subjectively felt need), which would only bring short-term pleasure to humans. In this case, the notion of well-being cannot explain why the research subject treated the family as the most vital aspect of their life.

To appreciate why the subject regards *jia* (family) as the first priority of life, Confucian and Daoist frameworks are helpful to comprehend Chinese perspectives. Confucian education emphasises on *wu lun* (the five cardinal relations). *Wu lun* includes: (1) a ruler and a subject (superior and subordinate); (2) father and son (parent and child); (3) husband and wife; (4) elder brother and younger brother (siblings); and (5) friends (Bockover, 2010). According to *wu lun*, three of the relations are about the family. This reflects the significance of family in Confucian teaching. Confucians recognise family as the most fundamental factor in one's life (Ames, 2009) because family is the chief platform for individuals to acquire, exercise, cultivate and extend *ren* (benevolence) – the principle virtue for Confucians.

Is family perceived as important from Daoist perspective? It seems that Daoists do not directly address family. Instead, it pays attention to *dao* – "the way of nature" (Morris, 1994, p.110). In Daoist thinking, *dao* is the origin of the world and it is the base of all creations, including family. That is to say, family is formed due to people following *dao* – the pattern of Nature. From this perspective, family is seen as essential when it is formed in accordance with natural rhythm of life. Hence, following Confucian and Daoist teachings, one would be able to recognise 'family' as the most important aspect of human life.

(a) Xing Fu Jia Ting (Good family)
Xing fu jia ting is an expression that the subject would use to describe a good family. Based on the data in Chapter 4, four values emerge under the context of *xing fu jia*

ting. They include completeness, role obligations, healthiness and spiritual peace. In seeking these values, different practices are embodied in the subject's daily lives. The practices consist of: (i) Seeking completeness through building a family with children; (ii) Fulfilling role obligations by feeding family and shaping a good child (supporting family); (iii) Maintaining health through physical exercises and good sleep; and (iv) Gaining spiritual peace through rituals and gestures (see Tab. 5.1). The following discussion is the interpretation of these values and practices based on the mainstream and Chinese perspectives.

Tab. 5.1: Local Concepts: *Xing fu* and *Xin*.

Local terms/concepts of living well	Embodiment of living well	Themes
Xing fu (Living well)		
(1) Xing fu jia ting 幸福家庭 (Good family)		
Qi zheng 齊整 (Orderly complete)	Build a family with children	Completeness: Build a family with children
Yang jia 養家 (Feed family)	Support family: – Buy one's own place – Shape *quai* 乖 (good) children	Role obligations: Support family – Feed family – Teach children
Jian kang 健康 (Healthy)	Physical exercises, good sleep	Healthiness: Physical exercises and good sleep
Ping jing c靜 (Peace and at ease)	Rituals and gestures	Spiritual peace: Rituals and gestures
(2) Peng you 朋友 (Friends)		
Xin 信 (Trust)	Work with *peng you*	Trust and work with friends
Xin (Heart-mind)		
(3) Kai xin gong zuo 開心工作 (Happy work) *You xing qu* 有興趣 (Have interests)		Work for interests, affection, satisfaction and creativity
Zhong yi 鍾意 (Affection)		
You man zu gan 有滿足感 (Have satisfaction)		
Chuang zuo 創作 (Creativity)		
Contrast with *xin ku* 辛苦 (hardship)	Work hard and bear *xin ku* (hardship)	Work hard to bear hardship

Tab. 5.1 (continued)

Local terms/concepts of living well	Embodiment of living well	Themes
(4) ***Xin zhong fu you*** 心中富有 **(Being rich at heart-mind)**		
Wo yao zhen pu xuan (I want real universal suffrage)	Social protests	Being rich at heart-mind: Social protests

i. Completeness: Build a Family with Children

Some of my female informants (e.g. Ada, Mrs. Cindy and Hestia) live with the aim of building a complete family which consists of a father, a mother and children (see Section 4.2.1). Hence, they put efforts in getting marriage and giving birth. Based on Eudaimonia, building a family with children can be viewed as a life purpose that contributes to one's psychological well-being. Nevertheless, the Eudemonic approach cannot explain why those informants could have such life objective. The mainstream framework does not discuss why people seek for building a complete family.

Both the Confucian and the Daoist frameworks could offer an understanding on why those informants would aim at building a complete family. As mentioned in Section 1.2.1, *jun zi* (a virtuous person) has three delights. The second delight occurs when his father and mother are both alive. This does not only explain why Mrs. Cindy had a feeling of loss when his husband (as well as the father of her family) passed away, but it also reflects the importance of having a complete family (which consists of a father, a mother and children). Confucius encourages individuals to build their own families and have children. He teaches people to pursue four missions in life: (1) *xiu shen*修身 (cultivation of moral characters), (2) *qi jia*齊家 (establishment of a harmonious family), (3) *zhi guo*治國 (governance of a state) and (4) *ping tian*平天下 (maintenance of harmony in the world). These four missions are to be achieved in accordance with its order and represents what a person should target on for his/her life journey. Among these four duties, *qi jia* (establishment of a harmonious family) is the second mission of individuals before they could order well in their own states. *Qi jia* means to establish a complete and harmonious family. Therefore, the basic tasks of *qi jia* are to build a new family through marriage and having children. Only after an individual have created a complete family, he/she could try to regulate the family and make it become harmonious.

What is Daoist view on marriage and having children? Even though Daoist teaching does not discuss marriage and children explicitly, its ideas of 'yin' and 'yang' suggest the importance of a harmonious marriage – matrimony between a man and a woman. Men present *yang*; while women represent *yin*. According to Daoist teaching, *yin* and *yang* are opposite but mutually interdependent. Therefore, a balance between *yin* and *yang* should be maintained. *Yin* and *yang* symbolize the significance of harmony.

Marriage (between a man and a woman) illustrates that a family is built with a balance between *yin* and *yang*. From Daoist perspective, marriage is a part of nature if forming a new family could help to maintain a harmonious balance in the system of the world. This can also explain why some of the informants (e.g. Ada and Eden) seek to have both a son (*yin*) and a daughter (*yang*) in a family – *You nu you zi* (have a daughter and a son) can help to maintain a balance in a family.

Although forming a complete family can be a life goal for the Chinese, the pressure for getting marriage and giving birth had also created distress to some informants (e.g. Betty and Hestia). How can Daoist thinking explain this kind of frustration? How would Daoists encourage a family to be harmonious? Daoists advocate living along with the pattern of nature. They preserve *zi ran* (nature, spontaneity) and *wu wei* (non-assertive action). Hence, they believe that marriage and giving birth should all be taken place spontaneously. That is, these events of life are in need to occur along the pattern of nature. With Daoist attitude of *wu wei*, patience and non-interference should be maintained along the life process. In this case, Daoist would not support any assertive intentions and acts on marriage and having children, such as speed dating, *cui hun* 催婚 (pressing for getting married) and artificial insemination. Hence, this can explain why some of the informants felt uncomfortable in attending any planned dating arrangements (e.g. Betty) or striving for pregnancy (e.g. Hestia). They felt frustrated because these arrangements are regarded as not spontaneous – given they may have to interfere the natural order of things and violate the way of nature (*dao*). Based on Daoist tradition, individuals engaging in these arrangements would be criticized as not possessing *de* (potency) – because they are unable to drop their egos and live harmoniously with nature. That is why they would feel uneasy when they do not follow the pattern of nature.

ii. Role Obligations: Support Family

Once a complete family is formed, the informants are obligated to carry out their family roles. They would provide supports to their families in terms of (1) feeding the family (*yang jia*) and (2) teaching their children to be *quai* (good) (see Tab. 5.1). These roles are aligned with the Chinese literal meaning of *jia ting* (family). *Jia ting* is the place where a family can physically live in there and be fed. *Jia ting* is regarded as the home of a family. How could the mainstream approach to well-being explain the above familial role obligations? Given Hedonism concerns on life satisfaction only, it does not offer any discussion on family roles. According to Maslow's (1943) hierarchy of needs, feeding the family and educating children can satisfy one's physiological needs and social belongingness respectively. In addition, Eudaimonia would perceive supporting family as a way to build positive relatedness. Hence, this practice would contribute to one's psychological well-being. However, both approaches do not explain why familial role obligations are seen as essential to the subject. The mainstream framework provides no clues on why feeding the family and teaching the children would be an embodiment of good family.

How could one understand the local familial role obligation through Confucian teaching? Familial role obligation is related to *yi* (appropriateness) and *li* (ritual propriety), the two key *de* (virtues) in Confucian education. *Yi* highlights the importance of behaving appropriately in the social relations; while *li* defines the rules that govern and guide peoples to perform their roles in *wu lun* (the five cardinal relations). Parents cultivate *yi* by taking their role obligations to look after the family. Family is treated as the first major platform for observing and following *li*. In a family, "*fu fu you bie*" (between husband and wife, attention to their separate duties) (Mencius: Teng Wen Gong I, 4; in Legge, 1985). That is to say, father and mother have separate duties in the family. According to *Chunqiu fanlu* written by Dong Zhongshu, it introduces *sang gang* 三綱 which are the three cardinal guides for individuals to observe their social roles. *Sang gang* consists of:

> Ruler guides subject; father guides son; and husband guides wife

Based on the three cardinal guides, two of them are related to the family. *Sang gang* specifies the role obligations of a father and a husband in the family. Father (the husband) is treated as *yi jia zhi zhu* 一家之主 (the head of a family) who is responsible for looking after his sons (children) and wife. That is why the findings in Section 4.2.1 showed Uncle Carl took the responsibility of feeding his family. In the *Three Character Classic*, it specifies:

> To feed without teaching is the father's fault. To teach without severity is the teacher's laziness.
> (Three Character Classic: 5, in Giles, 1910)

The above Chinese saying highlights the ritualized duties of a father – He is not only responsible for feeding but also teaching. If a father fails to offer guidance to his children, he would be at fault in failing to fulfil the obligation of his role as a father. Hence, father bears the responsibilities of both feeding and teaching. Nowadays fathers are often not the sole breadwinners of families. Both fathers and mothers are obligated to support the family. They try to develop *yi* (appropriateness) by taking up their familial role obligations and act in accordance to *li* (ritual propriety) through feeding and teaching their children. In Confucian teaching, these practices are regarded as a self-cultivation of *de* (virtues) and would be seen as the ways to attain *xing fu*.

Furthermore, teachers also held accountable to their students. Both FB 1 and FB 2 have their role obligations in teaching. Teachers in FB 1 and FB 2 target on the whole-person development of students, because they are obligated to teach severely. If not, they would be regarded as lazy. This explains why the teaching style of FB 1 is seen as rigorous and disciplinary. The third delight of *jun zi* (a virtuous person) (see Section 1.2.1) indicates that one would be able to derive satisfaction from teaching.

This explains why the teachers in FB 1 and FB 2 are willing to teach their children (students) to be *quai* (good).

How could the Daoist teaching explain the local familial role obligations? As discussed before, Daoism inspires individuals to drop their egos and live in harmony with nature. From that perspective, parents are advised to follow *dao* (the way of nature). They are encouraged to take up their *tian zhi* (bounden duties) – To support their families by feeding and teaching. Although Daoists value the bounden duties of parents, they believe that the growth and development of children should not be carried out in an assertive manner. Freedom should be offered to children so that they can grow and develop spontaneously (according to the way of nature – *zi ran*). Daoists perceive everything comes from the same origin (*dao*) and such pattern of nature should be followed. In that case, Daoists would not appreciate FB 2's promotion on enabling the kids to *ying zai qi pao xian* (win at the starting line), because any deliberate control and supervision on the child development would violate *wu wei* (non-assertive action) and distort the pattern of nature.

iii. Being Healthy: Physical Exercises and Good Sleep

The findings show that the informants value health (see Section 4.2.1). They recognised the need to do exercise and sleep well. How is healthiness understood from the mainstream framework of well-being? Hedonism assumes human lives to obtain pleasure and avoids pain (illness). Physical condition is important in Hedonic approach because health affects one's subjective well-being. Eudaimonia also recognises the importance of physical health. Fitness helps to satisfy one's physiological and safety needs. Individuals would like to take control over their health. Eudaimonia perceives such sense of control as a way of environmental mastery. Hence, health contributes to human psychological well-being. Even though the mainstream perspective realises the importance of health, it offers little discussion on how individuals can become healthy. It would be difficult to apprehend why the informants would like to do exercises and sleep well through the mainstream framework.

How important is health in Chinese linguistics and traditions? Do Confucian and Daoist teachings suggest any ways for individuals to become healthy? In Chinese language, *wu fu* 五福 represents the five signs of abundance, which includes longevity, prosperity, health and peace, virtue and a comfortable death (see Section 1.2.1). Health is part of *wu fu*. That means, Chinese thinks physical fitness is an imperative element in lives. Although Confucius stresses on self-cultivation of virtues and spiritual attainment, it does not deny the need for maintaining good health. Confucian teaching promotes *liu yi* 六藝 (six arts), which consists of *li* 禮 (rites), *le* 樂 (music), *she* 射 (archery), *yu* 御 (riding chariots), *shu* 書 (calligraphy), *shu* 數 (mathematics). Among the six arts, *she* (archery) and *yu* (riding chariots) are physical exercises that are promoted in Confucian education. Although Confucius does not discuss health in details, his training on *she* (archery) and *yu* (riding chariots) reflects the significance of doing physical exercises in daily lives. Furthermore, *The Analects* points out:

> When eating, he did not converse. When in bed, he did not speak.
> (The Analects: Xiang Dang, 8; in Legge, 1985)

The above Chinese saying highlights a person does not speak while he is sleeping. One needs to fall into sleep peacefully. Hence, this portrays that it is crucial to have a good quality of sleep in daily lives.

Following Daoist thoughts, harmony is the way to stay healthy. That means a balance between *yin* and *yang* should always be maintained. Doing exercises can be associated with *yang* since it symbolizes *dong* 動 (movement); while sleeping can be associated with *yin* because it implies *jing* 靜 (quietness). Daoists recognise the interdependence between *dong* (*yang*) and *jing* (*yin*). In that perspective, doing exercises (*dong*) and sleeping well (*jing*) are mutually supportive to healthiness given they are carried out to maintain a balance between *yang* and *yin*. Both of them are mutually important to lives, and therefore they represent the embodiment of good health.

iv. Spiritual Peace: Rituals and Gestures

The informants did not only concern with physical fitness (*jian kang*), they also valued spiritual health. They seek for spiritual peace (*ping an, ping jing* or *an xin*) through performing rituals (such as ancestor worship) and wearing symbolic accessories (such as jade accessories) (see Section 4.2.1). Is spiritual peace also considered as important in the mainstream perspective? Are local rituals and decorations appropriate to Hedonic and Eudemonic approaches to well-being? Hedonism pays attention to both physical and mental pleasure. It defines happiness as subjective well-being, which consists of life satisfaction, the presence of positive mood and the absence of negative emotion (Ryan and Deci, 2001). Hence, happiness (subjective well-being) signifies a positive state of mind. Is spiritual peace implies a positive state mind? According to the findings, the informants (e.g. Ada, Mrs. Alice, Brenda and Uncle Carl) looked for *ping an, ping jing, an xin, tai ping or ping wen*. All these local terms indicate a tranquil life encompassed of peace and stability. They imply a well-balanced spiritual state, neither positive nor negative. In this case, Hedonism cannot interpret why a well-balanced spiritual state is important.

To what extend would Eudaimonia help to explain spiritual peace? According to Maslow's (1943) theory, spiritual peace would be regarded as a safety need. For security purpose, a human would demand a life with stability as they prefer to maintain control over their lives (environmental mastery). Hence, spiritual peace contributes to individual psychological well-being. However, if the informants perceive they can take control over their lives, why do they need to perform rituals and wear symbolic accessories in order to gain spiritual comfort? It is unlikely that the mainstream approaches would appreciate the local rituals and decorations because these practices tend to undermine the human potential and self-governance.

If one finds it difficult to understand the local value of spiritual peace through rituals and decorations, could Confucian and Daoist thoughts help to explain these local practices? As mentioned in Section 1.2, peace and health are one of *wu fu* (five signs of abundance). Confucians value harmony, which indicates that a balance between physical and spiritual aspects should always be maintained in order to become healthy. *Zhong yong* 中庸 (equilibrium) is the way to form a harmonious whole person. In that perspective, spiritual peace and comfort imply *ping he* 平和 (harmony) in every aspect of a person – a well-balanced state between both physical and spiritual elements. In Confucian teaching, harmony can be achieved and maintained through *li* (ritual propriety). *Li* refers to sacrifice to the ancestors and spirits. Ancestor worship is considered as a kind of ritual (*li*). The informants would perform rituals (e.g. ancestor worship) and wear symbolic accessories because these practices are appropriate ways (*li*) for individuals to seek for *shen xin ping he* 身心平和 (a well-balanced state between physical and spiritual aspects). These practices are ways for one to become a harmonious whole person.

How would Daoists value harmony in a person? Daoists support the notion of harmony. Based on Daoist perspective, physical body represents *yang*; while spiritual mind represents *yin*. Daoists perceive that individuals would naturally become healthy if there is a harmony between human body (*yang*) and spirit (*yin*). Similar to Confucian thoughts, Daoists would value spiritual peace, given it symbolizes the state of *shen xin ping he* (a well-balanced state between physical and spiritual aspects). However, Daoists suggest individuals to let go of themselves (*wuwo*) in order to become spiritually at peace and stable. Individuals need to accept what life gives them, rather than seeking for personal desires and pre-conceived preferences. To Daoists, performing rituals and wearing symbolic accessories would be considered as assertive actions that target on fulfilling individual desires and wants. Hence, it is likely that Daoists would discard any assertive rituals and behaviours, because these practices may interfere the pattern of nature (*dao*).

The theoretical discussion of *xing fu jia ting* is summarised (see Appendix D: Tab. D1). The similarities and differences among the four perspectives are illustrated (see Fig. 5.1). As a summary, Hedonism interprets *xing fu jia ting* as a happy family; while Eudaimonia realizes building a family as a life purpose to satisfy one's social need. Although Confucian framework also values human need for affiliation, Confucius does not agree with Eudaimonia that individuals have to control their environment and health. Rather than focusing on personal autonomy, Confucians target on *qi jia* (establishing a harmonious family) as a life mission. It is because family is treated as a platform for cultivating virtues. Both Confucian and Daoist frameworks recognize that parents have their natural role obligations to family. They need to maintain harmony in the family. However, Daoists insist that any familial duties should be carried out spontaneously (in accordance with the pattern of nature).

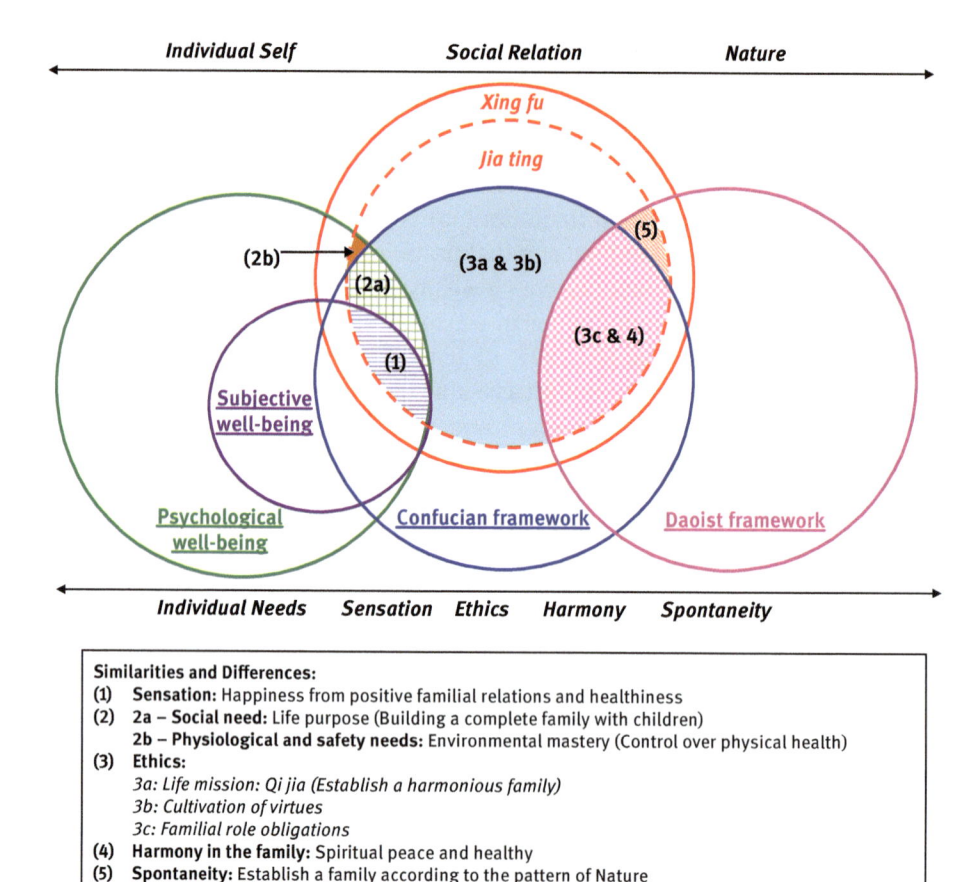

Fig. 5.1: Theoretical Discussion of *Xing Fu Jia Ting*.

(b) Peng You (Friends)

Friends in the local term is called '*peng you*'. *Peng you* are regarded as the second main element of life to the subject. *Peng you*, in Chinese is written as 朋友. 朋 is a measurement unit of the Chinese currency in the Ancient time. By that time, the Chinese regarded five shells as one *peng*. This implies *peng* 朋 has a connotation of 'forming a unit'. According to the Oracle Bronze inscription, 朋 is also written as 佣, in which *ren* 人 (human) is added to 朋. Thus, it implies the meaning of 'friends'. In particular, it denotes a companionship with those who have good moral conducts, similar goals and interests. For *you* 友, the Oracle Bone Inscription is written as . This character signifies two hands are moving towards the same direction. Hence, it indicates two persons associate with one another, and they would offer helping hands to each other. Again, it refers to friendship. As a consequence, *peng you* are contemporarily defined as 'friend'; 'companion'; 'acquaintance 'or 'fraternity'.

Chinese families tend to extend their familial network to friendships (see Appendix D: Fig. D1). For Chinese, *peng you* are regarded as a part of *jia ting* – an extended family. In particular, the informants (e.g. Mrs Alice, Ada and Betty) expressed their high preference over working with their *peng you* (acquaintance). Why are friends seen as essential to the informants? How would the mainstream framework interpret the demand for friends? Similar to family, Hedonism values companionship because individual is able to derive happiness and pleasure from amity. By the same token, Eudaimonia treats friendship as a kind of relations that enables individuals to satisfy their social needs. In such perspective, the informants need friends because of positive relatedness, which could contribute to their psychological well-being. Even though friends are constructive to one's well-being, social belongings are categorised as a lower level of needs only. In the mainstream perspective, friends are separated from work, and they are not necessary to be extended to comradeship (working associates). In the current case, the mainstream perspective might find it difficult to understand why the informants were inclined to work with friends who were regarded as trustworthy.

i. Trust and Work with Friends
Is *peng you* substantial to Chinese traditions? How might Confucian and Daoist frameworks help to explain the practice of working with *peng you*? Confucius views *peng you* as 'tong zhi' 同志, meaning those who possess the same mind. In that case, Confucian view reflects that the inherent philological meaning of *peng you* is: Companionship with those who have similar thoughts, goals and interests. The term, *tong zhi*, portrays that *peng you* can be treated as members of an extended family whose relationship can be as close as *xiong di* 兄弟 (brothers). In Confucian education, *peng you* can play a role of *juan zi* 君子 (virtuous person), who can help to exchange views on virtues and provide supports on cultivating *ren* (benevolence). That is why Confucius views *peng you* as critical to one's virtuous training. The informants highlighted the importance of *xin* 信 (trust) among friends. Their notion of *xin* can be well understood based on Confucian framework. According to *li* (ritual propriety) in the Confucian education, *xin* (fidelity) is the basic governance of friendship, as well as a quality in a friendship. "Trustworthiness is one of the five fundamental the Confucian virtues" and "quality" valued in a friendship (Cheung, 2011, p.136). Hence, my informants' perceived trust is an important element in friendship. If trust is built in a friendship, they would feel comfortable and reassured to work with *peng you* (friends). They would feel more *an xin* (spiritually secure) to work with friends. How is trust built in a friendship? One way to build trust is through *zhong cheng* 忠誠 (loyalty and sincerity). *Zhong cheng* is seen as a reciprocal

obligation between friends. One would trust their friends who are loyal and sincere. On the contrary, *xiao ren* 小人 (mean men) are not trustworthy. When loyalty cannot be maintained, trust in a friendship would be destroyed. As a consequence, *peng you* (friends) would be turned into *xiao ren* (mean persons).

How do Daoists look at *peng you*? Daoist teachings offer not much discussion on friendship. It does not examine the notion of *xin* (fidelity) directly given that Daoists stress on the relationship with nature, rather than people. Nonetheless, in *Zhuangzi*, it contrasts differences between the intercourse of *jun zi* (superior/virtuous men) and that of *xiao ren* (mean men) *(Zhuangzi: The Tree on the Mountain,* 5; in Legge, 1891b). Although the intercourse with *jun zi* could be tasteless, it can lead to affection. Conversely, the intercourse with *xiao ren* could be sweet, yet it can become an aversion. Similar to Confucian thoughts, Daoists encourage the communication with *jun zi*, rather than *xiao ren*. The informants regard their friends as *jun zi* (superior/virtuous men) who they show affection to; while they averse to dealing with *xiao ren* (mean men) who have betrayed them (or have been disloyal to them). Hence, the informants prefer working with *peng you* (friends), instead of *xiao ren*.

To sum up, the discussion of *peng you* (see Appendix D: Tab. D1) highlights the similarities and differences among the four perspectives (see Fig. 5.2). Hedonism regards *peng you* as one source of happiness. Eudaimonia does not only value such joy from companionship, it regards *peng you* as constructive to individual psychological well-being. Positive relatedness is able to fulfil the individual need for belongings. However, the mainstream is not able to explain why the locals prefer to work with friends. Therefore, the Chinese perspectives offer further understanding. The Confucian teaching treats *peng you* as an extended family and *tong zhi* (people with the same mind) – who can encourage intellectual inspiration on virtues. Chinese would feel more comfortable to work with *peng you* because Confucian education uses *xin* (fidelity) as a governance and quality in the friendship. As a result, both Confucian and Daoist teachings show affection to deal with *jun zi* – friends who are superior in ethics.

5.1.2 *Xin* (Heart-mind)

Xin 心 is pronounced as hsin. According to the *"Shuowen Jiezi"* written by Xu Shen (2006), the early Chinese inscriptions of *xin* are as following:

(Jia gu wen 甲骨文)   (Jin wen 金文)   (xiao zhuan 小篆)

Similarities and Differences:
(1) **Sensation:** Happiness from companionship
(2) **Social need:** Positive relatedness
(3) **Ethics** (to *peng you* – an extended family):
  3a: Role obligation: Xin (trust)
  3b: Intellectual inspiration on virtues
  3c: Affection to jun zi (virtuous person)

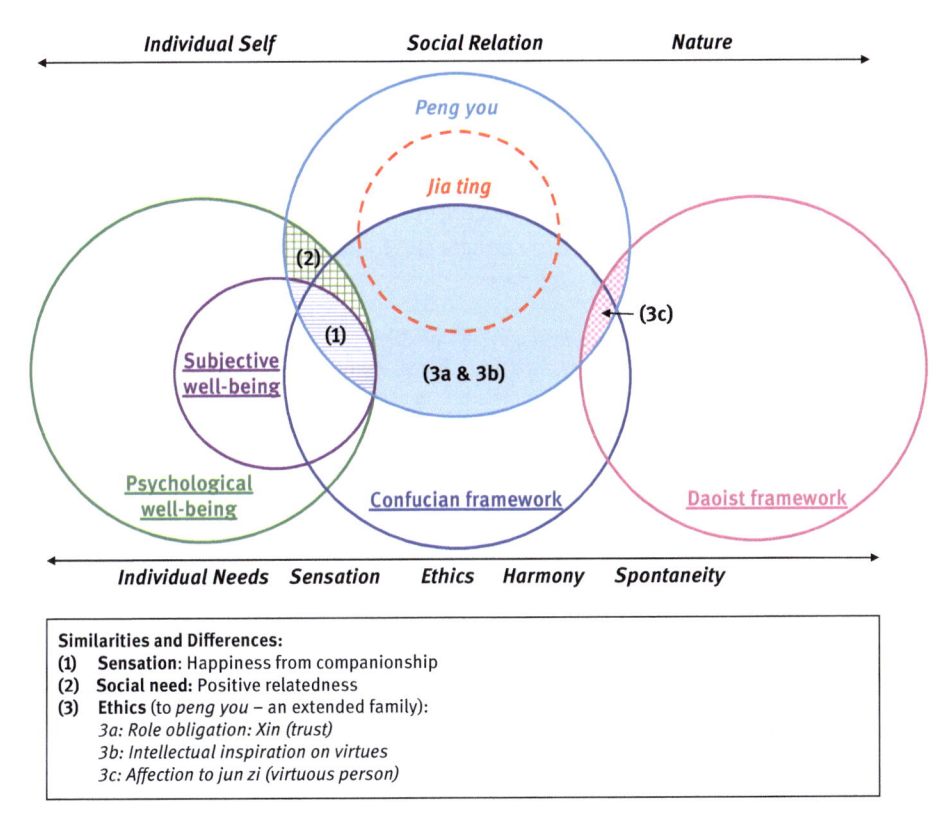

Fig. 5.2: Theoretical Discussion of *Peng You*.

Based on the above characters, *xin* is symbolised as an organ – the heart of human being and animals (Zhang, 1993) and it is situated in the centre of a body. That is why *xin* is often being directly translated as 'heart' in English. The contemporary dictionaries, such as *A Modern Chinese-English Dictionary* (Chen, 2001), *Zhongda Chinese-English dictionary* (Liang and Zheng, 2003) and *Longman concise Chinese-English dictionary* (Chan, 2007), commonly translate *xin* as heart; feeling; centre; intention; mind. From a philological perspective, *xin* is a morpheme, and it can be used to form numerous compounds. For example,
1. *xin zang* 心臟 (*xin* organ): 'heart organ.'
2. *xin si* 心思 (*xin* thoughts): 'thoughts; thinking'
3. *xin ling* 心靈 (*xin* spirit): 'soul.'
4. *xin xing* 心性 (*xin* nature): 'one's nature.'
5. *xin qing* 心情 (*xin* feeling): 'emotion.'
6. *dao de xin* 道德心 (morals *xin*): 'virtue, morality, ethic.'

The above compounds illustrate that *xin* can be linked to various human aspects, such as 'heart and feeling' (refer to 1 and 5); 'mind and thinking' (refer to 2); 'soul and spirit' (refer to 3); 'human inner nature' (refer to 4); and ethical qualities (refer to 6). In Zhang's (1993) book, titled "*Xin*", he outlines and explicates the historical transformations of *xin* from an Ancient China, Imperial China to the Contemporary Republic of China. He illustrates that the concept of *xin* bears strong Chinese historical and cultural salience. Following Zhang's (1993) precedent, Li et al. (2013) criticize a simple translation of *xin* as follows:

> In English, xin is often translated as 'heart' or 'mind'. This translation fails to transit the full meaning of the word that is deeply rooted in Chinese culture, thereby omitting or obscuring much of xin's significance in cultural knowledge. In academic scholarship, the over-simplified definition of xin can create difficulties in transmitting Chinese concepts that span many generations in various fields, such as traditional Chinese arts, sports, philosophy and medicine.
>
> (p.76)

They argue that the word, *xin,* is rooted in Chinese culture and it portrays some specific Chinese values, beliefs and idiosyncratic cultural essence. Therefore, they demystify *xin* and examine its meaning within the context of *qigong* (a Chinese health maintenance system and healing tradition). By using natural semantic metalanguage (NSM), they scrutinise *xin* based on the Chinese classical philosophies (mainly Confucian and the Daoist traditions) and Chinese medicine. Their analysis uncover that *xin* can be related to the eight dimensions: (1) *emotion*; (2) *physical heart*; (3) *mind*; (4) *virtue and vision*; (5) *ability to think and know*; (6) *concentration*; (7) *desire*; and (8) *a way of life and attitude* (pp. 77–78).

The findings in Chapter 4 reflect the concept of *xin* in which it plays a significant role in my informants' daily lives. They expressed '*kai xin gong zuo*' and '*xin zhong fu you*' are important to their lives. These two local expressions contain the Chinese word – *xin*. Therefore, the theoretical analysis below elucidates these two expressions in accordance with the distinctive contextual meaning(s) of *xin*.

(a) Kai Xin Gong Zuo (Happy Work)

As described in Section 4.2.3, *kai xin gong zuo* is important to the informants. This expression is made up of two terms: '*kai xin*' and '*gong zuo*'. Most dictionaries translate *kai xin* as happy, joyful and having fun; while *gong zuo* means works, jobs or tasks (Chen, 2001; Liang and Zheng, 2003; Chan, 2007). Here, *kai xin* is treated as an adjective to describe *gong zuo* (work). In Chinese, the compound *kai xin* is made of two morphemes, *kai* and *xin*. While *kai* can literally mean 'open', the meaning(s) of *xin* cannot be easily defined. From a philological perspective, *kai xin gong zuo* implies: When the individuals are able to open their *xin* at work, they would feel happy and joyful. Given the concept of *xin* can be associated with different human aspects (Li et al., 2013), its meanings are to be revealed layer by layer through the following interpretations.

How could the mainstream framework grasp the meaning of *xin*? In the mainstream perspective, the body, heart, mind and soul are four distinctive human elements:
1. The body represents physical being;
2. The heart is related to feelings and emotions;
3. The mind refers to the rational and intellectual aspect of a person (such as knowledge, critical thinking and logics)
4. The soul stands for human spirit.

According to the mainstream framework, these four aspects can be interrelated, but yet they are separated. Body and mind can exert influence over the heart (feeling and emotion) and soul (spirit) of a person. For example, based on Hedonism, one can obtain happiness from bodily pleasure; while according to Eudaimonia, one would feel spiritually satisfied due to intellectual growth and development. In this light, Hedonism might conceivably perceive *xin* as 'heart' while Eudaimonia could interpret *xin* as 'soul'. That means, Hedonism would look at *kai xin* as a feeling or an emotion which is directly equivalent to 'happiness'; whereas Eudaimonia would see *kai xin* as a 'spiritual fulfilment'.

i. For Interests, Affection, Satisfaction and Creativity
When did the informants open their *xin* in work? The informants felt *kai xin* (happy) when they were able to demonstrate interests, affection, satisfaction and creativity at work. Both Hedonism and Eudaimonia would probably perceive such *kai xin* as job satisfaction. In particular, this kind of job satisfaction is derived from interest, affection and creativity at work. In this case, Eudaimonia would categorise such *kai xin* as an intrinsic motivation. According to Maslow's (1943) hierarchy of needs, intrinsic motivation tends to fulfil one's esteem and self-actualization needs (the higher order of needs). Individuals would be motivated when they are capable of exercising autonomy and taking control (environment mastery) over their works. An individual's self-acceptance and personal growth are intrinsically related to any challenging jobs that are offered to them. Hence, *kai xin* could be due to an intrinsically motivated work.

How could Chinese construe such *kai xin* at work? Do Chinese think body, heart, mind and soul are distinguishable? Does *xin* imply either heart or mind or spirit? Chinese perceive that *shen* (body) and *xin* are connected. In Chinese, we call it *shen xin xiang lian* 身心相連 (literally means: body and *xin* are joined). That is to say, physical body and *xin* are interdependent and integrated to become a harmonious whole person. According to Confucian and Daoist thoughts, harmony between body and *xin* should always be maintained. In Chinese perspective, *xin* embodies heart, mind and soul. That means heart, mind and soul are not discrete. Instead, they are interchangeable, and they can all be represented by a single Chinese word – *xin*. Hence, *kai xin* can mean opening one's heart, mind and soul. On one hand, *kai xin* is attached to feeling or spiritual attainment, as it is interpreted by Hedonism and Eudaimonia respectively. On the other hand, *kai xin* can have more connotations if one uncovers its meanings based on Chinese philosophical traditions. How would Confucius look at *kai xin*? Given self is perceived as relational and interdependent in Confucian framework, *kai xin* would most likely be associated with the social nexus. The findings showed that the informants felt *kai xin* when they were able to work with their *peng you* (friends). Working with friends allows the informants to open up themselves (including their hearts, minds and spirits). In this case, *xin* can be referred as *xin xin* 信心 (belief *xin*) and *cheng xin* 誠心 (honest *xin*). *Xin xin* literally means 'trust; confidence; faith'; whereas *cheng xin* refers as 'sincerity'. From this perspective, working with *peng you* guarantee sincerity and confidence (*cheng xin*誠信) in the workplace. Since the informants were able to trust (*xin*信) their friends, they felt *kai xin* at work. In such viewpoint, *kai xin* can imply trust and sincerity in social intercourse.

In Confucian thinking, *kai xin* can also point towards intellectual inspiration. According to Confucian teaching, people can demonstrate interests, fondness, satisfaction and creativity during the intellectual intercourse with *peng you* (friends). In Chinese, *peng you* can be considered as *tong zhi* 同志 (people with the same mind). The informants felt *kai xin* because they were able to work with *tong zhi*, whose minds (such as interests, goals and thinking) are aligned with theirs. This represents an intellectual alignment. Confucius believes friendship can facilitate intellectual exchange on virtues. One may obtain *zhi* (wisdom) through friends. For instance, innovation and creativity can be stimulated in social discussion. The informants felt *kai xin* because they were allowed to interact intellectually with *peng you*. In that case, they were able to open up their minds and spirits by cultivating virtues at work. Hence, Confucian thinking emphasises on *dao de xin*道德心 (morals *xin*) 'virtue, morality, ethic'. Under this circumstance, *kai xin* is direct towards virtues and vision (Li et al., 2013).

What would Daoists say about *kai xin*? Daoists believes that *kai xin* arises when one lives in accordance to *dao* (the way of nature). In this view, *xin* can be referred as *xin xing* 心性 (*xin* nature; one's nature). That means, individuals are encouraged to open up their *xin* to nature and follow spontaneously with nature. This principle applies to work as well. Laozi treasures *zi ran* (nature) and believe *kai xin* comes spontaneously when one is working on what they innately like. The informants (e.g. Betty, Bonnie, Uncle Carl and Doris) felt *kai xin* at work because they were inherently interested in their jobs. Nevertheless, Daoists do not regard creativity as central to work. Daoist advocates to *wu wei* (non-assertive action) and perceives that innovation comes spontaneously. Individuals are not encouraged to invent sedulously. It seems that the informants took a different view. They thought *chuang zuo* 創作 (creativity) is important to their works. They seek for *chuang zuo kong jian* 創作空間 (room for creativity) and derive satisfaction from their *chung zuo* (creative works). To Daoists, these desires and behaviours might be considered as assertive.

ii. Work Hard to Bear Hardship

The subject demonstrated a strong willingness to bear *xin ku* (hardship) at work. They strived to make their businesses survive in the market. Why did they accept and allow any torments at work? Could the mainstream perspective of well-being understand such work practice? It seems that Hedonism might not understand such assiduous attitude and behaviour. Hedonic approach targets on maximising human pleasure and minimising pain. It tries to seek for happiness and avoid any discomfort. In such perspective, Hedonism might not appreciate the informants' willingness to bear hardship, because it interprets toils as a kind of suffering which would lower one's subjective well-being. For Eudaimonia, it assumes humans live for contentment, and therefore they seek for personal growth. It prompts individuals to actualise their potentials actively and take control over their works. The informants did not take an aggressive approach to work. Instead of acquiring a complete mastery on work, the informants abide any travails. To Eudaimonia, their work style might be interpreted as passive and might possibly lower one's psychological well-being. Hence, Eudaimonia might not apprehend why the subject's accepted the pain at work.

It seems that the mainstream perspective of well-being is unable to justify the subject's perseverance. What would Confucians and Daoist say to enlighten one's understanding on the subject? In Chinese, there is a saying: "*chi de ku zhong ku, fang wei ren shang ren*" 吃得苦中苦,方為人上人 (If you wish to be the best man, you must suffer the bitterest of the bitter). This indicates that Chinese see sufferings as live experiences which would train a person to become stronger and better. In Confucian teaching, it tends to agree with the above Chinese saying because Confucius emphasises on self-cultivation of *de* (virtues). Confucians perceive that hardship would facilitate one's development. Mencius highlights that a person needs to first experience suffering before he/she can be assigned to any great mission (*The Work of Mencius: Kao Tsz II*, 15(2), in Legge, 1949, p.447). In that case, suffering "*stimulates his mind, hardens his nature and supplies his incompleteness*". In other words, suffering can stimulate one's mind, strengthen one's inherent quality and overcome one's weaknesses. That means suffering can build up one's *nai xin* 耐心 (enduring *xin*). *Nai xin* means 'patience' and 'endurance'. Hence, Confucian teaching treats suffering as an exercise for developing the virtue of endurance. In this perspective, Confucians would probably recognise the subject's devotion to bear any hardship at work because such experience would enable individuals to become better and stronger in the future. Hence, their tolerance is an embodiment of *nai xin* (endurance). They are trained up to become more patient and wait for a better life in the future.

How would Daoist look at *xin ku*? Daoist think *yin* and *yang* do not exist in pure form. Instead, the equilibrium between them should always be maintained. Such harmony is necessary along the natural order of things. Correspondingly, although *kai xin* (happiness) and *xin ku* (hardship) are opposite, they need to be on an equal footing. Daoist perceive *xin ku* arises in order to be in harmony with *kai xin*. In other words, *xin ku* occurs because of the existence of *kai xin*. Individuals have to strike a balance between *kai xin* (*yang*) and *xin ku* (*yin*). That was why the subject accepted *xin ku* and worked hard to bear *xin ku*. To Daoist, patience to *xin ku* represents compliance to the pattern of the world, so that a sense of balance between *kai xin* and *xin ku* is preserved.

A summary of explaining *kai xin gong zuo* is provided (see Appendix D: Tab. D1). Connections among the four perspectives are shown (see Fig. 5.3). Confucians interpret *kai xin* as open *xin* (mind) – People would be able to open up their minds for intellectual inspiration if they are able to work with their *peng you* (friends). Daoists explain that when individuals are able to work on what they innately like, they would feel *kai xin* (happy). Both Hedonism and Eudaimonia treat *kai xin gong zuo* as job satisfaction. Eudaimonia would even regard such satisfaction is derived from intrinsic motivation, in which individual growth need is being fulfilled. However, the mainstream is unable to understand why locals are willing to bear hardship in work. Hence, Confucian and the Daoist frameworks are brought in to explain such phenomenon. Confucians highlight that endurance is one important work ethic. Difficulties in work can train individuals to become patient and better at finishing their tasks. Both Confucians and Daoists uphold harmony, appreciating hardship at work because a balance between *kai xin* (happiness) and *xin ku* (hardship) is to be preserved.

(b) Xin zhong fu you (Being rich at heart-mind)

The findings indicate that some of the informants (particularly the youth) look for *xin zhong fu you* 心中富有. This term consists of two phrases: *xin zhong* and *fu you*. *Xin zhong* can be referred as 'inside the heart-mind'; while *fu you* means 'richness'; 'abundance' and 'wealthy'. Hence, *xin zhong fu you* can be literally defined as 'being rich at heart-mind'. The local youth seeks for 'being rich at heart-mind'. How might the mainstream perspective understand this value? According to the mainstream framework, it might mostly interpret richness in heart-mind as happiness (in Hedonism) and spiritual contentment (in Eudaimonia). Happiness is the presence of positive mood; while *eu* and *demonia* in Greek mean good and spirit respectively. Both happiness and Eudaimonia direct towards emotional and spiritual aspects of an individual. That means *xin zhong fu you* could mean richness in feeling (excitement) in Hedonism; whereas it would mean spiritual fulfilment in Eudaimonia.

The data highlights that some of the local youth seek for being rich at heart-mind through demanding for a real universal suffrage and participating in social

5.1 Demystifying Chinese Notions — 127

Similarities and Differences:
(1) **Sensation:** Job satisfaction
(2) **Growth need:** Intrinsic motivation
(3) **Ethics:**
   3a: Role obligation (xin) and intellectual inspiration on virtues among pengyou (friends)
   3b: Endurance
   3c: Affection to jun zi (virtuous person)
(4) **Harmony:** Balance between *kai xin* (happiness) and *xin ku* (hardship)
(5) **Spontaneity:** Work on what one innately likes

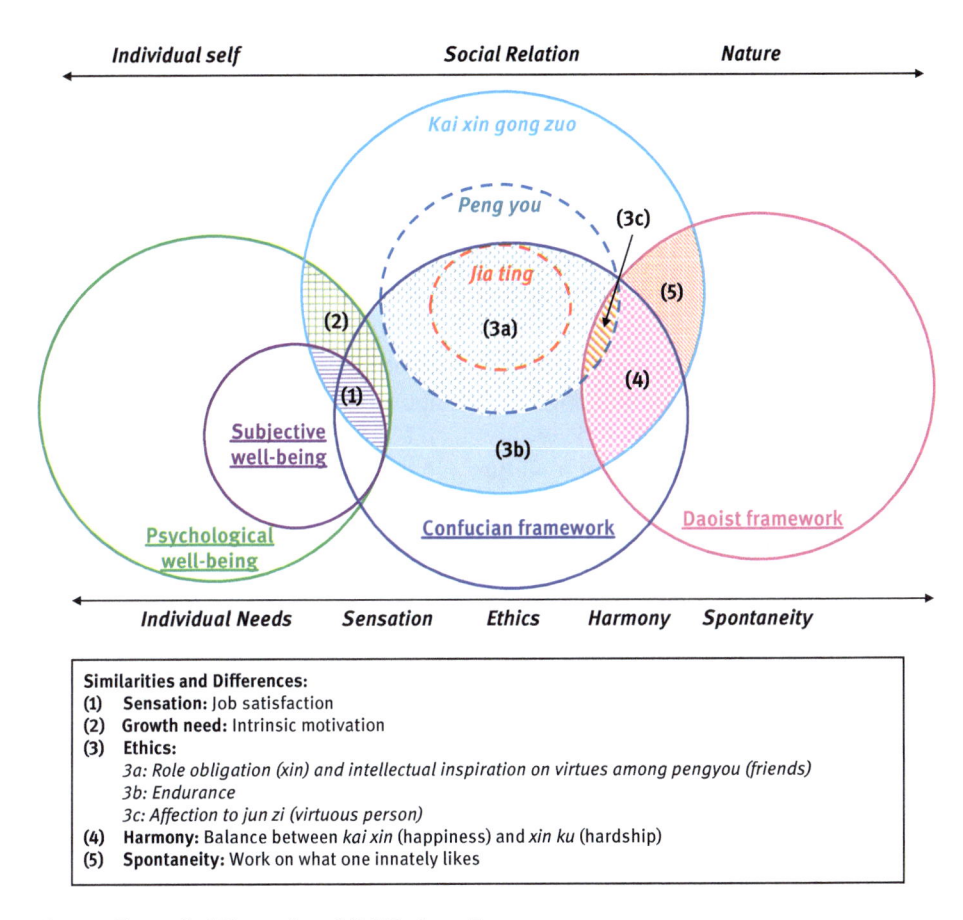

Fig. 5.3: Theoretical Discussion of *Kai Xin Gong Zuo*.

protests. How could one understand these requests and actions through the mainstream framework? It seems that Hedonic approach to well-being might not support any participation in social protests if they would result in pain and disappointment. On the other hand, Eudaimonia understands why individuals could participate in social protests. Aristotle (1985) perceives that well-being is constituted by being morally good. Therefore, individuals should try to uphold their moral standard in lives. That was why some locals would fight for justice through social protests. Some locals demand the voting right for electing their own Chief Executive, so that they can have a certain degree of democracy over the public governance. Eudaimonia considers their request will probably increase their psychological well-being because they were asking for autonomy and environment mastery.

Nonetheless, does Chinese view *xin zhong fu you* the same as the mainstream? As mentioned, *xin* can mean much more than simply heart and spirit. *Xin* can include heart, mind and soul. That means *xin zhong fu you* can imply an abundance in emotions, knowledge (mind) and spirit (soul). Again, the meaning(s) of *xin* can be further contextualised based on Chinese philosophical traditions. For instance, what would Confucius say about *xin*? In Confucian teaching, *xin* is particularly linked with *dao de* 道德 (virtues). In this perspective, *xin zhong fu you* is referred to the richness in virtues. Confucius focuses on four main virtues, which are *ren* (benevolence), *yi* (appropriateness), *li* (ritual propriety), *zhi* (acting wisely). In particular, *ren* is the most important virtue among all. Hence, Confucius would likely interpret *xin* as *ren xin* 仁心 (benevolent *xin*) – 'benevolence'. Given Confucius values *ren xin* (benevolence), how could one promote *ren xin* in the world? He contends for *Wei zheng yi de* 為政以德 (government by means of virtues), especially on *ren zheng* 仁政 (government by benevolence and humanity). He considers that "to establish a righteous government, the ruler and his minsters must act according to what was established in ancient rites because what made a government good was the power of moral virtues rather than the power of cruel and punitive laws. Moral virtues could produce trust and faith in the people, while punitive measures might stop wrongdoing only for a moment" (Yao, 2000, p. 22). Given that Confucian teaching stresses on *wei zheng yi dei*, it is reasonable for the locals to demand a government or a leader to possess an appropriate degree of virtues. Ling and Shih (1998) critically examine the application of the Confucian tradition in a postcolonial context. They highlight that governance is developed in accordance with the Confucian approach to leadership, advocating to *Minben Zhengzhi* 民本政治 ("People-Based Government") – "*The prince (jun) achieves lordly power only through the consent (tong yi) of the people (renmin)*" (p. 61). In the light of such governance, it seems that Confucians would possibly accept the local demands for true universal suffrage, if it is a means to demonstrate public consent and trust on virtuous leadership. The true universal suffrage can be seen as a mechanism to reflect and retrieve public consensus on selecting a virtuous leader.

How about Daoist view? Daoists view 'self' as part of nature, probably relating *xin* with nature – *xin xing* 心性 (*xin* nature) 'one's nature'. That means the people would feel *xin zhong fu you* (richness in heart-mind) when they live in accordance with the way of nature (*dao*). There is a Chinese compound, *xin dao* 心道 (*xin* the way) – which indicates *xin* as the way of life (Li et al., 2013). Laozi believes everything comes from the same origin – *dao*. Therefore, all things (including human beings) are on equal footing and should be weighted in the same way. In this light, Daoist may consider that it is reasonable for the local to ask for a true universal suffrage because each individual should be treated as the same and everyone is deserved to have identical voting rights. Nonetheless, Daoists encourage one to attain *dao* (the way of nature) by preserving *zi ran* (nature, spontaneity). That means, though each individual is deserved to be treated equally, such human rights should be given spontaneously and non-assertively (*wu wei*). Therefore, in this view Daoists may not support any social protests because demonstrations and movements are considered as assertive and intentional activities that may jeopardise the harmony of nature. Daoist would prefer individuals to defer their responses and follow the natural progress of universal suffrage (*pu xuan*). That was why some informants (e.g. Mrs. Cindy and Uncle Carl) would be willing to pocket (accept) the 831 decision first and not agree with the protesters. The Umbrella movement was blamed since it led to a social cleavage that has destroyed the harmony of the society.

A summary of the discussion on *xin zhong fu you* (see Appendix D: Tab. D1) compares and contrasts the views from the four frameworks (see Fig. 5.4). Hedonism interprets *xin zhong fu you* as positive mood (happiness); while Eudaimonia regards it as spiritual contentment, which is derived from fighting for democracy and righteousness in the society. The Confucians would refer *xin* as *ren xin* (benevolence) and explains *xin zhong fu you* as the demand for *wei zheng yi de* (governance by means of virtues) and collective welfare. However, in Daoist thinking, democracy should be obtained spontaneously and harmony in the society should always be preserved. That is why Daoists would not support any social protests that aim at universal suffrage.

5.2 Theoretical Dialogues

Up to this point, the findings is first interpreted through the mainstream framework of well-being (mainly Hedonism and Eudaimonia) and then through the Chinese perspectives (mainly the Confucian and the Daoist frameworks). Section 5.1 still represents a monologue from each perspective. How could one bring different perspectives together and engage them for a dialogue? Cheung (2011) took an experiment of theoretical dialogues in her study of the Chinese employees. She brought both western and Chinese conceptual frameworks of self into analysis and engaged them in conversations. She specified the following advantages of using such theoretical dialogues:

> By engaging them in dialogue, one may be able to see what the common focal points of interest and shared concerns are, what is absent in one which is found in the other, and what is crucial to one but less important to the other.

This section will adopt Cheung's (2011) idea of theoretical dialogues. Each perspective (including Hedonic, Eudemonic, and the Confucian and the Daoist frameworks) would initiate a dialogue. Each dialogue begins by highlighting the crucial ideas and concerns of life from a particular framework. Then, space will be provided for other perspectives to speak back as an equal partner, and response to any focal points of interest that is being raised. A total of four dialogues are created: (1) A dialogue on sensation and desires, which is initiated by Hedonism; (2) A dialogue on individual needs, which is started by Eudaimonia; (3) A dialogue on relation, ethics

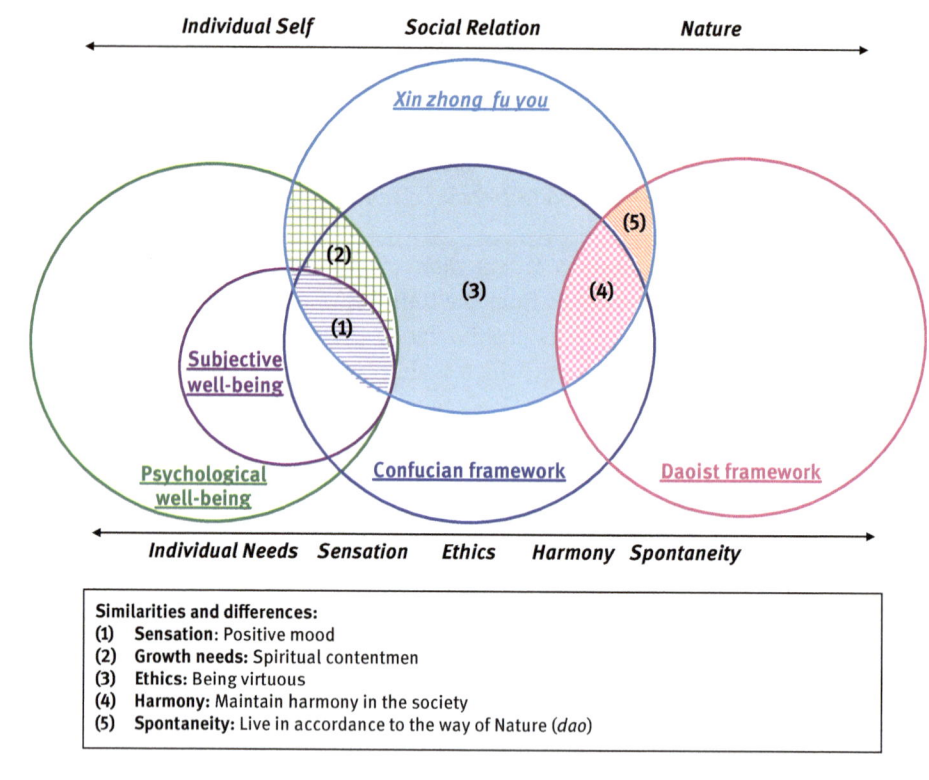

Figure: Venn diagram showing Individual Self, Social Relation, Nature axes, with circles for Psychological well-being, Subjective well-being, Confucian framework, and Daoist framework. Bottom axis: Individual Needs, Sensation, Ethics, Harmony, Spontaneity. Central region labeled *Xin zhong fu you*.

Similarities and differences:
(1) **Sensation**: Positive mood
(2) **Growth needs**: Spiritual contentmen
(3) **Ethics**: Being virtuous
(4) **Harmony**: Maintain harmony in the society
(5) **Spontaneity**: Live in accordance to the way of Nature (*dao*)

Fig. 5.4: Theoretical Discussion of *Xin Zhong Fu You*.

and harmony, which is begun by Confucians and (4) A dialogue on nature, *yin* and *yang* and spontaneity, which is opened up by Daoist. At last, based on the dialogues being made, the four frameworks are put together into Fig. 5.5 to illustrate their interpretations on the notion of *xin* and highlight the similarities and differences among the four perspectives.

5.2.1 Sensation and Desires

Hedonism is the first philosophical perspective discussed in Chapter 1. Hedonism assumes self as an individual and human organism is initially empty. Its core interest is to seek for happiness and pleasure, so as to fill up such emptiness. That is why in the previous section, it interprets *xing fu jia ting* as happiness from a family and pleasure from healthiness; *peng you* as happiness from friendship; *kai xin gong zuo* as happy work and *xin zhong fu you* as positive mood. Hedonism highlights that *xin* as 'heart' and links *xin* as a site for all *xin qing* 心情 (*xin* feeling) – feelings and emotions (Li et al., 2013). According to Hedonism, personal sensation is the only

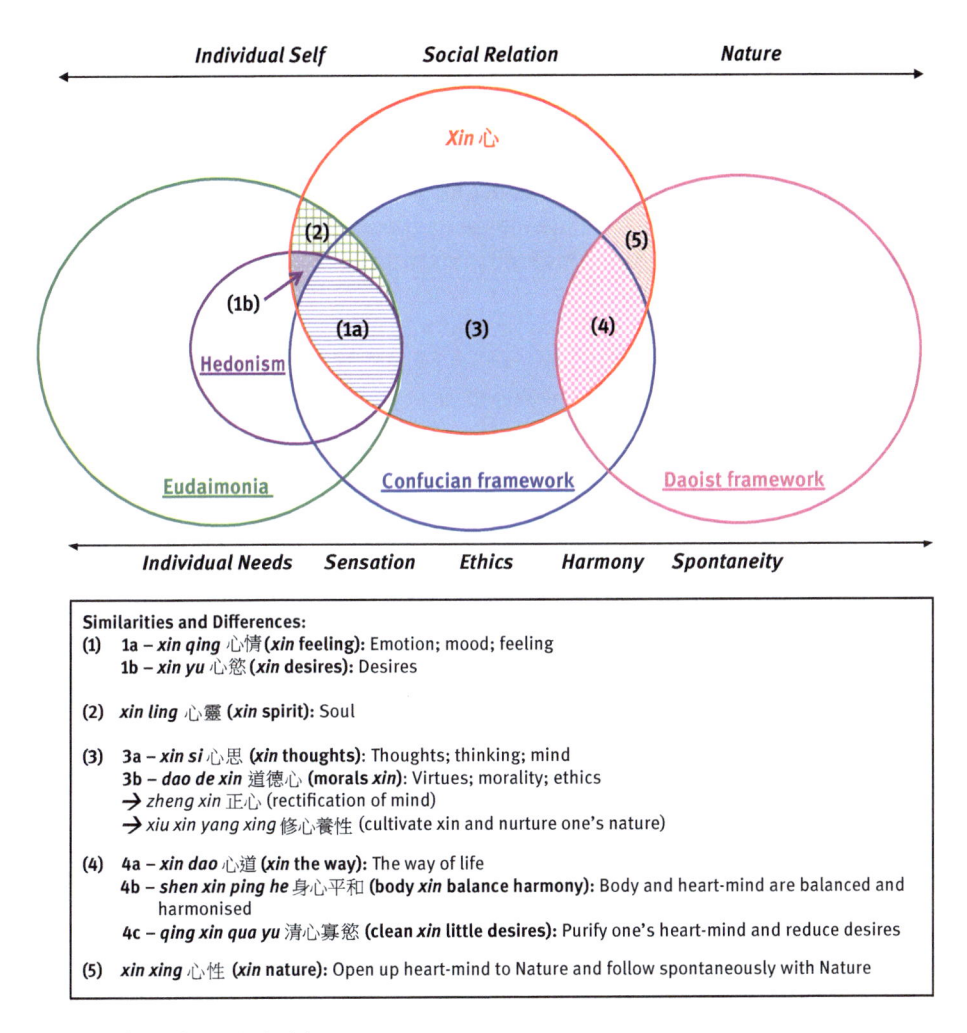

Fig. 5.5: *Xin*: A Theoretical Dialogue.

major concern of life. Hedonism believes that fulfilling personal desires is important to life. In that perspective, *xin* is correlated to the Chinese word – *yu* 慾 (desires). Li et al. (2013) highlights that:

> The concept of xin also can be illustrated by Chinese character: xin 心 is a radical in the lower part of the word 'desire慾', which has 'want 欲' on the top of the 'xin 心' implies that desires arise from the Heart. (p.84)

They explained that "*xin* is the origin of desire" (p.84). Hedonism targets on satisfying personal desires in order to gain happiness and pleasure. Among the four frameworks, Hedonism is the least sufficient for understanding the local expressions.

How would Eudaimonia respond to the Hedonic view of life? Eudaimonia would agree with Hedonism's notion of self, because both of them believes in individual self; whereas others are less important. Therefore, Eudaimonia would recognise the human need for positive sensation and desires. However, Eudaimonia perceives humans have their own potentials, and hence they are not initially vacant. It believes that humans should realise their potentials, rather than being slavish adherents of happiness and pleasure. In that case, Eudaimonia perceives that life should be more than happiness.

What about Chinese perspective on Hedonic happiness? According to *wu lun* (five cardinal relations), Confucian emphasises on social relations and collective welfare. Hence, Confucius would mostly understand the Hedonic view – one could be able to get happiness from family and friendship. Nevertheless, Confucius would reject any egoist happiness. Confucian teaching identifies self within the social nexus (Chang and Holt, 1996). It sees self as relational, rather than an individual. In Confucian education, the worth and acceptability of self are dependent on one's appropriateness of social behaviours (*yi*). In that case, Confucius would possibly discourage the pursuit of personal joy (sensation), because he believes that private desires would lead to egoism and selfishness. He sees *si xin* 私心 (selfish *xin*) 'selfishness' as a bad and unethical (Li et al., 2013). He would recommend people to self-cultivate themselves to become *jun zi* (virtuous persons). *Jun zi* pursues *yi* (appropriateness) and does not seek for self-indulgence (Cheung, 2011).

Does Laozi agree with Hedonism? He holds an opposing view of self against Hedonism and Eudaimonia. He perceives self as part of nature (*dao*), because everything comes from *dao*. "He advocates *wuwo* (no self, no I)" (Cheung, 2011, p. 205). That means, Daoists require people to *wang wo* 忘我 – "forgetting of one's own life/self" (Villaver, 2007, p. 2). Hence, Daoists do not agree with individualism in Hedonism and Eudaimonia. Laozi would likely oppose the Hedonic vision that people should focus on sensation – happiness and pleasure, because he believes that excessive desires would violate the pattern of nature (*zi ran*) and lead to a chaotic life (Cheung, 2010). On the contrary, Laozi encourages *wu wei* – individual should get rid of their own desires. He suggests people be *qing xin gua yu* 清心寡慾 (purify one's *xin* and reduce desires). That means, one should live with simplicity and tranquillity. Laozi ascertains that people can be truly happy, if they are able to contain excessive desires, accept what has been offered to them and live in accordance with the way of nature.

5.2.2 Human Needs

Eudaimonia is another western philosophical perspective which is discussed in Chapter 1. Similar to Hedonism, Eudaimonia builds on individualism which presumes self as autonomous and independent. In this perspective, individuals' life goals are based on their own preference and needs. Maslow (1943) organises human needs in a hierarchical order, starting from physical to psychological and spiritual (see Appendix A: Fig. A1). Alderfer (1969) further develop ERG theory, which classifies human needs into existence, relatedness and growth. Relationships such as *xing fu jia ting* (good family) and *peng you* (friendship), are regarded as social needs. Eudaimonia believes building a complete family can be a life purpose among the locals and such an intention is originated from one's demand for affiliation. In this case, others are positioned as instrumental – a channel for satisfying social needs. Self-actualization is the life goal in Eudaimonia. Therefore, all the six aspects of psychological well-being (autonomy, environmental mastery, life purpose, personal growth, self-acceptance and positive relatedness) are all directed towards self-actualisation. In Eudemonic approach to life, self-interest is the critical centre of concern.

Although positive belongings are important to life, Eudaimonia never perceives social desire as the most essential. Henceforth, Eudemonic framework fails to explain why locals see family and friendship as the fundamental elements of their livings. Eudaimonia would rather encourage people to realize their potentials and fulfil their growth needs. According to Fredrick Herzberg's (1959) two-factor theory, people would derive satisfaction from motivators – the intrinsic factors of the job itself (Herzberg et al., 1967). For example, personal advancement, achievement, recognition or growth. Eudaimonia views *kai xin gong zuo* as job satisfaction, which is mainly derived from the intrinsic motivation. In particular, Eudaimonia interprets autonomy, environmental mastery and personal growth as predominantly important to human lives. For instance, Eudaimonia recognises that the locals need for self-control, freedom and advancement on health, as well as work and society. In addition, Eudaimonia would mostly perceive *xin* as 'heart' (feelings) or/and 'soul' (spirit). Given that Eudaimonia is defined as 'good spirit', it would probably link *xin* with mental and spiritual fulfilment. This explains why Maslow (1969) later added 'self-transcendence' as the highest level of need beyond 'self-actualization'. According to Maslow (1993),

> Transcendence refers to the very highest and most inclusive or holistic levels of human consciousness, behaving and relating, as ends rather than as means, to oneself, to significant others, to human beings in general, to other species, to nature, and to the cosmos. (Holism in the sense of hierarchical integration is assumed; so also is cognitive and value isomorphism.).
> (p.66)

Maslow has included numerous explanations in the writing, *"Various meanings of transcendence"*, such as transcendence in the sense of loss of self-consciousness, self-awareness, self-forgetfulness; being intrinsic to the *Self* itself; time; culture; one' past; ego self and selfishness; mystical experiences; death, pain, sickness and evil; acceptance to the natural world; negatives and space etc. (p.56–65). Koltko-Rivera (2006) interprets Maslow's meaning of transcendence as to "seek to further a cause beyond the self and to experience a communication beyond the boundaries of the self through peak experience" (p.303). Koltko-Rivera further explains peak experience as "amalgamation of mystical experiences and certain experience with nature, aesthetic experiences, sexual experiences, and/or other transpersonal experiences, in which the person experiences a sense of identity that transcends and extends beyond the personal self" (p.303). Gomez and Fisherself (2005) classify transcendence as part of the spiritual well-being and is regarded as a spiritual attainment – the highest level of human needs in Eudaimonia. Is that really what Chinese demand for life? How could other frameworks respond to Eudemonic interpretation?

Although Hedonism would agree with Eudaimonia that life should focus on the individual self, Hedonism does not focus on individual needs. Hedonism concerns more on sensation (i.e. the ends rather than the means). In other words, as long as individuals are able to obtain happiness and pleasure in lives, the ways on fulfilling desires are not the focus of the discussion. Hence, Hedonism pays less attention to factors that are contributing to growth and development of self, such as self-sufficiency, self-mastery and self-development. Hedonism regards that all individual needs are simply human desires in lives. Thus, it is neither necessary to differentiate needs into orders nor classify motivation into intrinsic or extrinsic, so long as they all help to gain happiness in lives. Hedonism considers happiness is the life target/the end state. In other words, in Hedonic perspective, there are no differentiations between happiness and transcendence.

How would Confucius respond to the Eudemonic focus on individual needs? Confucius would most likely agree with Eudaimonia that humans have different kinds of needs, ranging from existence, relatedness to growth. In particular, Confucius would recognise the importance of social and developmental needs. He realizes the significance of *wu lun* (five cardinal relations) in one's life. His disciple, Mencius, has emphasised the needs for building up positive relations among *wu lun*:

> between father and son, there should be affection; between sovereign and minister, righteousness; between husband and wife, attention to their separate functions; between old and young, a proper order; and between friends, fidelity.
>
> (Mencius: Teng Wen Gong I, 4; in Legge, 1985)

Confucius would also agree that individuals should constantly learn and cultivate themselves. That is why he insists:

> Is it not pleasant to learn with a constant perseverance and application?
> (Analects: Xue Er: 1; in Legge, 1949, p.137)

Although Confucian teaching focuses on relations and self-cultivation, its purposes and directions for love and learning are different from Eudemonic approach. While Eudaimonia regards self-fulfilment as the prime intention for any relationships and growth, Confucius defines self-based on one's concern for other human beings. Unlike Eudaimonia, Confucius never treats others as instrumental. In Confucian education, others become the major concerns in social connection and ethical training.

Instead of putting self as the centre, Confucius establishes self within the social nexus. That means, our relations with others become part of ourselves. That is why much of the Confucian teaching covers how one should cultivate virtues in his or her interactions with others. The Five Constant Virtues (*ren, yi, li, zhi* and *xin*) in the Confucian thinking are associated with social relations (Cheung, 2010). The content of Confucian self-cultivation is mainly focus on ethics. Confucian thinking and its education aims to develop an individual to become *jun zi* (virtuous person), who acts as a moral agent to manifest virtues (*de*). *Jun zi* plays his or her appropriate role in the social intercourse with others. Therefore, in Confucian framework, 'others' are critical to the formation of self and one's life.

How would Confucians react to Eudemonic demand for autonomy and control? In Cheung's (2010) theoretical dialogue on self, she highlights that Confucians would probably oppose self-autonomy if it is being placed above other people. Confucians regard any individuals who uphold self-interest higher than others as *xiao ren* (a mean-spirit person). On the contrary, *jun zi* (virtuous person) is able to get rid of his or her own selfishness (*si xin*) and place others or public interest into priority. Instead of going for self-determining freedom, Confucian teaching suggests people be bound by virtues and follow *li* (ritual property). Only when *de* (virtues) are deeply rooted in an individual *xin* (heart-mind), he or she would enjoy autonomy by acting according to the heart-mind without violating any virtues (Liu, 2004). In that case, Confucians take self-autonomy and control as "an ethical achievement" (Cheung, 2010, p.218), rather than self-preference (Wong, 2004).

How would Daoist reply? Would Daoists recognise Eudemonic approach to life? Daoists teaching does not explicitly discuss individual needs. However, Daoist would most likely condemn Eudemonic approach to life as overly egoistic and assertive. Daoist target on living up the way of *dao* (the way of nature) and advice individuals to get rid of their own selves. They encourage people to follow the natural rhythms of lives. Therefore, rather than focusing on the individual needs for positive affiliation, growth and development, Daoists pay attention to the pattern of nature. Although the Daoists do not restrict any individuals from nurturing themselves, they encourage development to be taken spontaneously without sedulity and assiduity. In this case, Daoist would probably regard Eudemonic self-actualization as overly deliberate, because any aggressive self-determination for growth could violate the way of nature. Daoists therefore, respect the individual autonomy to live in accordance with the way of nature. It believes freedom and control are given to allow one to live in harmony with nature, rather than persevering self-interest and personal goals.

What about the notion of 'transcendence"? Is there such a concept in Chinese culture? Transcendence is always brought to interpret the Chinese culture, such as using altruism as transcendence of self (beyond the personal self) to interpret Confucian virtue of *ren*; taking Daoist view on *dao* and *zi ran* as transcendence of time and space – the mystical and cosmological experience (Gomez and Fisherself, 2005; Hall et al., 1998; Koltko-Rivera. 2006). Nevertheless, in the book, *"Thinking from the*

Han: Self, truth, and transcendence in Chinese and Western culture" written by Hall et al. (1998), they illustrate that the concept of transcendence is absent in the Chinese community. He argues:

> there is no effective appeal to transcendence in the mainstream Chinese tradition, neither as a means of shoring up one's spiritual sensibilities nor of stabilizing the character of one's social relationships. (p.253)

Confucian cultivation of *ren* is different from altruism, because "altruism entails self-abnegation"; whereas the cultivation of *ren* entails "the full self-other relationship" (p.259). Altruism presumes there is a need to reduce individual self by overcoming any selfishness and ego. On the contrary, Confucian virtues of *ren* do not require any deduction of self. They insist that:

> Ren describes a cultivated and mutually beneficial relationship between self and other, and it references a complementary grounded in the specific conditions of one's cultivated relationship with another person. The cultivation of ren is thus irreducibly other-entailing. (pp.258–259)

Unlike altruism that requires individuals to lose their sense of selves, *ren* could contribute to personal realization of self and bring in communal harmony. In addition, Hall et al. (1998) elucidated that Daoist concepts of *dao* and *zi ran* bear no transcendent status or pattern. Transcendence could be referred as going beyond either time or space (Maslow, 1969), which indicates that western metaphysical tradition sees the cosmos as a single-ordered form, which separates space with time – assuming that the world is a single space; and "time is duration while space is extension" (Hall et al., 1998, p. 250). That is to say, western philosophy assumes that: (1) the world is a single space, (2) things in the world (including time and space) are fixed and limited in nature and (3) anything happens outside such nature is regarded as supernatural. However, Hall et al. (1998) clarify that Daoist notion of *dao* is not made "in the sense of a single-ordered cosmos", but rather in the sense of *wan you* 萬有 (all things). *Dao* is the "process of the world itself" (Hall et al., 1998, p. 245) since *dao* produces all things (*Dao De Jing*, 42; in Legge, 1891). In other words, *dao* represents 'non-being', which is nameless, formless and even timeless. The Chinese compound, *shi jie* 世界 (literally means the boundary of generations), highlights that rather than separating space with time, Chinese would regard place is time (Hall et al., 1998). That is why *dao* is not equivalent to the western idea of cosmos. In Daoist tradition, *zi ran* (nature, spontaneity) is the way to preserve *dao*. *Zi ran* is translated as 'nature', which means everything should be attained in their 'natural state' (Lai, 2007). In other words, *zi ran* is to follow along with the nature, instead of going beyond nature. In Daoist perspective, *zi ran* should never be seen as supernatural. Hence, *dao* and *zi ran* are never the same as transcendence of time and space – the mystical and cosmological experience. There is no such a notion of transcendence in Chinese culture. Hall et al. (1998) condemn "the causal or improper use of the concept of transcendence to articulate the Chinese sensibility" (p.190). Hall et al. criticises that the scholars often used the term – transcendence, to refer to anything that could not be explained and were classified under the Aristotelian categories. Their critique is therefore in line with the postcolonial argument against "essentialism".

5.2.3 Human Relations

The next dialogues would be initiated by the Chinese philosophical frameworks: Confucianism and Daoism. This is a space where Chinese are able to "speak back", with an equal footing to the mainstream frameworks: Hedonism and Eudaimonia. Confucian tradition is the first Chinese philosophical framework discussed in Chapter 1. Therefore, the coming dialogue will be led by Confucians.

Among the four philosophical frameworks mentioned, Confucian framework is regarded as the most relevant perspective that helps to generate an understanding of the local lives. Confucian framework is highly significant to the locals, because Confucian thinking portrays most Chinese value on social relations, particularly on *jia ting* (family) and *peng you* (friends: an extended family). For illustration, *wu lun* (five cardinal relations) is central to Confucian teaching. Among *wu lun*, three of the relations are governed by a family. In this light, Confucius assumes self is placed within social nexus, particularly in the family. That means the self is formulated only in the social network and interactions with others. Individuals would define themselves based on their relationships with other people. That is why they emphasise on how they speak and treat with others. Hence, Confucians perceive self as relational and interdependence.

As Confucius positions self as interpersonal, he teaches people to maintain a harmonious relationship with others. He sets a key life goal for humans – Living in harmony with other people. In Confucian teaching, this target means living in accordance to *dao* (the way of Heaven). Under this context, *xin* would be connected to *xin dao* 心道 (*xin* the way) – which indicates *xin* as the way of life (Li et al., 2013). Confucius believes *tian* (the Heaven) creates everything and therefore humans should live in line with *tian dao* (the way of Heaven). How could one live with *tian dao*? In Confucian framework, one could live with *dao* by manifesting *de* (virtues). If an individual who is able to act and live according to *dao*, he/she is regarded as a sage (an ideal moral agent). That is why Confucian teaching focuses on ethics (*de*). The Five Constant Virtues in Confucian teaching are: *ren* (benevolence); *yi* (appropriateness); *li* (ritual propriety), *zhi* (wisdom) and *xin* (trustworthiness). These five virtues direct and govern individual attitude and behaviours with others. They are the principles and ways for guiding individuals to live harmoniously with others. That is why Confucius accentuates *xin* to *dao de* 道德 (virtues and ethics). He teaches people the way to *xiu xin yang xing* 修心養性 (cultivate *xin* and nurture one's nature). That means, people is encouraged to cultivate virtues and nurture the virtuous nature of humankind. Hence, cultivating and demonstrating virtues in lives (work) is an important life goal in Confucian teaching.

Ethics and social relations are two fundamental elements in Confucian thinking, and they are closely connected. The Confucian education suggests three main life objectives: (1) *ming de* 明明德 (Illustrate illustrious virtue); (2) *qin min* 親民 (Renovate the people); and (3) *zhi shan* 至善 (The highest excellence). In Chinese, they are called *san gang ling* 三綱領. These three objectives are stated in *The Great Learning* – one of the "Four Books" in Confucian teaching:

> What the Great Learning teaches, is to illustrate illustrious virtue; to renovate the people, and to rest in the highest excellence. (Liji: Da Xue: 2; in Legge, 1985)

These three objectives help to develop individuals to become virtuous both internally and externally. In Chinese, we use the term, *nei sheng wai wang* 內聖外王. *Nei sheng* 內聖 refers to a self-cultivation of virtues within an inner self (i.e. an ethical self); whereas *wai wang* 外王 is a demonstration of virtues in the outer world (i.e. social ethics). In other words, the first objective, *ming de* 明明德 (illustrate illustrious virtue) is for the cultivation of ethical self (*nei sheng* 內聖); while the second objective, *qin min* 親民 (renovate the people) is for extension of ethical self to the outer world (*wai wang* 外王). To achieve *nei sheng wai wang*, *The Great Learning* further proposes eights steps. These eight steps include: (1) *ge wu* 格物 (investigation of things); (2) *zhi* 致知 (extension of knowledge); (3) *cheng yi* 誠意 (sincere in thoughts); (4) *zheng xin* 正心 (rectification of mind); (5) *xiu shen* 修身 (cultivation of person); (6) *qi jia* 齊家 (regulate family); (7) *zhi guo* 治國 (order states); (8) *ping tian xia* 平天下 (maintain harmony in the world). The Chinese called the above eights steps as *ba mu* 八目. The first five steps are related to the cultivation of a person; while the last three steps are associated with social relations. It states that individuals can cultivate themselves by investigating on things, extending their knowledge, being sincere in thoughts and rectifying their *xin*. Mencius specifies the role of *xin*:

> To the mind belongs the office of thinking. By thinking, it gets the right view of things; by neglecting to think, it fails to do this. (Mengzi: Gaozi I: 15; in Legge, 1985)

Here, *xin* is referred as 'the mind'. *Xin* is the mind (the office of thinking). Mencius stresses on using mind to think in order to get the right view of things. Then, what is the meaning of *zheng xin* 正心 (rectification of mind)? *Zheng xin* (rectification of mind) means to correct one's mind by removing any negative thoughts and unethical intentions, such as desire, terror, a personal favour, sorrow and distress etc. (*Liji: Da Xue*: 9; in Legge, 1985*)*. Rectification of mind is the prerequisite of personal cultivation (*xiu shen* 修身). After the individuals have cultivated themselves, the next three stages emphasise on constructing social relations. It is deemed to be constructed through regulating families, ordering states and maintaining harmony in the world. By following these eight steps, one could initially cultivate and illustrate virtues (*ming ming de* 明明德) within a person and then demonstrate and extend the virtues along the social nexus in order to renovate others (*qin min* 親民). Ethics are brought from inner self to various social relations (outer world) under this manner. The ultimate accomplishment of an individual is to achieve the highest excellence (*zhi shan* 至善), in both personal and social ethics (see Appendix A: Fig. A2).

How could one achieve the highest excellence (*zhi shan* 至善) in life? In Confucian teaching, harmony is the way to achieve the highest excellence. Harmony in Chinese is *he* (和). *He* implies the means. *He* (harmony) is a core concept in Confucian framework, particularly in the *Doctrine of the Mean*. In this doctrine, *zhong yong* 中庸 ("equilibrium" – being balanced and upright") is the way to achieve harmony (in Li, 2008, p.425). Harmony should be maintained between *shen* (body) and *xin*. In that case, *xin* is related to *shen xin ping he* 身心平和 (body and *xin* are balanced and harmonised). Furthermore, harmony is extended to the relations with others. That means, one should always maintain harmonious social relationships. Confucius regards:

> Perfect is the virtue which is according to the Constant Mean.
> (Analects: Yung Ye, 27; in Legge, 1949, p.194)

The above indicates the importance of acting according to the mean in our daily lives (Ames, 2009). That is why most of the virtues in Confucian framework stress on inducing harmony within an individual, among others and in the world (Wong, 2011). In the *Five Classics*, it highlights harmony should always be maintained among virtues – This is the way to the highest excellence (*zhi shan* 至善) (in Ames, 2009, p. 86–87). Hence, this is the way to *ren dao* (the human way) as well as *tian dao* (the way of Heaven). To summarise, living in accordance to *dao* (the way of Heaven) is an ideal life for Confucians. This could be attained through (1) self-cultivation of virtues within the inner self, (2) extending virtues to social relations (outer world), and (3) maintaining harmony in social lives.

How would the mainstream perspective respond to Confucian view on social relations? Would the mainstream accept self as relational and interdependent? Both Hedonism and Eudaimonia agree with Confucius that social relations are critical factors to human life. Hedonism would value happiness derived from social network; while Eudaimonia would recognize human need for affiliation. However, neither Hedonism nor Eudaimonia would understand why Confucians place self within the social nexus. Both Hedonism and Eudaimonia treat self as an individual, independent and autonomous. Given everyone is self-governed, Maslow's (1943) hierarchy of needs puts 'self or I' as the focus of life. For instance, self-esteem, self-actualization and self-transcendence are the highest concerns in life. Since the mainstream emphasises on self-determining freedom to fulfil individual desires and needs, it may probably regard Confucian view of relational self as irrational and even dangerous. If individuals have to rely on others to realise themselves, they will lose their own sense of control over lives. As a consequence, it would adversely affect their degree of well-being. That is why the conventional approach would probably reject on defining self based on social relations.

How would the mainstream look at *tian dao* – The Confucian way of life? Neither Hedonism nor Eudaimonia discusses the notion of *tian dao*. In their analysis of Chinese and western culture, Hall et al. (1998) identify that *tian* has often been interpreted and grouped by the west counterpart as a 'transcendent' category, which is associated with cosmology and mysticism. They clarify that *tian* should not be defined as "Heaven", "Providence" nor "God "because these interpretations somehow mislead people towards the western concept of transcendence. They insist that *tian* is distinctively nontranscendent, culturally specific and functional because *tian* facilitates the possibilities of harmony at all aspects. In this light, *tian dao* implies living harmoniously with others by demonstrating *de* (virtues) in the world. Then, what are the mainstream view on virtues and harmony? While Hedonism provides no discussion on virtues and harmony, Eudaimonia considers virtues as important to life. In *Nichomacean Ethics*, Aristotle (1985) posits that true happiness is attained when one is able to express virtues. Aristotle regards virtues as a state of mind that allows individual to choose a mean – a right desire that is neither too excessive nor deficient. Aristotle inspires individuals to realise their rationality and wisdom in order to distinguish between right or wrong desires. He recognises that virtuous training would help individuals to develop insights for preserving a meaning in their lives. Under this light, Eudaimonia would probably appreciate Confucian cultivation of virtues.

Although Aristotle's concept of the mean can be compared to Confucian notion of harmony, they have different purposes and ways to attain equilibrium in lives. Confucians maintain harmony in order to live in accordance to *tian dao*, whereas Aristotle preserves a mean in order to realise the human virtuous potentials and gain personal contentment. Confucian attains harmony by promoting both personal as well as social ethics, while Aristotle tends to uphold the mean through exercising individual ethics. Given that Eudaimonia puts the centre of interest on individual self, it would certainly agree with Confucius's idea of *nei sheng* 內聖 (self-cultivation of virtue within the inner self). For example, Maslow's (1943) higher order of needs (such as gaining esteem, actualizing individual potentials and transcending oneself) are directed towards developing individual capacities to develop personal virtues in lives. Nevertheless, Eudaimonia puts a little weight on social ethics and seldom discuss extending virtues to the community (*wai wang* 外王). Hence, The Eight Steps (*ba mu* 八目) in Confucian education offers an additional reference for the mainstream, to understand how Chinese would be able to cultivate an ethical self as well as demonstrate the virtues within the social nexus (including family, country and the world). Confucian teaching helps to extend the ethics from personal (inner self) to societal level (outer world).

How would the Daoist respond to the Confucian views on life? Laozi would agree that life should live in accordance to *dao*. *Xin* in Daoist tradition would also refer to *xin dao* (*xin*, the way) – the way of life. However, Daoist interpretation of *dao* is different from Confucian *dao*. Laozi concerns more on the way of nature (*dao*), rather than the human way (*ren dao*) advocated by Confucius. Laozi encourages individuals to understand the pattern of nature, follow *zi ran* (nature) and live in harmony with *wanwu* (ten thousand things in nature). Therefore, he stresses on the virtue of naturalness, rather than social virtues promoted by Confucius. He does not pay much attention to social relations. Although Laozi does not emphasise on social virtues, he upholds equal respect to others. Since *wanwu* are created by *dao*, he believes everything should deserve equal status (Cheung, 2011). That is why respect should be given to others. Nevertheless, Daoists oppose to any deliberate virtuous trainings because they value *wu wei* (non-assertive action). They would probably regard Confucian ritual education as artificial and hypocritical (Cheung, 2011). In *Dao De Jing*, Laozi specifies:

> If we could renounce our benevolence and discard our righteousness, the people would again become filial and kindly (Dao De Jing, 19; in Legge, 1891)

> When we renounce learning we have no troubles (Dao De Jing, 20; in Legge, 1891)

The above writings highlight that the Laozi disapproves Confucian social virtues, such as *ren* (benevolence) and *yi* (appropriateness). He does not recognise any cultivation of virtues. Hence, he would probably disagree *san gang ba mu* 三綱八目 (The Three Objectives; The Eight Steps) raised by Confucian teaching. Cheung (2011) provides justification on why Daoist reject any ethical learning. She points out that Daoist's concept of *ci* 施 (compassion) is a spontaneous kindness that could be lived up effortlessly. For instance, in the findings (see Section 4.2.1), the local parents are willing to look after their children because feeding and teaching their children are regarded as their *tian zhi* (natural duties and responsibilities).

For the notion of harmony, would Laozi agree with Confucius? Laozi would certainly support harmony in lives. *Dao De Jing* specifies *wanwu* (ten thousand things in nature) are sustained by two opposite forces: *yin* (darkness) and *yang* (brightness) (in Legge, 1891). *Yin* and *yang* are coexisting and complementary, in which they need to be maintained in a balanced portion. That means, they symbolise the significance of harmony in *wanwu*. In that case, Daoist would support Confucian view on maintaining harmony among the four virtues. They would also agree with Confucians that the way to *zhi shan* 至善 (the highest excellence) is to preserve harmony in the social lives. Nonetheless, the target of harmony is different between Daoism and Confucianism. The former focuses on harmony with nature, whereas the later pay attention to the harmony with other peoples. Daoists do not only encourage people to live harmoniously with other human beings but also *wanwu* (everything) in nature.

5.2.4 Nature, *Yin/Yang*, Spontaneity

The last dialogue is initiated by Daoists. Laozi, the founder of Daoist tradition, suggests people living in harmony with *dao* (the way of nature). In order to achieve this life goal, he asks people to *wang wo* 忘我 (forget one's self). *Wang wo* enables individuals to get rid of any personal desires. Here, *xin* is a way of life (Li et al., 2013). Daoist view of *xin* would be associated with *xin xing* 心性 (*xin* nature) and *qing xin* 清心 (purify *xin*). *Xin xing* indicates the nature of *xin*. That means, Daoists support living in accordance with the way of nature. They encourage individuals to *qing xin*, meaning to keep their minds and thoughts away from any excessive desires and intentions. In Daoist term, *qing xin* means *xu xin* 虛心 (empty *xin*) or *xin zhai* 心齋 (xin fasting). Laozi describes that sages would empty their minds without desires and follow the governance of nature (*Dao De Jing*, 42; in Legge, 1891). Similarly, Zhuangzi (one key follower of Daoist teaching) illustrates *xu xin* with fasting:

> Such freedom is the fasting of the mind   (Zhuangzi, 4, in Legge, 1891)

Zhuangzi insists that only when individuals are able to restrain their desires like fasting their minds, they will obtain freedom and peace. In other words, Daoist supports *wuwo* 無我 (no self, no I), in which self-individualism, egoless and selfishness should be eliminated. When one becomes *wuwo*, he or she is able to understand, accept and follow the way in which *dao* (nature) operates.

While *dao* is the source of everything, *wanwu* (everything) is coordinated by *yin* (darkness) and *yang* (brightness). That is to say, Daoists believe every phenomenon has two sides: *yin* and *yang*. Mun (2011) in his book, *"Yin-Yang in Traditional Chinese Thought and its Modern Practices"*, highlights that *yin* and *yang* are embodied in every aspect of our lives. For instance, there are *yin* and *yang* in individual personality and behaviours; in business practices; in government policies and in the contemporary financial investment and social ethics. He points out the dynamics of *yin* and *yang* – they are constantly changing and interacting. Hence, Daoists consider that retaining a balance between *yin* and *yang* is important to life. For instance, Daoists interpret *xing fu jia ting* (good family) as the state where harmony is achieved. Therefore, Daoists regard there are both *yin* and *yang* in every domain of human values and practices.

According to Daoist tradition, one needs to follow *dao* by manifesting *de* (the potency of realizing oneself within nature) (Lai, 2007). *Zhen ren* 真人 (real or true persons) are individuals who possess *de* (Morris, 1994). They practically preserve *zi ran* and practice *wu wei* in their daily lives. In Section 1.2.2, *zi ran* is referred as nature or spontaneity; while *wu wei* means non-assertive action. That means, *zhen ren* can restrain their control, interference and confrontation against any situations in lives and accept what life gives to them. In such way, they would live spontaneously and harmoniously with the pattern of nature. That is why Daoists believe that spontaneity is the vital way to life.

How could the mainstream respond to Daoist way of life? The mainstream framework may find it difficult to agree with Daoist style of life. First, Daoist ideas of *wu wo* (no self) or *wang wo* (forget one's self) is totally contradict with the conventional notion of individual self. Both Hedonism and Eudaimonia target on confirming self by making self as the centre of focus in lives. Personal desires and needs are essentials for individuals. That is why Hedonism fulfils self by gaining happiness; while Eudaimonia realizes self by actualising one's potentials. In this light, Daoist view of abandoning self and getting rid of desires are completely unacceptable to the mainstream.

Daoist preference on following *dao* (the pattern of nature) is distinguished from the Eudemonic beliefs of rationality and environmental mastery. Daoist tradition emphasises on *wu wei* (non-assertive action) and *zi ran* (spontaneity), whereas Eudemonic approach perceives humans should have the ability to master the environment (Ryff and Singer, 2008). Eudaimonia encourages individuals to exercise control over their own life in order to achieve self-chosen goals. In that sense, Eudaimonia may regard Daoist approach as too passive, while Daoist may consider the mainstream as overly aggressive and egocentric. Hence, Daoist framework is not matched with the conventional approach to well-being. There is a Chinese saying: *dao bu tong, bu xiang wei mou*「道不同,不相為謀」, which means "Those whose courses are different cannot lay plans for one another" (The Analects: Wei Ling Gong, 40 in Legge, 1985). Given the mainstream, to a large extent, is opposite to Daoist way of life, the conventional and Daoist can hardly counsel one another.

How about Confucians? Would they agree with Laozi's style of life? Unlike Laozi, who asks people to forsake self, Confucius encourages self to be defined and developed based on social bonds. Confucius targets on living harmoniously with other peoples and uses virtues as the basic governance mechanism in social relations. His follower, Mencius once said:

> To nourish the mind, there is nothing better than to make the desires few.
> (Mengzi: Jin Xin II: 81; in Legge, 1985)

In this case, Confucians would probably accept Daoist thought of *qing xin gua yu* (purify *xin* and reduce desires). They would agree with Daoism that people should eradicate any self-centred thoughts and desires because any *si xin* (selfishness) would be considered as unethical and harmful to others. They believe that by removing egoism, one could be able to retain the intrinsic goodness– the original nature of mankind. Under this circumstance, Confucians would appreciate Laozi's goal on living with *dao* (the way of nature) because Daoist naturalistic life approaches could enable people to live up the innate goodness of human beings.

Although there are no such concepts of *yin* (darkness) and *yang* (brightness) in Confucian tradition, Confucius would mostly accept the concept of balance in Daoist teaching. Confucius highlights that *he* 和 (harmony) is the way to the highest excellence of life. He suggests people to attain harmony within the individual self, among relations with others and the world (Wong, 2011). Mun (2011) highlights that there are *yin* and *yang* aspects in Confucian teaching. Among the Four Constant Virtues, *ren* (benevolence) and *zhi* (wisdom) are associated with *yin*; while *yi* (appropriateness) and *li* (ritual propriety) are linked with *yang*. For example, *ren* is a cultivation of inner self. Therefore, *ren* is related to *yin*; while *li* is a ritual propriety that should be performed in the outer world, thus *li* is linked to *yang*. In Confucian teaching, one does not only develop *ren* internally but also need to demonstrate *ren* in the outer world through performing *li*. In that case, a balance among the four virtues should always be maintained. Indeed, Mun (2011) points out that there are *yin* and *yang* in every virtue. He explains that virtue, by its nature, is supposed to be an inner characteristic of a person. Therefore, virtue itself represents *yin*. On the contrary, any behaviours that demonstrate virtues are seen as *yang*. Based on such perspective, *zhong* 中 (equilibrium) becomes a rule of thumb of putting virtues into practice. People need to reveal both *yin* and *yang* aspects of each virtue. That is to say, they should possess virtues to cultivate inner self (*yin*); while they demonstrate virtues to the outer world through actions (*yang*). Under such circumstance, they need to behave according to the mean and never act in an extreme manner. In this context, Confucian notion of 'harmony' is similar to Daoist concept of 'balance', because both of them insist on upholding the equilibrium in any aspects of lives.

Confucians may find it hard to recognise Daoist idea of 'spontaneity', as Confucian education consists of *san gang ba mu* 三綱八目 (The Three Objectives; The Eight Steps) that teaches individuals to actively foster both personal as well as social ethics in their own lives. Hence, Confucians believe in deliberate cultivation and extension of virtues. For instance, Confucians promote *wei zheng yi de* (government by means of virtues). Confucians perceives that virtues are the key governing mechanism in lives. In that circumstance, Confucians would possibly feel uncomfortable with Daoist concepts of *wu wei* (non-assertive action) and *zi ran* (spontaneity). They would not appreciate Daoist beauty of *wu wei er zhi* 無為而治 (rule in the way of non-action). If they follow Daoist thought of abandoning all intended efforts for virtuous training, they may lose their sense of purpose and direction in life.

As a summary, both Hedonism and Eudaimonia assumes self as independent and autonomous. They perceive that life must be focused on one's own individual self. Hedonism takes sensation (happiness and pleasure) as the centre of life. However, Eudaimonia perceives that life should be more than just happiness. Eudaimonia targets on individual needs for existence, relatedness and growth. According to Maslow's hierarchy of needs, the highest concern for life is self-actualization and self-transcendence. For Confucian framework, it understands the Hedonic demand for happiness and Eudemonic approach for growth and development (self-actualization). However, Confucians place self within the social nexus and its teaching stresses on ethics. Confucians believe that living in accordance to *tian dao* (the way of Heaven) is the goal in lives. In order to achieve such a life goal, Confucian teaching encourages people to cultivate virtues and live harmoniously with other peoples. Lastly, Daoist framework is fundamentally diverse with the mainstream because of their opposing view on self. Daoists support *wuwo* (no self, no I) and situate self as part of nature. They aim at living in accordance to *dao* (the way of nature) and maintain balance (harmony) between *yin* and *yang* in lives.

Based on the above theoretical dialogues, each perspective would have their own interpretations on the Chinese notion of *xin*. As shown in Fig. 5.5, it portrays similarities and differences among the four frameworks. Hedonism refers *xin* as 'heart' and associates *xin* with feelings and emotions (心情; *xin* feeling) and desires (心慾; *xin* desire); while Eudaimonia would view *xin* as 'soul' (心靈; *xin* spirit) and links *xin* with spiritual attainment. However, the Chinese notion of *xin* bears much more meaning than feelings and spirit. Chinese perspectives reveal more layers of understanding regarding the indigenous connotations of *xin*. In addition to the meaning of 'heart', Confucians would look at *xin* as 'mind' (心思; *xin* thought). They believe people would open up their *xin* (heart-mind) in the process of self-cultivation of virtues. Confucians emphasise on *dao de xin* 道德心 (moral *xin*) and relate *xin* to ethics and virtues. That is why Confucian teaching targets on *zheng xin* 正心 (rectification of mind) and *xiu xin yang xing* 修心養性 (cultivation of *xin* and nurturing one's nature). Daoists would view *xin* as *xin xing* 心性 (xin nature) and connect *xin* with nature. This indicates Daoists suggest people open their *xin* (heart-mind) to nature and live spontaneously with nature. Both Confucian and Daoist frameworks target on living in harmony with *dao*. In that case, *xin* would mean *xin dao* 心道 – the way of life. Both Confucians and Daoists encourage harmony between body and *xin* (*shen xin ping he* 身心平和). That is to say, purifying one's *xin* and reducing personal desires (*qing xin gua yu* 清心寡慾). Towards the end, the next chapter concludes by drawing implications from the data analysis.

Chapter 6
Conclusion

This book offers answers to the following research questions (RQ):

> RQ 1: How does the discourse of well-being emerge and transform in a Chinese context?
>
> RQ 2: Do members of family business in China (Hong Kong specifically) draw upon the discourse of well-being in their daily practices? If not, what relevant concepts *do they refer to and make use of in a given time period?*

The archaeological examination (see Chapter 3) scrutinises the (trans)formations of well-being in a Chinese context. The 'thick description' (see Chapters 4 and 5) shows that the research subject did not draw upon the discourse of well-being in their daily lives. Instead, some more salient Chinese expressions, including *jia ting* (family), *peng you* (friends), *kai xin gong zuo* (happy work) and *xin zhong fu you* (being rich at heart-mind) were used. These expressions are interpreted through the framework of well-being, Chinese language and its philosophies. Two Chinese notions, *xing fu* (living well) and *xin* (heart-mind) are further contextualised. Based on the analysis, this chapter draws implications on theory, methodology and relevant work practices. The contributions of this book are also highlighted. This research contributes to theoretical debates regarding the application of well-being in Chinese context. The benefits of taking an indigenous perspective to understand a Chinese subject are implied. Concerning methodology, the value of drawing from both archaeology and anthropology is highlighted; ethics in research is emphasised; and the advantages of formulating a dialogue within 'thick description' are explained. The practical implications for business practitioners and researchers are discussed and some suggestions for multinational corporations (MNCs) to handle the international human resource management (IHRM) issues in China are offered. At the end of this chapter, limitations and recommendations for future research are put forward to enhance self-reflexivity.

6.1 Implications

6.1.1 Theoretical Implications

Three theoretical implications are derived from the investigation. First, the assumed universality of well-being is challenged. In response to the limitations of well-being, the book draws upon the indigenous language and philosophies to understand a Chinese subject. Second, it highlights the importance of examining change in discourse and generating cross-cultural analyses. Third, it explores conditions of the possibility of founding a theory for a Chinese subject.

(a) Challenging Globalisation of Well-being: Exploring its limitations

As discussed in Chapter 1, *objectification* and *essentialism* challenged globalisation of well-being in Chinese context. An archaeological and anthropological examination was conducted to investigate how the notion of well-being was relevant to a Chinese subject. In other words, some limitations of well-being are explored.

Based on the archaeological and anthropological examination, well-being is shown to have has its discursive boundary. The archaeological analysis examines the ontological nature of the notion – Well-being is indeed culturally bound and dynamic. Well-being has its root based on certain European values on happiness. Hence, well-being could be less applicable to Chinese. Well-being and *xing fu* are two distinct concepts and each have its own cultural origin. However, when well-being is being appropriated to a Chinese context, *xing fu* is made as an equivalent to well-being. In that case, a concern of *essentialism* is raised in the well-being discourse.

The anthropological analysis further highlights certain limitations of deploying a mainstream framework of well-being to interpret the data. The framework of well-being is less able to explain the Chinese concepts of *xing fu* and *xin*. For instance, the notion of well-being could hardly explain why the research subject: (1) views family as the most vital element of life; (2) eagers to build up a family; (3) treats feeding family and teaching children as an embodiment of *xing fu*; (4) prefers doing exercises and sleeping well; (5) seeks spiritual peace through rituals; (6) tends to work with friends who are trustworthy; and (7) is willing to bear hardship (see Section 5.1.1). These aspects reflect the inherent theoretical restrictions of well-being in terms of making sense of how the Chinese subject may think and behave.

The book does not necessarily disregard the notion of well-being. Well-being can be used to explain human behaviour in family businesses (Astrachan and Jaskiewicz, 2008; Ceja, 2009; Danes et al., 1999; Shepherd, Marchisio and Miles, 2009). Nevertheless, while well-being can be drawn to understand a phenomenon under investigation, one should not overlook its constraints, particularly when the latter may not be immediately noticeable in a cross-cultural management discourse.

Given well-being is made as a universal concept, it is important to examine its usefulness in an international business management context. Researchers such as Banerjee (2003), Learmonth (2009) and Xu (2008) have argued that any attempt of globalising management concepts, grand theories and even language could run a danger of colonisation of the mind. This book supports such an argument by unveiling a similar threat – a colonisation of well-being in Chinese context. The archaeological examination highlights the moment when Chinese subject was being dragged into the dominant discourse of well-being, causing a misrepresentation of the subject – Chinese were often marginalised because they were found to have a lower degree of well-being (e.g., Diener et al., 1995; Wang and Wang, 2016); while the indigenous notion of *fu* was made silent in the management discourse. As a consequence, the appropriation of well-being to Chinese subject can be another example of a subtle colonisation of management ideologies and practices.

Management discourse is rarely drawn by the Chinese research subject. For instance, 'thick description' (see Chapter 4) indicates: (1) the term – *'well-being'* has not been spontaneously expressed in any of my field visits; and (2) the research subject neither adopts *'management'* nor *'strategy'* at work. The findings show that management discourse has seldom appeared in the research setting. As shown in the Section 4.3, such an absence is often being essentialised as if the Chinese family business (CFB) is having a distinctive managerial mechanism that is different from professional management and business strategy (Chen, 1995; Redding, 1990; Poutziouris et al., 2002; Whiteley, 1992). Accordingly, the book illustrates that globalising strategic management can represent domination in cross-cultural management discourse.

To resist the above dominance, this book opens up a discursive space for a Chinese subject to speak in its own terms. Local expressions are therefore put as the centre of concern. These expressions can offer insights related to the local living styles: The research subject tends to *strive to survive* and *move on as life unfolds*. The book also demonstrates how Confucian and Daoist philosophical traditions can add another layer of understanding to the phenomenon under investigation. Yet, in international business management discourse, they are often not presented or not being adopted as equally important as the mainstream framework. Hence, the book calls for understanding Chinese subject based on its indigenous language and philosophies.

(b) Generating Cross-cultural Analyses: Examining Discursive Changes
The discourse of well-being can be dynamic. This book highlights that it is worthwhile to examine change in discourse. Discursive change represents history and development of knowledge. The discursive transformation from happiness to well-being indicates how knowledge of well-being is produced and developed. Furthermore, this book opens a discursive space to examine some Chinese concepts (such as *xing fu* and *xin*).

As mentioned in Chapter 1, the general conceptualisation of well-being is vague (Danna and Griffin, 1999). Well-being is a difficult term to define, because it is a multidimensional concept that encompasses all aspects of human life (Blaxter,1990; Conceição, and Bandura, 2008). Veenhoven (2000a; 2000b) criticises that there are too many objects within the discourse of life, such as *'quality of life'*, *'well-being'* and *'happiness'* etc. These concepts are often denoted with diverse meanings – "sometimes they are used as an umbrella term for all of the value, and the other times to denote special merits" (p. 1) (Veenhoven, 2000b). As a consequence, too many objects are emerged along the discursive transformation and they can cause misunderstanding and confusion. Veenhoven (2000b) and Wong (2011) therefore call for an examination of each discursive object. They encourage researchers to examine the substantive meanings of each individual object and clarify its specific connotations. This book may now respond to their call – by opening a discursive space where various expressions can be uncovered and examined. Each expression has its own contextual meanings and therefore an analysis across different cultural expressions is provided (see Fig. 6.1).

	Expressions	Social roles	Discipline	Context	Differentiation
	Happiness	Intellectuals	Philosophy and Psychology	Individual Self	Working
Mainstream	**Well-being** Psychological well-being Subjective well-being	Elites: e.g. academics, scholars, professional management (HR)	Healthcare, Positive Psychology, Business management		Managing
Local	*Xing fu* 幸福 *Xin* 信 / 心 *Kai xin gong zuo* 開心工作	Local family businesses: e.g. business owners, parents, employees	Chinese Family Business	Relational *Jia ting* *Peng you* Work relations	Living — *Yang sheng* 養生 (Feeding life) — *Yang xin* 養心 (Nurturing xin)
	Xin zhong fu you 心中富有	Local youth: e.g. students, post 70s, 80s & 90s	Hong Kong's Politics	Societal Citizens	
	(I)	(II)	(III)	(IV)	(V)

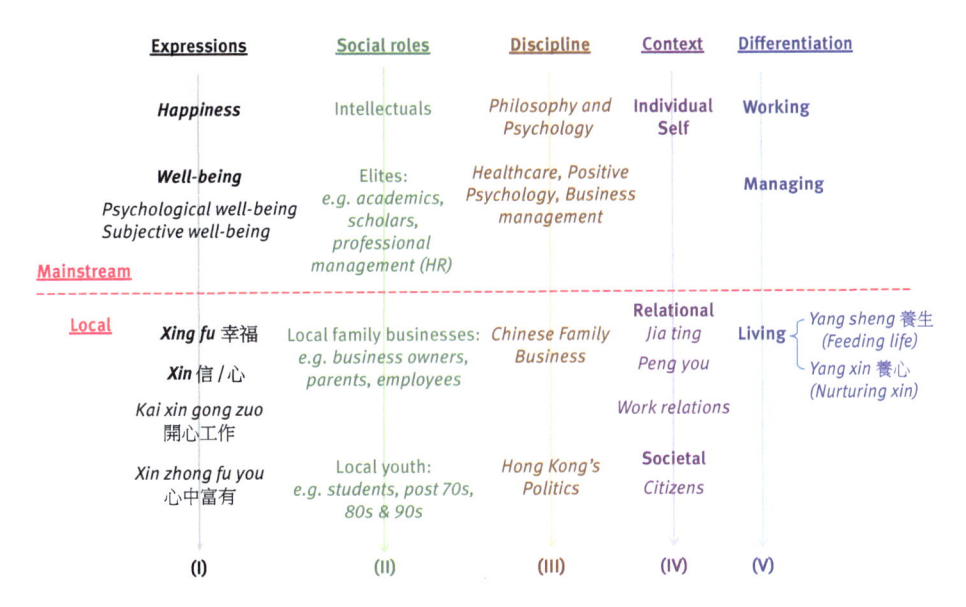

Fig. 6.1: A Cross-cultural Analysis: From Mainstream to Local Expressions/Concepts.

The discourse changes from the mainstream to local expressions (see Fig. 6.1: Part I). According to Foucault (1979), discourse can be transformative under different "conditions of possibility" (Preface: p. xxiv). His archaeology examines the conditions that give rise to discourse. Fig. 6.1 contextualises each expression according to its 'conditions of possibility'. In other words, the conditions that gave rise to each expression were examined. Each expression was made possible within certain conditions, such as among certain groups of key social players (see Fig. 6.1: Part II) in a particular discipline of study (see Fig. 6.1: Part III) and in a specific context (see Fig. 6.1: Part IV). The archaeology of well-being (see Chapter 3) demonstrated that: (1) the discourse of happiness was formed by the intellectuals in Philosophy and practiced by the politicians through law and regulations; (2) well-being began in the field of Positive Psychology, and well-being was often constructed by the elites, such as human resource management professionals, managers and academics. The anthropological examination (see Chapters 4 and 5) showed that: (1) *xing fu* was contextually related to *jia ting* (family) and *peng you* (friends); (2) *xin* (trust) was important to *peng you*; (3) *kai xin gong zuo* (work happily) was appeared within the work context; and (4) *xin zhong fu you* (being rich at heart-mind) was demanded among the local youth, particularly in the political arena. These expressions are discursive objects. Given each object is made under a unique set of conditions, the analysis implies differentiations among various expressions (see Fig. 6.1: Part V). For instance, in an organisational context, happiness is referred to an individual pleasure at work (i.e. regarding working); while well-being is regarded an aspect of human resource management (i.e. regarding managing). In contrast, *xing fu* and *xin* are a day-to-day concern of a Chinese subject (i.e. regarding living), particularly on the relational aspects. These disparities do not only imply transformations (movements) within the discourse, but also illustrate some cross-cultural differences between the mainstream and local expressions

The anthropological examination further implies a discursive change within local context – From *yang sheng* (feeding life) to *yang xin* (nurturing heart-mind) (see Fig. 6.1: Part V). *Xing fu* is usually related to family. Practices such as building a family with children, supporting family and being physically healthy and spiritually peaceful are the embodiments of *xing fu*. These practices define the manner on how the research participants feed themselves and their families. Accordingly, the notion of *xing fu* can be inferred as *yang sheng* (feeding life). In addition to *xing fu*, the findings show two other indigenous expressions: *kai xin gong zuo* and *xin zhong fu you*. These two terms indicate the significance of *xin*. As explained in Section 5.1.2, *xin* can be referred as heart-mind. The research subject also pays attention to nurturing its heart-mind, which is called *yang xin* in Chinese. Here, a change in local expressions is found: from *xing fu* to *xin*, which indicates that the research subject does not only focus on *yang sheng* (feeding life), but also *yang xin* (nurturing heart-mind). In other words, an examination on discursive transformation does not only uncover intercultural differences, but also reveal intra-differences within the local discourse.

(c) Conditions of Possibility: Founding a Theory for a Chinese Subject

In order to avoid the problem of *allochronism* identified by Fabian (1983, p.32), the researcher of this book is reluctant to apply any given theory. As discussed in Section 2.2, Fabian criticises that the positivist approach would require the researchers to employ a given theory for organising an observed phenomenon. In such a way, the theory or the category of the theory is adopted to study the subject. Any aspect of the subject, which is not covered by the theory, might be ignored or treated as unimportant or irrelevant. As a result, the subject is made an object of knowledge for establishing the theory. Fabian (1983) calls such a constitutive phenomenon, *allochronism* – a denial and suppression of the subject's voice. Therefore, in order to avoid *allochronism*, this book does not apply a given theory or model to assess the subject.

Furthermore, this book positions itself not for the purpose of constructing any theory. Why not? There are two reasons. First, it is impossible for this book to derive a theory of Chinese management/organisation or a Chinese theory of management. The archaeological examination (see Chapter 3) diagnoses the problems of objectification and essentialism in the well-being discourse. They indicate that an indigenous subject is still being deprived of its voice in the management discourse. Under such a condition, it is not possible for researchers to found any indigenous concept or/and theory. That is why this book does not intend to formulate any theory about a Chinese subject.

The second reason is that this book stays consistent with Foucault's (1972) archaeology. Archaeology is to "establish a possibility", not for founding a theory (Foucault, 1972, p. 114–115). In his *Order of Things*, Foucault (1970) states that:

> it seems to me (him) that the historical analysis of scientific discourse should . . . be subject, not to a theory of the knowing subject . . . . (Forward, p. xv)

According to Foucault, rather than generating any theory of the knowing subject, he focuses on discursive practices and transformation. He is not interested in formulating a theory related to human consciousness. Likewise, if one reads Foucault carefully, it is necessary to avoid appropriating Foucault for the purpose of constructing any organisational theory or vice versa – creating organisational theory into Foucault (Knights, 2004). Hence, this book does not intend to develop a management theory onto Foucault either.

If this book does not aim at theory-building, what are its intention and contribution? Before answering this question, it would be helpful to spell out the contribution of Foucault's archaeology. Foucault (1970) hopes that his work "would be an indispensable step if, one day, a theory of scientific change and epistemological causality was to be constructed" (Forward, p. xiv). His attempt is to shed some light on "the epistemological field" (Preface, p. xxiii) for further discussion. In doing so, he examines "the conditions of possibility" – "rediscover on what basis knowledge and theory became possible" (Preface, p. xxiii). For instance, in *The Birth of the Clinic*, Foucault (1973) states that:

> The research that I am (he is) undertaking here therefore involves a project that is deliberately both historical and critical . . . with determining the condition of possibility of medical experience in modern times. (Preface, p. xix)

By the same token, this book intends to study 'the conditions of two possibilities':
(1) *the conditions that made the discourse of well-being possible in a Chinese context;*
(2) *the conditions that could make an indigenous voice possible in management discourse.*

The conditions of the first possibility are revealed by way of an archaeological examination; while the conditions of the second possibility are uncovered by way of an anthropological examination and upholding ethics in research. Even though the book does not emphasize on theory-building, such an archaeological and anthropological examination begins to shed some light on the conditions of possibility for a Chinese theory.

In the archaeological examination, the problem of essentialism is diagnosed in the well-being discourse. Due to essentialism, the Chinese (*the Other's*) voice is marginalised or almost silent. That means, essentialism is hindering the emergence of any indigenous theory. Hence, one key condition that would make a Chinese theory possible is to first steer away from essentialism. How? Sheridan (1990) remarks that "the interests of the oppressed are best expressed in their own words" (p.221). Therefore, the researcher of this book suggests accounting for the subject's own expressions. Then, in what ways can the subject's expression become possible? The book proposes ethnography. In *The Order of Things*, Foucault (1970) specifically highlights ethnology at the end of his discussion. He considers that ethnology deliberately "seek its object in the area of the unconscious processes that characterize the system of a given culture; in this way it would bring the relation of historicity" (p.414). That means, ethnography requires a researcher to get close with an indigenous subject and to pay attention to local expressions, so as to make an indigenous historicity and authenticity visible. Expressions can consist of any objects or concepts. In Foucault's (1972) archaeology, objects, enunciative modalities and concepts gave rise to themes and theories. Working along such a sequence, the formation of any indigenous theory could be possible after certain local objects and concepts are formed and transformed. For this reason, this book treats ethnography as a crucial condition of possibility of founding any indigenous object and concept before the formation of any indigenous theory. In other words, this ethnography represents an early work that contributes to providing a condition of the possibility of founding a theory of Chinese management/organisation.

Nevertheless, ethnography alone may not be enough, given there is a possibility of "allochronism" (Fabian, 1983) in anthropology, in which the subject's voice is being suppressed. If so, under what conditions could the subject has liberty to express themselves? For Foucault, in order to exercise freedom appropriately, one necessary condition is to care for the self (Bernauer and Rasmussen, 1988; Hahm, 2001). Foucault explains further:

> One cannot care for self without knowledge. The care for self is of course knowledge itself . . . but it is also the knowledge of a certain number of rules of conduct or of principles which are at the same time truths and regulations. To care of self is to fit one's self out with these truths. That is where ethics is linked to the game f truth. (Bernauer and Rasmussen, 1988, p. 5)

According to Foucault, ethics is necessary for the practice of freedom and care for the self (Hahm, 2001). Hence, the book highlights that a crucial condition that makes the subject's voice possible is to advocate ethics in research. Xu (2008) suggests replacing ontology with ethics as the first philosophy. Indeed, she proposes three principles in research: (1) "ethics before knowledge", (2) "justice before power", and (3) "dialogue before vision" (p.267). The researcher of this book follows Xu's ethical principles. This research is one illustration of how an ethical discursive practice enables a subject to exercise some freedom to speak in its own terms. Hence, ethics is considered a necessary condition for making a Chinese theory possible not now as yet, but in future.

Finally, what are the conditions of possibility of ethics in research? This book highlights reflexivity as a condition for ethics. This book is an attempt to move from theory to reflexive analysis. By definition, "theory is simply a way of imposing conceptual order on the empirical complexity of the phenomenal world" (Suddaby, 2014, p.407). In Suddaby's (2014) examination of *'Why Theory?'*, he highlights that academics with diverse ontological and epistemological preferences would have different views concerning the roles of theory. For him, debates and tensions over the values of theory are actually productive to knowledge production. His primary concern lies in "the lack of reflexivity with theory". He encourages research community to have constant reflection on knowledge and its system. This book may now respond to his call. Rather than focusing on building a Chinese theory (Tsui, 2006; Child, 2009), this thesis pays close attention to reflexivity. Aligning with Foucault's (1997a) idea of *'governmentality'*, critical self-reflection and transformation would enable the constitution of ethics. In other words, reflexivity could be a condition of the possibility of ethics in research. Following Xu's (2008) "ethics before knowledge" (p. 267), this book illustrates that reflexivity could enable the researcher to stay critical; question the conventional concepts and theories; and generate a contextualised analysis of an indigenous subject. Hence, this book is an attempt to show that reflexivity becomes a discursive practice of ethics.

To summarise, the contribution of this book does not lie in theory-building, but in epistemological considerations – offering insights to the conditions of the possibility of founding a theory for a Chinese subject. To do so, this book uses archaeology as a way of diagnosing a possibility of essentialism in the well-being discourse; while using anthropology as a provisional solution to overcome essentialism. More importantly, ethics is the key for making an indigenous subject's voice becoming possible in management discourse, while reflexivity is a condition for exercising ethics in research. To that end, the book invites further discussion to explore conditions of possibility, so that formation of theory regarding Chinese subject may be possible in the not too distant future.

6.1.2 Methodological Considerations

Three implications on methodology are considered. Firstly, the book shows how research can overcome the problem of *essentialism* by drawing upon archaeology and anthropology. The complimentary value of the two methodologies is demonstrated. Secondly, this book upholds ethics in research by doing justice to its Chinese subject. Lastly, the book formulates a dialogue within 'thick description'. By this, the value of 'thick description' is recognised and its content is further extended through a dialogue.

(a) Archaeology and Anthropology

This book demonstrates that archaeology and anthropology can be complementary – While Foucault's archaeology is able to dissect *essentialism*, anthropology is able to offer a solution to *essentialism*. The literature review (see Chapters 1 and 2) signposts a possible threat of *essentialism* within the discourses of Chinese family business and well-being. In order to support the above claim, gaining an understanding of *essentialism* is the first step. For that reason, the book draws from Foucault's (1972) *Archaeology of Knowledge* to diagnose *essentialism* in the well-being discourse. As highlighted by Foucault (1972), "discourse produces reality; it produces domains of objects and rituals of truth" (p.194). Chapter 3 does not only uncover how the discourse of well-being has produced various kinds of objects (such as *subjective well-being, psychological well-being* and *quality of life*), but also traces how the discourse of well-being produces the practice of *essentialism* as the ritual of truth. That means, chapter 3 provides a picture of the problem, because the archaeological examination traces at which layer of text the discourses of *well-being* and *xing fu* have merged and examines the conditions that gave rise to such an integration (see Fig. 3.4: 4th layer of text). Foucault's archaeology indicates how, where and when *essentialism* has occurred in the discourse of well-being. Hence, the book demonstrates how Foucault's archaeology is able to reveal and dissect the problem of *essentialism* within a discourse.

How could researchers avoid *essentialism*? The book suggests a plausible way of decolonisation – Rather than dragging the Chinese subject into the dominant discourse of well-being, an interstitial space is released to allow the subject to speak in its own expressions. Yet how could researchers find out the subject's expressions? This book suggests a feasible methodology – using anthropology to study the Chinese subject. Given post-colonial epistemology aims to open a space to recognise any viable alternative knowledge system and local voice, Jack and Westwood (2006) highlight the values of "critically-inspired ideographic methods, for example, critical ethnography" (p. 493). Critical ethnography helps locating research in a particular historical, cultural and institutional context and takes local self-representation as the prime resource that drives research conceptualisations and practice. The study demonstrates how critical ethnography can contribute to an understanding of a Chinese subject. By conducting a critical ethnography, the ethnographer was able to get close to her research participants, observe their lives, socially interact with them and even 'live' with them. The fieldwork allows the ethnographer to pay attention to the participants' local expressions (verbal and non-verbal; written and spoken), daily practices, culture, tradition, customs, values and beliefs. That is how some indigenous expressions are found, including *jia ting* (family), *peng you* (friends), *kai xin gong zuo* (work happily) and *xin zhong fu you* (rich in heat-mind). *Xing fu* and *xin* are even further scrutinised. Consequently, this research has illustrated how anthropology can be taken as a methodological solution to avoid *essentialism* in research.

(b) Ethics in Research
The book advocates ethics in research. To uphold ethics in research, Xu (2008) follows Levinas' solution to a question of knowledge – replacing ontology with ethics as the first philosophy (p. 242). She encourages researchers to engage with a Chinese subject through conversation and treat the subject as their interlocutors so that both "the writer and subject share the same discursive space of theory in dialogue" (p.271). By that, she means one needs to "abandon the "monologue" of the researchers", "be prepared for a clearing operation with the familiar vocabulary and categories", and be "sufficiently attentive to other's (a non-western subject's) expression" (p.271). The questions of "Who is talking?" and "How does talking take place?" (p.271) should be emphasised. In other words, researchers (who are the key social players in the discourse) need to take up the responsibility of finding ways to address an imbalance of power, such as to welcome expressions from the indigenous communities and place these expressions ahead of the vision of Self (the researcher).

In response to Xu's (2008) call, this study is an attempt to put her ethical considerations in research into practice. Specifically, here are a few steps the author has taken to safeguard the voice of her research subject. First, I am conscious of my pre-understanding and existing knowledge on business management. In Chapters 1 and 2, I steer clear of an application of management knowledge to a Chinese context. A critical approach to existing knowledge is necessary. Second, I formulate an alternative and introduce ideas from Confucian and Daoist perspectives to contextualise well-being in a Chinese context (see Chapter 1). Third, from an archaeological analysis (see Chapter 3), I gain some in-depth understanding about *essentialism* and carefully proceed by avoiding *essentialism*. By opening up an interstitial space between *well-being* and *xing fu*, an indigenous voice is brought into a shared discursive space where Chinese subject can be treated on equal footing. Forth, in the ethnography, I engage with the locals through conversations, pay attention to the context and welcome indigenous expressions. Fifth, 'thick description' (see Chapter 4) is used to scrutinise the subject's lived experience and expressions. Here, the indigenous voice has occupied much space in the text. Finally, I examine the indigenous expressions in context and conduct a cross-cultural examination in such a way that both western and Chinese perspectives are set in dialogue (see Chapter 5). Because of the above steps, this book begins to show what one could do in order to do justice to Chinese subject. When Chinese subject is treated equality, a dialogue can be opened.

(c) Dialogue within 'Thick Description'

This book shows how 'thick description' and dialogue can offer further understanding of a Chinese subject. Rather than simply recording what the subject has done, 'thick description' comprehends details and interprets the symbolic meanings and implications of the phenomenon under investigation. Such an interpretation is able to provide an understanding of the subject's expressions. Chapters 4 and 5 offer a 'thick description' of the subject's lived experience. The 'thick description' here does not only present findings, but also captures the thoughts, emotions and web of social interactions among the participants within the operating context. As a result, each expression could be further interpreted by entailing its specific intention, contextual meanings and implications. That is how *xing fu* and *xin* have been illuminated within 'thick description'. Accordingly, 'thick description' is able to provide an in-depth understanding of the research subject.

How about the use of dialogues? How could dialogues be beneficial to international business management? Cheung's (2011) research on dialogues is worthy of note. She finds ways to include both western and non-western perspectives and explains:

> the new framework developed here advocates not a substitute, but inclusion. To reach a broad understanding of the phenomenon under examination, both western and non-western conceptual frameworks should be engaged in a dialogue. (p.263)

This book gives support to Cheung's (2011) argument. The cross-cultural analysis in Chapter 5 enables both western and Chinese perspectives to be in dialogue. The dialogue reflects their similarities and differences and indicates the hybridity of the research subject. Hence, the dialogue serves as enrichment to existing knowledge.

Where could dialogues take place in the discourse? This book formulates a dialogue within 'thick description'. Such a methodological experiment can derive two implications: (1) Dialogues can provide a possible extension to 'thick description; while (2) 'thick description' can be served as a home for dialogue. One of the possible concerns related to 'thick description' is how far it could be manifested within the qualitative research (Ponterotto, 2006). Even though 'thick description' has its significant role in ethnography, Geertz (1973) has never mentioned what come next after 'thick description'. In response to this gap, the book has demonstrated how a 'thick description' can be extended so that both western and Chinese perspectives are engaged in a dialogue. In other words, creating dialogues on theoretical level could methodologically offer an extension to 'thick description'. Congruently, 'thick description' provides a condition for dialogue. 'Thick description' offers an understanding of the subject's lived experience. This in-depth account of the subject is important because local expressions have to be revealed and contextualised through 'thick description' before any cross-cultural dialogues could be formed. The book has illustrated that within a 'thick description', both western and Chinese perspectives can be placed in the same discursive space for a dialogue. Hence, 'thick description' can become a home for dialogue.

6.1.3 Work Practices

Below explains some practical implications on IHRM and management research:

(a) To Business Practitioners: Diversity

The book reminds business practitioners (such as managers and IHRM professionals) in the multinational corporations (MNCs) to critically examine their management practices in Chinese context. MNCs are encouraged to "analyse the Western organisation management concepts and methods critically in light of their cultural assumptions and how their core values differ from those in China" (Wang, Wang, Ruona and Rojewski, 2005, p.323). For example, this study shows that the concept of well-being is not necessarily significant to the members of Chinese family business (CFB); and the boundary between work and family in CFB is not clear. Hence, the notion of work-family conflicts (WFC) and some global work-family balance (WFB) initiatives may be of little value to the Chinese subject. Xiao and Cooke (2012) draw similar implication in their investigation on the major sources of work-life conflicts encountered by workers in China. They indicate that:

> Chinese workers are faced with a very different set of incentives and disincentives in their choices regarding work-life, and consequently, work-life balance often becomes, in reality, more like a work-life trade-off . . . As Ling and Powell (2001) pointed out, the western (US) perspective of work-life conflict (WLC) is not adequate in explaining work-life issues in the Chinese context. (p. 19)

For that reason, business practitioners in MNCs can pay attention to those positive IHRM practices, such as work-life balance initiatives, wellness program, employee assistance program and employee satisfaction survey etc. and evaluate whether these so called 'best practices' are attractive to Chinese employees (Ariss and Sidani, 2016; Ballard and Grawitch, 2017; Burke, 2017; Cooke et al., 2014; Jacques, 1996; Liu and Yu, 2021; Wright et al., 2017; Xiao and Cooke, 2012). In particular, the instruments that are commonly used to measure employee well-being could be less applicable to Chinese workers (Ariss and Sidani, 2016; Liu and Yu, 2021). Hence, it would be appropriate to critically review any global managerial concepts, theories, models, tools and even practices before applying them to Chinese context.

Although Chinese culture may not be the only explanation for an absence of management discourse in a given context (Child, 2009), this ethnography shows that language in use is significant in organisations. Chia and King (2001) regard language as an organisation and vice versa. They indicate the significance of language in organisational communication and sense-making. Westwood (2001) also highlights that:

> Language and culture are inseparable – if one is lost then so is the other. (p. 241)

In other words, language and culture go hand in hand – if management language is absent in a Chinese context, then so is the management culture which is originated from the west (Jacques, 1996). Similarly, if an indigenous language is present, then so is the local culture. Hence, this ethnography argues that Chinese language and culture can be one explanation for the findings. The 'thick description' (see Chapters 4 and 5) can imply that indigenous language and culture play a significant role in CFBs. The research subject speaks in its own dialect and lives according to its own cultural values and beliefs. For instance, the notion of *xing fu* (living well) highlights the significance of *jia ting* (family) in a Chinese society. That is why the anthropological study shows a familial culture in all the four CFBs. The Confucian value of *zi qiang bu xi* (positive self-striving) enables a Chinese subject to strive for survivals; while the Daoist concept of *zi ran* (spontaneity) leads the subject to move along as life unfolds. Hence, the daily practices of the Chinese subject are shaped by its indigenous values. In regards to this, a diverse approach in IHRM is recommended so that the views of Chinese employees could be taken into consideration. For example, a cafeteria benefit plan could be implemented, because it allows each individual employee to choose from a variety of benefits and formulate a plan that suits his/her own needs. Based on the 'thick description', below are some choices of benefits that could be made available to Chinese employees:

i. Concerning Xing Fu (Living Well)

The 'thick description' shows that the locals values *xing fu*. One of their life missions is to build up a *xing fu jia ting* – a complete family with children. Therefore, they put effort into getting married and giving birth. In response to the significance of *jia ting* (family), offering marriage opportunities in the workplace may be valuable to Chinese employees. For instance, Hitachi in Japan offers free marriage agency service for its staff (Chan, 2008). Employees who are single and would like to enrol in this service can submit their applications with relevant information (such as academic background, family background, hobbies, personalities, weight, height and preferences, etc.) to the Human Resources Management Department. And then, the information will be updated in the internet website called *que qiao* 鵲橋 (Magpie Bridge). Employees (who have enrolled for this service) can browse through *que qiao* in their free time. Once they have found the person they would like to date, they can send their requests for dating via *que qiao*. If there is a mutual agreement between both parties, the Human Resources Management Department could arrange a date for them. This is a real life example to illustrate how a company can help its staff to search for their *xing fu* – finding a right partner for life. In other words, it facilitates its staff to *qi jia* (establish a harmonious family).

Supporting family is another embodiment of *xing fu*, which requires individuals to fulfil their familial role obligations. The findings indicate one basic familial duty is *yang jia* (feeding the family), which can include buying a place for the family to live and shaping children to be good. In that case, MNCs can consider supporting their members to accomplish their familial responsibilities – perhaps in terms of purchasing a residential place for living. For example, KPMG and The University of Rochester offer a mortgage housing incentive program to their staff (Petroff, 2014; The University of Rochester, 2017). They partner with some private banks and offer preferential mortgage plans and services to their employees. Since the data demonstrates that while *mai lou* (buying a residential place) is one key concern of the locals, *shang che* (owning one's own place first) seems to be difficult (especially for the young couples). This kind of mortgage program aims to help "people get on the property ladder early, rather than having to wait a few years" (Martindale, 2015). Hence, this kind of benefit can be specifically designed for Chinese employees who would like to purchase a residential place for their family.

ii. Concerning Xin (Heart-mind)

Xin (heart-mind) is related to *yang xin* (nurturing heart-mind). The research subject seeks *jian kang* (physically healthy) and *ping an* (spiritually peaceful). The analysis illustrates that maintaining a harmony between *shen* (body) and *xin* (heart-mind) is important. Hence, Chinese employees may seek to maintain such a balance in lives. For example, participating in regular sports activities, interest classes, entertainments, stress management in the workplace may help Chinese employees to sustain a balance between physical and spiritual health. In particular, in order to preserve spiritual peace in lives, many locals nowadays would participate in classes like yoga, *tai chi*, Chinese painting and calligraphy, etc. Hence, it may be worthwhile for MNCs to provide these activities or services to Chinese employees.

The 'thick description' also shows that Chinese subject prefers working with *peng you* (friends). In that case, business practitioners are able to derive benefits from using referrals and word of mouth as their key recruitment and selection methods. Furthermore, the anthropological study shows that the meaning(s) of *xin* (heart-mind) should be specifically contextualised. By offering a cafeteria benefit plan, each Chinese employee can then customise his/her own benefits plan based on individual *xin yi* 心意 (thoughts and preferences). Hence, a diverse approach can help practitioners to understand on how and when Chinese employees would feel *kai xin* (happy) and *xin zhong fu you* (being rich in heart-mind).

These suggestions are tailor-made based on the local expressions – *xing fu* (living well) and *xin* (heart-mind). They are designed for *yang sheng* (feeding life) and *yang xin* (nurturing heart-mind). Future research can carry out to examine the details, implementation and effectiveness of the above practices in Chinese contexts.

The key practical implication of this study is on changing management perspectives. Rather than relying on the global 'best practices' of IHRM, a diverse management approach that advocates multiple values and perspectives is suggested. Dialogues between perspectives (such as the management in MNCs and local employees) are encouraged, so as to derive a comprehensive understanding of the phenomenon.

(b) To Researchers: Pluralism
This part draws implications on management research practices. Majority of the international management studies remain firmly in the traditional-functionalist-positivism (Jack et al., 2008). As discussed in Chapters 2 and 3, a weakness of positivism is that it tends to be unreflective about its ontology, epistemology and representation. With regards to this shortcoming, Jack and Westwood (2006) recommend management researchers to increase reflexivity by taking a critical perspective. As shown in this study, a critical approach that accounts for social structure and change in discourse can offer insights to functionalist-positivist research. These insights move beyond the explanation offered by a mainstream approach and provide another view on the phenomenon under investigation. To generate knowledge, the study therefore calls for more critical management studies (CMS) to be carried out in international business management.

How can CMS be encouraged in research? A fundamental channel to arouse more attention to CMS is through management learning and education. One important job of CMS researchers is to introduce such a perspective and emphasise its importance in teaching to improve curricula (Learmonth, 2017). Yet, the book does not aim at narrowing research horizons by substituting positivism with a critical stance. Instead, the author advocates "pluralism", which is a diverse approach to knowledge proposed by Morrell, Learmonth and Heracleous (2015) in their examination of evidence-based management (EBMgt). Morrell and Learmonth (2015) explain that:

> Recognizing difference in intellectual traditions and celebrating their respective contribution is important not because it will lead to the triumph of the humanities over the sciences; rather, because pluralism promotes a balance between them as complementary ways of thinking about the problems facing people in work organisations. (p.529)

Their argument is to encourage researchers to appreciate different ontologies, epistemologies and standpoints, because organisational issues can be understood in various ways and angles.

How can researchers uphold pluralism? Above all, we as researchers need to always maintain an open attitude by accepting knowledge in a variety of approaches. Pluralism is a basis for meaningful dialogue (Morrell and Learmonth, 2015). The dialogue within 'thick description' (see Chapter 5) is an illustration to recognise the value of including multiple perspectives (both western and Chinese perspectives), so as to derive a better understanding of the phenomenon under investigation. Furthermore, researchers who identify themselves as critical thinkers are reminded not only to be critically aware of the dominant works, but also be self-reflexive on their own critical views and practices so that more multi-faceted debates on improving management learning and education can be generated (Ford, Harding and Learmonth, 2010). In general, researchers should preserve intellectual flexibility and critical reflexivity.

6.1.4 Contribution

This book intends to make three kinds of contribution to international business management. First, the study contributes to the literature of well-being by offering a cultural perspective of the notion. It engages in the debate related to the significance of well-being in a Chinese context. The archaeological examination opens a discursive space where examining well-being per se is plausible. Such an investigation uncovers an ontological nature of well-being – Well-being is *dynamic* and *culturally distinctive*. Hence, this book makes a contribution to knowledge by revealing two additional characteristics of well-being. Accordingly, well-being is culturally rooted based on European value, without any equivalent concept in a Chinese context. The assumed universality of well-being is therefore challenged. A discursive weakness of well-being is revealed – it is a culturally bound concept. The examination further reveals the problem of *essentialism* in the well-being discourse when the notion is unintentionally being misappropriated to Chinese subject. Globalisation of well-being in Chinese context is shown as another example of a subtle colonisation and marginalisation of the mind. Another theoretical contribution is that this book opens a discursive space where a Chinese subject is allowed to express in its own language and practices. Within this space, some more salient Chinese expressions and concepts are contextualised and their differences with well-being are unveiled. In this way, the book widens the scope of knowledge by bringing in a Chinese perspective into the discursive space.

Second, the book gives insights into research methodology. The study offers insights to operationalise both archaeology and anthropology. This research demonstrates how Foucault's (1979) archaeology is able to dissect *essentialism*, while Geertz's (1973) 'thick description' is able to offer a solution to *essentialism*. By drawing from both archaeology and anthropology, a new insight about well-being is derived. This insight could be neglected if only a mainstream approach was followed. Besides, the value of using 'thick description' is demonstrated given it is able to generate an understanding of a phenomenon under investigation. Within 'thick description', local expressions are revealed and an additional source (i.e. Chinese philology and its philosophical traditions) is introduced to interpret the data. Instead of merely discussing well-being – a western perspective, this study offers a Chinese perspective and put the two into a dialogue. By engaging the two perspectives in dialogue, their similarities and differences are examined. Hence, the benefits of following both western and Chinese sources are shown. Such knowledge may help both sides to understand each other better, and shed some light on understanding a Chinese subject. More importantly, the book contributes to the epistemology – the conditions of the possibility of formulating any theory for a Chinese subject. Ethics in research is highlighted as a crucial condition.

Third, this book contributes to an understanding of a phenomenon from a Chinese perspective, which can help business practitioners and researchers to critically examine the existing management and research practices in Chinese context. To business practitioners, the study encourages them to review their global management ideologies and examine whether the worldwide managerialist measures and practices are applicable across cultures. To manage employees with various cultural backgrounds, a diverse approach which takes indigenous perspective into account is suggested. In addition, this research is a critical management study (CMS) on well-being. Such a critical approach can provide an additional understanding of the topic. Therefore, to researchers, this book calls for more CMS in order to enhance reflexivity in research. Given the study demonstrates that an organisational phenomenon can be understood in multiple ways, the value of pluralism is recognised. Intellectual flexibility is encouraged so that researchers can accept, appreciate and demonstrate a variety of approaches to research.

6.2 The Future of Well-being?

This research has five key limitations. These limitations can be served as possible directions for future research of well-being. The first limitation is related to the local expressions being revealed. These expressions are derived from a majority of participants, whose age was around 30 to 45 years old. Only a few of them were less than 25 years old or more than 50 years old. In that case, the themes of this study are mainly constructed based on the expressions given by the middle-aged group. The 'thick description' indicates that local expressions can vary across generations. For instance, *xin zhong fu you* is particularly raised among the local youth. However, while the study tends to focus on the perspectives of the middle-aged group, alternate views from other age groups are being marginalised. Therefore, future investigations on different generational expressions would help to explore changes within the local discourse. In addition, the expressions are derived from a majority of participants, who are regarded as core members of the business. In Chinese, they are regarded as part of the family. Given the size of the firms is microbusiness which usually consists of less than 10 persons, the data collected tends to concentrate on the views of these core family members. The researcher finds it difficult to contact the non-core members because of either they have already left the firms or they were reluctant to talk with the researcher. The researcher considers that gaining rapport from those non-core members may run the risk of losing the trust from the central family members. Therefore, the researcher decides not to emphasise the views of the non-core members. In that case, while the study tends to focus on the views of the central family members, alternate views from non-core members (e.g. Ms. Abegail, Ms. Ally and Ms. Apple in FB 1) are marginalised. Hence, future research on expressions from non-core members would help to explore the dynamics and roles of power within the context.

The second limitation is related to sampling. The study adopts snowball sampling. One major weakness of snowball sampling is it may result in biased samples (Cohen and Arieli, 2011). That means, the sampling relies on the social network of the researcher, which may post constraint on the variety of participants. For instance, most field sites are restricted to microbusinesses in similar industries. Since majority of the family businesses in Hong Kong are SMEs, this study focuses on microbusinesses. The industries of the four sites are mainly education (FB 1 and FB 2) and retail (FB 3 and 4). Given there are little varieties of companies under study, it may affect the transferability of the study. The book may not be able to transfer its findings to different social groups. For instance, the lived experience could be very different for one working for a large multinational corporation versus a small firm. Future research on different types and sizes of Chinese family businesses (CFBs) are encouraged in order to gain further understanding of their practices. As the literature indicates that there is a tendency of partial representations of CFBs in the management discourse, the book particularly calls for more critical ethnographies to examine the practices of CFBs.

The third limitation is related to the period that the ethnography was conducted. The period of field visit is between 2012 and 2015 (i.e. most of the data presented is collected two years ago). Although visits were made occasionally during the years of 2016 and 2017, these follow-ups were mainly for clarifying some existing findings, instead of exploring new themes. However, changes in terms of the subject's lived experience have occurred in the recent two years. For instance, Betty and Bonnie decided to close down FB 2 at the end of 2016 because of financial difficulties and additional familial responsibilities. As a result, their lives would not be the same as before. However, due to the time constraint, this ethnography is unable to account for such a change. The book suggests conducting an updated or continuous investigation in the future, so that changes in the subject's lived experience can be examined.

The forth limitation is related to the place of research. The study is carried out in Hong Kong. Given China has 34 provinces, it is reasonable to argue that the dialect, culture, practice and living style of Chinese vary across provinces, cities and districts. These variations would definitely affect how one lives. The lived experience and the views among the locals in Hong Kong could be dissimilar with the Chinese living in other areas. In that case, the analysis and practical implications offered by this study may be less applicable to the family businesses operated in other parts of China. Again, the transferability of the study may be confined to its specific context only. To explore more Chinese expressions, future investigations in various parts of China are encouraged. To add a layer of understanding of the local discourse, comparisons among these expressions are also recommended.

The fifth limitation is related to the dialogue. This study initiated a dialogue on theoretical level only, rather than on an actual level. In that case, a question on whether the theory is closely consistent with the practice is raised – To what extent does the cross-cultural theoretical analysis apply to the real practice? In response, more dialogues are encouraged. The dialogues are not only limited to theoretical level. They can be carried out in actual conversations, such as between the business practitioners in different countries, between the managers and the employees (Cheung, 2011), between the members and non-members of family business. These dialogues may aid in developing mutual respect and understanding between both parties. To enable two-way communication, each participant should be able to share the same discursive space, be treated as an equal partner and be allowed to speak out his/her opinions. In other words, the book calls for a continuous effort to overcome the problems of *objectification* and *essentialism*.

The book examines the concept of well-being and other local expressions within the context of Chinese family business in Hong Kong. The theoretical scope is clearly specified. Nevertheless, this study proposes critical examinations on other popular global management concepts such as teamwork, flexibility, sustainability and work-life balance. The author encourages future research to examine these notions per se and investigate their significance across cultures.

A Closing Remark . . .
The book starts by questioning the implicit universalism of a management concept: well-being. The problems of *objectification* and *essentialism* were suspected in the cross-cultural management discourse. To diagnose and overcome the problems, the book proposes taking both Foucault's (1979) archaeology and Geertz's (1973) 'thick description' respectively. The 'thick description' is further extended through a theoretical dialogue between both western and Chinese perspectives. Such a methodology is seldom in use in the management research. However, the book has demonstrated that its approach was capable of uncovering further layers of understanding about the phenomenon. These layers would be neglected if the mainstream positivist-functionalist approach was solely followed. Hence, the book calls for management diversity in which multiple perspectives and research methods are encouraged to broaden our horizons on various organizational phenomena and issues. Diversity requires business practitioners and researchers to put ethics in practice (Cummings et al., 2017). That means, they are encouraged to accept and recognise the views of each individual, and at the same time remain reflexive and critical. This is a key condition in which indigenous theories can be made possible in the future.

Appendices

Appendix A

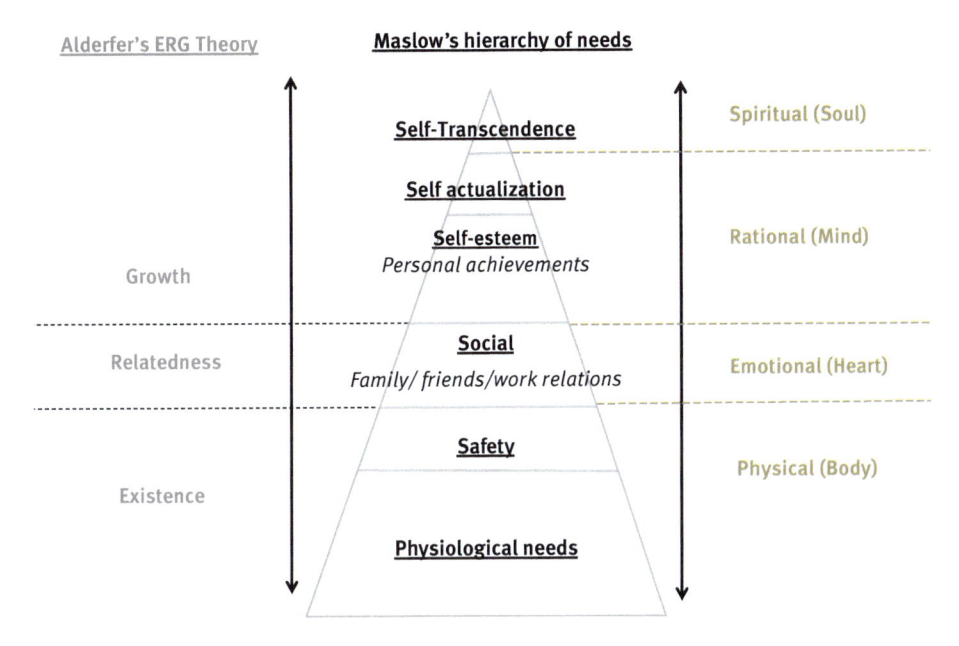

Alderfer's ERG Theory — Growth, Relatedness, Existence

Maslow's hierarchy of needs (pyramid, bottom to top):
- Physiological needs
- Safety
- Social — Family/ friends/work relations
- Self-esteem — Personal achievements
- Self actualization
- Self-Transcendence

Spiritual (Soul) / Rational (Mind) / Emotional (Heart) / Physical (Body)

Fig. A1: A Mainstream Perspectives on Human Needs. (Alderfer, 1969; Maslow, 1943; Maslow and Lowery, 1998)

Notes A1: Discursive Formation and Transformation Through Thresholds

1 Discursive Formation

Foucault (1972) explains that discursive formation "deals with system of dispersion between a number of statements" and "defines regularity (an order, correlations, positions and functionings, transformations) between objects, types of statement, concepts and thematic choices" (p. 38) (see Tab. A1). Such system of dispersion and regularity can be revealed on the basis of the unities of discourse that represent "the history of ideas, or of thought, or of science, or of knowledge" (p.21). Foucault comprehends that "if there really is a unity, it does not lie in the visible, horizontal coherence of the elements formed, it resides, well anterior to their formation, in the system that makes possible and governs that formation" (p.72). Hence, archaeology uncovers such unities and continuity, question them, and then disconnect them within the discourse. Foucault posits that "as soon as one questions that unity, it loses its self-evidence; it indicates itself, constructs itself, only on the basis of a

Nei sheng 內聖
(The cultivation of ethical self)

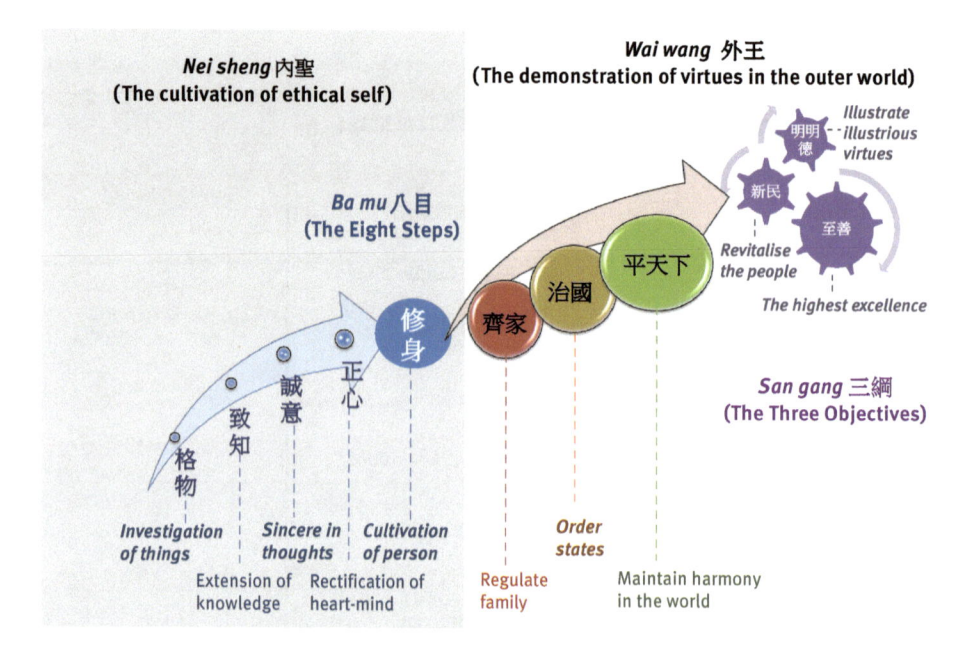

Wai wang 外王
(The demonstration of virtues in the outer world)

明明德 — Illustrate illustrious virtues
新民 — Revitalise the people
至善 — The highest excellence

Ba mu 八目
(The Eight Steps)

San gang 三綱
(The Three Objectives)

格物 — Investigation of things — Extension of knowledge
致知 — Sincere in thoughts — Rectification of heart-mind
誠意
正心
修身 — Cultivation of person
齊家 — Regulate family
治國 — Order states
平天下 — Maintain harmony in the world

Fig. A2: Confucian *San Gang Ba Mu*. (Legge, 1985)

Tab. A1: Discursive (Trans)Formation (Foucault, 1972).

Discursive Formation
Definition: Whenever one can describe, between a number of statement, such system of dispersion, whenever, between objects, types of statement, concepts, or thematic choices, one can define regularity (an order, correction, positions and functionings, transformations), we will say, for the sake of convenience, that we are dealing with a discursive formation . . . The conditions to which the elements of this division (object, mode of statement, concepts, thematic choices) are subjected we shall call the rules of formation. The rules of formation are conditions of existence (but also of coexistence, maintenance, modification, and disappearance) in a given discursive division (p.38).

Type of formation	Meaning	Ways to account for the formation
(1) Formation of objects	Examines a question: "what has ruled their existence as objects of discourse?" (p.41)	I. "map the first surface of their emergence" (p.41) II. "describe the authorities of delimitation" (p.41) III. "analyse the grid of specification" (p.42)
	"One might say, then, that a discursive formation is defined (as far as its objects are concerned, at least) if one can establish such a group; if one can show how any particular object of discursive finds in its place and law of emergence" (p.44).	

Tab. A1 (continued)

Discursive Formation		
(2) Formation of enunciate modalities	"discover the law operating behind all these diverse statements, and the place from which they come" (p.50).	Ask: I. "Who is speaking?" (p.50) – 'Who is qualified to speak?' II. 'Where is the speaking taking place?' (p.50). III. 'How is the discourse made possible?' (p.50).
(3) Formation of concepts	Describes the "group of relations that constitutes a system of conceptual formation" (p.60)	Defined through: I. "forms of succession" (p.56) II. "forms of co-existence" (p.57) III. "procedures of intervention" (p.58).
(4) Formation of strategies	Examine the formations of any 'themes' or 'theories' (p.64)	I. "Determine the possible points of diffraction of discourse" (p.65) II. study "the economy of the discursive constellation to which it belongs to" (p.67) III. examine how "the determination of the theoretical choices that were actually made is also dependent upon another authority" (p.67).

Ways of Transformation

(1) may undergo a number of intrinsic mutations that are integrated into discursive practice without the general form of regularity being altered (pp.74–75) **Meaning:** Although the elements in the discourse may change, the rules and laws of the formation are the same. Thus, the system itself preserves individuality, with the same group of relations being established.	(2) the discursive practices modify the domains that they related to one another (p.75). **Meaning:** The elements in the discourse would be articulated with one another, which lead to changes and modifications on the group of relations that has been established and developed.

Operated through:

I. "a single positivity" (p.171) in each level of events	II. "the analysis of transformations" (p.172)	III. "new rules of formation" (p.173);	IV. "the appearance and disappearance of positivities" (p.175).

complex field of discourse" (p.23). Therefore, he regards archaeology as "the project of a pure description of discursive events as the horizon for the search for the unities that form within it" (p.27).

How can one uncover unity and disconnect it? It is inclusive of two approaches. First, Foucault suggests to seek 'a secret origin' (p.25) in the discourse. He highlights that "the irruption of a real event; that beyond any apparent beginning, there is always a secret origin – so secret and so fundamental that it can never be quite grasped in itself" (p.25). Secondly, one can define the rules and conditions that enable the possibility of a particular statement, making it legitimate and inclusive and vice versa.

In Foucault's writing, he divided discursive formations into four types: (a) Formation of objects, (b) enunciate modalities, (c) concepts and (d) strategies.

(a) The Formation of Objects

In Foucault's archaeology, he discusses the formation of objects as the first type of discursive formation. The formation of objects examines a question: "what has ruled their existence as objects of discourse?" (p.41). Foucault considers "this formation is made possible by a group of relations established between authorities of emergence, delimitation and specification" (p.44). He further explains that "discursive formation is defined (as far as its objects are connected, at least) if one can establish such a group; if one can show how any particular object of discourse finds its place and law of emergence; if one can show that it may give birth simultaneously or successively to mutually exclusive objects, without having to modify itself" (p.44).

Foucault devises three ways which can aid in the examination of the formation of the objects: (1) "map the first surface of their emergence" (p.41); (2) "describe the authorities of delimitation" (p.41) and (3) "analyse the grid of specification" (p.42). First, archaeology highlights the rules and object in which an object emerges in a particular context (societies, periods and forms of discourse). This level of analysis reveals "initial differentiation, in the distances, the discontinuities, and the thresholds that appear within it (the discourse)". It examines how a particular discourse finds "a way limiting its domain, of defining what is talking about, of giving it the status of an object – and therefore of making it manifest, nameable, and describable" (p.41). Second, archaeology describes the individuals or groups who have major authority to "delimit, designate, name, and establish" (p.42) the objects. Hence, "this formation is made possible by a group of relations established between authorities of emergence, delimitation, and specification" (p.44). Lastly, archaeology examines "the grid of specification", a system wherein the objects are "divided, contrasted, related, regrouped, classified, derived from one another as objects" (p.42) of a particular discourse.

For the feasibility of the above mentioned three tasks, there are several conditions that are imperative for the occurrence of an object: (1) a positive condition of a complex group of relations; (2) a system of relations, including both primary and secondary relations; and (3) "a group of rules that are immanent in a practice, and define it in its specificity" (p. 46). With these conditions, the discourse is regarded as a practice rather than a text.

(b) The Formation of Enunciate Modalities
The formation of enunciate modalities is to "discover the law operating behind all these diverse statements, and the place from which they come" (p.50). According to Foucault, the ways to discover the law operating behind the discourse is to ask: (1) Who is speaking?; (2) Where is the speaking taking place?; and (3) How is the discourse made possible?

The first question – 'Who is speaking?' could be more accurately referred as 'Who is *qualified* to speak?'. For Foucault, archaeology investigates the one who has prestige and right to legitimately define, spontaneously accept or reject any offers of a discourse. For example, the status of one profession, institutions, system, social norms, economic and legal conditions may have given 'the right' and 'limitations' to practice and to further extend the knowledge within a discourse. The second question – 'Where is the speaking taking place?' describes the "institutional *sites*" from which the qualified individuals (in the first question) make their discourse, "and from which this discourse derives its legitimate source and point of application (its specific objects and instruments of verification)" (p.51). The last question – 'How is the discourse made possible?' examines the contexts that enable "the position of the subject" "to occupy in relation to the various domains or groups of objects" (p.52). It looks for "a field of regularity (for various position of subjectivity)" (p.55).

As a summary, the above three questions scrutinise "the various status, the various sites, the various positions that he (the subject) can occupy or be given when making discourse" (p.54). The formation of enunciate modalities shows the manner in which the discourse is established and "linked by a system of relations" (p.54).

(c) The Formation of Concepts
The formation of concepts describes the "group of relations that constitutes a system of conceptual formation" (p.60). Foucault highlights that conceptual formation can be defined through: (1) "forms of *succession*" (p.56); (2) "forms of *co-existence*" (p.57) and (3) "procedures of intervention" (p.58). First, "forms of succession" includes "the various *orderings of enunciative series*" and "*types of dependence* of the statement" (pp. 56–57). These forms relate to "a set of rules for arranging statements in series, an obligatory set of schemata of dependence, of order, and of successions, in which the recurrent elements that may have value as concepts were distributed" (p.57).

Second, 'forms of co-existence' details all the statements that are involved within the discourse (no matter they are formulated, accepted, criticized, discussed, judged, rejected or excluded). It involves outlining: (1) "a field of presence" (p.57);

(2) "a field concomitance" (p.58); and (3) "a field of memory" (p.58). Foucault explains that "in this field of presence, the relations established may be of the order of experimental verification, logical validation, mere repetition, acceptance justified by tradition and authority, commentary, a search for hidden meaning, the analysis of error; these relations may be explicit (and sometimes formulated in types of specialized statement: references, critical discussion), or implicit and present in ordinary statement" (p.57). 'A field of concomitance' is inclusive of statements that are active among the studied statements. On the contrary, 'a field of memory' refers to "statements that are no longer accepted or discussed, and which consequently no longer define either a body of truth or a domain of validity, but in relation to which relations of filiation, genesis, transformation, continuity and historical discontinuity can be established" (p.58).

Third, "procedures of intervention" refers to the ways that determine the manner in which the statements are *rewritten, transcribed, translated, approximated, delimited, transferred, systemized, redistributed or rearranged* from one discourse to another (p. 59). For instance, the rewriting techniques, modes of translation, ways of appropriation and transfer and systems of redistribution. To summarise, the formation of concepts defines a system wherein varied elements that are part of the discourse are related to one another.

(d) The Formation of Strategies

The formations of objects, enunciative modalities and concepts could give rise to certain 'themes' or 'theories' in discourse. Foucault mentioned these themes and theories as "strategies" (p.64). He indicated three possible research directions that can lead to the formation of strategies: (1) "Determine the possible points of diffraction of discourse" (p.65); (2) study "the *economy of the discursive constellation* to which it belongs to" (p.67); and (3) examine how "the determination of the theoretical choices that were actually made is also dependent upon another authority" (p.67). For points of diffraction, they include (a) "*points of incompatibility*: two objects, or two types of enunciation, or two concepts may appear, within the same discursive formation, without being able to enter under pain of manifest contradiction or inconsequence – the same series of statement; (b) *point of equivalence*: the two incompatible elements are formed in the same way and on the basis of the same rules; the conditions of their appearance are identical; they are situated at the same level; and instead of constituting a mere defect of coherence, they form an alternative; and (c) *link points of systematization*: on the basis of each of these equivalent, yet incompatible elements, a coherent series of objects, forms of statement, and concepts has been derived" (p.66). These points "form discursive subgroups" "as if they were immediately unity and raw material out of which larger discursive groups ('theories', 'conceptions' and 'themes') are formed" (p.66).

Second, the *economy of the discursive constellation* can be studied by depicting the particular authorities that has been directed by one's own theoretical choice. The discursive constellation represents the role(s) played by the discourse being examined, in relation to other discourses that are currently with it or related to it.

Third, the determination of the theoretical choices can be "dependent upon another authority" (p.67). Foucault specifies that such an authority can be characterized by: (1) the *function* that the discourse under examination has to be carried out in a field of non-discursive practices, (2) "*the rules and processes of appropriation* of discourse" (p.68) and (3) "the possible positions of desire in relation to discourse" (p.68). These are the "formative elements" (p.68) that are made possible in the field of non-discursive practices.

The above description highlighted that under a system of formation, "there exists a vertical system of dependence" (p.73). However, the defined four levels of formation (formations of objects, enunciated modalities, concepts and strategies) are not independent and "there exists a whole hierarchy of relations" (p.73) among them. Thus, archaeology helps to discover "the complex group of relations that functions as rules", in which "it lays down what must be related, in a particular discursive practice" (p.74). Besides, Foucault specifies that "as a group of rules for discursive practice, the system of formation is not a stranger to time" and "*must not be taken as blocks of immobility, static form*" (pp. 73–74). Thus, discursive formations are susceptible to changes; therefore, archaeology helps to account for changes in the discourse. It seeks to study the transformation within a discourse.

2 Discursive Transformation

How can archaeology examine the mobility and changes in discourse? Foucault's archaeology is an "archaeological description of change" (p.166). It accounts for discursive transformations in two ways (see Tab. A1). First, discursive elements "may undergo a number of intrinsic mutations that are integrated into discursive practice without the general form of regularity being altered" (pp.74–75). In other words, even if the elements in the discourse might alter, the rules and laws of the formation remain unchanged. Thus, the system itself preserves individuality, within the same groups of relations that are being established. Conversely, the other way of mobility is "the discursive practices modify the domains that they related to one another" (p.75). The elements in the discourse would be articulated with one another which leads to modifications within the group of relations that has been established and developed.

How does archaeology examine the above two kinds of mobility? First, it suspends any "temporal succession" (p.167), that is, "this suspension is intended precisely to reveal the relations that characterize the temporality of discursive formations and articulate them in series whose intersection in no way precludes analysis" (p.167). This can be achieved by (1) defining "the rules of formation of a group of statement" and examining the hierarchy of rules, and (2) showing "how a succession of events may, in the same order in which it is presented, become an object of discourse, be recorded, described, explained, elaborated into concepts, and provide the opportunity for a theoretical choice" (p.167). Second, archaeology analyses the changes through speaking of "discontinuities, ruptures, gaps, entirely new forms of positivity, and of sudden redistributions" (p.169). Archaeology handles the occurrence of differences in a serious manner. Hence, "its aim is not to overcome differences, but to analyse them, to say what exactly they consist of, to differentiate them" (p.171).

How does archaeology analyse differentiations? It sees differences operate through: (1) "a single positivity" (p.171) in each level of events; (2) "the analysis of *transformations*" (p.172); (3) "new rules of formation" (p.173); and (4) "the appearance and disappearance of positivities" (p.175). To begin with, archaeology differentiates between varied levels of events: statement themselves, objects, types of enunciation, concepts, strategic choices and new rules of formation and more. Archaeology believes there is always "single positivity" in each level of events. Hence, its aim is to reveal such single positivity in each level, so that differentiations between various levels of element can be known.

Second, "archaeology tries to establish the system of transformations that constitute 'change'" (p.173) by conducting 'the analysis of transformations'. 'The analysis of transformations' examines the disappearance of one positivity and emergence of another through different kind of formation. It also considers "how the different elements of a system of formation were transformed"; "how the characteristic relations of a system of formation were transformed"; "how the relations between different rules of formation were transformed"; and "how the relations between various positivities were transformed" (p.172).

Third, differentiations can be operated with the help of new rules of formation. Foucault regarded the new rules of formation as "the principle of their multiplicity and dispersion" (p.173). These new rules "describe and analyse phenomenon of continuity, return, and repetition" and distinguish formations of various elements as heterogeneous.

Forth, Foucault believes "it is always a discontinuity specified by a number of distinct transformations, between two particular positivities" (p.175). Not only does archaeology identify appearance and disappearance of positivities, it also examines "the system of interpositivity" (p.176). It signifies the linkages between various positivities and examines the generation of symmetrical effects by such linkages.

Archaeology does not examine the discursive transformation on the sole basis of chronology. Instead, it considers the distribution of time in accordance to the "different thresholds, succession and possible coincidence (or lack of it), the way in which they govern one another, or become implicated with one another, the conditions in which, in turns, they are established . . . " (p.187). Therefore, the next section explains different thresholds for discursive (trans)formation.

3 Different Thresholds for (Trans)Formation

To describe discursive (trans)formations and to comprehend how the discourses could have developed into science, Foucault highlighted the importance of different thresholds. He outlined the mentioned four thresholds to describe various emergencies of discursive formations and transformations: (1) "Threshold of positivity"; (2) threshold of epistemologization"; (3) "threshold of scientificity"; and (4) "threshold of formalization" (p.187) (see Tab. A2). The chronology of the four thresholds "is neither regular nor homogeneous" (p.187). The discursive formations do not cross such thresholds at regular interval period of time nor at the same time. Instead, archaeology divides the history of discursive (trans)formations through different thresholds. It outlines the unique order of thresholds being crossed in a discourse, in order to scrutinise its discursive transformations and signify the hierarchy of relations and corrections between various elements.

Tab. A2: Types of Thresholds (Foucault, 1972).

Type of Threshold	Description
(1) Threshold of positivity	The moment at which a discursive practice achieves individuality and autonomy, the moment therefore at which a single system for the formation of statement is put into operation, or the moment at which this system is transformed, might be called **the threshold of positivity** (p. 186).
(2) Threshold of epistemologization	When in the operation of a discursive formation, a group of statement is articulated, claims to validate (even unsuccessfully) norms of verification and coherence, and when it exercises a dominant function (as a model, a critique, or a verification) over knowledge, we will say that the discursive formation crosses **a threshold of epistemologization** (pp. 186–187).
(3) Threshold of scientificity	When the epistemological figure thus outlined obeys a number of formal criteria, when its statements comply not only with archaeological rules of formation, but also with certain laws for the construction of propositions, we will say that it has crossed **a threshold of scientificity** (p.187).
(4) Threshold of formalization	And when this scientific discourse is able, in turn, to define the axioms necessary to it, the elements that it uses, the propositional structure that are legitimate to it, and the transformations that it accepts, when it is thus able, taking itself as a starting-point, to deploy the formal edifice that it constitutes, we will say that it has crossed **the threshold of formalization** (p.187).

Notes A2: Critiques of Foucault

Before going into critiques of Foucault, it is useful to understand how Foucault considers critique. In *The Politics of Truth,* Foucault (1997b) speaks about the question of *'What is critique?'*. For him, critique indicates a "critical attitude as virtue in general" (p.25). He regards critique as "the art of not being governed quite so much" (p.29). This definition implies a confrontation with power. In other words, there is an "interplay of governmentalization and critique" (p.31), in which "the subject gives himself the right to question truth on its effects of power and question power on its discourses of truth" (p.32). Hence, Foucault places critique in the context of "the politics of truth" (p.32). That is why his work does not only represent his critique of power, but also his devotion to the truth (Sheridan, 1990).

While debates about Foucault's work as a whole are sometimes intense (Bevir; 1999; Barratt, 2002; Knights, 2002; Rowlinson and Carter; 2002), it is useful to consider his work by following his ideas in two periods: (a) The archaeological and (b) the genealogical phases (Dreyfus and Rainbow, 1982; Burrell, 1984; Knights, 2002; Barratt; 2008). Most criticisms of his archaeology of knowledge are related to epistemological aspects; while comments on genealogy are about political and ethical aspects.

1 Archaeological Phase: Epistemological Aspects

Foucault's early work is about his critiques of structuralism. In the Classical period, knowledge is produced based on structuralism – representation and the sign; and analysis of the relationship between fixed elements (Sheridan, 1990). Foucault (1972) regards structuralism as a methodological problem. Therefore, he uses archaeology to "question teleologies and totalizations" (p.16) in structuralism. His books, such as *Madness and Civilisation, The Birth of the Clinic and The Order of Things*, represent his critique to structuralism; while *Archaeology of Knowledge* is written to provide a rigorous elucidation of his epistemology.

Foucault is aware of criticisms against his archaeological approach. In the final chapter of *Archaeology of Knowledge*, Foucault (1972) offers a response to an imaginary opponent. He replies to questions regarding the scope and limitations of his archaeology. His response covers the following: (a) anti-structuralism, (b) history, (c) non-science and (d) revolution.

(a) Anti-structuralism

First, the opponent challenges Foucault's dissociation from structuralism. On the one hand, Foucault refuses to locate his archaeological enterprise within structuralism. On the other hand, his approach applies some themes of structuralism. The opponent, therefore, argues that Foucault denies his archaeology as a structural analysis. For instance, the opponent claims that it is impossible to make discourse neither dispensing with the speaking subject nor removing away from history itself; otherwise, the discourse fails to account for its anthropological references and actual and successive events. Foucault (1972) responds by clarifying his aim – instead of isolating structuralism beyond its legitimate recognition; he intends to conduct an analysis that shows how discursive practices differ from one another. For instance, he has "never once used the word 'structure' in *The Order of Things*" (p.200–201). Although such an analysis does not rely on structuralist principles, he never intends to discard the speaking subject and history. On the contrary, he approaches the subject by defining its diverse positions and functions within discourse; and examining the history of ideas by revealing discursive transformation at different levels.

(b) History

Second, the opponent does not accept Foucault's approach to history, in which he frees discourse from its "constituent activity", "fundamental teleology" and "subjectivity" (Foucault, 1972, p.201). The opponent questions the status of archaeology – is it history or philosophy? In response, Foucault insists that his archaeology is "a discourse about discourse" (p.205), which differentiates from philosophy as well as history. He highlights that:

> If philosophy is memory or a return of the origin, what I am (he is) doing cannot, in any way, be regarded as philosophy; and if the history of thought consists in giving life to half-effaced figures, what I am (he is) doing is not history either. (p. 206)

If archaeology is neither philosophy nor history of thought, what is it? Foucault specifies that archaeology is "a diagnosis" (p.206) of the potential problems in knowledge production. He treats archaeology as:

> a search for the origin, for formal a prioris, for founding act, in short, as a sort of historical phenomenology (when on the contrary, its aims is to free history from the grip of phenomenology). (p.203)

Why is it called archaeology? Alan Sheridan offers an answer by an illuminating reading of Foucault. Sheridan is the first one who translates a number of Foucault's works in English. In *Michel Foucault: The Will to Truth*, Sheridan (1990) offers a useful elucidation of Foucault's archaeology. He distinguishes the positions held by Foucault and Marx, in terms of their views of the subject and history. Marx's historical analysis is built ultimately on "the founding function of the subject" and "of human consciousness" (p. 91) – what we can call "total history" and "humanism" (p. 91–92). On the contrary, Foucault tries to move away from 'totalities' and generates a different form of historical analysis which undermines the primacy of the subject in order to uncover and examine the existence, functions and relations between various discursive practices. In doing so, Sheridan (1990) highlights that Foucault's methodological approach is different from 'total history', in terms of "the attribution of innovation, the analysis of contradictions, comparative descriptions, and the mapping of transformation" (pp.102–103). Given Foucault writes a different form of history that moves away from what men have said, he would rather use a term, "archaeology" (Sheridan, 1990, p. 102). Hence, the term 'archaeology' is coined in order to separate what he was doing from the established norm in the history of thought.

Following Foucault's archaeology, Jacques (1996) writes about history to interpret the present. He examines American management history in order to understand a direction for the future. He insists that:

> This history is written to show some of the patterns made by the present as its kaleidoscopes into the immediate future. It does not yield to prediction, but seeks to throw into relief the fault lines and points of leverage marking the points at which intentional action is most likely to have results. (pp.13 – 14)

Hence, Jacques's archaeological examination "seeks to change work practices by changing the way we think about what can be changed, what should be changed and what possibilities exist for those involved in change" (p.14).

Another example is Xu's (1997; 2000) assessment of Total Quality Management (TQM). She follows Foucault's archaeological approach to trace the formation of knowledge on quality. In doing so, she studies historical details in order to address the problems in the established management knowledge, such as an imbalance operating modes of thought in the discourse on quality and a gap in the division of 'theory and practice' (Xu, 2000, p.447). She highlights that:

> Paradoxically, asking questions backward does allow me (her) to think forward. Not only does a way of thinking produce knowledge, its production cannot be separated from its discursive condition. (p. 447)

Even though Foucault, Jacques and Xu have clearly indicated their purposes and ways of accounting for history, archaeology is still being disapproved by those historians who tend to have a very different commitment in terms of what history should be about. For instance, Rowlinson and Carter (2002) identify six criticisms of archaeology, which are "(1) impenetrable style; (2) avoidance of narratives; (3) ambivalence to truth; (4) errors in historical facts; (5) neglect of relevant historiography; and (6) questionable historical explanations" (p.527). They articulate these arguments and assess the works of Clegg, Jacques and Burrell, who took a Foucauldian approach in their organisational analyses. For example, Rowlinson and Carter (2002) suspect that Jacques (1996) has failed to engage with appropriate historiography and generalize with adequate textual evidence. To such a review, Knights (2002) argues that Foucauldian analysis should not be seen as a conventional style of history. Foucault does not show much interest in staying in the past nor resolving the scholarly debates (Barratt, 2008). Indeed, Foucault has never claimed that his archaeological approach represents an evolutionary development of history. In particular, Foucault's analyses are not equivalent to historical stages from feudalism to socialism through the process of capitalism in Marx's materialism (Knights, 2002). Rather than framing history in a linear sequence (i.e. the pre-modern, modern and postmodern times), Foucault looks at the conditions of historical possibility. He examines the conditions of and "an effect of 'problem' of the present, not the past" (Knights, 2002, p.579). Given that 'history' in the Foucauldian style has shed some light on management (Jacques, 1996; Savage, 1998; McKinlay, 2006); 'history' becomes a resource for understanding the present (Barratt, 2008). The historical nature of Foucault's archaeology highlights a sense of contingency and fluidity in the present day practices (Sheridan, 1990; Barratt, 2002). This is perhaps why Foucault (1977a) describes his distinct form of examination as "history of the present" (p. 31), and not about the past.

Barratt (2008) outlines three ways to construct a history in the Foucauldian style: (1) start to diagnose any problems of the present; (2) explore the complex and contingent process regarding how and when the present took shape; and (3) examine governmentality by studying the languages used by the authorities to analyse the objects and process of governance. Working along those three steps, Barratt highlights that the purpose of a Foucauldian history is to:

> seek to capture not only the rationalities or games of truth that underpin the activity of government, but how these particular ways or style of ordering, defining and regulating human being have come into being. (p.520)

Hence, Foucault considers that there is always a complex history underlying concepts, classification and instruments of control which consist of a given rationality (Barratt, 2008). That is why Barratt (2008) regards a Foucauldian history as:

> fictional narratives – not in the sense of a falsehood – but in the sense that through the ordering placed on historical data (Falzon, 1998) and the deployment of language. (p.521)

Thinking along this direction, one can appreciate that a Foucauldian history lies in the way it enables and "seeks to transform the understanding of the reader" by moving away from the orthodoxy representation of historical truth (Barratt, 2008, p.521).

(c) Non-science

Third, the opponent argues that Foucault's archaeology is not a science. Archaeology is challenged for not being able to establish rigorous scientificity and create future generality (Foucault, 1972). Foucault defends that he has "never presented archaeology as a science, or even as the beginning of a future science" (p.206). That is to say, archaeology should never be treated as a science, because it is not supposed to be so.

Nevertheless, archaeology is related to sciences, given archaeology describes many science-objects and touches on questions raised by psychoanalysis, philology, epistemology, political sciences, sociology and biology.

In his careful reading of Foucault, Sheridan (1990) offers some explanation of the archaeological enterprise. Sheridan highlights that the nature of archaeology cuts across both science and non-science domains, because archaeology functions in between scientific and non-scientific streams. For that reason, archaeology produces non-scientific knowledge which is not supposed to be judged by scientific criteria. To Sheridan, the key contribution of Foucault is his attempt to avoid Marxist analyses, and to inspect the system of articulation between discursive and non-discursive practices.

Although Foucault himself and Sheridan have clarified the scope and nature of archaeology, much criticism against archaeology is based on the rules of science. One condemnation is Foucault's analyses lack implications that can unify theories with current practices (Smart, 1983; Barratt, 2004). For instance, Foucault is challenged by Marxist supporters for discounting the economic, social and political practices at that time (Sheridan, 1990). The empirical weakness of Foucauldian studies of management is that they provide little proof and evidence in telling the truth (Guest, 1999). Legge (1995) calls this problem as "relativism" – "a rejection of the existence of fundamental truths, in the power of reason and observation" (p. 301). However, in his defence, Foucault (1970) insists that it is not possible to generate any 'final' or 'definite truth'. *Archaeology of Knowledge* is written to extend his previous outputs (such as *Madness and Civilisation* and *The Order of Things*) and that represents his own elucidation and reflection of his analyses regarding certain theoretical and methodological problems. Foucault (1972) states that:

> Rather than founding a theory – and perhaps before being able to do so, (I (he) do not deny that I (he) regret(s) not yet having succeeded in doing so) – my (his) present concern is to establish a possibility. (pp.114–115)

Instead of constructing a rigorous theoretical model, he uses archaeology to open up and establish a possibility of mapping the linkages between discursive and non-discursive practices. To that end, Sheridan (1990) clarifies that Foucault does not intend to develop a theory of history. Nor does he support any theories related to political, social or economic practices. His archaeology is not meant to be a "pure theory", but "an invitation to discussion" (p. 213).

Foucault's distinctive form of analysis is "not 'grand narrative' or 'totalizing theory'" (Knight, 2002, p.579). The objective of Foucault's analysis is neither theory building nor preserving a particular 'truth' within a theory (Smart, 1983; Barratt, 2002; Knight, 2002). His archaeology focuses on examining:

> the interrelationship between formation of domains and objects (e.g. madness and sexuality, etc.) and their articulation within discourse itself subject to rules and procedures of verification and falsification – and the effects of this complex relationship 'in real'.
> (Smart, 1983, p.136)

That means, the theoretical and practical implications of his work lie in revealing complicated processes and practices in which power relations are regulated, governed and rationalised, instead of a definite representation of an individual or a particular field of experience (Barratt, 2002). Foucault's analyses contribute to "an understanding of the historical conditions of possibility of the human sciences and their social and political effects" (Smart, 1983, p. 73). Hence, Foucault's (1972) archaeology is an analysis of conditions of possibility in the discursive (trans)formation.

Foucault's writing represents a shift from theory to analysis. His work moves from a positivistic tendency towards a critical reflection upon the existing sets of stable and inviolable findings, concepts, principles and theories (Knights, 2002). One important practical implication from reading Foucault is to learn from his attitude and spirit which might guide one towards a distinctive form of reflexivity in scholarly practices (Barratt, 2002; 2004). In other words, a useful lesson from taking Foucault seriously is to: (1) follow his commitment to questioning conventional thought about what seems to be unthinkable (Knights, 2002); (2) maintain responsiveness to any danger and opportunities and (3) be willing to criticise and change one's values and thinking (Barratt, 2004). In such a spirit, the researcher of this thesis attempts to (1) challenge the mainstream discourse of well-being; (2) respond to any potential danger of objectification and essentialism in discourse and (3) evaluate one's values and practices in management and research.

(d) Revolution

Last, the opponent argues that Foucault is making a revolution that causes difficulties to others (Foucault, 1972). A warning is issued regarding the conditions of Foucault's archaeology. Foucault responds tactically by identifying a double mistake of the opponent. First, Foucault makes it clear that the discursive positivities he has formulated should not be interpreted as limitations imposed on the subjects, but rather an attempt to reveal a complexity and density of discursive practices. He specifies clearly at the introduction chapter that his aim "is not to transfer the field of history" (p.15). Second, Foucault asks a rhetorical question to his opponent:

> What is that fear that makes you reply in terms of consciousness when someone talks to you about practices, its conditions, its rules and its historical transformations? What is that fear that makes you seek, beyond all boundaries, ruptures, shifts and divisions, the great historico-transcendental destiny of the Occident?. (p. 210)

Foucault considers the only answer to the above questions is "a political one" (p.210). Hence, he implies that after all, the criticism against him comes from a political intention. While such a note closes his defence of archaeology, it opens up his mind to genealogy.

2 Genealogical phases: Political and Ethical Aspects

Foucault admits that a hidden criticism of archaeology is its lack of attention to power relations in discourse (Sheridan, 1990). Therefore, in the later stage, he takes an interest in examining the role of power in discourse and adopts Nietzsche's term of 'genealogy'. In his *Discipline and Punish: The Birth of the Prison* (1977a), he highlights the power/knowledge relations as follows:

> Power produces knowledge . . . Power and knowledge directly imply one another . . . There is no power relation without the correlative constitution of a field of knowledge, nor any knowledge that does not presuppose and constitute at the same time power relations. (p.27)

That means, power and knowledge are interdependent, in which "all knowledge is political" (Sheridan, 1990, p.220).

Foucault's genealogy arouses intense debates regarding power/knowledge relation. One typical argument against genealogy is that Foucault does not offer enough ground for any resistance or agency (Smart, 1983; Said, 1986; Barratt, 2003; 2004). Foucault has over-emphasised the effects of power. As a result, the subject is reduced as a passive recipient of power (Borg, 2015), who seems to be stripped off for any capacity to struggle (Gabriel, 1999; Newton, 1998; Reed, 1998). To defend against this denunciation, referring to Foucault's texts is necessary. In *the subject and power*, Foucault (1982) explains that:

> Power is exercised only over free subjects and only insofar as they are free. By this we mean individual or collective subjects who are faced with a field of possibilities in which several ways of behaving, several reactions and diverse comportments may be realised. (p. 790)

By this, Foucault actually highlights the importance of the free subject in the power relation. He emphasises that:

> In this game freedom may well appear as the condition for the exercise of power . . . The relationship between power and freedom's refusal to submit cannot, therefore, be separated. (p. 790)

Hence, Foucault suggests that power can be exercised only when the subject has a certain capacity of freedom to resist. That is to say, resistance represents a form of freedom of the subject. Hahm (2001), Barratt (2002), Knights (2004) and Borg (2015) derive a similar argument based on their thoughtful readings of Foucault. They argue that the existence of power implies the possibility of resistance – "whenever there is power, there is also resistance" (Knights, 2004, p. 22) or "there can be no power . . . without the possibility of resistance" (Borg, 2015, p.13). Therefore, according to Foucault, freedom and resistance are regarded as the conditions of possibility for power (Hahm, 2001; Barratt, 2002; Knights, 2004; Borg, 2015).

Given genealogy scrutinises the conditions of possibility of how the subject is able to act according to themselves within particular power relations, the notion of agency has been inwardly examined (Barratt, 2003). In his *Politics of Truth*, Foucault (1997b) highlights that:

> I will say that critique is the movement by which the subject gives himself the right to question truth on its effects of power and question power on its discourses of truth. (p. 32)

Hence, Foucault implies that one can exercise his/her agency to resist the normalizing effects of power (Bevir, 1999; Hahm, 2001). In other words, the subject can utilize the capacity for agency to question any received identity (Bevir, 1999). This is the moment when the subject has the right to question the power. That is why Barratt (2003) argues that:

> If Foucault fails to theorize agency in any formal sense, this can be defended as a deliberate move rather than an omission. (p. 1077)

His argument is based on the view that agency should not be assumed as an abstract capacity. Instead, agency should be examined in relation to any social practices regarding how peoples with different capacities, resources and possibilities are able to act on themselves within a specific social context. Then, what are the conditions that the subject can possibly exercise agency in a social relationship? Foucault's notion of *governmentality* sets out a condition of this possibility. In the *Ethics: Subjectivity and Truth*, Foucault (1997a) defines that *'governmentality'*:

> implies the relationship of the self to itself, and I (he) intend(s) this concept of 'governmentality' to cover the whole range of practices that constitute, define, organise, and instrumentalise the strategies that individuals in their freedom can use in dealing with each other. . . . Thus, the basis for all this is freedom, the relationship of the self to itself and the relationship to the other. . . . I (He) believe(s) that the concept of governmentality makes it possible to bring out the freedom of the subject and its relationship to others – which constitutes the very stuff of ethics. (p.300)

For Foucault, the subject is involved in an active constitution of the self via his/her conscientiousness and self-knowledge and this is referred as critical self-reflection and transformation (Foucault, 1977b). Along the process, the subject can govern oneself by exercising a certain capacity of freedom in order to produce ethical conducts in a social intercourse (Hahm, 2001; Borg, 2015). In other words, the subject exercise agency and resistance through the ethics of care for the self and its relations with others, instead of the suppression of power (Hahm, 2001). This is what Foucault (1977b) calls *an aesthetics of existence* (aesthetic self), which can be considered as a condition in which the subject would exercise his/her autonomy of resistance for the purpose of producing an ethical self. Therefore, the concept of agency is implied in Foucault's ideas of *governmentality* and *an aesthetics of existence*.

Foucault's ideas are arguably applicable in the workplace given the subject at work is positioned in economic relations that are as much as in the power/knowledge relations mentioned by Foucault (Barratt, 2002; Knights, 2002; 2004). For instance, it is arguable that Foucault's concern of power can be applied in relation to the limits of capitalism raised by Marx (Smart, 1983; Barratt, 2002; Bidet, 2016). Bidet (2016) has attempted to bring Marx and Foucault together. Bidet produced a synthesis of both Marx's capitalism and Foucault's liberalism. In particular, Bidet took Foucault's dimension of knowledge-power to demonstrate the incompleteness and missing links of Marx's theory of Capital. While Bidet's attempt is insightful and novel, it is also unjustified to selectively appropriate Foucault's power/knowledge without recognising the incompatibility between Marx and Foucault, in terms of their epistemologies and assumptions. This argument has been raised by Knights (2004) in his examination of organisational analysis. On one hand, Knights recognises the value of Foucault in management studies. On the other hand, he is also aware of a weakness in writing organisational analyses into Foucault – There is a strong tendency for organisational theorists to select Foucault's genealogy to examine the power and discipline within organisations. In particular, *Discipline and Punish: The birth of the prison* has become a popular representation of Foucault, in which a majority of organisational studies focuses and draws from this book. As a consequence, Knights warns that such a selective appropriation of Foucault could lead to the following danger:

> Accordingly, his (Foucault's) epistemology is often ignored, his uniquely sceptical approach to history marginalised, his analysis of power and resistance constrained by reading into it dualistic conceptions that are wholly inappropriate, his ethics seen as self-indulgent rather than a culmination of his life's work and a vivid example of his method of deploying universally-held values precisely to struggle against them.
>
> (p.590)

In order to avoid the above risks, Knights suggests pushing organisational analysis towards a manner that can fully engage with Foucault. One way to do so is to remain vigilant with Foucault's epistemological approach by constantly challenging what is taken for granted and examining the conditions of possibility. Therefore, following Knight's advice, this book deploys Foucault's archaeology to challenge the concept of well-being and scrutinise the conditions of subjectivity that made well-being possible in a Chinese context.

Postcolonial perspective is an example that builds from Foucault's idea of power/knowledge relations. Postcolonial studies challenge the politics of knowledge and examine the conditions of possibility of imperialism and colonialism. Given Foucault's epistemological approach tends to focus on 'how' and 'when' questions (Foucault, 1970; 1972), some postcolonial researchers have extended Foucault's inquiries and stepped further to address the 'why' question. They focus on investigating the details and impacts of the colonial projects. For instance, Stoler (1992) highlights the divisiveness of the colonial project by assessing its intentions, objectives, practices, interaction and impacts. Another example is Westwood (2001), who does not only examine the knowledge/power strategies of the colonist, but further analyse the purposes behind the strategies. He offers answers concerning why essentialism occurs in the comparative management discourse. In his examination, the three motives of essentialism are:

(1) The West would like to spread modernization and development and incorporate underdeveloped nations into the world economy;
(2) The process of incorporation reduce the uncertainties and threats posed by *the Other*;
(3) Making *the Other* amenable to a system of categorization, organization and order.

In addition to identifying the causes of essentialism, Westwood (2001) calls for strategies that examine how *the Other* can be relocated in terms of agency, reversal and hybridity. For instance, Ngugi (1981) demonstrates a decolonisation by resisting the language of dominance (i.e. English), writing in African language and focusing on the specificities of African language. Another example is from Tibi (1995) who illustrates a possibility of de-Westernising science in Muslim society. He insists on Muslim knowledge system – 'knowledge for living"; while rejecting Western "knowledge for power" in the Islamic world (Watt, 1988: 13). These examples show how researchers may respond to critiques of Foucault by defending their approaches based on Foucault and extending his enquiries.

Appendix B

Notes B1: Research Design and the Fieldwork

Research design is a strategic plan and structure of the research. It is a blueprint and a road map for ethnographers to conceptualise each step before they build knowledge and understanding (Fetterman, 2010). As suggested by Brewer (2000), an ethnographic research design can include the outline and features of the topic, the choice of research site or field, the form(s) of sampling employed, the resources available for the research, the sampling of the time and the events to be experienced in the field, the method(s) of data collection, negotiating access to the field, the nature of the fieldworker role(s), the form of analysis and dissemination to be used to report the results and more. Among the research process, fieldwork is one of the most significant elements of any ethnographic research design (Fetterman, 2010).

The fieldwork started on March 01 2012. The researcher selected four field sites: FB 1–4. All four companies are family business of small and medium-size. The fieldwork ended on December 31 2015. The amount of fieldwork (in terms of hours and periods) is shown in Tab. B1:

Tab. B1: Amount of Fieldwork in Each Field Site.

Field Site	Period	Hours
FB 1 (An Education Centre)	Mar 01 2012–Dec 31 2015	252 hours
FB 2 (A Dance Studio)	Sep 27 2013–Dec 31 2015	224 hours
FB 3 (A Jade Accessory Maker)	Jan 01 2013–Dec 31 2015	231 hours
FB 4 (A Fashion Business)	Feb 03 2014–Dec 31 2015	212 hours
	Total hours:	919 hours

The fieldwork is discussed in five aspects: (1) selection of field site, (2) sampling, (3) gaining access, (4) data collection and (5) reflexivity.

1 Selection of Field Site

In the context of post-colonial thought, Jack and Westwood (2006) suggest that local self-representation should be taken into account and become the key resource driving research. They encourage indigenous researchers from non-western contexts to engage in their own research practice and conduct truly emic studies. With the need for such studies, I chose a Chinese backdrop, Hong Kong as the site for research. Clifford (1986) referred to those researchers who act as insiders to study their own cultures as "indigenous ethnographer" (p.9). I took advantage of being a local, familiar with the Hong Kong dialect, Cantonese (which is the mother language of the researcher), its culture, lifestyle, weather and environment. Thus, the key advantage of being an 'indigenous ethnographer' is that I "know exactly what one is talking about" (Madden, 1999, p.260), thus such familiarity may "offer new angles of vision and depths of understanding" (Clifford, 1986, p.9).

The researcher would like to emphasise that this research is an ethnography, rather than a case study research. The researcher has never intended to produce case studies. Yin (1981) highlights that:

> A common misconception is that case studies are solely the result of ethnographies or of participant-observation, yet it should be quickly evident that numerous case studies have been done without using these methods (e.g., Allison, 1971). Conversely, using these methods does not always lead to production of case studies (e.g. the ethnographic and observational research on police behaviours by Reiss, 1971; Rubenstein, 1973; and Van Maanen, 1979; none of which had typically been designed as case studies). (p.59)

Cohen and Deborah (2003) make a clear differentiation between ethnography and case study. They highlight a crucial difference between ethnography and case study lies in the intention of the study. Ethnography is 'inward looking', which centres on 'culture' and intends to study ways of life for a particular cultural participant; while case study is 'outward look', that aims to delineate the phenomenon through a detailed examination of individual cases and their contexts (Cohen and Deborah, 2003). The purposes of the author are to get close with an indigenous subject and understand its culture by capturing its local expressions which are embedded in its everyday lives. Hence, judging from the intention of this book, it is an ethnography, instead of a case study.

Based on the methodological position, this study belongs to ethnography. According to Guba and Lincoln (2005), they position case study within the 'post positivism' – the conservative end of the qualitative research continuum which seeks to exclude researcher's influence on the data or evidence. That is why case study can be regarded as a part of the conventional methodology that insists on rigour, validity, reliability and objectivity (Stake, 2005). Although individual case study does not aim at generalisation, the accumulation of case studies does target on generalisation (Cohen and Deborah, 2003). On the contrary, ethnography is situated along the critical perspective and social constructivism which allows researchers to be part of the researched (Guba and Lincoln, 2005). Based on the ontological and epistemological assumptions of this study, the researcher holds a critical perspective, rather than positivism nor post positivism (see Tab. B2). Hence, ethnography is chosen because it would be more aligned with the philosophical position of the researcher.

Tab. B2: Philosophical Perspectives in Social Sciences.

Assumptions		Positivism	Interpretivism	Critical perspective
1.	**Ontology:**			
a.	*Reality is/are*	− objective, 'out there' to be found − perceived through the senses − perceived uniformly by all peoples − governed by universal law − based on integration	− 'subjective', in people's minds − created, not found − interpreted differently by people − objectified through human interaction	− both 'out there' and in people's minds − complex: appearance is not reality − created by people, not by nature − in tension / full of contradictions − based on oppression and exploitation
b.	*Human beings*	− rational individuals − obeying external laws − without free will	− creators of their world − making sense of their world − not restricted by external laws − creating systems of meanings	− creators of their destiny − oppressed, alienated, exploited, restricted − brainwashed, misled, conditioned − hindered from realizing their potential
2.	**Epistemology:**			
a.	*Science*	− based on strict rules and procedures − deductive − relying on sense impression − value free	− agreement with actor's common sense interpretation − inductive − relying on logical consistency and interpretations − not value free	− conditions shape life but can be changed − emancipating, empowering − relying on sense impression and values − temporal and context-bound − not value free
b.	*Knowledge in the form of*	Explanation	Interpretation	Understanding

Tab. B2 (continued)

Assumptions	Positivism	Interpretivism	Critical perspective
c. *Research aims to*	– explain social life – predict course of event – discover the laws of social life – seek out causes	– interpret social life – understand social life – discover people's meanings	– explain, interpret and elucidate – reveal myths and illusions – reveal power and mechanisms – emancipate and empower – identify and challenge/question domination and ideological practices
d. *Data*	– social facts	– social interaction	– historical, structural and ideological
e. *Researcher*	– independent observer	– part of what is observed	– engager and actor of reality

(Modified from: Chua, 1986; Harvey and MacDonald, 1993; Sarantakos, 1998)

Based on the above justification, the researcher regards this study as a critical ethnography, instead of a case study. The researcher chooses the four Chinese family businesses in order to examine the local expressions of a Chinese subject in its everyday lives. Hence, the four family businesses are regarded as four field sites for the ethnography. Due to the small amount of the field sites, classification into cases is insignificant and even impossible. The researcher actually declines to do so because this book has never been a case study research that requires classification and generalisation among the four businesses.

2 Sampling

Snowball sampling is also known as chain-referral sampling, in which researchers develop contacts with informants through referral (Cohen and Arieli, 2011). Snowball sampling is commonly used in ethnography because it helps ethnographers to gain access to the field sites and develop contacts (Grbich, 1999). This research employs snowball sampling given developing trust is necessary if one wants to gain access to the Chinese family business. Firstly, I used my local network to develop contacts. To begin the fieldwork, I contacted my relatives and friends to see if they could participate in my research or refer anyone to me. That was how the snowball started rolling. Then, close contacts recommended other participants to me. The snowball kept rolling until I was able to gain access to the four field sites: FB 1 to 4. Regular field site visits to the four companies ensued. At the end, the four family businesses should be enough to generate sufficient data for the research. The profiles of my informants can be referred to Tab. B3.

Tab. B3: Profiles of Informants.

a. Profiles of informants in the four field sites.

Family business	People	Descriptions	Remarks	Interview
FB 1: An education centre	Mrs. Ada	Role: Family worker Age: 40s Education: Bachelor business degree	Ada is referred by Gigi. Ada is a family worker of a family business, owned by her mother. She is married and has a daughter and a son.	√
	Mrs. Alice	Role: Owner Age: 60s	Alice is the mother of Ada and an owner of FB 1. FB 1 has two branches in the same district and offers educational services, mainly to the primary school and secondary school students.	√
	Ms. Amy	Role: Teacher Age: 20s	Amy is working as a full-time teacher in FB 1 for several years. She is mainly responsible for the teaching and administration work.	√
	Mrs. Ann	Role: Teacher Age: 30s	Mrs. Ann is working as a full-time teacher in FB 1 for several years. She is mainly responsible for the teaching and administration work.	√
	Mrs. Ashley	Role: Employee Age: 40s	Ms. Ashley is working as a full time employee since 2005. She is mainly responsible for pantry work.	√
	Mrs. Audrey	Role: Teacher Age: 40s Education: Bachelor degree	Mrs. Audrey is working as a full-time teacher in FB 1 for several years. She studied in the same college with Ada's sister, and therefore has a close and long friendship with Ada's family. She is mainly responsible for the teaching and housekeeping in another branch. She is married and has children.	√

Tab. B3 (continued)

a. Profiles of informants in the four field sites.

Family business	People	Descriptions	Remarks	Interview
	Ms. Averi	Role: Tutor (part-time) Age: 20s	Ms. Averi is working as part-time tutor in FB 1. She also works for the family business (FB 8) owned by her father.	√
	Ms. Alysia	Role: Tutor (part-time) Age: 20s	Ms. Alysia is working as a part-time tutor in FB 1. She is a new tutor.	√
	Ms. Abbey	Role: Tutor (part-time) Age: 40s	Ms. Abbey is working as a part-time tutor in FB 1 for around 6 years.	√
	Ms. Abegail	Role: Teacher Age: 20s	Ms. Abegail was a full-time teacher in FB 1. She worked there for a few years and has resigned.	
	Ms. Ally	Role: Teacher Age: 20s	Ms. Ally was a full-time teacher in FB 1. She has resigned. She was once referred by Alice's neighbor.	
	Ms. Apple	Role: Tutor (part-time) Age: 40s	Ms. Apple is a new part-time tutor. Due to her poor performance, she was being terminated.	
	Part-time employees		FB 1 employs part-time teaching staff to conducting tutorials. Most of them are university's students or housewives.	
FB 2: A dance studio	Ms. Betty	Role: Owner Age: 30s Education: Master degree in Accountancy	Ms. Betty is the owner of FB 2. She is a ballet dancer. Opening a dance studio is her dream. She initiated to start the business with her close friend, Mrs. Bonnie.	√
	Mrs. Bonnie	Role: Owner Age: 30s Education: Diploma in Hospitality	Mrs. Bonnie is the owner of FB 2. She has a full-time job as a flight attendant. She is married and has a 3 years old daughter.	√
	Mr. Bob	Role: Limited partner Age: 50s	Mr. Bob was once Betty's superior. He seldom engages in the operation of FB 2. He mainly offers financial support to Betty.	√
	Ms. Brenda	Role: Full-time employee Age: 20s	Ms. Brenda was the first full time employees of FB2. She was responsible for teaching, as well as administration work. Her employment ended due to the economic problem of FB 2.	√

Tab. B3 (continued)

a. Profiles of informants in the four field sites.

Family business	People	Descriptions	Remarks	Interview
	Mrs. Blossom	Role: Full-time employee Age: 30s	Ms. Blossom was the second full-time employees of FB 2. She was responsible for teaching, as well as administration work. Her employment ended due to the economic problem of FB 2.	√
	Ms. Bessy	Role: Part-time teacher Age: 30s	Ms. Bessy is Betty's friend. They usually dance together. She teaches the Yoga course.	√
FB 3: A jade accessory maker	Uncle Carl	Role: Owner Age: 60s Education: Primary school level	Uncle Carl is a jade accessory maker for over 30 years. He has a retail store, selling his products. He also works at home. He is the sole work in the business.	√
	Auntie Connie	Role: Carl's wife Age: late 50s Education: Primary school level	Auntie Connie is Carl's wife. They have been married for over 20 years. She is a full-time housewife.	√
	Mr. Carson	Role: Carl's eldest son Age: 30s Education: Secondary school level	Mr Carson is Carl's eldest son. He is working as a driver in a logistic company. He seldom involves in the FB 3.	√
	Mrs. Cindy	Role: Carl's eldest sister Age: 60s Education: Primary school level	Mrs. Cindy is Carl's sister. She is the wife of Mr. Isaac (FB 10). She often visits Carl and Connie for social chats and family gatherings.	√
FB 4: A fashion business	Ms. Doris	Role: Owner Age: 40s Education: Master degree in Art and Fashion Design	Ms. Doris is a fashion designer. She opens FB 4 with her boss, Dave. She runs a fashion retails store in Central.	√
	Mr. Dominic	Role: Full-time driver Age: late 40s	Mr. Dominic is the full-time driver of FB 4. He is mainly responsible for the office technical maintenance and logistic arrangement.	√

Tab. B3 (continued)

a. Profiles of informants in the four field sites.

Family business	People	Descriptions	Remarks	Interview
	Mr. Dave	Role: Owner Age: 50s	Mr. Dave is Doris's boss. He trusts Doris and relies very much on her to run the business. He is the key financial provider of the business.	√
	Ms. Daisy	Role: Part-time employee Age: 20s	Ms. Daisy is studying fashion in the Honk Kong Polytechnics University. She is working as a part-time employee in FB 4. When Doris and I are unable look after the retail store, Daisy would work and manage the operation.	√
	Mr. Daniel	Role: Doris's brother-in-law Age: 40s	Mr. Daniel is Gigi's husband. He often helps Doris in graphic designs.	√

b. Profiles of Human Resources Professional (HRP).

HRP	Company	Descriptions	Remarks	Interview
Mr. Peter	A trading MNC	Role: HR director Age: 50s Education: Bachelor degree in Engineering	Mr. Peter works in a trading MNC which its operates across Asia, Europe and Australia. Peter is referred to by my colleague. He was previously an Engineering manager, and had been transferred to the works of training and development since 1992. Now, he is the Group Human Resource Director.	√
Ms. Paris	Educational Institute	Role: HR Officer Age: 20s Education: Master degree in Project Management	Ms. Paris is working as a HR officer in one educational institute. She was my past students. Her HR work focuses on training and development. Her family runs a family business- a restaurant.	√
Mrs. Pansy	Banking	Role: Training Officer Age: 30s Education: Bachelor degree in Hospitality	Mrs. Pansy is referred by my colleague. She is a training officer in one international bank.	√
Ms. Patricia	Accounting and Auditing Firm	Role: HR consultant Age: 30s Education: Master degree in Organisational Psychology	Ms. Patricia is my previous colleague. She is an organisational psychologist. She is responsible for organising training and development for her company.	√

Tab. B3 (continued)

b. Profiles of Human Resources Professional (HRP).

HRP	Company	Descriptions	Remarks	Interview
Ms. Pauline	Consultancy Firm	Role: HR Consultant Age: 40s	Ms. Pauline is referred by Patrica. They worked together as HR consultants before.	√

c. Profiles of informants in other companies.

Family business	People	Descriptions	Remarks	Interview
FB 5: A logistics company	Mr. Edmond	Role: Managing Director Age: 30s Education: Bachelor business degree from overseas	Mr. Edmond is my contact in church. He was the successor of FB 5. His family business was sold in the early 2012. He is now an employee of a logistic multinational firm, and is responsible for work related to sales and marketing. He is married and has a one-year old child	
	Mrs. Eden	Role: Housewife Age: 30s Education: Full-time PhD student and received her college and university education from overseas	Mrs. Eden is the wife of Edmond. She is currently a full-time PhD student in Hong Kong, and a full-time housewife.	
FB 6: A trading company	Fiona	Role: Employee Age: 30s Education: Received education from overseas	Fiona is referred by my friend. She had lived and studied in Canada for many years. Few years ago, she decided to come back to Hong Kong. She was an English teacher of my friend. Few months ago, she has changed to work for a family business, which is a trading company. Her roles in that trading firm are to improve the efficiency of its business process, offer suggestions for change and manage the change process.	√

Tab. B3 (continued)

c. Profiles of informants in other companies.

Family business	People	Descriptions	Remarks	Interview
FB 7: A graphic design and illustration business	Mrs. Gigi	Role: Graphic designer and illustrator Age: 40s Education: Bachelor degree in Hong Kong	Mrs. Gig is my close contact. She has started her graphic design business in 2012. While she is running her business, she is also a working as full-time graphic designer in a company.	√
FB 8: A transportation service company	Ms. Averi	Role: Family worker Age: 20s	FB 8 is a small family business, offering transportation service for some schools. Ms. Averi is a family worker of that family business, which owned by her father. She is responsible for taking care of the school's kids during the transportation.	√
FB 9: Local Bank (MNC)	Ms. Hestia	Role: Manager Age: 30s	FB 9, a local bank, which is found by a family business. It has become a MNC.	√
FB 10: A metal work company	Mr. Isaac	Role: Retired owner Age: 70s Education: Up to college level	FB 10 was a metal work company, founded by Mr. Isaac's father. Isaac was the successor of FB 10. He closed the business in 2005.	

Sampling within each fieldsite is another aspect that deserves attention (Hammersley and Atkinson, 1995). Once the researcher could feel free to chat with the people in FB 1 since June 2012, I adopted a 'big-net approach' (Fetterman, 2010). As the study progressed, I gradually refined and narrowed the focus to specific portions of the population under study. Fetterman (2010) admits that most ethnographers employ the big-net approach in their participant observations, because it "ensures a wide-angle view of events before the microscopic study of specific interactions begins" and "this big picture helps refine an ethnographer's focus and aids the fieldworker in understanding the finer details that he or she will capture on film and in notes for further analysis" (p.35).

Fetterman (2010) indicates that "anthropologists have traditionally relied most heavily on one or two individuals in a given group", given "time is always a factor" and the "key actors are excellent source of information and important sounding boards for ethnographers . . . (who) can provide detailed historical data, knowledge about contemporary interpersonal relationship (including conflicts), and a wealth of information about the nuances of everyday life" (Fetterman, 2010, p.50). Although I tried to speak with as many people as possible, I still relied heavily on some key players in the business. In each family business, there are various members in the company. For example, FB 1 has different groups[1] of people. I looked for some key actors of the business. For example, major players include Ada, Mrs. Alice, Amy, Ann and Audrey in FB 1; Betty and Bonnie in FB 2; Uncle Carl in FB 3 and Doris in FB 4. These players were able to provide background stories and keep me updated on relevant issues and events occurring in the business.

Five local HR practitioners are selected for semi-structured interviews. They are mainly selected due to their close friendship with the researcher. The main purpose of including their views is to indicate that they are familiar with the concept of well-being. Such a finding is aligned with the archaeological examination of this study, which shows that HR professional is the one who speaks for the well-being. However, the researcher does not intend to compare any differences in terms of how the local HR professional expresses well-being. It is because that is not the focus of this ethnography. The purpose of this ethnography is on uncovering the local expressions and concepts in a Chinese context – Chinese family business in Hong Kong. The local HR views on well-being are mostly expressed within the mainstream interpretation, in which well-being is associated with benefits, work-life balance and job satisfaction etc. Instead of following the mainstream debate that argues well-being can be measured by a number of variables, this study would like to open a discursive space outside the boundary of well-being. As a result, alternate local expressions can be revealed and emphasised. In other words, local HR views are not the focus in the research questions nor in the data analysis. They are taken as an empirical supplement to support the archaeological analysis.

3 Access

Once the decision was made to examine the family businesses in Hong Kong, the first potential opportunity was the logistics company (FB 5) inherited by Mr. Edmond from his father. Before I went to the United Kingdom to complete the first year of PhD study, I had used his personal contacts to establish talks with the respective firm for the research. Thus, the fieldwork was established with FB 5. Nevertheless, as indicated by

---

1 Basically, the staff of FB 1 can be ranged from:
 - family workers versus non-family workers;
 - employees versus management;
 - full-time versus part-time staff;
 - teaching staff versus non-teaching staff.

Hammersley and Atkinson (1995), "the course of ethnographic work cannot be predetermined" (p.24). In early 2012, shortly after I went back to Hong Kong for the fieldwork, I was told by the owner of FB 5, Edmond that the sale of his family business was confirmed. Given such situation, I needed to look for another firm to conduct a pilot study.

Although the way of conducting ethnography cannot be definitely set out, this does not mean "the researcher's behaviour in the field can be haphazard" given the researcher can make adjustments to events by "taking 'the line of least resistance'" (Hammersley and Atkinson, 1995, p.21). Therefore, in searching for another firm to start my fieldwork, I used my personal contacts to conduct the research with an acquaintance. I gained access to FB 1 (An education center) through Ada, who is the youngest daughter of the owner in FB 1. My first meeting with Ada was arranged by Gigi wherein we had a casual dinner together. In the dinner, Ada accepted my request to conduct a study about her business and agreed that I could regularly visit her company.

Blomberg, Giacomi, Mosher and Swenton-wall (1993) remind the field-worker that:

> jeopardizing one's position in the community by insisting on observing or participating in an activity, when doing so is deemed inappropriate in the community, could easily spell disaster for the project. It is more advantageous to proceed slowly, gaining trust before insisting on access to certain events, people and activities. Often patience and greater familiarity with local custom will pay off. What was off limits initially may become open in time. (p.132)

I was therefore cautious about the possible consequences of being too 'pushy' with participants. Brewer (2000) point out that "the time spent in the field can even be restricted at the beginning in order for people to get used to the presence of the ethnographer slowly, although thereafter it needs to be intensive" (p. 85). Therefore, to start the fieldwork in FB 1, I visited the company on a bi-weekly basis. Initially, I usually talked with Ada only, as I aimed to develop a close relationship with her, before gaining the trust of other people on site. I was aware of the significance of gaining trust with Ada and making people in the company feel comfortable with my presence. Meanwhile, being a relatively silent observer at the beginning of the visits, would allow me to learn about the company's culture, custom and routines. Thus, considerable time was spent for the research and other employees to be at ease within the new dynamics.

Since first visit on 1st March 2012, I was waiting for 'signs' which indicate a certain degree of trust has been established, before I could move further to chat with other people openly and freely in the company. However, "trust is rarely instantaneous and is usually like any friendship in being a slow, steady process" (Brewer, 2000, p.85). After 3-month visits, the 'signs' came in June, when I received Whatapps messages from Ada in response to regular request for company's visit:

> Remember please do NOT buy anything if u come this time. (5 June 2012)

> Okay, actually u can come anytime u like . . . U can come without prior notice . . . . (14 June 2012)

Even upon the visit on 29 June 2012, the owner of FB 1, Mrs. Alice told me:

> You can come whenever you like.

At the beginning of June 2012, I was introduced to some colleagues in the company. Following this, I was able to chat with them, observe their daily routine operations, offer some ad hoc clerical assistance and have lunch with them occasionally. As recorded in the field note:

> This time, I also had chance to get involved in some ad hoc administrative tasks. The staff and owners started getting familiar with my regularly visit and I started feeling I'm being part of the company. (14 June 2012)

> When I arrived to the centre, Ada and Mrs. Alice were having lunch with the other staff. I was invited to join them for lunch and we have a casual chat over various topics, such as family lives, work, current educational issues and hobbies etc. (29 June 2012)

The above were perceived as 'signs' which show that a certain level of rapport has been established between the informants and me. With these 'signs', I started to move to the next stage since June 2012 where (1) increase the frequency of visit to around 1-2 times per week, (2) lengthen the duration of each visit from within 2 hours to more than 3 hours, and (3) go and chat with the people in the company. That was how I began my ethnographic journey in FB 1, which was treated as the pilot study of this book.

Research design can involve extending field sites (Hammersley and Atkinson, 1995). However, a major difficulty in extending the pilot study is the access to further sites. As a response, I started to work on with the informants who are considered as potential gatekeepers, like Uncle Carl and Ms. Doris. Moreover, I did not exclude data from the informants who previously worked or have worked in family businesses (such as Mr. Edmond and Mrs. Eden E in FB 5 and Mr. Isaac in FB 10 in Tab. B3). At last, I am able to gain access to FB 2, 3 and 4.

I gained access to FB 2 because its owners – Betty and Bonnie are my close friends. I shared close relationships with both of them for nearly twenty years, since we were at the same secondary school. Given we are very *shu* 熟 (familiar with each other), it was not difficult to gain access. The access was naturally obtained, without much hesitation nor obstacles. The close relation with the two owners affected how I conducted the fieldwork in this company. In FB 1, I had taken a relatively conservative and passive approach given trust and rapport had not yet been built at the beginning. I would always remind myself to be cautious about my responses and behaviours. To play safe, I would rather be less intrusive and focus more on participant observations. In contrast, more aggressive and active roles at FB 2 were taken. With a close peer relation with Betty and Bonnie, I would share the views about the business, and participate in the business operation and evolution in FB 2.

For FB 3, its owner was one of my personal contacts. Therefore, gaining access was straightforward. The request for including this business as part of the study was simply made by a phone call. As Uncle Carl always said to me: *'You can visit me at anytime you like. We are one family. You are always welcome to have a chat with me and your auntie (his wife, Auntie Connie) when you are free. We can go for lunch or tea'*. As an ethnographer, it was concluded that I acted on various roles. In FB 1, I would normally be a participant observant and did not disturb the daily operation of the tutorials. In FB 2, I would behave as a *peng you* (friend), whom Betty and Bonnie would be able to freely share their feelings and thoughts. As *peng you*, I would also offer assistance to them and share my advice with them. In FB 3, since Uncle Carl and Auntie Connie are seniors and I respect them dearly. I call them Uncle and Auntie, instead of calling them directly by their first name. Hence, in FB 3, I would take a role as a patient listener when they shared their stories and experiences. This business is of a different nature from FB 1 and FB 2 and I have limited knowledge in this industry. Thus, while visiting FB 3, I acted like a journalist.

The journey in FB 4 began in February 2014 when I had an afternoon tea with my close contact, Doris. On that day, she shared her good news: *"I'm going to open my own retail store"*. Doris had been working in the fashion field for number of years. After the tea, she immediately brought us to PMQ, where her new shop would be situated. The shop was still under renovation and was not yet ready for business. After visiting her shop, I asked if I could make regular visits to the shop and invited her to participate in my research. She instantly made a casual respond with a joke to indicate her agreement: *"Of course, you definitely need to come regularly. I need you to look after the shop! Ha ha ha!"* . Her reaction signified that my roles as an ethnographer would be different in FB 4, when compared to that in FB 1, 2 and 3. Provided the close relationship between I and Doris, I regarded myself as a key family member who should bear social obligation and responsibilities to look after her business. Hence, in FB 4, I would be an active participant in the business.

4 Data Collection Methods

In this study, the data was obtained mainly by: (a) participant observation, (b) informal conversation, (c) documentary and photos evidence, (d) writing interpretive field notes and diary and (e) semi-structured interviews.

(a) Participant Observation

Brewer (2000) regards participant observation as the data collection technique that is most closely associated with ethnography. Ethnographers would collect data by participating in the daily life of informants in natural settings. They would watch, observe and talk to informants in order to understand their interpretations, social meanings and daily routines. During the field visits, I had the opportunity to walk around and observe how my informants perform their daily activities. Though I was an overt observer, I aimed not to create any disturbance over my informants' work, especially when they are conducting lessons. For instance, in FB 1, I would normally sit at the corner of the room, taking my notes and observing without much intrusion. Nevertheless, I occasionally offered assistance by engaging in some clerical ad hoc tasks. The purpose was not only "to generate data through watching and listening to what people naturally do and say, but also add the dimension of personally experiencing and sharing the same everyday life as those under study" (Brewer, 2000, p.59). The personal reflection, attitude and social meanings when engaging in and living with the people in the field form part of the data

(b) Informal Conversations

Another main method of data collection is informal conversations. This method is common in ethnography (Fetterman, 2010). For instance, in FB 1, I would usually have informal conversations with the informants before the start of any classes at 3:00pm. These conversations cover wide range of topics, such as family, hobbies, current news, TV programs, food and issues in work and more. Most often, I would attempt to have 'informal interviews' with them. Thus, I have "a specific but implicit research agenda", in which there are series of questions listed in the field diary and will "wait for the most appropriate moment to ask them during informal conversations" (Fetterman, 2010, p.41). Indeed, casual conversations are a major method to collect data, particularly in FB 2, 3 and 4, given the close relationships developed by the researcher. In addition, living in Hong Kong, I also had chance to chat with some local citizens, youth, Human Resource Professionals and academics. Having dialogues with them enables me to gain a better understanding of the phenomenon.

(c) Documentary and Photo Evidence

The companies' and participants' Facebooks, documents and photographs, such as the company's brochures, photographs of the office environment and events previously organized etc. were examined. All hard-copy documentary evidence is filed and stored according to different categories. Although, these sources of data may not provide a direct link to the topic, they can reflect the company's value, area of concern and culture implicitly (Fetterman, 2010). Hence, proper use of them would be helpful and relevant.

Despite the focus of the study is the concept of well-being in China, the researcher makes reference to secondary data: the published documents and records regarding aspects of Hong Kong communities, such as news reports, public speeches, government reports, census and reference books. These sources of information could help to understand the lives of the locals on a macro level.

(d) Field Notes and Dairy

I took notes on every fieldwork activity, such as company visits, informal conversations and social gatherings. However, the process of note-taking varies depending on different sites and occasions. In FB 1, I usually sat in the corner of the classroom to observe and take notes; in FB 2, I normally sat in the reception counter, chatted with the owners and staff while jotting down the notes; in FB 3, I often sat next to the owner, asked him questions, observed his works and wrote down the notes; in FB 4, I always first oversaw the operation, then chatted with the owner when she came back and finally wrote the notes in the last hour of my visit. Various approaches in note-taking could generate impacts on what was observed. For instance, in FB 1, I usually acted as an observant and described things and incidents based on my observation and feelings. In FB 2 and 3, I often chatted with the owners and staff during the operation. In that case, I was able to write down their answers, describe their feelings and comments in the notes. In FB 4, I often participate in the operation. As a result, I described the working lives I experienced and jotted down the conversation with the owners. In general, the content of the field notes covers my feeling, experience, activities, incidents, events, observations and conversations occurred in each fieldwork. I tried to write as many as I could in every fieldwork, so that I did not need to repeat the same description in the dairy. Afterwards, when I went back home, I read my field notes and wrote diary. The diary is mainly my personal interpretations and critical reflections (both emotionally and intellectually) on each visit. Occasionally, I included some key references or quotations that are relevant to my interpretations. I also marked down the things I need to follow-up in the next visit. The field notes are written on the notebook during each visit. The field notes are consisted of 603 A5 handwritten pages; while the dairy consists of 152 A4-typed pages. The diary is stored as encrypted Microsoft Word files and is indexed onto the encrypted USB memory stick and PC hard drive.

(e) Semi-structured Interviews

Following Learmonth's (2009) methodological approach, semi-structured interviews were conducted at the later stage of the ethnography where a certain degree of trust has been established. In total, 33 semi-structured interviews with the participants were conducted. The interviewees range from family business owners, family workers, their family members, employees and Human Resource professionals. The questions asked in the interviews are related to the interviewees' past and present living experience and their expectations in the future.

5 Reflexivity

Reflexivity is defined as "a turning back on oneself, a process of self-reference" (Davies, 1999, p.4). It refers to a concern on how the selves and identities of the researchers and subject influence the research process, given the ethnographers are part of the context, setting and culture they are trying to understand and represent (Brewer, 2000). Reflexivity needs to be maintained throughout the whole research process (Davies, 1999).

Stanley (1996) asserted two forms of reflexivity: descriptive and analytical. Descriptive reflexivity involves reflection on the impact of various contingencies which may affect the research outcome, such as the geographical and social location of the research, the preconceptions of the researcher and the relationship between the researcher and the researched among others. This kind of reflexivity assumes knowledge of the process of knowledge production, is shaped by the social context or power structure (Collyer, 2011). Therefore, descriptive reflexivity requires ethnographers to develop a critical attitude towards their data (Brewer, 2000).

Analytical reflexivity demands reflection on the epistemological matters and knowledge claims (Brewer, 2000). It requires ethnographers to explicitly explain the process through which they reach their understanding and interpretation of the phenomena (Collyer, 2011). Thus, the ethnographers need to reflect upon areas, such as the theoretical or conceptual framework and methodology they are using; the values, commitments and preconceptions they bring to work; their ontological assumptions about the social reality and nature of society; and the topic and the approach of research in which they are interested (Brewer, 2000). Hence, analytical reflexivity reflects upon the process by which ethnographers reach their conclusion and looks at how they 'construct' their knowledge claims (Collyer, 2011).

Reflexivity is of utmost essence for this study as it provides a solution for the legitimacy of my interpretation and representation of data (Davies, 1999; Brewer, 2000). Therefore, this study would reflect on the following aspects:

(a) The Researcher

The personal history of researchers, as well as the disciplinary and broader sociocultural circumstances they are faced with, can have a profound effect on the entire research process, from the initial topic selection to final writing up (Collyer, 2011). I come from a family wherein the family members were engaged in family business founded by my grandparents. Thus, due to this, I experienced the dynamics in a family business and the complex relation within a family tie. For instance, the boundary of the family and work lives were not distinctly defined and the family obligation was often overlapped with the work duties. Given such family background, I recognise the importance of well-being in such type of business. Thus, this provides me with the research interest towards the lives and well-being of people in family businesses.

The topic of this study is well-being. The choice of this topic is due to my interest over the issue of work-family conflict in the Human Resource Management field during my postgraduate study in Australia. Such area of study is largely quantitative, which relies greatly on western assumptions and models, such as the segmentation model, integration model or boundary theory etc. Given the fact that little examination has been carried out to question whether the segmentation model (which is based upon the western assumption of treating work and family as two distinct domains) is appropriate in a Chinese context, my initial proposal (July 2010) aims to offer a new variable: work-family harmonisation and look at its linkage with well-being through a qualitative approach. The intent of the researcher was to use structured interviews, focus groups and participant observations to obtain data to examine the relationship between work-family harmonisation and well-being. Hence, the original proposal was situated within the neo-positivism/neo-empiricism with realist ontology and objectivist epistemology (Johnson, et al., 2006).

After reviewing the literature related to post-colonialism and discussions with my research supervisors, I realised that examining the indigenous culture would be more interesting to me. Therefore, I chose to employ an anthropological approach to reveal the current local expressions and concepts. Once I chose an anthropological study as my primary methodology, the next step was to determine an appropriate method. Several possibilities were taken for consideration, such as grounded theory, hermeneutics, phenomenology, critical discourse analysis and Foucault's (1972) discourse.

Since the ontological nature of well-being was considered, I began to scrutinise the concept from a critical stance given such a methodology would be more aligned with the ontological assumption of reality, epistemology and moral concern described in this study. Given the post-colonial perspective (particularly Said's (1978) Orientalism) is influenced by Foucault's idea of power and knowledge, I began to pay attention to Foucault's discourse since August 2012. As a result, the possibility of using Foucault's (1972) archaeology as another part of the methodology to demystify the mainstream framework of well-being was considered. By May 2013, the research evolved into one which employs both archaeological and anthropological examination.

I am a Chinese with both local and overseas educational background. Therefore, my prior knowledge in the context of well-being can consist of both western perspectives and Chinese point of view. Therefore, I would aim to demystify the mainstream framework through archaeology, and reveal local expressions and concepts through 'thick description'. Since I was born in Hong Kong, there are personal experiences in relations to the political, economic, social and historical changes of Hong Kong, both before and after its Handover (1997). Such experience and prior understandings would be taken into account while interpreting the findings. Hence, the interpretation of the data would account for my prior knowledge of the Chinese language, local traditions and societal changes.

(b) Difficulties and Challenges

Globalisation has raised questions on the traditional anthropological values of 'locality', 'primitive' and 'tribalism'. The emergence of urban anthropology also required appropriate modifications to traditional anthropological methods of investigation. In assessing methodological issues of anthropological field research in the 21st century, Teshome-Bahiru and Negash-Wossene (2007) underline the challenges of urbanisation and cultural pluralism. They compare village communities with urban areas and described that urban cities are comparatively more congested, more diverse in population and bigger in size. Hence, researchers who conduct anthropological studies in towns and cities may encounter problems such as lack of time and space to privately stay with the people involved in the investigations; communication problems due to the diversity of languages in urban areas; and difficulties in dealing with various social life and complexity of the urban centre. This research takes place in Hong Kong, a modern metropolis which is perceived to be crowded, busy and time-conscious with varieties of social life and urban complexities. There were a few challenges I encountered which are mentioned previously by Teshome-Bahiru and Negash-Wossene (2007). Those challenges are described as follows:

i Researcher in the Field

Choosing Hong Kong, an urban city, as the site of fieldwork is regarded as both an advantage and a challenge for me. On one hand, I am an indigenous ethnographer who can enjoy the advantage of being familiar with the local culture, language, living style and environment. On the other hand, going back 'home' imposes challenges, as I need to take up multiple roles at the same time based on my obligations to the family, work and study. Not only do I need to spend time with my family and participate in the family social gatherings, I also had to engage in a full-time job to financially support my family and study. Therefore, after the return to Hong Kong, I got a full-time job in January 2012, working as an Assistant Lecturer in The Open University of Hong Kong. This job allowed me to go for the fieldwork as long as the research activity did not restrict my work performance. Nevertheless, taking up multiple roles has created time-management problems and stress. As reflected in the field note:

> I have just finished a company visit and now I need to rush back to the office for work. I start feeling a bit tired to go for fieldwork, rush back to work for teaching and meeting and write up diary at night (after a full-day work). (5 April 2012)

In an attempt to resolve the above problem, I altered the mode of study as part-time since July 2012.

An ethnographer often encounters difficulties in balancing the dual role of being both an insider and outsider (Brewer, 2000; Sherif, 2001; Fetterman, 2011). In terms of macro level, I am a local, an insider; although, "sometimes a familiar setting is too familiar . . . and the researcher takes events for granted, leaving important data unnoticed and unrecorded" (Fetterman, 2011, p.39). For instance, I received local education and have worked in an academic field for more than 5 years. I am used to the teaching culture that is prevalent in Hong Kong, which may sometimes lead me to take for granted the teaching approach adopted by the staff in FB 1. In regards to this potential problem, after each company visit, I would retreat from the setting and go to a quiet place at night to write my diary. While writing the diary, I would reflect, examine and question every tiny detail of that visit and reassess the roles and interactions during the day.

Researchers need to spend time in building trust with different participants in the site (Brewer, 2000). I gain access to the four field sites by having close contacts with a senior figure in each firm. In that case, I may run the risk of forming an impression of the business solely based on the perspectives of those in power; while marginalizing the lives and views of other members of the business. In order to reduce such a risk, I tried to get in touch with other staff. In particular, the experience in FB 1 can illustrate my role in the research process, in terms of how the relations with a senior position may have impacts on me as a researcher. Although the initial access to FB 1 is granted by Ms. Ada (who is the successor, the family worker as well as the management of the company), I still have to build trust with other staff in FB 1. When I was introduced by Ada, I was cautious that the other employees may perceive me as a 'spy' or 'power broker'. Hence, I aimed to perform a "non-threatening role in the field" (Fetterman, 2010, p.82). Paradoxically, I tried to prevent cutting off other lines of communication by establishing independence in the field (Fetterman, 2010). For example, in the first few visits, I bought cakes and cookies for the staff and told them that my presence was solely for the academic purpose of my PhD study. In the beginning, I acted like a complete observer (Gold, 1958) without much participation in the field. Thus, I adopted a subtle observation especially when the teachers are conducting classes. This can convey a message to the staff that they are the ones who can 'control' the class. In the first two months of visits, the part-time teachers and students were curious. As a result, I spent time to develop relationship and trust with them. After 3-month visits, they started to see me differently. They began to get used to my presence and chat with me naturally. Since then, my role has changed to more like an observer-participant (Gold, 1958). Another example is the experience in FB 2. To begin my field visit in FB 2, I was introduced by the owners, Ms Better and Mrs. Bonnie. In the first few weeks, I found it difficult to chat freely with Ms. Brenda (i.e. a full-time employee) since she was aware that I was a close friend of Ms Better and Mrs. Bonnie. In order to break the ice, I enrolled in a one-to-one Chinese dance course taught by Ms. Brenda. After attending her class for a month, I developed a closer bond with Ms. Brenda. We could then have more casual chats on a range of matters, such as family, love, study, hobbies, dream and even work. The experience in FB 1 and FB 2 made me aware that "trust has to be continually worked at, negotiated and renegotiated, confirmed and thereafter repeatedly reaffirmed" (Brewer, 2000, p.86). Hence, building rapport is an on-going concern along the research process (Sherif, 2001).

My roles entailed are varied in the fieldwork and are constantly changing as "there are no clear boundaries between researchers and ethnographic contexts, but where in reality, the boundaries are more entrenched and yet constantly shifting than initially imagined" (Sherif, 2001, p.445). Here is an illustration: Since most of the informants come from the local network, some of them are regarded as my close contacts. While engaging in informal conversations with them, I would sometimes struggle between the roles of being a close contact (i.e. a relative or a close friend) and a researcher. When discussing issues that are regarded as emotional and controversial, such as the conflicts in the family or work, I occasionally chose to remain neutral and suppress any personal comments, beliefs, emotions and political sympathy to these issues. My aim is to avoid increasing the tension between the parties involved. However, while I would retain neutrality in those sensitive issues, as a close contact, there is also a need to demonstrate care and concern to the feelings of my close contacts. This role ambiguity reminds me to be constantly reflexive upon the multiple selves, experience and potential interpretations.

ii Choices in the Academic Community

The "hegemony of apparent rationality that typifies conventions in academic publishing" (Learmonth, 1999, p. 1010) may restrict researchers from taking a critical position. Johnson and Duberley (2003) acknowledge that researchers who take on a critical position could face resistance and challenges from a community whose quality and validity criteria are at odds with their ontological and epistemological commitments. As a researcher taking a critical stance, there were certain personal experiences that were difficult during the journey of research. For instance, I received the following comments from my academic work colleagues and friends:

> How can you 'prove' your interpretation represents the truth of reality?
> (from one who takes on a positivist epistemology)

> Em . . . given your research is not in the mainstream . . . would you consider to change the direction back to the conventional approach so that you can gain more acceptances?
> (suggested by one who takes on a neo-positivist epistemology)

> To what extent can your findings claim to have high validity and reliability?
> (questioned from one who is familiar a quantitative approach)

> This kind of research is not from the mainstream. You can hardly get publications!
> (commented by one who comes from the mainstream)

Johnson and Duberley (2003) remind us that "we must not underestimate the role that researcher's own community plays in sanctioning particular representative practices, whose norms may exclude the dissemination of the outcomes of collaborative inquiry" (p. 1296). Their remarks sensitised me to the existence of potential concerns and challenges, their dynamics and the political and ethical implications underlying the knowledge production process. Taking a critical research approach is never easy and straightforward. While working on such challenges, researchers are encouraged to stay sensitive to one's ontological, epistemological and political position and welcome dialogue for promoting critical consciousness (Johnson and Duberley, 2003).

iii Ethical Issues

Teshome-Bahiru and Negash-Wossene (2007) remind researchers to pay attention to ethical issues when conducting anthropological studies in cities. Researchers may consider the three principles suggested by the University of Victoria in its "*Protocols and principles for conducting research in an indigenous context*" (2003): (1) partnership, (2) participation and (3) protection. 'Partnership' means that the working relationship with the indigenous people should be based on collaboration. 'Protection' refers to protecting the individuals who participate in the research process through informed consents, maintaining confidentiality of any research material and safeguarding them from any negative impact of the results. 'Participation' implies indigenous people have the right to participate in the research and derive benefits that might result from the research. They also have the right to not participate if they do not feel comfortable with the research.

With regards to the above three principles, this thesis aims for partnership and participations in a respectful manner. For every informant, I would explain the aims, approach, confidentiality and possible outputs of my research. There will be protection of the welfare, health and right of the people under investigation. The ethical review checklist has been sent to the University for approval at the beginning of the fieldwork in 2012. Direct quotes may be used to illustrate participants' expressions in everyday lives. However, to protect the confidentiality of their identity, they will be referred to by pseudo-names. For easy reference, the pseudo-names of the participants in FB 1 start with 'A'; while those in FB 2 begin with 'B" and so on. The pseudo-names of the Human Resource Professionals start with "P". Similarly, the organisations they are working with are anonymised as FB 1, 2, 3 or 4 and so on.

Most importantly, this research would be accountable to the locals in family businesses, who may be traditionally treated as an "object" in Eurocentric representations. Reflexivity, respect and account for the diversity of human experiences are always the priorities in this research.

Notes B2: Interview Transcription and Data Consolidation

1 Transcribing Interviews

A notation system is used in order to capture some non-verbal expressions, such as pauses, emphasis and laughter. The main target of this ethnography is to uncover the current local expressions, rather than tacit reasoning procedures nor sequences of interaction. A conversational analysis which demands a relatively detailed notation to produce orderly social interaction (Silverman, 2001) is regarded as overly detailed and time consuming. For that reason, this research adopt a simplified notation system (see Tab. B4), which is based on Poland's (1995) alternative abbreviated instructions and Silverman's (2001) simplified transcription symbols. One of the limitations of such a notation system is it is unable to capture information related to the setting, atmosphere and some facial or bodily expressions such as smile, wink and gesture. Poland (1995) considers this constraint as unavoidable. In this case, some non-verbal clues, such as the context and posture are written in my field notes. Field notes can be used it as a "partial interpretive account" (Poland, 1995, p.306) to supplement the interview transcription.

The whole process of each semi-interview is recorded. These recordings need transcription as it would help to organise the disorderliness of natural conversations (Silverman, 2001). The transcription is made in Chinese. Initially, I tried to do the transcription. However, it took me 15 hours to transcribe one 45-minute interview. After transcribing a few interviews, the experience was considered to be inefficient. Therefore, I decided to hire a transcriber to do the transcription. The transcriber is Hong Kong Chinese and speaks both Cantonese (the most common Chinese dialect in Hong Kong) and English. Since all of my interviews were in Cantonese and occasionally with some English words, the chosen transcriber is qualified to undertake transcription. Although I hired transcriber, I collaborated with her as a team to ensure the transcription quality. Before the actual transcription, I had a face-to-face meeting with the transcriber wherein a brief understanding of the thesis, including the topics, objectives, methodology and research questions were mentioned. Afterwards, I had regular meetings with the transcriber as they help to provide feedback to the

Tab. B4: Simplified Notation System (Adapted from Poland, 1995 and Silverman, 2001).

Feature	Transcription symbols	Explanations and Examples
Pauses	. . .	Use series of dots to denote short pauses E.g. I think . . . is also important.
	. . . (long pause)	Use series of dots and (long pause) to indicate long pause of 4 or more seconds E.g. Em . . . (long pause) may be you are right!
Interruption	– –	Use a hyphen to show someone's speech is broken off midsentence E.g. What do you –
Emphasis	Capital letters	Use capital letters to denote strong emphasis E.g. WHAT?
Garbled speech	( )	Use empty bracket to indicate the transcriber's inability to hear what was said E.g Yes, I like () because of you.
	[?/?]	Use square brackets and question mark to flag words that are not clear and are based on guessing. E.g. At that time, Harry just [doubled? / glossed?]
Non-verbal expressions	{expressions}	Indicate expressions in the curly brackets. E.g. You are right {laugh}!

transcriber. At the same time, the transcriber shared with me her difficulties in the transcription process. Every transcript was reviewed. Since I establish communication with the transcriber, difficulties and problems were also resolved in the early stage of the transcription. For instance, regarding the interviews with the HR Professionals, the transcriber commented that she finds it difficult to understand some jargons in Human Resource Management, such as 360 degree feedback, flexitime, Quality of Work Life (QWL) etc., given she is not working in this field. As a result, I listened to the particular audio clip, find out those jargons that she is not familiar with, and explain the terms to her. The above process is regarded as transcription training, which is an important strategy to enhance transcription quality (Poland, 1995). The key problems that were encountered in the transcription process and their respective resolutions are summarised in Tab. B5.

Tab. B5: Problems in the Transcription.

Problems	Description	Solutions
Alteration of data	Before the first meeting with the transcriber, I asked the transcriber to transcribe a 15-minute interview as a tester to access her quality of transcription. In the trial transcription, the transcriber tended to 'tidy up' the discussion by herself. For example, she altered the testimonies of the interviewees to make the conversation flows more logical.	Poland (1995) suggested that it is vital to fully inform the transcriber the nature and purpose of the research in the initial stage of transcription. **Actions taken:** – I immediately arranged a first meeting with the transcriber to clarify the background of my research and the requirement of the transcription. – I specified to her the importance of verbatim record. I also went through a section of the audio record with her and demonstrate in details about the notation system, requirements and standards of the transcription. – For illustration, I gave her few of the transcriptions. The transcriptions do not only provide a sample of reference to the transcriber. They also serve to ensure that the researcher has a good grasp of the data.
Run-on sentences	There are a number of run-on sentences in the interviews	The transcriber needs to decide where to start and end the sentences (Poland, 1995). However, incorrect judgement can change the interpretation of the data. **Actions taken:** – The transcriber was asked to highlight those run-on sentences in each transcription. – The run-on sentences were reviewed carefully and discussed in the meetings to decide the most appropriate treatment.
Difficulty in recognizing participants	Since some interviews are conducted in a group, the transcriber found it difficult to recognise and identify the voice of each participant.	Provide information that would help the transcriber to get familiar with the setting of the interview before the transcription. **Actions taken:** – For each interview, I would list the number of participants, their names and basic background. – Short description about the context and general content of each interview were given. – In case, the transcriber is still unsure about who is doing the talking, she would highlight that part in her transcription. – Discussions were made in our regular meetings.

2 Consolidating Data

After the fieldwork, there is an abundant amount of data derived from field notes, diary, interviews, documentary and photos. On one hand, a large body of data may help to generate a 'thick description' (Greertz, 1973). On the other hand, the amount of data can be so overwhelming that it creates anxiety to the researchers. To consolidate the data, data management is an important technique in qualitative research (Ryan and Bernard, 2003). The thesis employs thematic analysis to sort out the ethnographic data. Thematic analysis is a process for locating codes and themes in qualitative information (Boyatzis, 2000Braun and Clarke, 2006). Boyatzis (1998) identified the purposes of thematic analysis as follows:

1. "A way of *seeing*
2. A way of *making sense* out of seemingly unrelated material
3. A way of *analysing* qualitative information
4. A way of *systematically observing* a person, an interaction, a group, a situation, an organisation, or a culture
5. A way of *converting* qualitative information into quantitative data" (p. 4).

Generally, thematic analysis is regarded as one of the generic skills shared across qualitative analysis (Braun and Clarke, 2006). One key benefit of thematic analysis is its flexibility (Braun and Clarke, 2006) (see Tab. B6). It enables researchers to communicate their findings and interpretation to the readers using different methods. For this advantage, this thesis adopts thematic analysis as a way to process the qualitative data so as to identify themes and patterns of living or behaviours of the research subject. Then, the themes and patterns are analysed and presented through 'thick description' (Geertz, 1973).

Tab. B6: Advantages of Thematic Analysis (Braun and Clarke, 2006).

Advantages of thematic analysis
Flexibility
Relatively easy and quick method to learn, and do.
Accessible to researchers with little or no experience of qualitative research.
Results are generally accessible to educated general public.
Useful method for working within participatory research paradigm, with participants as collaborators.
Can usefully summarise key features of a large body of data, and / or offer a 'thick description' of the data set.

Tab. B6 (continued)

Advantages of thematic analysis
Can highlight similarities and differences across the data set.
Can generate unanticipated insights
Allow for social as well as psychological interpretations of data
Can be useful for producing qualitative analyses suited to informing policy development.

Braun and Clarke (2006) outline six phases in the process: (1) Familiarising yourself with your data, (2) Generating initial codes, (3) Searching for themes, (4) Reviewing themes, (5) Defining and naming themes and (6) Producing the report (see Tab. B7). The thesis follows the above six steps to consolidate the data. First, I familiarised myself with the data. The data was classified into three sets: (1) family business, (2) HR professional and (3) miscellaneous (including data from local academics, youth, citizens and secondary data). The semi-structured interviews were transcribed. While re-reading the data, the initial ideas for coding were developed. At this stage, I tried to get a general understanding of the data.

Tab. B7: Steps of Thematic Analysis (Adapted from Braun and Clarke, 2006).

Process	Phrase of thematic analysis	Application
1. Transcription	1. Familiarising yourself with your data	– Classify and file the data into three sets: (1) Family business (2) HR professional (3) Miscellaneous – In the family business data set, classify and file the data according to each organisation. – Transcribe semi-interviews. – Read and re-read the data, including field notes, diary, transcripts, documents and photos. – Note down initial ideas for coding.
2. Coding	2. Generating initial codes	– Code manually by writing notes next to the texts, using different coloured pens to indicate potential patterns. – Create three excel spreadsheets: (1) Family business, (2) HR Professionals and (3) Miscellaneous. In each spreadsheet, list out all possible codes found and support each code with surrounding data.

Tab. B7 (continued)

Process	Phrase of thematic analysis	Application
3. Analysis	3. Searching for themes	– For each family business, analyse all the codes, sort them into potential themes and subthemes based on the patterns found, and collate all relevant coded data extracts within the identified themes and sub-themes. – Analyse the themes in each family business, compare the themes among different family businesses and group similar themes together. – Analyse the codes found in the spreadsheets of HR Professionals and miscellaneous. Associate these codes with the themes found in the data set of family business – Create a new spreadsheet – Themes, list all the potential themes and support each theme with subthemes and surrounding data from different data sets
	4. Reviewing themes	– Check if the themes works in relation to the coded extracted and the three data sets. – Generate a coherent pattern among the themes and sub-themes and create a thematic map – Code any additional data within the themes, which have been missed in the earlier coding. Re-coding if appropriate.
4. Overall	5. Defining and naming themes	– Ongoing analysis to define and refine the essence of each theme. – Provide a clear definition and name for each theme. – Generate a story that each themes tells. Briefly write down the scope and content of each theme.
5. Written report	6. Producing the report	– Final analysis and write up. – Generate a thick description for each story. In each story, spells out the theme and sub-themes clearly and select relevant examples from data. – Relate the analysis back to the research question 2 and literature to create a thick description and theoretical dialogues.

After data collection data, coding ensued. At this stage, initial codes were generated. I went through the notes of initial thoughts for coding; the data was read several times. Manual coding was pursued; at this stage, an effort was made to situate the data in the context. Coloured pens were used to indicate potential patterns. After the initial coding, three excel sheets were created, including family business, HR professional and miscellaneous. In each spreadsheet, all possible codes were listed out along with the data that supported each code. There are three main difficulties at this stage. One is the data itself sometimes is contradicting. Following the advice given by Braun and Clarke (2006), the accounts that departed from the dominant story were retained and were reviewed later in the analysis stage. Another problem is that some data can be coded with different 'themes'. Initially, I tried to write down as many codes as possible. Later on, I would do the re-coding and encoding again when the themes were searched. The last issue was when to stop coding. The process of coding can be long and tedious and ongoing; however, the researcher should decide when to move to the next phase. According to Braun and Clarke's (2006) guideline, I began to move to the subsequent stage when each data item has been given an equal amount of attention.

In the third stage, I searched for themes. Different codes were reviewed (including codes that are contradicting) and were compared them to find the patterns. I started with the spreadsheet and data set of family business. Based on the data of each family business, all the codes were analysed, sorted into potential themes and sub-themes based on the pattern found. For each themes and sub-themes, relevant data as evidence was extracted for illustrations. After finding the themes for each family business, the themes among the different organisations were compared similar themes were grouped together. Next, I read the spreadsheets of HR professional and miscellaneous. Again, the codes were analysed. Then I associated the codes with the themes found in the family business data set. After all the themes have been searched, a new spreadsheet called 'Themes' was devised. In this spreadsheet, all the potential themes and sub-themes were noted and were supported with surrounding data. The main challenge in this stage is grouping and screening. I need to search for the pattern among the codes and group the similar codes into one theme. During the process, the irrelevant themes were screened. In short, I need to decide what to include and what to exclude. To handle this question, I referred back to my research questions and literature review. Since the key objective of the anthropological study was to reveal other local expressions made by the research subject, I tried to include those themes that are relevant to the research questions. The relevant themes were prioritised according to their significance which is reflected by their frequencies of occurrence, emphasis made by the research subject and amount of supporting data. Themes and codes of less importance were screened out. For instance, *kuai le* 快樂 and *fu zi* 福祉 are found in the written brochures of FB 1. Nevertheless, these two Chinese terms only appear once and they are seldom used as oral language. They seem to be comparatively less significant to the locals. Therefore, I decided to exclude these two terms in the findings. All the themes are checked in relation to the codes extracted and the three data sets, so as to make sure they are presented with thorough, inclusive and comprehensive details and examples from the data sets.

In the fourth stage, I reviewed the data sets again and coded any additional data within the themes which have been missed out in the earlier coding. The themes were checked against one another and back to the original data. Some of the data was re-coded to enhance accuracy and coherency. At last, the themes are rearranged into the four key local expressions: (1) *jia ting*, (2) *peng you*, (3) *kai xin gong zuo* and (4) *xin zhong fu you*.

In the fifth stage, I defined and refined the essence of each theme. The four themes were grouped into two specific indigenous notions – *xing fu* and *xin* and generated a final version of thematic map. Based on the thematic map, a story was generated for each theme. To prepare for the writing up, the scope and content of each theme was written. At last, I related the analysis back to the research questions and produced 'thick description'.

To reflect upon the entire process, thematic analysis is never as systematic as described above. Instead, it is long, tedious, repetitive and even chaotic, because it is difficult to go along each phrase step by step. Often times, I felt the need to go back to the data sets and spreadsheets to recode and encode again in order to improve the conciseness, preciseness and coherence of the analysis.

Appendix C

Fig. C1: Yellow Ribbon.

Tab. C1: Living Well in Family Business.

Local terms of living well	Embodiment of living well				
	Daily practices	Work practices: From managing to living			
		FB 1	FB 2	FB 3	FB 4
Xing fu jia ting 幸福家庭 **(Good family)**		(1) Familial culture: Blurring the boundary between business and family			
Qi zheng 齊整 (Orderly complete)	Build a family with children	Work like a family	My own baby	Home office	Family helper
Yang jia 養家 (Feed family)	Support family: – *Mai lou* 買樓 (Buy a Place) – shape *quai* 乖 (good) children	Buy one's own place Emphasise on comprehensive development for children		Craftsmanship for a living	Having a residential place for living
Jian kang 健康 (Healthy)	Physical exercises and good sleep	Health – a key topic of social chats	—	Avoid the wife to get hurt in craftsmanship	—
Ping jing 平靜 **(Peace and at ease)**	Rituals and gestures	(2) **Move on as life unfolds** → *Jian bu xing bu* (See one step, take one step) → No strategy			
An xin 安心 (Secure)		Value *tai ping* (Peace and stability)	Prefer to have no monetary pressure	Value *ping wen* (Peace and stability)	Be relax

		—	Ancestors worship at the opening	Selling symbolic accessories	—
		Act in the right timing	Jian bu xing bu (See one step, take one step)	No perfect plan	Keep going until opportunities arise

(3) Absence of / Resistance to management

		Hire shu ren (acquaintance); Zi dong bo (work automatically)	Rely on zi ji ren (ingroup members)	Take care shi fu (master) and shi mu (the master's wife)	Work wholeheartedly
		Management: No need	Management: Troublesome	—	Management: A challenge

(4) Strive to survive
- persistently being able to maintain existence in the market
- trying to handle most of the tasks by themselves
- working hard with heart and mind

Peng you 朋友 (Friends)

Xin 信 (Trust)	Trust and work with friends

Kai xin gong zuo 開心工作 **(Happy work)**

You xing qu 有興趣 (Have interest)

Zhong yi 鍾意 (Affection)

You man zu gan 有滿足感 (Have satisfaction)

Chuang zuo 創作 (Creavity)

(continued)

Tab. C1 (continued)

Local terms of living well	Embodiment of living well				
	Daily practices	Work practices: From managing to living			
		FB 1	FB 2	FB 3	FB 4
Contrast with *xin ku* 辛苦 (hardship)	Work hard to bear *xin ku* (hardship)	*Liu de qing shan zai, na pa mei chai shao* (Strive to maintain existence in the market)	*Shou zhu xian* (Hold on to survive)	One man band; *Zi ji zuo* (Do it by oneself)	Work as part of self; *Gong fu* and *xin ji* (Work hard with heart and mind)
Xin zhong fu you 心中富有 (Being rich at heart-mind)	Social Protest			—	

Appendix D

Tab. D1: Interpretations from Hedonism, Eudaimonia, the Confucian and Daoist Frameworks.

Themes / Findings	Hedonism	Eudaimonia	The Confucian Framework	The Daoist Framework
(1) *Xing fu jia ting* 幸福家庭 **(Good family)**	Derive happiness from familial lives	Fulfil social needs Contribute to positive relatedness	Perceive family as the most fundamental to one's life Among *wulun*, three of the relations are belonged to the family	Family is originated from *dao* (the Nature)
Completeness: **Build a family with children**	No discussion	Can been seen as a life purpose Does not discuss why building a family is important	*Qi jia* (establish a harmonious family) is a life mission of an individual	Family is formed due to people following the pattern of nature A family is built to balance *yin* and *yang* Marriage and having children should be taken place spontaneously
Role obligations: **Support family**	No discussion	Satisfy one's physiological and social needs No clues on why role obligations are essential	Family is the key platform for cultivating virtues According to *yi* and *li*, feeding and teaching are the ritualised duties of parents	Parents are encouraged to take up their *tian zhi* (bourdon duties) According to *wuwei*, it does not support any deliberate control over the development of children

https://doi.org/10.1515/9783110684643-010

Tab. D1 (continued)

Themes / Findings	Hedonism	Eudaimonia	The Confucian Framework	The Daoist Framework
Healthiness: Physical exercises and good sleep	Obtain pleasure from being physically healthy Avoid any pain and illness	Satisfy one's physiological and safety needs Represent environmental mastery on physical health Does not explain the ways to healthiness	Health is part of *wufu* Promote archery and riding chariots as exercises Emphasise the importance of sleeping peacefully Harmony between *shen* and *xin*	Harmony is the way to stay healthy Balance between *yin* and *yang* should always be maintained Doing exercises (*dong*) and sleeping (*jing*) are mutually supportive to healthiness
Spiritual peace: Rituals and gestures	No discussion on spiritual peace – a well-balanced spiritual state	Regard spiritual peace as a safety need Does not appreciate any local rituals and decoration, given these practices may undermine human potentials and self-governance	According to *zhong yong*, harmony between physical and spiritual aspects of lives should be maintained Seek spiritual peace through *li* (rituals)	Harmony between *yang* (body) and *yin* (*xin*) should be maintained Discard any assertive rituals and behaviours
Themes / Findings	Hedonism	Eudaimonia	Confucian	Daoist
(2) Peng you 朋友 (Friends)	Happiness from friendship	Fulfil social needs Contribute to positive relatedness	*Peng you* are the extended family *Peng you* are *tong zhi* (people with the same mind) The role of *peng you* (especially for *junzi*) is to exchange views on virtues	Not much discussion on *peng you*

Tab. D1 (continued)

Themes / Findings	Hedonism	Eudaimonia	Confucian	Daoist
Trust and work with friends	No discussion on trust	No discussion on trust	*Xin* is the basic governance of friendship Due to *xin*, people would be comfortable to work with friends *Zhong cheng* (loyalty and sincerity) is a way to build *xin*	No discussion on trust Prefer to work with *junzi*
(3) *Kai xin gong zuo* 开心工作 **(Happy work)**	Happiness from work	Job satisfaction	*Kai xin* is due to being able to work with *tong zhi*	*Kai xin* is due to the affection of *junzi*
For interests, affection, satisfaction and creativity	No discussion on what constitute such happiness	Gain satisfaction due to intrinsic motivation Fulfil the growth needs Allow autonomy and environmental mastery over work Increase self-acceptance and personal growth	Able to obtain *zhi* (wisdom) from *peng you* Able to open up one's mind and spirit through intellectual inspiration with *peng you*	Able to work on what one innately likes Not encourage to invent sedulously due to *wuwei* Believe innovation should come spontaneously
Work hard to bear hardship	Interpret *xin ku* as a suffering Does not understand local assiduous attitude and behaviours	Interpret such tolerance as a passive response Does not understand why local accept the pain in work	Treats suffering as an exercise for cultivating endurance Hardship facilitate one's strength and growth	*Xin ku* arises in order to be in harmony with *kai xin* Patience to *xin ku* represents compliance to the pattern of the world Balance between *kai xin* (yang) and *xin ku* (yin) should always be preserved

Tab. D1 (continued)

Themes / Findings	Hedonism	Eudaimonia	Confucian	Daoist
(4) *Xin zhong fu you* 心中富有 **(Being rich at heart-mind)**	Positive mood	Good spirit	Xin is particularly linked with *dao de* 道德 (virtues) Richness in virtues	Relate *xin* with nature – *xin xing* 心性 (one's nature) Rich in heart-mind when one lives in accordance to the way of nature (*dao*)

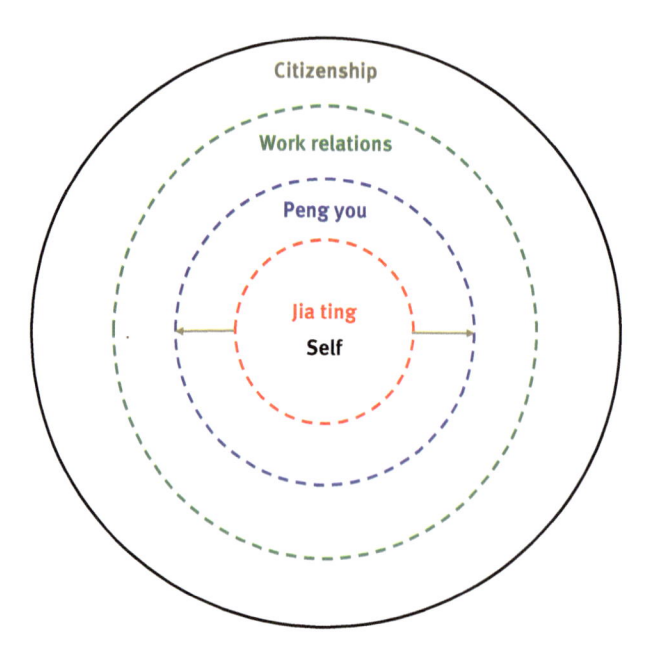

Fig. D1: Confucian Perspective on Self.

References

Abbas, A. (1997). *Hong Kong: Culture and the politics of disappearance.* Hong Kong: Hong Kong University Press and University of Minnesota Press.

Acquaah, M. (2016). Family business theories and Sub-Saharan African family businesses. In *Family businesses in Sub-Saharan Africa* (pp. 9–42). Palgrave Macmillan US.

Ahrentzen, S.B. (1990). Managing conflict by managing boundaries: How professional homeworkers cope with multiple roles at home. *Environment and Behavior,* 22(6),723–752.

Ailon, G. (2008). Mirror, mirror on the wall: Culture's consequences in value test of its own design. *Academy of Management Review,* 33(4),885–904.

Alderfer, C. P. (1969). An empirical test of a new theory of human needs. Organizational Behaviour and Human Performance, 4(2), 142–175.

Allen, T.D., Herst, D.E.L., Bruck, C.S. and Sutton, M. (2000). Consequences associated with work-to-family conflict: A review and agenda for future research. *Journal of Occupational Health Psychology,* 5, 278–308.

Allport, G. W. (1961). *Pattern and growth in personality.* New York: Holt, Rinehart and Winston.

Alvesson, M., and Deetz, S. (2005). Critical theory and postmodernism: Approaches to organizational studies. In C. Grey and H. Willmott (eds). *Critical management studies: A reader.* Oxford: Oxford University Press.

Ames, R. T. (2009). *Seeking harmony rather than uniformity.* Beijing: Peking University Press

Ammons, S. and Markham, W. (2004). Working at Home: Experiences of skilled white collar workers. *Sociological Spectrum,* 24, 191–238.

Angrosino, M. (2007). *Doing ethnographic observation al research.* London: Sage.

Ariss, A.A. and Sidani, Y. (2016). Comparative international human resource management: Future research directions. *Human Resource Management Review,* 26(4),352–358.

Aristotle (1985). *Nichomachean ethics,* T. Irwin, translator, Hackett, Indianapolis.

Aryee, S. (1993). Antecedents and outcomes of work-family conflict among married professional women: Evidence from Singapore. *Human Relations,* 45, 813–837.

Aryree, S., Luk, V., Leung, A. and Lo, S. (1999). Role stressors, work-family conflict and well-being: An examination of the effects of the spouse support and coping behaviors among employed parents in Hong Kong. *Journal of Vocational Behavior,* 54, 259–278.

Ashforth, B., Kreiner, G. and Fugate, M. (2000). All in a day's work: Boundaries and micro role transitions. *The Academy of Management Review,* 25(3),472–491.

Astrachan, J. H. and Jaskiewicz, P. (2008). Emotional returns and emotional costs in privately held family businesses: advancing traditional business valuation. *Family Business Review,* 21 (2),139–149.

Australian Business Deans Council (2010). Australian business deans council journal quality list. Retrieved on September, 24, 2012.

Au-yeung, A. (2015), "Number of social enterprises in Hong Kong reaches all-time high", *South China Morning Post,* October 8 2015, Retrieved from: http://www.scmp.com/news/hong-kong/education-community/article/1865071/number-social-enterprises-hong-kong-reaches-all (accessed March 10 2022).

Ballard, D. W. and Grawitch, M. J., (2017). Psychologically healthy workplace practices and employee well-being. In R. Burke and K. M. Page, *Research handbook on work and well-being.* UK: Edward Elgar, pp. 3–36.

Banerjee, S. B. (2003). Who sustains whose development? Sustainable development and the reinvention of nature. *Organization Studies,* 24(1),143–180.

Barratt, E. (2002). Foucault, Foucauldianism and human resource management. *Personnel Review*, 31(2),189–204.

Barratt, E. (2003). Foucault, HRM and the ethos of the critical management scholar. *Journal of Management Studies*, 40(5), 1069–1087.

Barratt, E. (2004). Foucault and the politics of critical management studies. *Culture and organization*, 10(3),191–202.

Barratt, E. (2008). The later Foucault in organization and management studies. *Human Relations*, 61(4), 515–537.

Baruch, G.K. and Barnett, R.C. (1986). Role quality, multiple roles involvement and the psychological well-being in mid life women. *Journal of Personality and Social Behaviour*, 3, 578–585.

Bate, S. P. (1997). What happened to organizational anthropology? A review of the field of organizational ethnography and anthropological studies. *Human Relations*, 50(9),1147–1175.

Bauer, W. (1976). *China and the search for happiness recurring themes in four thousand years of Chinese cultural history*. New York: Seabury Press.

Beer, M., Spector, B., Lawrence, P., Mills, Q., and Walton, R. (1984). Managing human resource management. In R. E. Walton and P. R. Lawrence (eds), *Human resource management trends and challenges*. Boston: Harvard Business School Press.

Bellah, R. N., Madsen, R., Sullivan, W. M., Swidler, A., and Tipton, S. M. (1985). *Habits of the heart: Individualism and commitment in American life*. New York: Harper and Row.

Bernauer, J. W., and Rasmussen, D. M. (Eds.). (1988). *The final Foucault*. MIT Press.

Bevir, M. (1999). Foucault and critique: Deploying agency against autonomy. *Political theory*, 27 (1),65–84.

Bhabha, H. K. (1984). Of mimicry and man: The ambivalence of colonial discourse. *Discipleship: A special issue on psychoanalysis*, 28, 125–133.

Bhabha, H. K. (1985). Signs taken for wonders: Questions of ambivalence and authority under a tree outside Delhi. *Critical Inquiry*, 12(1),144–165.

Bhabha, H. K. (1990). *Nation and narration*. London and New York: Routledge.

Bhabha, H. K. (1994). *The location of culture*. London and New York: Routledge

Bhabha, H. K. (1996). Culture's In-Between. In S. Hall and P. du Gay (Eds), *Question of cultural identity*, London: Sage Publishing, 53–60.

Bidet, J. (2016). *Foucault with Marx*. London: Zed Books Ltd.

Birch, A. (1991). *The colony that never was*, Hong Kong. Twin Age Ltd.

Bird, B. Welsch, H., Astrachan, J.H. and Pistrui, D. (2002). Family business research: The field evolution of an academic field. *Family Business Review*, 15(4),337–350.

Blackburn, Simon (2008). *Oxford dictionary of philosophy*, second edition revised. Oxford: Oxford University Press.

Blaxter, M. (1990). *Health and lifestyle*. London: Tavistock /Routledge.

Blomberg, J., Giacomi, J., Mosher, A. and Swenton-wall, P. (1993). Ethnographic field methods and their relation to design. In D. Schuler and A. Namioka, *Participatory design: Principles and practices*. New Jersey: Lawrence Erlbaum Associate, Inc., 123–156.

Bluedorn, A. C. and Martin, G. (2008). The time frames of entrepreneurs. *Journal of Business Venturing*, 23(1),1–20.

Bockover, M. (2010). Confucianism and ethics in the Western philosophical tradition I: Foundational Concepts. *Philosophy Compass*, 5/4, 307–316.

Boje, D., Oswick, C. and Ford, J. (2004). Language and organization: The doing of discourse. *Academy of Management Review*, 29(4),571–577.

Borg, K. (2015). Conducting critique: reconsidering Foucault's engagement with the question of the subject [a]. *Symposia Melitensia*, 11, 1–15.

Boyatzis, R. E. (1998). *Transforming qualitative information: Thematic analysis and code development*. London: Sage.
Braun, V., and Clarke, V. (2006). Using thematic analysis in psychology. *Qualitative research in psychology*, 3(2),77–101.
Brewer, J. D. (2000). *Ethnography*. Open University Press: Buckingham.
Brickman, P. D. and Campbell, D. T. (1971). Hedonic relativism and planning the good society. In M. H. Appley, *Adaptation level theory*. New York: Academic Press.
Brigham, K. H., De Castro, J. O. and Shepherd, D. A. (2007). A person-organization fit model of owner-managers' cognitive style and organizational demands. *Entrepreneurship Theory and Practice*, 31(1),29–51.
Brunstein, J. C. (1993). Personal goals and subjective well-being: A longitudinal study. *Journal of Personality and Social Psychology*, 65(5),1061–1070.
Burke, R. (2017). Work and well-being. In R. Burke and K. M. Page, *Research handbook on work and well-being*. UK: Edward Elgar, pp. 3–36.
Burke, R. and Page, K. M. (2017). *Research handbook on work and well-being*. UK: Edward Elgar.
Burrell, G. (1984). Sex and organizational analysis. *Organization Studies*, 5(2),97–118.
Burrell, G. (1992). The organization of pleasure. Critical management studies, 66–89.
Burrell, G. and Morgan, G. (1979). *Sociological paradigms and organizational analysis*. Portsmouth: NH: Heinemann.
Calestani, M. (2009). An anthropology of 'the good life' in the Bolivian Plateau. *Social Indicator Research*, 90, 141–153.
Calestani, M. (2013). Suma Jakaña. In An Anthropological Journey into Well-Being (pp. 13–29). Springer: Dordrecht.
Cameron, N. (1991). *An illustrated history of Hong Kong*. Hong Kong: Oxford UP.
Carney, M. (1998). A management capacity constraint. Obstacles to the development of the oversea Chinese family business, *Asia Pacific Journal of Management*, 15, 137–162.
Carney, M., and Jaskiewicz, P. (2015). Six books that have shaped the landscape of family business scholarship. *Academy of Management Learning and Education*, 14(3), 423–429.
Carver, C. S., & Scheier, M. F. (1999). Themes and issues in the self-regulation of behavior. Advances in social cognition, 12(1), 1–106.
Casillas, J. and Acedo, F. (2007). Evolution of the intellectual structure of family business literature: A bibliometric study of FBR. *Family Business Review*, 20(2),141–162.
Ceja, L. (2009). Subjective well-being and families in businesses: A study using experience sampling. Working paper: University of Barcelona.
Census and Statistics Department. (2021). *Labour Force, Employment and Unemployment*. Retrieved from: https://www.censtatd.gov.hk/en/scode200.html#section4 (accessed March 23 2022).
Cepeda, G. and Martin, D. (2005). A review of case studies publishing in Management Decision 2003–2004. *Management Decision*, 43(6),851–876.
Chakrabarty, D. (2000). *Provincializing Europe: Postcolonial thought and historical difference*. Princeton, N.J: Princeton University Press.
Chan, P. F. (2008). *100 stories of management*. Taiwan: Yu Ho Cultural
Chan, S. W. (2007). *Longman concise Chinese-English dictionary*. Hong Kong: Pearson Longman.
Chan, W. (1963). *A source book in Chinese philosophy*, Princeton, NJ: Princeton University Press.
Chandler, G. N. and Lyon, D. W. (2001). Issues of research design and construct measurement in entrepreneurship research: The past decade. *Entrepreneurship, Theory and Practice*, 25, 101–113.
Chang, H and Holt, G. (1996). An exploration of interpersonal relationship in two Taiwanese computer firms. *Human Relations*, 49(12),1489–1517.

Chang, K. and Lu. L (2007). Characteristics of organizational culture, stressors and wellbeing. The case of Taiwanese organizations. *Journal of Managerial Psychology*, 22(6),549–568.

Chen, J., Zhou, F., He, Z., and Fu, H. (2020). Second-generation succession and the financialization of assets: An empirical study of Chinese family firms. *Emerging Markets Finance and Trade*, 56 (14), 3294–3319.

Chen, M. (1995). *Asian management systems: Chinese Japanese and Korean styles of business*, London: Routledge.

Chen, Z. (2001) (Ed.). *A modern Chinese-English dictionary*. Beijing: Foreign Language Teaching and Research Press.

Cheung, E. M. K. (2001). The Hi/stories of Hong Kong. *Cultural Studies*, 15(3),564–590.

Cheung, L. W. (2011). Managing Chinese employees: Dialogues from the notion of self. PhD thesis, University of Nottingham

Chew, M. (2001). An alternative metacritique of postcolonial cultural studies from a cultural sociological perspective. *Cultural Studies*, 15(3),602–620.

Chia, R., and King, I. (2001). The language of organization theory. *The language of organization*, 310–328.

Chiang, S. (1996). *The philosophy of happiness: A history of Chinese life philosophy*, Hong Yei Publication, Taipei.

Chichao, L. (2000). *History of Chinese political thought: During the early Tsin period*. London: Routledge.

Child, J. (2009). Context, comparison, and methodology in Chinese management research. *Management and Organization Review*, 5(1), 57–73.

Childe, V. G. (1946). Archaeology and Anthropology. *Southwestern Journal of Anthropology*, 2(3),243–251.

Chiu, C. (1998). *Small family business in Hong Kong: Accumulation and accommodation*. Hong Kong: The Chinese University Press.

Chow, R. (1992). Between colonizers: Hong Kong's postcolonial self-writing in the 1990s'. *Diaspora*, 2(2),151–170.

Chow, R. (1993). *Writing diaspora: Tactics of intervention in contemporary cultural studies*. Bloomington: Indiana University Press.

Chow, R. (1998). King Kong in Hong Kong: Watching the "Handover" from the USA, *Social Text: Intellectual Politics in Post-Tiananmen China*, 55, 93–108

Chrisman, J., Chua, J. and Sharma, P. (2005). Trends and directions in the development of a strategic management theory of the family firm. *Entrepreneurship Theory and Practice*, 555–575.

Chrisman, J., Kellermanns, F., Chan, K. and Liano, K. (2010). Intellectual foundations of current research in family business: an identification and review of 25 influential articles. *Family Business Review*, 23(1),9–26.

Christopher, J. (1999). Situating psychological well-being: exploring the cultural roots of its theory and research. *Journal of Counselling and Development*, 77, 141–152.

Chua, W. F. (1986). Radical development in accounting thought. *The Accounting Review*, 61 (4),601–632.

Chung, W. W. C. and Yuen, K. P. K. (2003),Management succession: a case for Chinese family-owned business, *Management Decision*, 41(7),643–655.

Clark, A. E. (2005). Your money or your life: Changing job quality in OECD countries. *British Journal of Industrial Relations*, 43(3),377–400.

Clark, A. E. and Oswald, A. J. (1994). Unhappiness and unemployment, *Economic Journal*, I(4), 648–59.

Clark, A. E., Georgellis, Y., Lucas, R. E., and Diener, E. (2004). Unemployment alters the set point for life satisfaction. *Psychological Science*, 15, 8–13.

Clifford, J. (1986) Introduction: Partial truths, in J. Clifford and G. Marcus, *Writing culture: The poetics and politics of ethnography*, University of California Press: Berkeley, pp. 1–26.

Cohen, A. and Deborah, C. (2003). Ethnography and case study: A comparative analysis. *Academic Exchange Quarterly*, 7(3), 283–288.

Cohen, N., and Arieli, T. (2011). Field research in conflict environments: Methodological challenges and snowball sampling. *Journal of Peace Research*, 48(4),423–435.

Collyer, F. (2011). Reflexivity and the sociology of science and technology: The invention of "Eryc" the antibiotic. *The Qualitative Report*, 16(2),316–340.

Compton, W. C., Smith, M. L., Cornish, K. A., and Qualls, D. L. (1996). Factor structure of mental health measures. *Journal of personality and social psychology*, 71(2),406–413.

Conceição, P. and Bandura, R. (2008). Measuring subjective wellbeing: A summary review of the literature. Retrieved from: http://www.undp.org/developmentstudies/docs/subjective_wellbeing_conceicao_bandura.pdf (accessed March 10 2022).

Cooke, F. L., Saini, D. S., and Wang, J. (2014). Talent management in China and India: A comparison of management perceptions and human resource practices. *Journal of World Business*, 49 (2),225–235.

Cooper, A. C. and Artz, K. W. (1995). Determinants of satisfaction for entrepreneurs. *Journal of Business Venturing*, 10(6),439–457.

Costa, P. T. and McCrae, R. R. (1980). Influence of extraversion and neuroticism on subjective well-being: Happy and unhappy people. *Journal of Personality and Social Psychology*, 38 (4),668–678.

Coviello, N. E. and Jones, M. V. (2004). Methodological issues in international entrepreneurship research. *Journal of Business Venturing*, 19, 485–508.

Croon, M.A., De Vries, J., Michielsen, H.J., Van Heck, G.L. and Willemsen, T.M. (2007). Which constructs can predict emotional exhaustion in working population? A study into its determinants. *Stress and Health*, 23, 121–130.

Cua, A. S. (1975). Confucian Vision and Experience of the World. *Philosophy East and West*, 25(3),319–333.

Cua, A. S. (1981). Opposites as Complements: Reflections on the Significance of Tao. *Philosophy East and West*, 31(2),123–140.

Cua, A. S. (1998). *Moral vision and tradition: Essays in Chinese ethics*. Washington, DC: Catholic University of America Press.

Cummings, S., Bridgman, T., Hassard, J., & Rowlinson, M. (2017). *A new history of management*. Cambridge University Press.

Cummins, R. A. (1995). On the trail of the gold standard for life satisfaction. *Social Indicators Research*, 35, 179–200.

Curtis, J. and Harrison, L. (2001). Beneath the surface: Collaboration in alcohol and other drug treatment. An analysis using Foucault's three mode of objectification. *Journal of Advanced Nursing*, 34(6),737–744.

Czarniawska-Joerges's, B. (1992). *Exploring complex organizations. A cultural perspective*. London: Sage.

Danes, S. M., Leichtentritt, R. D., Metz, M. E., and Huddleston-Casas, C. (2000). Effects of conflict styles and conflict severity on quality of life of men and women in family businesses. *Journal of Family and Economic Issues*, 21(3),259–286.

Danes, S. M., Zuiker, V., Kean, R. and Arbuthnot, J. (1999). Predictors of family business tensions and goal achievement. *Family Business Review*, 12(3),241–252.

Daniel, C. O. (2019). Effects of job stress on employee's performance. International Journal of Business, Management and Social Research, 6(2), 375–382.
Danna, K. and Griffin, R. W. (1999). Health and well-being in the workplace: A review and synthesis of the literature. *Journal of Management*, 25, 357–384.
Davidsson, P. (1989). Entrepreneurship – And after? A study of growth willingness in small firms. *Journal of Business Venturing*, 4(3),211–226.
Davies, C. A. (1999). *Reflexive ethnography: A guide to researching selves and others*. Routledge: London.
Davis, E. (2005). *Encyclopaedia of contemporary Chinese culture*. Routledge: New Work.
de Saussure, F. (1983), *Course in General Linguistics*, trans. by Harris, R., Open Court Classics, Chicago, IL.
Dean, M. A., Shook, C. L., and Payne, G. T. (2007). The past, present, and future of entrepreneurship research: Data analytic trends and training. *Entrepreneurship Theory and Practice*, 31(4),601–618.
Deci, E. and Ryan, R. (2008). Hedonia, eudaimonia, and well-being: An introduction. *Journal of Happiness Studies*, 9, 1–11.
Deci, E. L., & Ryan, R. M. (1985). The general causality orientations scale: Self-determination in personality. Journal of research in personality, 19(2), 109–134.
Denzin, N. K. (1989). *Interpretive biography*. Newbury Park, CA: Sage.
Derne, S. (2010). Well-being: Lesson from India. In G. Mathew and C. Izquierdo, *Pursuits of happiness: Well-being in anthropological perspective*. Oxford: Berghahn Books, 127–146.
Desrochers, S. and Sargent, L. (2004). Boundary/Border theory and Work-family integration. *Organization Management Journal*, 1(1),40–48.
Desrochers, S., Hilton, J. M., and Larwood, L. (2002). Measuring work-family boundary ambiguity: A proposed scale. *Bronfenbrenner Life Course Center Working Paper* #02–04.
Dess, G. G., Pinkham, B. C. and Yang, H. (2011), Entrepreneurial Orientation: Assessing the Construct's Validity and Addressing Some of Its Implications for Research in the Areas of Family Business and Organizational Learning. *Entrepreneurship Theory and Practice*, 35: 1077–1090.
Diener, E. (1984). Subjective well-being, *Psychological Bulletin*, 95, 542–575.
Diener, E., Diener, M. and Diener, C. (1995). Factor predicting subjective well-being of nations. *Journal of Personality and Social Psychology*, 69, 851–864.
Diener, E., Lucas, R. E., and Scollon, C. N. (2006). Beyond the hedonic treadmill: revising the adaptation theory of well-being. *American psychologist*, 61(4),305–314.
Diener, E., Oishi, S., and Tay, L. (2018). Advances in subjective well-being research. *Nature Human Behaviour*, 2(4),253–260.
Diener, E., Suh, E. M., Smith, H. and Shao, L. (1995). National and cultural differences in reported subjective well-being: Why do they occur? *Social Indicators Research*, 31, 103–157.
Dodd, S. D. (2011). Mapping work-related stress and health in the context of the family firm. *The International Journal of Entrepreneurship and Innovation*, 12(1),29–38.
Dreyfus, H. and Rainbow, P. (1982), The Subject and Power, In *Michel Foucault: Beyond structuralism and hermeneutics*. The University of Chicago Press.
Easterby-Smith, M., Thorpe, R. and Jackson. (2012) *Management Research*. (4th eds). London: Sage.
Easterlin, R. A. (1974). Does economic growth improve the human lot? Some empirical evidence. In P. A. David and M. W. Reder (Eds), *Nations and households in economic growth* (pp. 89–125). New York: Academic Press.
Easterlin, R. A. (2005). Building a better theory of well-being. In L. Bruni and P. Porta (Eds.), *Economics and happiness: Framing the analysis*. Oxford: Oxford University Press.

Easter-Smith, M. Thorpe, R. and Lowe, A. (1991). *Management research: An introduction*. London: Sage.
ECIC. (2005). Tips for SME: Director's rights and responsibility: Improving corporate governance in SMEs. *Compass*, 11(1),20–26.
Ed, D., Suh, E. M., Lucas, R. E., and Smith, H. L. (1999). Subjective well-being: Three decades of progress. *Psychological Bulletin*, 125(2),276–302.
Edwards, J. R., and Rothbard, N. P. (1999). Work and family stress and well-being: An examination of person-environment fit in the work and family domains. *Organizational Behavior and Human Decision Processes*, 77(2),85–129.
Erikson, E. H. (1959). Identity and the life cycle: Selected papers. *Psychological Issues*, 1, 1–171.
Erni, J. N. (2001). Like a postcolonial culture: Hong Kong re-imagined. *Cultural Studies*, 15 (3),389–418.
Fabian, J. (1983). *Time and the Other: How anthropology makes its object*, Columbia University Press: New York.
Falzon, C. (1998). *Foucault and social dialogue*. London: Routledge.
Fan, G. and Frisbie, W. (2009). How do multiple roles affect young and middle-aged women's health? The impact of employment and family roles. *Journal of Population Studies*, 38, 33–65.
Fei, X. (1939). *Peasant Life in China*. London: Routledge.
Fei, X. (1948) *Xiangtu Zhongguo (Rural China)*. Shanghai: Guancha.
Fei, X. (1953). *China's gentry: essays in rural-urban relations*. Chicago: University of Chicago Press.
Fei, X. (1997). Investigating ethnicity: My studies and views of ethnic groups in China, *Journal of Peking University (Humanities and Social Sciences)*, 2, 4–12.
Fetterman, D. M. (2010). *Ethnography: Step by step*. (3rd eds). Sage Publications, Inc: Los Angeles
Fleuret, S. and Atkinson, S. (2007). Wellbeing, health and geography: A critical review and research agenda. *New Zealand Geographer*, 63, 106–118.
Foley, S. and Powell, G. N. (1997). Reconceptualising Work-Family Conflict for Business/Marriage Partners: A Theoretical Model. *Journal of Small Business Management*, 35, 36–47.
Foo, M. D. (2009). Emotions and entrepreneurial opportunity evaluation. *Entrepreneurship Theory and Practice*, 35(2),375–393.
Ford, J., Harding, N., and Learmonth, M. (2010). Who is it that would make business schools more critical? Critical reflections on critical management studies. *British Journal of Management*, 21, S71–S81.
Foucault, M. (1970). *The order of things: An archaeology of human sciences*. London: Tavistock.
Foucault, M. (1972). *The archaeology of knowledge*. London: Routledge.
Foucault, M. (1973). *The birth of the clinic*. London: Routledge
Foucault, M. (1977a). *Discipline and punish: The birth of the prison*. New York: Vintage Book.
Foucault, M. (1977b). An aesthetics of existence. *Politics, philosophy, culture: Interviews and other writings*, 1984, 47–53.
Foucault, M. (1979) *Discipline and punish*. New York: Vintage.
Foucault, M. (1982). The subject and power. *Critical Inquiry*, 8(4),777–795.
Foucault, M. (1997a). *Ethics: Subjectivity and truth*. New York: New Press.
Foucault, M. (1997b). *The politics of truth*. New York: Semiotext.
Frederick, S., and Loewenstein, G. (1999). Hedonic adaptation. In D. Kahneman, E. Diener and N. Schwarz (Eds.), *Well-being: The foundations of hedonic psychology* (pp. 302–329). New York: Russell Sage.
Frenkel, M. (2008). The multinational corporation as a third space: Rethinking international management discourse on knowledge transfer through Homi Bhabha. *Academy of Management Review*, 33(4),924–942.

Frey, B. S. (2021). What future happiness research?. In *A modern guide to the economics of happiness*. Edward Elgar Publishing.

Fromm, E. (1979). Primary and secondary process in waking and in altered states of consciousness. *Journal of Altered States of Consciousness*, 4(2),115–128.

Frone, M.R., Yardley, J.K. and Markel, K.S. (1997). Developing and testing an integrative model of the work-family interface. *Journal of Vocational Behaviour*, 50, 145–167.

Fung, A. (2001). What makes the local? A brief consideration of the rejuvenation of Hong Kong identity. *Cultural Studies*, 15(3),591–601.

Fung, Y. (1952). *A history of Chinese philosophy*, Princeton, NJ: Princeton University Press

Gabriel, Y. (1999), Beyond happy families, *Human Relations*, 52(2),179–203.

Gadamer, H. G. (1989). *Truth and Method*, 2nd edn (J. Weinsheimer and D. G. Marshall, Trans.). New York: Continuum. (Original work published in 1960)

Gargan, E. (April 22 1997). Chinese soldiers march into Hong Kong. *New York Times*. Retrieved from: http://www.nytimes.com/1997/04/22/world/chinese-soldiers-march-into-hong-kong.html (accessed March 10 2022).

Geertz, C. (1973). *The interpretation of cultures*. New York: Basic Books.

George, J. M, and Brief, A. P. (1990). The economic instrumentality of work: An examination of the moderating effects of financial requirements and sex on the pay-life satisfaction relationship. *Journal of Vocational Behavior*, 37, 357–368.

Gerris, J., Kinnunen, U., Makikangas, A. and Vermulst, A. (2003). Work-family conflict and its relations to well-being: the role of personality as a moderating factor. *Personality and Individual Differences*, 35, 1669–1683.

Gibbons, M., Limoges, C., Nowotny, H., Schwartzman, S., Scott, P. and Trow, M. (2005). *The new knowledge production of knowledge*. London: Sage

Gielnik, M. M., Zacher, H. and Frese, F. (2010). Focus on opportunities as a mediator of the relationship between business owners' age and venture growth. *Journal of Business Venturing*, 27(1),127–142.

Giles, H. (1910). *San Tzu Ching – Elementary Chinese*. Retrieved from: http://ctext.org/three-character-classic (accessed March 10 2022).

Giovannini E., Hall J. and D'Ercole M.M. (2006), Measuring Well-being and societal progress, Background paper for the conference 'Beyond GDP', 19–20 November 2006, Brussels. Retrieved from: http://www.beyond-gdp.eu/background.html (accessed March 10 2022).

Gold, R. (1985). Roles in sociological field observation. *Social Forces*, 36, 217–233.

Gomez, R. and Fisherself, J. W. (2005). Item response theory analysis of the spiritual well-being questionnaire. *Personality and Individual Differences*, 38, 1107–1121.

Good, L.K., Sisler, G.F. and Gentry, J.W. (1988). Antecedents of turnover intentions among retail management. *Journal of Retailing*, 64, 295–314.

Goodman, J. (1997). History and anthropology. In J. Rutherford (Eds.), *Identity, community, culture, differences*. London: Lawrence and Wishart, 222–237.

Goody, J. (1996). *The east in the west*. Cambridge University Press.

Goody, J. (2012). *The theft of history*. Cambridge University Press.

Gosden, C. (2002). *Anthropology and archaeology: A changing relationship*. London and New York: Routledge.

Graham, A. C. (1965). 'Being' in linguistics and philosophy: A preliminary inquiry. *Foundations of Language*, 1 (3), 223–231.

Grbich C. (1999). *Qualitative research in health. An introduction*. London: Sage Publications.

Greenhaus, J.H. and Beutell, N.J. (1985). Sources of conflict between work and family roles. *Academy of Management Review*, 10, 76–88.

Greenhaus, J.H. and Powell, G.N. (2006). When work and family are allies: a theory of work-family enrichment. *Academy of Management Review*, 31, 72–92.

Grzyacz, J.G. and Bass, B.L. (2003). Work, family, and mental health: testing different models of work-family fit. *Journal of Marriage and Family*, 65, 248–262.

Gu, Z. (1995). *Lao Zi: The book of Tao and Teh*. Beijing: Peking University Press

Guba, E. G. and Lincoln, Y. S. (2005). Paradigmatic controversies, contradictions, and emerging confluences. In N. K. Denzin and Y. S. Lincoln (Eds.), *The Sage handbook of qualitative research* (3rd ed.), Thousand Oaks, CA: Sage, 191–215.

Guest, D.E. (1999). Human resource management – the worker's verdict. *Human Resource Management Journal*, 9(2),5–25.

Hahm, C. (2001). Confucian ritual and the technology of the self: A Foucaultian interpretation. *Philosophy East and West*, 51(3),315–324.

Hall, A., Melin, L. and Nordqvist, M. (2001). Entrepreneurship as radical change in the family business: Exploring the role of cultural pattern. *Family Business Review*, 14, 193–208.

Hall, A., Melin, L. and Nordqvist, M. (2006). Understanding strategizing in family business context. In P.Z. Poutziouris, K.X. Smyrnios and S.B. Klein (Ed.), *Handbook of Research on Family Business*. Cheltenham: Edward Elgar, 253–268

Hall, D. L. and Ames, R. T. (1987). *Thinking through Confucius*. New York: State University of New York Press.

Hall, D., Ames, Roger T., and EBSCO Industries. (1998). *Thinking from the Han self, truth, and transcendence in Chinese and Western culture*. Albany, N.Y.: State University of New York Press.

Hammersley, M. (1990). *Reading ethnographic research: A critical guide*. New York: Longman.

Hammersley, M. and Atkinson, P. (1995). *Ethnography: Principles in practice*. (2nd eds). London and New York: Routledge.

Hansen, C. (1993). Classical Chinese ethics. In P. Singer, *A companion to ethics*, Oxford: Blackwell Publishing, 69–81.

Hanson, G.C., Hammer, L.B. and Colton, C.L. (2006). Development and validation of a multidimensional scale and perceived work-family positive spillover. *Journal of Occupational Health Psychology*, 11, 249–265.

Harrington, R. (2013). *Stress, Health and Well-being: Thriving in the 21st century*, U.S.A: Wadsworth.

Harvey C., Kelly A., Morris, H. and Rowlinson, M. (2010). The Association of Business Schools: Academic Journal Quality Guide. Version 4. Retrieved from: http://www.associationofbusiness schools.org/node/1000257 (accessed March 10 2022)

Harvey, L. and MacDonald, M. (1993). *Doing sociology*. London: Macmillan Press Ltd.

Haworth, J. and Hart, G. (2007). *Well-being: Individual, community and social perspectives*. London: Palgrave Macmillan.

He, Y. (2007). Confucius and Aristotle on friendship: A comparative study. *Frontiers of Philosophy in China*, 2(2),291–307.

Headey, B. W. (2008). The set point theory of well-being: Negative results and consequent revisions. *Social Indicators Research*, 85, 389–403.

Headey, B. W. (2010). The set point theory of well-being has serious flaws: On the eve of a scientific revolution? *Social Indicators Research*, 97, 7–21.

Headey, B. W. and Wearing, A. J. (1989). Personality, life events, and subjective well-being: Toward a dynamic equilibrium model. *Journal of Personality and Social Psychology*, 57(4),731–739.

Helliwell, J. F., Huang, H., Wang, S., and Norton, M. (2021). World happiness, trust and deaths under COVID-19. *World Happiness Report*, 13–56.

Herr, R. S. (2003). Is Confucianism compatible with care ethics? A critique. *Philosophy East and West*, 53(4),471–489.

Herzberg, F., Mausner, B. and Snyderman, B.B. (1967). *The Motivation to Work* (2nd ed.), Wiley: New York.

Higginbottom G. M. (2004). Sampling issues in qualitative research. *Nurse Researcher*, 12, 7–19.

Higgins, C.A., Duxbury, L.E. and Irving, R.H. (1992). Work-family conflict in the dual-career family. *Organizational Behaviors and Human Decision Processes*, 51, 51–75.

Hill, E. J., Hawkins, A. J., and Miller, B. C. (1996). Work and family in the virtual office: Perceived influence of mobile telework. *Family Relations*, 45, 293–301.

Hmieleski, K. M. and Corbett, A. C. (2008). The contrasting interaction effects of improvisational behavior with entrepreneurial self-efficacy on new venture performance and entrepreneur work satisfaction. *Journal of Business Venturing*, 23(4),482–496.

Ho, H. and Kuvaas, B. (2020). Human resource management systems, employee well-being, and firm performance from the mutual gains and critical perspectives: The well-being paradox. *Human Resource Management*, 59(3), 235–253.

Ho, L. (1990). *Qoulou de xianggangren (The Ugly Hon Konger)*. Hong Kong: Chiwenhuayouxiangongci.

Hofstede, G. (1993). Cultural constraints in management theories. *Academy of Management Perspectives*, 7(1), 81–94.

Holloway, I. (1997). *Basic concepts for qualitative research*. London: Blackwell Science.

Hong Kong Society of Accountants (1997). *Second report of the corporate governance working group*. Hong Kong: HKSA

Hornsby, J. S., Kuratko, D. F. and Montagno, R. V. (1999). Perception of internal factors for corporate entrepreneurship: A comparison of Canadian and U.S. managers. *Entrepreneurship Theory and Practice*, 24, 9–24.

Hu, Q., and Schaufeli, W. B. (2011). Job insecurity and remuneration in Chinese family-owned business workers. *Career Development International*, 16(1),6–19.

Huppert, F. (2005). Positive mental health in individuals and populations. In F. Huppert, N. Baylis, and B. Keverne (Eds.), *The science of well-being* (pp. 307–340). Oxford: Oxford University Press.

Huppert, F. A. and Linley, P. A. (2011). *Happiness and well-being: Critical concepts in psychology*, London and New York: Routledge.

Hwang, K. and Chang, J. (2009). Self-Cultivation: Culturally sensitive psychotherapies in Confucian societies. *The Counselling Psychologist*, 37(7),1010–1032.

Innes, C. L. (2007). *The Cambridge introduction to postcolonial literatures in English*. Cambridge University Press.

Jack, G. and Westwood, R. (2006). Postcolonialism and the politics of qualitative research in international business. *Management International Review*, 46(4),481–501.

Jack, G.A., Calas, M. B., Nkomo, S. M. and Peltonen, T. (2008). Critique and international management: An uneasy relationship. *Academy of Management Review*, 33(4),870–884.

Jacques, R. (1996). *Manufacturing the employee: Management knowledge from the 19th to 21st centuries*. London: SAGE Publications Ltd.

Jahoda, M. (1958). *Current concepts of positive mental health*. New York: Basic Books.

Jankowiak, W. (2010). Well-being, cultural pathology and personal rejuvenation in a Chinese City, 1981–2005. In G. Mathew and C. Izquierdo, *Pursuits of happiness: Well-being in anthropological perspective*. Oxford: Berghahn Books, 147–166.

Ji, Cheng (2011) *Discourse politics: How symbolic power works during the social transformations in China's countryside*. Beijing: China's Social Science Publisher.

Jiang, Z., and Korczynski, M. (2016). When the 'unorganizable'organize: The collective mobilization of migrant domestic workers in London. *Human Relations*, 69(3),813–838.

John, O. P. (2009). Berkeley Personality Lab. Retrieved from: https://www.ocf.berkeley.edu/~john lab/index.htm (accessed March 10, 2022).

Johnson, P., Buehring, A., Cassell, C. and Symon, G. (2006). Evaluating qualitative management research: Towards a contingent criteriology. *International Journal of Management Reviews*, 8 (3),131–156.

Johnson. and Duberley, J. (2003). Reflexivity in management research. *Journal of Management Studies*, 40(5),1279–1303.

Jung, C. G. (1933). *Modern man in search of a soul*. New York: Harcourt, Brace and World.

Kahn, C. H. (1966). The Greek verb 'to be' and the concept of being. *Foundations of Language*, 2 (3),245–265.

Kahneman D., Diener E. and Schwarz N. (1999). *Well-Being: The Foundations of Hedonic Psychology*, New York: Russell Sage Foundation

Kaltenmark, M. (1969). *Lao Tzu and taoism*. Stanford University Press.

Kansikas, J. and Laakkonen, A. (2009). Students' perception of family entrepreneurship – A study on family business academic education. *Management International*, 14(1),55–65.

Kao, J. (1993). The worldwide web of Chinese business. *Harvard Business Review*, 71, 24–36.

Karofsky, P., Smyrnios, K., Romano, C., Tanewskil, G., Millen, R. and Yilmaz, M. (2001). Work-family conflict and emotional well-being in American family business. *Family Business Review*, 14 (4),313–324.

Kashdan, T. B., Baswas-Diener, R. and King, L. A. (2011). Reconsidering happiness: The cost of distinguishing between hedonics and eudaimonia. In F. A. Huppert and P. A. Linley, *Happiness and well-being: Critical concepts in psychology*, London and New York: Routledge.

Katz, J. A. (1993). How satisfied are the self-employed: A secondary analysis approach. *Entrepreneurship Theory and Practice*, 17, 35–51.

Katz, J. and Csordas, T. (2003). Phenomenological ethnography in sociology and anthropology. *Ethnography*, 4(3),275–288.

Kelloway, E.K., Gottlieb, B.H. and Barham, L. (1999). The source, nature and direction or work and family conflict: a longitudinal investigation. *Journal of Occupational Health Psychology*, 4, 337–346.

King, A. Y. C. and Bond, M. H. (1985). The Confucian paradigm of man: A sociological view. In W. Tseng and D. Y. H. Wu (Eds.), *Chinese Culture and Mental Health*. Orlando, FL: Academic Press, 29–45.

King, R. and Peng, W.Q. (2007). *Family control longevity: Evidence from the S and P 500*, Department of Finance, Hong Kong University of Science and Technology.

Kinnuneb, U., Pulkkinen, L. and Rantanen, J. (2005). The big five personality dimensions, work-family conflict, and psychological distress. A longitudinal view. *Journal of Individual Differences*, 26 (3), 155–166.

Kinnunen, U. and Mauno, S. (1998). An antecedents and outcomes or work-family conflict among employed women and men in Finland. *Human Relations*, 51, 157–177.

Klein, H.K. and Myer, M.D. (1999). A set of principles for conducting and evaluating interpretive field studies in information systems. *MIS Quarterly*, 23(1),67–94.

Knibbe, K. and Versteeg, P. (2008). Assessing phenomenology in anthropology. Lesson from the study of religion and experience. *Critique of Anthropology*, 28(1),47–62.

Knights, D. (1992). Changing Spaces: The disruptive impact of a new epistemological location for the study of management. *Academy of Management Review*, 17(3),514–536.

Knights, D. (2002). Writing organizational analysis into Foucault. *Organization*, 9(4),575–593.

Knights, D. (2004). Michel Foucault. In S. Linstead (Eds), *Organizational Theory and Postmodern Thought*, London: Sage, 14–33.

Koltko-Rivera, M. E. (2006). Rediscovering the Later Version of Maslow's Hierarchy of Needs: Self-Transcendence and Opportunities for Theory, Research, and Unification. *Review of General Psychology*. 10(4),302–317.

Kondo, D. K. (1990). *Crafting selves: Power, gender, and discourses of identity in a Japanese workplace*. The University of Chicago Press: London.

Kontinen, T. and Ojala, A. (2010). The internationalization of family businesses: A review of extant research. *Journal of Family Business Strategy*, 1, 97–107.

Kossek, E.E. and Ozeki, C. (1998), Work-family conflict, policies, and the job-life satisfaction relationship: A review and directions for organizational behavior-human resources research. *Journal of Applied Psychology*, 83, 139–149.

Kreiner, G.E. (2002). Boundary preferences and work-family conflict: A person-environment fit perspective. Paper presented at the annual meeting of the Academy of Management Conference, Denver, CO.

Krumeich, A., Weijts, W., Reddy, P. and Meijer-Weitz, A. (2001). The benefits of anthropological approaches for health promotion research and practice. *Health Education Research Theory and Practice*, 16(2),121–130.

Lai, K. (2007). Ziran and Wuwei in the Daodejing: An Ethical Assessment. *Dao*, 6, 325–337.

Landy, F.J. (1997). Early Influences on the Development of Industrial and Organizational Psychology. *Journal of Applied Psychology*, 82, 467–477.

Lau, S. K. and Kuan, H. C. (1988). *The ethos of the Hong Kong Chinese*. Hong Kong: The Chinese University Press.

Learmonth, M. (1999). The National Health Service manager, engineer and father? A deconstruction. *Journal of Management Studies*, 36(7),999–1012.

Learmonth, M. (2009). Girls' working together without 'teams': How to avoid the colonization of management language. *Human Relations*, 62(12),1887–1906.

Learmonth, M. (2017). Making history critical: Recasting a history of the "management" of the British National Health Service. *Journal of Health Organization and Management*, 31 (5),542–555.

Lee, F.L.F. (2015). Social movement as civic education: communication activities and understanding of civil disobedience in the Umbrella Movement, *Chinese Journal of Communication*, 8:4, 393–411.

Lee, L., Wong, P. K., Foo, M. D. and Leung, A. (2011). Entrepreneurial intentions: The influence of organizational and individual factors motivated reasoning in new product introductions. *Journal of Business Venturing*, 26(1),124–136.

Lee, S. J. (2022). Determinants of Happiness. *Public Happiness*, 105–142.

Legge, J. (1891a). *The Dao De Jing*. Retrieved from: http://ctext.org/dao-de-jing (accessed March 10 2022).

Legge, J. (1891b). *The Writings of Chuang Tzu*. Clarendon. Retrieved from http://ctext.org/zhuangzi

Legge, J. (1949). *The Chinese classics I: Confucian Analects, The Great Learning and The Doctrine of the Mean*. Oxford: Oxford University Press.

Legge, J. (1985). *The Analects*. Clarendon. Retrieved from: http://ctext.org/analects (accessed March 10 2022)

Legge, J. (1985). *The Work of Mencius*. Clarendon. Retrieved from: http://ctext.org/mengzi (accessed March 10 2022)

Legge, K. (1995). *Human resource management: Rhetorics and realities*, Macmillan, Basingstoke.

Leppäaho, T., Plakoyiannaki, E., & Dimitratos, P. (2016). The case study in family business: An analysis of current research practices and recommendations. *Family Business Review*, 29 (2),159–173.

Li, C. (2008). The Philosophy of Harmony in Classical Confucianism. *Philosophy Compass*, 3/3, 423–435.

Li, D. (2005). Motivation in Chinese and its use, June 10–12, *Proceeding for the 2005 International Symposium on Operational Strategies and Pedagogy for Chinese Language programs in the 21st Century*, Taipei, Taiwan.

Li, J., Ericsson, C. and Quennerstedt, M. (2013). The meaning of the Chinese cultural keyword *xin*. Journal of Language and Culture, 4(5),75–89.

Liang, D. and Zheng, J. (2003). *Zhongda Chinese-English dictionary*. Hong Kong: Chinese University Press.

Liang, X., Wang, L., and Cui, Z. (2014). Chinese private firms and internationalization: Effects of family involvement in management and family ownership. *Family Business Review*, 27 (2),126–141.

Ling, L. H. M. and Shih, C. (1998). Confucianism with a liberal face: The meaning of democratic politics in postcolonial Taiwan. *The Review of Politics*, 60(1),55–82.

Link, H.C. (1924). *Employment psychology*, New York: Macmillan.

Liu, J., Siu, O. L., & Shi, K. (2010). Transformational leadership and employee well-being: The mediating role of trust in the leader and self-efficacy. *Applied Psychology*, 59(3), 454–479.

Liu, L., and Yu, J. (2021). Guanxi HRM and employee well-being in China. *Employee Relations*, 43(4), 892–910.

Liu, X. (2009). Daoism (I): Lao Zi and the Dao-De-Jing. In B. Mou, *Routledge history of world philosophies, Volume 3: History of Chinese philosophy*, Routledge: London and New York, 209–236.

Liu, Y. (2004). The self and li in Confucianism. *Journal of Chinese Philosophy*, 31(3),363–376.

Loy, J. T. (2012). Overseas Chinese family business research: a comparative analysis. *Journal of family business management*, 2(1),31–39.

Lu, L. (2001). Understanding happiness: A look into the Chinese folk psychology. *Journal of Happiness Studies*, 2, 407–432.

Lu, L. (2009). 'I or we': Family socialization values in a national probability sample in Taiwan, *Asian Journal of Social Psychology*, 12, 145–150.

Lu, L. (2010). Chinese well-being. In M. H. Bond (eds), *The Oxford handbook of Chinese psychology*, Oxford: Oxford University Press, 327–342.

Lu, L. and Gilmour, R. (2006). Individual-oriented and socially oriented cultural conceptions of subjective well-being: Conceptual analysis and scale development. *Asian Journal of Social Psychology*, 9, 36–49.

Lu, L., and Yang, K. S. (2006). Emergence and composition of the traditional-modern bicultural self of people in contemporary Taiwanese societies. *Asian Journal of Social Psychology*, 9, 167–175.

Lu, L., Kao, S. F., Chang, T. T., Wu, H. P. and Jin, Z. (2008). The individual- and social-oriented Chinese bicultural self: A subcultural analysis contrasting mainland Chinese and Taiwanese. *Social Behavior and Personality*, 36 (3), 337–346.

Lucas, R. E., Clark, A. E., Georgellis, Y., and Diener, E. (2003). Re-examining adaptation and the set point model of happiness: Reactions to change in marital status. *Journal of Personality and Social Psychology*, 84, 527–539.

Luechapattanaporn, T., and Wongsurawat, W. (2021). Cultural factors in Chinese family business performance in Thailand. *International Journal of Entrepreneurship*, 25(2), 1–15.

Luk, D. M. and Shaffer, M. A. (2005). Work and family domain stressors and support: Within- and cross-domain influence on work-family conflict. *Journal of Occupational and Organizational Psychology*, 78, 489–508.

Luo, L. and Chou, C. Y. (2020). Protecting job performance and Well-Being in the demanding work context: The moderating effect of psychological detachment for Chinese employees: International review of applied psychology. *Applied Psychology*, 69(4), 1199–1214.

Madden, R. (1999). Home-town anthropology. *Australian Journal of Anthropology*, 10(3), 259–270.

Madigan, S. P. (1992). The application of Michel Foucault's philosophy in the problem externalizing discourse of Michael White. *Journal of Family Therapy*, 14, 265–279.

Mahto, R. V., Davis, P. S., Pearce II, J. A. and Robinson Jr, R. B. (2010). Satisfaction with firm performance in family businesses. *Entrepreneurship Theory and Practice*, 34(5),985–1001.

Manning, J. (2016). Constructing a postcolonial feminist ethnography. *Journal of Organizational Ethnography*, 5(2),90–105.

March, J. (2004). Parochialism in the evolution of a research community: The case of organization studies. *Management and Organization Review*, 1(1),5–22.

Martindale, N. (2015), "Mortgages as an employee benefit", *HR Magazine*, August 14 2015, Retrieved from: http://www.hrmagazine.co.uk/article-details/mortgages-as-an-employee-benefit (accessed March 10 2022)

Maslach, C., Leiter, M. P., & Schaufeli, W. (2009). *Measuring burnout.* Oxford University Press: UK

Maslow, A. (1943). A theory of human motivation. *Psychological Review*, 50(4),370–396.

Maslow, A. (1969). Various meanings of transcendence. Journal of Transpersonal Psychology, 1(1), 56–66.

Maslow, A. and Lowery, R. (1998). *Toward a psychology of being* (3rd ed.). New York: Wiley and Sons.

Maslow, A. H. (1969). Various meaning of transcendence. *Journal of Transpersonal Psychology*, 1 (1),56–66.

Mathew, G. and Izquierdo, C. (2010). *Pursuits of happiness: Well-being in anthropological perspective*. Oxford: Berghahn Books.

Mattew, G. (2010). Finding and keeping a purpose in life: Well-being and *Ikigai* in Japan and elsewhere. In G. Mathew and C. Izquierdo, *Pursuits of happiness: Well-being in anthropological perspective.* Oxford: Berghahn Books, 167–188.

McGillivray, D. (2003). Governing working bodies: a genealogical analysis of organizational wellness. Unpublished doctoral dissertation, Glasgow Caledonian University, Glasgow.

McGillivray, D. (2005). Fitter, happier, more productive: Governing working bodies through wellness. *Culture and Organization*, 11(2),125–138.

McGillivray, M. (2007). Human well-being: Issues, concepts and measures. In *Human Well-Being* (pp. 1–22). Palgrave Macmillan UK.

McGregor, I., and Little, B. R. (1998). Personal projects, happiness, and meaning: on doing well and being yourself. *Journal of personality and social psychology*, 74(2),494–512.

McKinlay, A. (2006). Managing Foucault: genealogies of management. *Management and Organizational History*, 1(1),87–100.

Michalos, A. C. (1985). Multiple discrepancies theory. *Social Indicators Research*, 16, 347–413.

Minkes, A. L., and Foster, M. J. (2011). Cross-cultural divergence and convergence: With special reference to the family firm in South East Asia and China. *International Journal of Cross Cultural Management*, 11(2),153–166.

Mok, H., and Cheung. I. (1992). Family control and return covariation in Hong Kong's common stocks. *Journal of Business Finance and Accounting*, 19 (2), 277–293.

Monsen, E. and Boss, R. W. (2009). The impact of strategic entrepreneurship inside the organization: Examining job stress and employee. *Entrepreneurship Theory and Practice*, 33 (1),71–104.

Moores, K. and Mula, J. (2000). The salience of market, bureaucratic, and clan controls in the management of family firm transitions: Some tentative Australian evidence. *Family Business Review*, 13, 91–106.

Morrell, K., and Learmonth, M. (2015). Against evidence-based management, for management learning. *Academy of Management Learning and Education*, 14(4),520–533.

Morrell, K., Learmonth, M., and Heracleous, L. (2015). An archaeological critique of 'evidence-based management': One digression after another. *British Journal of Management*, 26 (3),529–543.

Morris, B. (1994). *Anthropology of the self: The individual in cultural perspective*. London: Pluto Press.

Mosbah, A., and Wahab, K. A. (2018). Chinese family business in Malaysia: Development, culture and the family business philosophy. *International Journal of Academic Research in Business and Social Sciences*, 8(5),997–1006.

Mote, F. W. (1971). *Intellectual foundations of China*. New York: Knopf.

Moyer, S.K. and Chalofsky, N.E. (2008). Understanding the selection and development of life goals of family business owners. *Journal of Enterprising Culture*, 16(1),19–53.

Mun, K. C. (2011). *Yin-Yang in traditional Chinese thought and its modern practices*, Hong Kong: The Chinese University of Hong Kong.

Myer, M. D. (1997). Qualitative Research in Information Systems. *MISQ Discovery*, 21(2),241–242.

Nandy, A. (1983). *The intimate enemy: Loss and recovery of self under colonialism*. Oxford: Oxford University Press.

Nerkar, A. A., McGrath, R. G. and MacMillan, I. C. (1996). Three facets of satisfaction and their influence on the performance of innovation teams. *Journal of Business Venturing*,11(3), 167–188.

Netemyer, R.G., Boles, J.S. and McMurrian, R. (1996). Development and validation of work-family conflict and family-work conflict scales. *Journal of Applied Psychology*, 81,400–411.

Newton, T. (1998), Theorising subjectivity in organisations, *Organisation Studies*, 19(3),415–447.

Ngugiwa T. (1981). *Decolonising the mind: The politics of language in African literature*. Portsmouth, NH: Heinemann.

Nippert-Eng, C. (1996). *Home and work*. Chicago: University of Chicago Press.

Noon, M. (1992). HRM: A map, model or theory. In P. Blyton and P. Turnbull (eds), *Reassessing human resource management*. London: Sage Publication.

Nordqvist, M., Hall, A. and Melin, L. (2009). Qualitative research on family business: The relevance and usefulness of interpretive approach. *Journal of Management and Organization*, 15 (3),294–308.

O'Driscoll, M.P., Ilgen, D.R. and Hildreth, K. (1992). Time devoted to job and off-job activities, interrole conflict and affective experiences. *Journal of Applied Psychology*, 77, 272–279.

Oishi, S., Diener, E., Lucas, R. and Suh, E. (1999). Cross-cultural variations in predictors of life satisfaction: perspectives from needs and values. *Personality and Social Psychology Bulletin*, 25, 980–990.

Onnolee, N. and Jennings, J. E. (2018). Looking in the other direction: An ethnographic analysis of how family businesses can be operated to enhance familial well-being: ETandP. *Entrepreneurship Theory and Practice*, 42(2), 317–339.

Orlikowski, W.J. and Baroudi, J.J. (1991). Studying information technology in organizations: Research approaches and assumptions. *Information Systems Research*, 2:1, 1–28.

Oswald, A.J. (1997). Happiness and economic performance. *The Economic Journal*, 107, 1815–1831.

Page, K. M. and Vella-Brodrick, D. A. (2009). The 'what', 'why', and, 'how' of employee well-being: A new model. *Social Indicators Research*, 90, 441–458.

Palmer, C. (2001). Ethnography: A research method in practice. *International Journal of Tourism Research*, 3, 301–312.

Pancheva, M. G., Ryff, C. D., and Lucchini, M. (2021). An integrated look at well-being: Topological clustering of combinations and correlates of hedonia and eudaimonia. *Journal of Happiness Studies*, 22(5), 2275–2297.

Patzelt, H. and Shepherd, D. A. (2011). Negative emotions of an entrepreneurial career: Self-employment and regulatory coping behaviors. *Journal of Business Venturing*, 26(2), 226–238.

Perricone, P. J., Earle, J. R., and Taplin, I. M. (2001). Patterns of succession and continuity in family-owned businesses: Study of an ethnic community. *Family Business Review*, 14(2), 105–121.

Peterson, C. (2006). A primer in positive psychology. Oxford university press: UK

Petroff, A. (2014). "Let your employer get you a cheaper mortgage", Retrieved from: http://money.cnn.com/2014/09/25/real_estate/mortgages-uk-kpmg/index.html (accessed March 10 2022).

PMQ. (2015, 4 June). Floor Plan: Explore PMQ. Retrieve from: http://www.pmq.org.hk/the-site/floor-plan/ (accessed March 10 2022).

Poland, B. D. (1995). Transcription quality as an aspect of rigor in qualitative research. *Qualitative Inquiry*, 1(3), 290–310.

Ponterotto, J. G. (2006). Brief note on the origins, evolution, and meaning of the qualitative research concept thick description. *The Qualitative Report*, 11(3), 538–549.

Poutziouris, P., Yong W. and Chan, S. (2002). Chinese entrepreneurship: the development of small family firms in China, *Journal of Small Business and Enterprise Development*, 9(4), 383–399.

Poutziouris, P.Z., Smyrnios, K.X. and Klein, S.B. (2006). Introduction: the business of researching family enterprise. In P.Z. Poutziouris, K.X. Smyrnios and S.B. Klein (Ed.), *Handbook of Research on Family Business*. Cheltenham: Edward Elgar, 253–268

Prasad, A. (2003). The gaze of the other: Postcolonial theory and organizational analysis. In A. Prasad, *Postcolonial theory and organizational analysis: s critical engagement*. New York: Palgrave Macmillan, 3–46

Protocols and principles for conducting research in an indigenous context (2003). University of Victoria. Faculty of Human and Social Development. (Final version).

Pybus, M. and Thomas, M. (1979). Health awareness and health actions of parents. in J. Boddy (1985) *Health: perspectives and practices*. New Zealand: Dunmore Press.

Radford, G. P., and Radford, M. L. (2005). Structuralism, post-structuralism, and the library: de Saussure and Foucault. *Journal of Documentation*, 61(1), 60–78.

Rahula, W. (1974). *What the Buddha taught*. New York: Grove Press.

Rawls, J. (2009). *The justification of civil disobedience*, in Aileen Kavanagh, John Oberdiek, Arguing about the law, UK: Routledge.

Redding G. (2000) What is Chinese about Chinese Family Business? And How Much is Family and How Much is Business?. In: Yeung H.W., Olds K. (eds) *Globalization of Chinese Business Firms*. London: Palgrave Macmillan.

Redding, S.G. (1990). *The spirit of Chinese capitalism*, New York: De Gruyter.

Redding, S.G. and Wong, G.Y.Y. (1986). The psychology of Chinese organizational Behaviour. In M.H. Bond (Ed.), *The Psychology of Chinese People* (pp. 267–295). New York.

Reed, M. (1998), Organisational analysis as discourse analysis: a critique, In Grant, D. and Oswick, C. (Eds), *Discourse and Organisation*, London: Sage.

Robbins, S.P. and Coulter, M.A. (2010). Management. (10th ed). Pearson: UK.

Rode, J. C. (2004). Job satisfaction and life satisfaction revisited: A longitudinal test of an integrated model. Human relations, 57(9), 1205–1230.

Rose, N. (1990). *Governing the soul*. London: Routledge.

Rothausen, T. J. (2009). Management work-family research and work-family fit. Implication for building family capital in family business. *Family Business Review*, 22(3),220–234.

Rowlinson, M., and Carter, C. (2002). Foucault and history in organization studies. *Organization*, 9 (4),527–547.

Ryan R. and Deci, E. (2000). Self-determination theory and the facilitation of intrinsic motivation, social development, and well-being. *The American Psychologist*, 55, 68–78.

Ryan, G. W., and Bernard, H. R. (2003). Techniques to identify themes. *Field methods*, 15(1),85–109.

Ryan, R. and Deci, E. (2001). On happiness and human potentials: A review of research on hedonic and eudaimonic well-being. *Annual Review of Psychology*, 52,141–166.

Ryan, R. and Frederick C. (1997). On energy, personality and health: subjective vitality as a dynamic reflection of well-being. *Journal of Personality*, 65, 529–65.

Ryff, C. and Singer, B. (1998). The contours of positive human health, *Psychological Inquiry* 9 (1),1–28.

Ryff, C. and Singer, B. (2008). Know thyself and become what you are: A eudaimonic approach to psychological well-being. *Journal of Happiness Studies*, 9, 13–39.

Ryff, C. D. (1989). Happiness is everything, or is it? Explorations on the meaning of psychological well-being. *Journal of Personality and Social Psychology*, 57(6),1069–1081.

Ryle, G. (1971). *Collected Papers: Collected Essays, 1929–1968*. Vol 2. London: Hutchinson.

Said, E. (1978). *Orientalism*. New York: Vintage Books.

Said, W. E. (1986). Foucault and the imagination of power. In D. C. Hoy (Eds), *Foucault: A critical reader*, New York: Blackwell, 149–155.

Salaff, J. (1992). Women, and the family. And the State in Hong Kong, Taiwan, and Singapore, in R. Appelbaum and J. Henderson, J., *States and development in the Asian Pacific rim*. London: Sage, 267–288.

Salas-Vallina, A., Pasamar, S., and Donate, M. J. (2021). Well-being in times of ill-being: How AMO HRM practices improve organizational citizenship behaviour through work-related well-being and service leadership. *Employee Relations*, 43(4), 911–935.

Sarantakos, S. (1998). *Social Research*. London: Macmillan Press Ltd.

Sarvimaki, A. (2006). Well-being as being well – A Heideggerian look at well-being. *International Journal of Qualitative Studies on Health and Well-being*, 1, 4–10.

Savage, M. (1998). Discipline, surveillance and the "career". In A. McKinlay and K. Starkey, *Foucault, management and organization*, London: Sage, 65–92.

Scheier, M. F., and Carver, C. S. (2003). Self-Regulatory Processes and Responses to Health Threats: Effects of Optimism on Well-Being. *Social psychological foundations of health and illness*, 395–428.

Schjoedt, L. (2009). Entrepreneurial job characteristics: An examination of their effect on entrepreneurial satisfaction. *Entrepreneurship Theory and Practice*, 33(3),619–644.

Schjoedt, L. and Shaver, K. G. (2007). Deciding on an entrepreneurial career: A test of the pull and push hypotheses using the panel study of entrepreneurial dynamics data. *Entrepreneurship Theory and Practice*, 31(5),733–752.

Schwandt, T. A. (2001). *Dictionary of qualitative inquiry* (2nd ed.). Thousand Oaks, CA: Sage.

SCMP (2014). *NPC Standing Committee decision on Hong Kong 2017 election framework*, Retrived from: http://www.scmp.com/news/hong-kong/article/1582245/full-text-npc-standing-committee-decision-hong-kong-2017-election) (accessed March 10 2022).

Seal, C. (1999). *The quality of qualitative research*. London: Sage

Seligman, M. E. P. 2011. *Flourish: A visionary new understanding of happiness and well-being*. New York: Free Press.

Seligman, M.E.P. and Csikszentmihalyi, M. (2000). Positive psychology–an introduction. *American Psychologist*. 55(1): 5–14.

Shabbir, A. and Gregorio, S. D. (1996). An examination of the relationship between women's personal goals and structural factors influencing their decision to start a business: The case of Pakistan. *Journal of Business Venturing*, 11(6),507–529.

Sharma, P. (2004). An overview of the field of family business studies: Current status and directions for the future. *Family Business Review*, 17(1),1–36.

Sharma, P. (2010). Advancing the 3 Rs of family business scholarship: Rigor, relevance, research. *Entrepreneurship and Family Business*, 12, 383–400.

Sheer, V. C. (2013). In search of Chinese paternalistic leadership: Conflicting evidence from samples of mainland China and Hong Kong's small family businesses. *Management Communication Quarterly*, 27(1),34–60.

Sheldon, K. and Elliot, A. (1999). Goal striving, need satisfaction, and longitudinal wellbeing: the self-concordance model. *Journal of Personality and Social Psychology*, 76, 482–497.

Shen, V. (2009). Daoism (II): Zhuang Zi and the Zhuang-Zi. In B. Mou, *Routledge history of world philosophies, Volume 3: History of Chinese philosophy*, Routledge: London and New York, 237–265.

Shen, W., Kiger, T. B., Davies, S. E., Rasch, R. L., Simon, K. M. and Ones, D. S. (2011). Samples in Applied Psychology: Over a decade of research in review. *Journal of Applied Psychology*, 96 (5),1055–1064.

Shepherd C. D., Marchisio, G. and Miles, M. P. (2009). A conceptual model of burnout in individual, family Business, corporate, and social/not-for-profit entrepreneurship. Paper presented at Australian Center for Entrepreneurship Research.

Sheridan, A. (1990). *Michel Foucault: The will to truth*. London and New York: Routledge.

Sherif, B. (2001). The ambiguity of boundaries in the fieldwork experience: Establishing rapport and negotiating insider/outsider status. *Qualitative Inquiry*, 7(4),436–447.

Shizgal P. (1999). On the neural computation of utility in Kahneman D., Diener E. and N. Schwarz, *Well-Being: The Foundations of Hedonic Psychology*, New York: Russell Sage Foundation, 500–524.

Silver, H. (1993). Home and domestic work. *Sociological Forum*, 8, 181–204.

Silverman, D. (2001). *Interpreting qualitative data: Methods for interpreting talk, text and interaction*. London: Sage.

Simon, M., Shrader, R.C., (2011). Entrepreneurial actions and optimistic overconfidence: The role of motivated reasoning in new product introductions, *Journal of Business Venturing*, 27, 291–309.

Simon, R. I. and Dippo, D. (1986). On Critical ethnographic work. *Anthropology and Educational Quarterly*, 17(4),195–202.

Simona, M., Houghtonb, S. M. and Savellia, S. (2003). Out of the frying pan . . . ?: Why small business managers introduce high-risk products? *Journal of Business Venturing*, 18 (3),419–440.

Simsek, O. F. (2009). Happiness revisited: Ontological well-being as a theory-based construct of subjective well-being. *Journal of Happiness Studies*, 10, 505–522.

Sirgy, M. J. (2021). Effects of Personality on Wellbeing. In *The Psychology of Quality of Life*. Springer, Cham, 207–221.

Smart, B. (1983). *Foucault, Marxism and critique*. London: Routledge.

Smyrnios, K., Romano, C., Tanewskil, G., Karofsky, P., Millen, R. and Yilmaz, M. (2003). Work-family conflict: A study of American and Australian family business. *Family Business Review*, 16(1),35–51.

Social Enterprise (2017), What is social enterprise? Retrieved from: http://www.social-enterprises.gov.hk/en/introduction/whatis.html (accessed March 10 2022).

Sparkes, A. C. (2007). Embodiment, academics, and the audit culture: a story seeking consideration. *Qualitative Research*, 7(4) 521–55.
Spivak, G. C. (1981). French feminism in an international frame. *Yale French Studies*, 62, 154–184.
Spivak, G. C. (1985). The Rani of Sirmur: An essay in reading the archives. *History and Theory*, 24 (3),247–272.
Spivak, G. C. (1988). Can the subaltern speaks? In C. Nelson and L. Grossberg (Eds.), *Marxism and the interpretation of culture*, Macmillan Education: Basingstoke, 271–313.
Stafford, K. and Tews, M. J. (2009). Enhancing work-family balance research in family business. *Family Business Review*, 22(3),235–238.
Staines, G. (1980). Spillover vs. compensation: A review of the literature on the relationships between work and ironwork. *Human Relations*, 33, 111–130.
Stake, R. (2005). Qualitative case studies. In N. K. Denzin and Y. S. Lincoln (Eds.), *The Sage handbook of qualitative research* (3rd ed.), Thousand Oaks, CA: Sage, 443–466.
Stanley, L. (1996). The mother of invention: necessity, writing and representation, *Feminism and Psychology*, 6, 45–51.
Stanton, E. A. (2007). The human development index: A history. PERI Working Papers.
Steffy, B. and Grimes, A. (1992). Personnel / Organizational Psychology: A critique of the discipline. In M. Alvesson and H. Willmott (eds). *Critical Management Studies*. London: Sage.
Stewart, A. (2003). Help one another, use one another: Towards an anthropology of family business. *Entrepreneurship Theory and Practice*, 27(1),383–396.
Stier, S. (1993). Wellness in the family business. *Family Business Review*, 6(2),149–159.
Stoler, A.L. (1992). Rethinking colonial categories: European Communities and the boundaries of rule, In N.B.Dirks (ed.), *Colonialism and Culture*. Ann Arbor, MI: Michigan University Press, 319–52.
Suddaby, R. (2014). Editor's comments: Why theory?. *Academy of Management Review*, 39 (4),407–411.
Sullivan, J.J. (1986). Human nature, organizations, and management theory. *Academy of Management Review*, 11(3),534–549.
Szeto, M. M. (2006). Identity politics and its discontents. *Interventions*, 8(2),253–275.
Teshome-Bahiru, W. and Negash-Wossene, J. (2007). Anthropological field research in 21st century: Scope, challenges and ethics. *International Journal of Contemporary and Applied Studies of Man. Anthropologist Special Issue*, 3, 7–18.
The EU SME Centre. (2015). "HR Challenge in China". Retrieved from: http://www.eusmecentre.org.cn/es/article/hr-challenges-china (accessed March 10 2022).
The Hong Kong Institute of Directors. (2014). "Guidelines on corporate governance for SMEs in Hong Kong.", Retrieved from: https://www.charltonslaw.com/hong-kong-law/guidelines-on-corporate-governance-for-smes-in-hong-kong/ (accessed March 10 2022).
The University of Rochester. (2017). "Mortgage housing incentive program", Retrieved from: http://www.rochester.edu/working/hr/benefits/library/_mortg_bene_brochure.pdf (accessed March 10 2022).
Thomas, J. (1993). *Doing critical ethnography*. London: Sage Publications.
Tibi, B. (1995). Culture and knowledge: the politics and Islamisation of knowledge as a postmodern project? The fundamentalist claim to de-Westernization, *Theory, Culture and Society*, 12: 1–24.
Tooby, J. and Cosmides, L. (1992). The psychological foundations of culture, in J.H. Barkow, L. Cosmides and Tooby (eds.), *The Adapted Mind: Evolutionary Psychology and the Generation of Culture*, New York: Oxford University Press,19–136.
Townley, B. (1993). Foucault, power/ knowledge, and its relevance for human resource management. *Academy of Management Review*, 18(3),518–545.

Trompenarrs, F. and Hampton-Turner, C. (1998). *Riding the waves of culture*, London: Nicholas Brealey Publishing

Tsang, E. W. K. (2002). Learning from overseas venturing experience. The case of Chinese family business. *Journal of Business Venturing*, 17, 21–40.

Tsang, S. (2004). *Modern history of Hong Kong*. London and New York: I.B. Tauris. and Co Ltd.

Tsui, A. S. (2006). Contextualization in Chinese management research. *Management and Organization Review*, 2(1), 1–13.

Tu, W. (1985a). *Confucian thought: Selfhood as creative transformation*. Albany: State University of New York Press.

Tu, W. (1985b). Selfhood and otherness in Confucian thought. In A. J. Marsella, G. DeVos, and F. L. K. Hsu (Eds.), *Culture and self: Asian and Western perspectives*. New York: Tavistock Publications, 232–251.

Ullmann, S. (1962). *Semantics: An introduction to the science of meaning*. Oxford: Basil Blackwell.

UNDP (2007). Human Development Reports 2007/2008. Retrieved from: http://www.undp.org/en/reports/global/hdr2007-2008 (accessed March 10 2022).

Veenhoven, R. (2000a). Freedom and happiness: A comparative study in forty-four nations in the early 1990s. In E. Diener and E. M. Sul (eds), *Culture and subjective well-being*, Cambridge, MA: The MIT Press, 257–288.

Veenhoven, R. (2000b). The four qualities of life. *Journal of Happiness Studies*, 1(1), 1–39.

Vera, C.F. and Dean, M.A. (2005). An examination of the challenges daughters face in family business succession. *Family Business Review*, 18(4),321–345.

Villaver, R. B. (2007). *Wuwei* in the thoughts of *Zuang Zi*. *An Interdisciplinary Research Journal*, 18(2),1–15.

Vroom, V. H. (1964). *Work and motivation*. New York: Wiley.

Wah, S.S. (2004). Entrepreneurial leaders in family business organizations. *Journal of Enterprising Culture*, 12(1),1–34.

Wallace, B. and Shauna, S. (2006). Mental balance and well-Being. Building bridges between Buddhism and Western psychology. *American Psychologist*, 61(7),690–701.

Wang, F. and Wang, D. (2016). Place, geographical context and subjective well-being: State of and future directions. In D. Wang and S. He (eds.), *Mobility, Sociability and Well-being of Urban Living*, Springer-Verlag: Berlin Heidelberg, 189–230.

Wang, G. (2008). 中国传统幸福观的历史嬗变及其现代价值. Doctoral Dissertation, Heilongjiang University.

Wang, J., Wang, G. G., Ruona, W. E. A. and Rojewski, J. W. (2005). Confucian values and the implications for international HRD. *Human Resource Development International*, 8(3), 311–326.

Wang, X. (2009). "Being" must be dealt with contextualization, *Journal of Jiangsu Administration Institute*, 1, 26–30.

Warr, P. B. (1987). *Work, unemployment and mental health*. Oxford: Oxford University Press.

Warr, P. B. (1990). The measurement of well-being and other aspects of mental health. *Journal of Occupational Psychology*, 63, 193–210.

Warr, P. B. (2007). *Work, Happiness, and Unhappiness*. New York: Routledge.

Warr, P. B. (2009). Environmental "vitamins", personal judgments, work values, and happiness. Pages 57–85 in S. Cartwright and C. Cooper (eds.) *The Oxford Handbook of Organizational Well-being* (Oxford: Oxford University Press).

Warr, P. B. (2011). How to think about and measure psychological well-being. In M. Wang, R. R. Sinclair and L. E. Tetrick (eds.) *Research Methods in Occupational Health Psychology*. New York: Routledge.

Warr, P. B. (2017). Self-Employment, Personal Values, and Varieties of Happiness–Unhappiness. Journal of Occupational Health Psychology. Advance online publication: http://dx.doi.org/10.1037/ocp0000095. (accessed March 10 2022).

Warr, P. B. (2019). The psychology of happiness. Routledge.
Warr, P. B. and Nielsen, K. (2018). Wellbeing and Work Performance. e-Handbook of Subjective Wellbeing, edited by E. Diener, S. Oishi, and L., Published online with open access by NobaScholar: https://www.sheffield.ac.uk/polopoly_fs/1.740690!/file/wellbeing_and_performance.pdf (accessed March 10 2022).
Waterman, A. (1993). Two conceptions of happiness: Contrasts of personal expressiveness (eudaemonia) and hedonic enjoyment, *Journal of Personality and Social Psychology*, 64, 678–691.
Watt, W.M. (1988) Islamic Fundamentalism and Modernity. London: Routledge.
Webber, R.A. (1969) Convergence or divergence?, *Columbia Journal of World Business*, 4(3): 75–83.
Welsh, D.H.B, Kaciak, E., Memili, E. and Zhou, Q. (2017). Work-Family Balance and Marketing Capabilities as Determinants of Chinese Women Entrepreneurs' Firm Performance. *Journal of Global Marketing*, 30(3), 174–191.
Welsh, F. (1997). *A history of Hong Kong*. London: Harper Collins.
Wengle, H. (1986). The psychology of cosmetic surgery: A critical overview of the literature 1960–1982. Part 1. *Annals of Plastic Surgery*, 16, 435–443.
Westwood, R. (2001). Appropriating the other in the discourse of comparative management. In R. Westwood and S. Linstead (Ed.), *The Language of organization*. London: Sage, 241–282
Westwood, R. (2004). Towards a postcolonial research paradigm in International business and comparative management. In R. Marschan-Piekkari and C. Welch (Ed.), *Handbook of qualitative research method for international business*. Cheltenham: Edward Elgar, 56–83.
Westwood, R. (2006). International business and management studies as an orientalist discourse. A postcolonial critique. *Critical Perspectives on International Business*, 2(2),91–113.
Westwood, R., and Linstead, S. (Eds.). (2001). *The language of organization*. London: Sage.
Whitley, R. (1992). *Business systems in East Asia*. London: Sage.
Whyte, W. F. (1969). *Organizational behaviour: Theory and application*. Homewood: Richard D. Irwin.
Wijaya, A., Kasuma, J., Tasențe, T., and Darma, D. C. (2021). Labor force and economic growth based on demographic pressures, happiness, and human development. *Journal of Eastern European and Central Asian Research*, 8(1),40–50.
Wiklund, J., Davidsson, P. and Delmar, F. (2003). What do they think and feel about growth? An expectancy-value approach to small business managers' attitudes toward growth. *Entrepreneurship Theory and Practice*, 27(3),247–270.
Wilcock, A., Arend, H., Darling, K., Scholz, J., Siddall, R., Snigg, C and Stephen, J. (1998). An exploration study of people's perception and experiences of well-being. *British Journal of Occupational Therapy*, 61(2),75–82.
Wong, D. B. (2004). Relational and autonomous self. *Journal of Chinese Philosophy*, 31(4),419–432.
Wong, H. P (2011). Dao, harmony and personhood: Towards a Confucian ethics of technology. *Philosophy and Technology*, 24, 11–21.
Wong, H. W. and Chau, K. L. F. (2020). *Tradition and transformation in a Chinese family business*. Routledge
Wong, P. T. P. (2011). Positive Psychology 2.0: Towards a balanced interactive model of the good life. Canadian Psychology, 52(2),69–81.
World Health Organization, Health and Welfare, Canada, Canadian Public Health Association. (1986). *The Ottawa Charter for Health Promotion*. Ottawa, Canada: WHO.
World Health Organization. (1948). *Constitution of the WHO*. WHO, Geneva.
Wortman, C. B., and Silver, R. C. (1987). Coping with irrevocable loss. In G. R. Vanderbos and B. K. Bryant (Eds.), *Cataclysms, crises, catastrophes: Psychology in action*. Washington, DC, US: American Psychological Association.

Wortman, Jr. M.S. (1994). Theoretical foundations for family owned business: A conceptual and research based paradigm. *Family Business Review*, 7(1),3–27.
Wright, T. A. (2007). A look at two methodological challenges for scholars interested in positive organizational behavior. In Positive organizational behavior: Accentuating the positive at work, 177–190.
Wright, T. A., Emich, K. J. and Klotz, D. (2017). The many 'face' of well-being. In R. Burke and K. M. Page, *Research handbook on work and well-being*. UK: Edward Elgar, pp. 37–58.
Wu, M., Chang, C. C., and Zhuang, W. L. (2010). Relationships of work–family conflict with business and marriage outcomes in Taiwanese copreneurial women. The International *Journal of Human Resource Management*, 21(5),742–753.
Xiao, Y. and Cooke, F. L. (2012). Work-life balance in China? Social policy, employer strategy and individual coping mechanism. Asia Pacific Journal of Human Resources, 50, 6–22.
Xu, Q. (1997) The making of Total Quality Management (TQM): A supplementary examination, PhD thesis, University of Durham.
Xu, Q. (1999). TQM as an arbitrary sign for play: Discourse and transformation. *Organizations Studies*, 20(4): 659–681.
Xu, Q. (2000). On the way to knowledge: Making a discourse at quality. *Organization*, 7, 427–453.
Xu, Q. (2008). A question concerning subject in The Spirit of Chinese Capitalism. *Critical Perspectives on International Business*, 4(2/3), 242–276.
Xu, S. (2006). *Shuowen Jiezi*. Beijing: Jiuzhou Press.
Yao, X. (2000). *An introduction to Confucianism*. Cambridge University Press: UK.
Yin, R. K. (1981). The case study crisis: Some answers. *Administrative science quarterly*, 26(1), 58–65.
Young, R. J. C. (2004). *White mythologies: Writing history and the West*. Rutledge: London.
Yu, F. L. T., and Kwan, D. S. (2015). Coevolution of culture and technology: the business success of Lee Kum Kee. *Global Business Review*, 16(1),182–195.
Yu, F. T. (2001). The Chinese family business as a strategic system: an evolutionary perspective. *International Journal of Entrepreneurial Behavior and Research*, 7(1),22–40.
Yu, F., Wang, P., Bai, Y. and Li, D. (2018), Governance conflict in Chinese family firms: Managed by family-based managers or external managers?, *International Journal of Conflict Management*, 29 (4), 446–469.
Yu, J. (1998). Virtue: Confucius and Aristotle. *Philosophy East and West*, 48(2),323–347.
Zahra, S. A., Klein, S. B., and Astrachan, J. H. (2006). Epilogue: theory building and the survival of family firms–three promising research directions. *Handbook of research on family business*, 614–617.
Zahra, S. and Sharma, P. (2004). Family business research: A strategic reflection. *Family Business Review*, 17(4),331–346.
Zedeck, S. (1992). Introduction: Exploring the domain of work and family concerns. In S. Zedeck (Ed.), *Work, families and organizations*. San Francisco: Jossey-Bass, 1–32.
Zhang, D. (2002). *Key Concepts in Chinese Philosophy* (E. Ryden Trans.). Beijing: Foreign Languages Press. (Original work published in 1989).
Zhang, G. and Veenhoven, R. (2008). Ancient Chinese philosophical advice: Can it help us find happiness today? *Journal of Happiness Studies*, 9, 425–443.
Zhang, L. (1993). *Xin*. Beijing: Zhongguo Renmin Daxue Chubanshe.
Zhao, J. (2003). Views on the national happiness. *Journal of Ankang Teachers College*, 15, 38–44.
Zheng, W. (2002). The transfer of ownership and leadership: A study of Chinese family business and Inheritance, (Doctoral Dissertation, University of Hong Kong), [HKU Theses Online], Retrieved from: http://hub.hku.hk/handle/123456789/36034 (accessed March 10 2022).

List of Tables

Tab. 1.1	Hedonism Versus Eudaimonia	—— 9
Tab. 1.2	Proposed Conceptual Framework	—— 27
Tab. 1.3	An Archaeology of TQM (Xu, 1997)	—— 29
Tab. 1.4	An Archaeology of Well-being	—— 30
Tab. 3.1	Grids of Specification of Happiness (Aristotle, 1985)	—— 49
Tab. 5.1	Local Concepts: *Xing fu* and *Xin*	—— 111
Tab. A1	Discursive (Trans)Formation (Foucault, 1972)	—— 168
Tab. A2	Types of Thresholds (Foucault, 1972)	—— 175
Tab. B1	Amount of Fieldwork in Each Field Site	—— 187
Tab. B2	Philosophical Perspectives in Social Sciences	—— 189
Tab. B3	Profiles of Informants	—— 191
Tab. B4	Simplified Notation System (Adapted from Poland, 1995 and Silverman, 2001)	—— 210
Tab. B5	Problems in the Transcription	—— 211
Tab. B6	Advantages of Thematic Analysis (Braun and Clarke, 2006)	—— 212
Tab. B7	Steps of Thematic Analysis (Adapted from Braun and Clarke, 2006)	—— 213
Tab. C1	Living Well in Family Business	—— 218
Tab. D1	Interpretations from Hedonism, Eudaimonia, the Confucian and Daoist Frameworks	—— 221

https://doi.org/10.1515/9783110684643-012

List of Figures

Fig. 3.1	Discursive (Trans)Formation of Well-being ——	47
Fig. 3.2	Discursive (Trans)Formation of *Xing Fu* ——	56
Fig. 3.3	Discursive (Trans)Formation of Well-being and *Xing fu* ——	63
Fig. 3.4	A Discursive Space 'Outside' Well-being Discourse ——	68
Fig. 5.1	Theoretical Discussion of *Xing Fu Jia Ting* ——	118
Fig. 5.2	Theoretical Discussion of *Peng You* ——	121
Fig. 5.3	Theoretical Discussion of *Kai Xin Gong Zuo* ——	127
Fig. 5.4	Theoretical Discussion of X*in Zhong Fu You* ——	130
Fig. 5.5	*Xin*: A Theoretical Dialogue ——	131
Fig. 6.1	A Cross-cultural Analysis: From Mainstream to Local Expressions/Concepts ——	149
Fig. A1	A Mainstream Perspectives on Human Needs ——	167
Fig. A2	Confucian S*an Gang Ba Mu*. (Legge, 1985) ——	168
Fig. C1	Yellow Ribbon ——	217
Fig. D1	Confucian Perspective on Self ——	224

Index

affective well-being 11, 53–54
allochronism 37, 150, 152
anthropology 1, 3, 28, 37, 146, 152–154, 161
archaeology 1–2, 3, 28–30, 32, 42–45, 50, 61, 64, 66–67, 146, 149, 151–154, 161, 164

ba mu 138, 140–141, 144

Chinese well-being 13, 23–24
concepts 1–2, 3, 8, 11, 14–15, 20, 27, 42, 45, 50, 52–53, 55, 60, 64, 66, 68, 70, 75–76, 104, 106, 109, 122, 136, 143–144, 146–148, 152–153, 157, 161, 164
Confucianism 2–3, 14, 60, 137, 141
contribution 2–3, 8, 15, 34, 44–45, 64, 67, 146, 151, 153, 160–161

dao 18–21, 22, 83, 99, 106–108, 110, 113, 115, 117, 121, 124, 128, 132, 135–137, 139–140, 142–145
Daoism 2–3, 14, 20, 60, 105, 115, 137, 141, 143
de 15, 18–19, 21–22, 107, 113–114, 125, 128, 135, 137, 140, 142
desire 7–8, 13, 22, 55, 80, 110, 117, 122, 125, 129, 131–134, 138–140, 142–143, 145
dialogue 3, 31, 37, 50, 67, 109, 129, 135, 137, 142, 145–146, 153–156, 160–161, 164
discursive formation 29–30, 42, 45, 48, 52–53
discursive transformation 42, 52–54, 61, 64, 68, 148, 150

essentialism 1–2, 3, 32, 35, 37–38, 40, 43–45, 55, 64, 66–67, 102, 104, 137, 147, 151–155, 161, 164
Eudaimonia 2–3, 4, 6–8, 10, 15, 25–26, 31, 45, 48, 50, 52, 67, 110, 112–113, 115–117, 119–120, 123–127, 129, 132–134, 137, 139–140, 143–145

fu 13, 57–61, 68, 148

gestures 90, 111

Hedonism 2–3, 4, 6–10, 14, 25–26, 31, 45, 48, 110, 113, 115–117, 119–120, 123–126, 129–132, 134, 137, 139–140, 143–145

jia ting 3, 76, 79–83, 92, 109–110, 113, 117, 119, 130, 133, 137, 142, 146, 149, 155, 158
jian kang 86, 159
jun zi 107–108, 112, 114, 120, 132, 135

kai xin gong zuo 3, 109, 122, 126, 130, 133, 146, 149–150, 155
kuai le 87

li 15, 17, 19, 114–115, 117, 135, 137, 144

nature 20–22, 107–108, 110, 113, 115, 117, 120, 124, 128, 132, 135–136, 141–142, 145
needs 7–8, 10, 110, 113, 115, 119, 123, 133–135, 139–140, 143–144
neo-positivism 1, 24–25, 55

objectification 2, 32, 35–37, 43–45, 55, 64, 66–67, 147, 151, 164

peng you 3, 92–93, 95, 109, 118–120, 124, 126, 130, 133, 137, 146, 149, 155, 159
ping jing 87, 89, 116
positivism 1, 24–25, 55, 62, 160
psychological well-being 8, 11, 26, 50, 52–53, 62, 110, 112–113, 115–116, 119–120, 125, 127, 133, 154

relations 16, 103, 110, 137–138, 143
ren 15–16, 19, 107, 110, 119, 128, 136–137, 144
rituals 89, 111, 116–117

san gang 141, 144
sensation 4, 24, 130, 132, 134, 144
set-point theory 5, 10
spontaneity 21–22, 108, 142, 144
strategy 3, 25, 32, 34, 39–40, 44, 90–91, 99, 102–104, 148
structure 34–35, 41
subjective well-being 5, 11, 26, 50, 52–53, 62, 115–116, 125, 154

thick description 1, 3, 31, 71, 156, 158, 161–162, 164
thresholds 29–30

https://doi.org/10.1515/9783110684643-014

wu fu 14, 115, 117
wu lun 17–18, 103, 110, 114, 132, 134, 137
wu wei 22, 105–106, 113, 115, 124, 128, 132, 141–144

xin zhong fu you 3, 100–101, 109, 122, 126–128, 130, 146, 150, 155, 159, 162

yi 15, 17, 19, 105, 107, 114, 132, 137
yin and yang 20, 112, 141

zhen ren 142
zhi 15, 18–19, 107, 124, 137, 144
zi ran 21–22, 113, 115, 124, 128, 132, 135–136, 141–144, 158